A CONCISE DICTIONARY
OF THEOLOGY
Third Edition

A CONCISE DICTIONARY OF THEOLOGY
Third Edition

by

Gerald O'Collins, SJ,
and
Edward G. Farrugia, SJ

Paulist Press
New York / Mahwah, NJ

Cover design by Christina Cancel
Book design by Lynn Else

Library of Congress Cataloging-in-Publication Data

O'Collins, Gerald.
    A concise dictionary of theology / Gerald O'Collins, SJ and Edward G.
    Farrugia, SJ. — Third edition.
        pages cm
    Includes index.
    ISBN 978-0-8091-4827-1 (alk. paper) — ISBN 978-1-58768-236-0
    1. Theology—Dictionaries. I. Farrugia, Edward G. II. Title.
    BR95.O25 2013
    230.03—dc23
                                                2012042278

ISBN 978-0-8091-4827-1 (paperback)
ISBN 978-1-58768-236-0 (e-book)

Published by Paulist Press
997 Macarthur Boulevard
Mahwah, New Jersey 07430

www.paulistpress.com

Printed and bound in the
United States of America

De licentia superiorum ordinis

CONTENTS

PREFACE TO THE THIRD EDITION (2013)

The revised and expanded edition of this dictionary (published in 2000) has received encouraging accolades from teachers and students alike. One professor called it "a wonderful collection," marked by "fresh language" and an "evenness of style and consistency in the quality and accuracy of entries." A student reported that he used it every time he wrote his assignments and reviewed his class notes. Another student called it an "awesome and incredible resource" for her master's program, and added, "I highly recommend it for theology students as well as for anyone in ministry." Another student praised the dictionary as "the single most helpful work of reference" that he had used in his years of studying theology and remarked, "to my knowledge, there is no other work like this in print today." An editorial review characterized the dictionary as "balanced, clearly written, and ecumenical in perspective."

Such feedback has prompted us into preparing a third edition of our *Concise Dictionary of Theology*. This has involved correcting a few mistakes, updating some entries where this was necessary, and adding several new entries (e.g., "Sign" and "Virtue Ethics"), a chart of councils, and a timeline.

Some readers, while recognizing the need for a concise dictionary to be true to its name, have expressed a desire to have bibliographical help, at least for the most significant entries. A number of full-scale works provide such help for a wide range of topics. Let us list some, beginning with the most recent: E. G. Farrugia, SJ (ed.), *Encyclopaedic Dictionary of Eastern Christianity* (Rome: Pontifical Oriental Institute, 2012); J. A. McGuckin (ed.), *The Encyclopedia of Eastern Orthodox Christianity*, 2 vols. (Chichester: Wiley-Blackwell, 2011); Daniel Patte (ed.), *Cambridge Dictionary of Christianity* (New York: Cambridge University Press, 2010); E. Fahlbusch et al. (eds.), *The Encyclopedia of Christianity*, 5 vols. (Grand Rapids, Mich.: Eerdmans 1999–2008); Ken Parry (ed.), *The Blackwell Companion to Eastern Christianity* (Malden, Mass.: Blackwell, 2007); F. L. Cross and E. A. Livingstone (eds.), *The Oxford Dictionary of the Christian Church*, 4th ed. (Oxford: Oxford University Press,

2005); J.-Y. Lacoste (ed.), *Encyclopedia of Christian Theology*, 3 vols. (New York: Routledge, 2004); and *New Catholic Encyclopedia*, 2nd ed., 15 vols. (Washington, DC: Catholic University of America, 2003); Ken Parry et al. (eds.), *The Blackwell Dictionary of Eastern Christianity* (Oxford: Blackwell, 1999). The Brill Online Collection offers two excellent resources: *Encyclopedia of Christianity* and *Religion Past and Present*.

For further bibliographies on biblical questions, one could consult K. D. Sakenfeld (ed.), *The New Interpreter's Dictionary of the Bible*, 5 vols. (Nashville: Abingdon Press, 2007–9), and D. N. Freedman (ed.), *Anchor Bible Dictionary*, 6 vols. (New York: Doubleday, 1992).

Denzinger-Schönmetzer, *Enchiridion Symbolorum, Definitionum et Declarationum de Rebus Fidei et Morum*, 36th ed. (Freiburg im Breisgau: Herder, 1976) provided a classic collection of Church documents, arranged chronologically and in the original languages. Peter Hünermann edited a 37th edition (Freiburg im Breisgau: Herder, 1991), in which a German translation faces the original texts (DH in our abbreviations). This work has now appeared, with an English translation facing the original texts (San Francisco: St Ignatius Press, 2012).

As teachers and students of theology move further into the twenty-first century, we offer this third, revised edition of our *Concise Dictionary of Theology* in the hope of promoting a knowledge of what key terms mean, how they have been used, and where they came from. For help in producing this third edition, we wish to thank John Batt, Philip Moller, and Paul Pallath.

G. O'C and E. G. F.
Easter 2012

PREFACE TO THE
SECOND EDITION (2000)

For this new edition of our *Concise Dictionary of Theology*, we have enlarged a few entries, made some necessary corrections, inserted fifty new entries, and added an index of names. We have now provided precise references to the latest (1996) edition of Neuner/Dupuis, *The Christian Faith*. In some cases, only DH carries the relevant text; in a few cases, only ND. [A seventh edition of *The Christian Faith* appeared in 2001.] We have also added references to the *Codex Canonum Ecclesiarum Orientalium* or *Code of Canons of the Oriental Churches* (abbreviated CCEO), promulgated by Pope John Paul II on October 18, 1990. This code is an indispensable reference work on Eastern Christianity.

Some people continue to speak inaccurately of our "editing" this dictionary. Let us repeat what was indicated in the original preface. We did not recruit a team of contributors whose work we then edited; instead, we wrote together every entry—from "Abba" to "Zwinglianism."

We have drawn much encouragement from our readers, and from the fact that this dictionary has appeared in Indonesian, Italian, Polish, and Ukrainian. Spanish and other foreign language translations are being prepared. As the second Christian millennium gives way to the third, we once again offer our readers this dictionary with the desire of improving clarity and precision in Christian theology around the world.

G. O'C and E. G. F.
Easter 1999

PREFACE TO THE
FIRST EDITION (1990)

Over the past three decades. programs of Christian theological study have, by and large, been considerably improved. Historical and biblical sources are generally used more scientifically and fairly. Narrow debates have given way to dialogue and a readiness to learn from the best available authorities. Professors and students of the Latin West have discovered more and more the treasures of Eastern Christianity. A rigid reliance on just one philosophical tradition has been superseded by a healthier philosophical pluralism. In most quarters, theologians have appreciated and faced two great challenges. What is involved when we interpret our basic texts? What method(s) should we employ in developing our theological systems? Dialogue with Judaism, Islam, and other religions has flourished in a new and surprising way. In various parts of the world, local and regional expositions of Christian faith have emerged.

Despite some loss, there have been very many gains in Christian theology. At the same time, change, growth, and the new diversity have created a language problem—especially for those beginning the study of theology. Students can be confused about the meaning of important and even basic theological terms.

To help relieve this situation, we offer this concise dictionary. Our aim is not to smuggle in some system, but simply to identify key words and phrases that are used in contemporary theology sometimes in a variety of ways. We have included some biblical, catechetical, ethical, historical, liturgical, and philosophical terms that theological students will come across sooner or later. Although this dictionary is primarily designed for Westerners (particularly Roman Catholics), increased contacts with Eastern Christians have encouraged us to add some terms from the East.

In brief, the aim of this work is to clarify theological terminology and to promote accuracy in its usage. We shall be thoroughly satisfied if we make some contribution toward achieving these goals. In its entirety, this dictionary has been authored by both of us, and we assume equal responsibility for its whole content.

It did not seem appropriate to burden a concise dictionary with bibliographies. But we wanted to indicate some major sources: the Bible, whose two main parts, the Old and New Testaments, are abbreviated OT and NT, respectively; the documents of the Second Vatican Council (1962–65); the 1983 *Code of Canon Law* (abbreviated CIC); and the latest [now the 42nd of 2009] edition of H. Denzinger, *Enchiridion Symbolorum, Definitionum et Declarationum de Rebus Fidei et Morum* by Peter Hünermann (Freiburg i. Br., 1991, abbreviated DH). Those who have difficulty with the Greek and Latin texts provided by DH are referred to the translations of many of these documents provided by J. Neuner and J. Dupuis (eds.), *The Christian Faith*, 6th rev. ed. (New York, 1996; abbreviated ND) [now in its seventh edition of 2001]).

The expertise of various friends and colleagues has helped us clarify many terms more successfully: Giorgio Barone-Adesi, Jean Beyer, Charles Conroy, Mariasusai Dhavamony, Clarence Gallagher, Edouard Hambye, Eduard Huber, John Long, Antonio Orbe, Ronald Roberson, Tomas [later Cardinal] Spidlik, Frank Sullivan, Javier Urrutia, Jos Vercruysse, Jared Wicks, and Boutros Yousif. In a special way we wish to thank most sincerely John Michael McDermott and Robert Taft, who provided us with numerous corrections and challenges. With gratitude and affection, we dedicate this dictionary to those great supporters of theology and theologians, Eugene and Maureen McCarthy.

Gerald O'Collins, SJ, and Edward G. Farrugia, SJ
Rome, June 16, 1990

ABBREVIATIONS

Abbreviations for Documents of Vatican II

AA   *Apostolicam Actuositatem* (Decree on the Apostolate of Lay People)

AG   *Ad Gentes Divinitus* (Decree on the Church's Missionary Activity)

CD   *Christus Dominus* (Decree on the Pastoral Office of Bishops in the Church)

DHu   *Dignitatis Humanae* (Declaration on Religious Liberty)

DV   *Dei Verbum* (Dogmatic Constitution on Divine Revelation)

GE   *Gravissimum Educationis* (Declaration on Christian Education)

GS   *Gaudium et Spes* (Pastoral Constitution on the Church in the Modern World)

IM   *Inter Mirifica* (Decree on the Means of Social Communication)

LG   *Lumen Gentium* (Dogmatic Constitution on the Church)

NA   *Nostra Aetate* (Declaration on the Relation of the Church to Non-Christian Religions

OE   *Orientalium Ecclesiarum* (Decree on the Catholic Eastern Churches)

OT   *Optatam Totius* (Decree on the Training of Priests)

PC   *Perfectae Caritatis* (Decree on the Up-to-date Renewal of Religious Life)

PO   *Presbyterorum Ordinis* (Decree on the Ministry and Life of Priests)

SC   *Sacrosanctum Concilium* (Constitution on the Sacred Liturgy)

UR   *Unitatis Redintegratio* (Decree on Ecumenism)

Other Abbreviations

Arab.   Arabic

CCEO   *Codex Canonum Ecclesiarum Orientalium* (Code of Canons of the Oriental Churches)

CIC   *Codex Iuris Canonici* (Code of Canon Law)

DH   H. Denzinger/P. Hünermann (eds.), *Enchiridion Symbolorum, Definitionum et Declarationum de Rebus Fidei et Morum*

Gr.   Greek

Heb.   Hebrew

Lat.   Latin

ND   J. Neuner/J. Dupuis, *The Christian Faith*

NT   New Testament

OT   Old Testament

A

Abba. The familiar word in Aramaic for "father," applied to God by Jesus. Where it occurs in the NT (Mark 14:36; Rom 8:15; Gal 4:6), the Greek equivalent is always given. See *Adoption as God's Children; Father, God as*.

Abortion (Lat. "thwarted birth"). The intentional destruction of an unborn child in its mother's womb or removing it from its mother's womb. An unborn child's unintended death during surgery to save its mother's life is "indirect" abortion: the child's death is a tragic yet inevitable side effect of surgery that is good in itself (e.g., the removal of a cancerous uterus); the child's death as such is not the means that produces the mother's restored health. Respect for innocent human beings and human life at all stages pervades the scriptures; one text condemns violence that produces a miscarriage (Exod 21:22–25). Two early Christian documents, the *Didache* (5.2) and the *Epistle of Barnabas* (19.5), condemn abortion, and some patristic writers (e.g., St. Basil the Great [d. 379]) treat it as murder. The Synod of Elvira (306) excommunicates women procuring abortions, allowing those who repent to receive communion only at the time of death (canon 63), while the Synod of Ancyra (314) readmits them to communion after some years of penance (canon 21). The Quinisext Synod (692) calls those who procure abortion "murderers" (canon 91). When promoting married love and respect for human life, Vatican II (1962–65) describes infanticide and abortion as "abominable crimes" (GS 51; see also GS 27). The condemnation of abortion has been repeated by the 1995 encyclical of Blessed John Paul II (pope 1978–2005), *Evangelium Vitae*. The Catholic Church's two canonical codes treat abortion as a serious offense against human life (CIC 1397; CCEO 728 §2; 1450 §2). In the Latin Code of Canon Law, those who successfully procure an abortion incur an automatic (*latae sententiae*) excommunication (CIC 1398); in the Eastern code, the excommunication is not automatic but reserved to the bishop. See *Birth Control; Excommunication; Latae Sententiae; Quinisext Synod; Vatican Council, Second*.

Absolution. Pronouncing over repentant sinners the forgiveness of personal sins through Christ (see DH 1673). The absolution may be in the indicative form (e.g., "I absolve you") or the "precatory" form (e.g., "May almighty God have mercy on us and forgive us our sins"). Eastern formulas of absolution are generally "precatory" (e.g., "May God forgive you"). Absolution forms an essential part of the sacrament of penance and makes present Christ's ministry of forgiveness (Matt 18:21–35; Mark 2:1–12, 15–17; Luke 5:17–26; 7:36–50; 15:1–32; 19:1–10; John 8:3–11), and the powers he left to the church to "bind" and to "loose" (Matt 16:19; 18:18; John 20:22–23). In the Latin rite, the prayer of absolution runs as follows: "God, the Father of mercies, through the death and resurrection of his Son has reconciled the world to himself and

1

sent the Holy Spirit among us for the forgiveness of sins; through the ministry of the church may God give you pardon and peace, and I absolve you from your sins in the name of the Father, and of the Son, and of the Holy Spirit." The Council of Trent (1545–63) defined absolution to be not only a statement, but also a judicial act (DH 1685, 1709; ND 1628, 1649). Absolution is given by the bishop who heads the diocese and by the priests to whom he gives authority to hear confessions (see DH 1323; ND 1612). According to the 1983 Code of Canon Law, they then have this "faculty" to hear confession anywhere in the world, unless the bishop of another diocese expressly forbids them from doing so in his diocese (see CIC 967; CCEO 722 §4). Where there is imminent danger of death or large numbers who want to receive the sacrament of penance but cannot confess their sins individually, general absolution may be given (CIC 961; CCEO 720 §2). But those who receive the sacrament should be told to confess individually at their earliest convenience. The absolution at the beginning of Mass or during the Liturgy of the Hours is a sacramental, not a sacrament. See *Confession; Diocese; Epiclesis; Forgiveness of Sins; Jurisdiction; Ordinary; Penance, Sacrament of; Sacrament; Sacramental.*

Abstinence. Refraining from otherwise legitimate activities such as eating meat. In the West, the Catholic Church enjoins abstinence from meat on Ash Wednesday and Good Friday. As regards other Fridays, Episcopal conferences, however, may adapt the practice to local needs (see CIC 1249–53). In the East, where such practice depends on the law of each *sui iuris* church (CCEO 882), abstinence days are much more frequent and, as a rule, identified with fasting. See *Asceticism; Eastern Catholic Churches, Four Ranks of; Episcopal Conference; Fasting; Lent.*

Accident. A characteristic that inheres in a substance and cannot exist independently of it, but which as such is not essential to that substance. Aristotelian philosophy recognizes nine classes of accidents, which include quality, quantity, relation, space, and time. Quality and quantity are called absolute and intrinsic; the others, relative and extrinsic accidents. See *Substance and Accidents; Transubstantiation.*

Acoemetae (Gr. "nonsleepers"). Monks who took seriously the injunction of St. Paul to "pray without ceasing" (1 Thess 5:17), lived in absolute poverty, and devoted themselves to prayer, group by group, for twenty-four hours a day. Their founder was Abbot St. Alexander (ca. 350–ca. 430). They upheld the Council of Chalcedon (451), but were later unjustly accused of being Nestorian. With their center in Constantinople, they survived until the thirteenth century, having mitigated their poverty and built up a famous library. The Pauline ideal has also inspired Western contemplatives, in particular institutes of perpetual adoration. Both East and West have widely accepted the proposal of Origen (ca. 185–ca. 254) to unite prayer with necessary work, so that the whole of life becomes "prayer without ceasing." See *Asceticism; Chalcedon, Council of; Hesychasm; Liturgy of the Hours; Monasticism; Nestorianism; Prayer.*

Acolyte (Gr. "follower"). See *Lector; Tonsure.*

Adam (Heb. "man"). The biblical designation for the first man, created with Eve in the image and likeness of God (Gen 1:26–27) and the original ancestor of Jesus (Luke 3:38). As Second or Last Adam (Rom 5:14; 1 Cor 15:45), Christ restored to the human race the righteousness and life lost by the first Adam (see DH 901, 1524; ND 1928). See *Eve; Justification; New Eve; Original Sin; Polygenism.*

Ad Limina Visit (Lat. "to the threshold"). The visit that bishops make every five years to the pope in order to give an account of the state of their dioceses (see CIC 400, 395). Some articles (28–32) of the apostolic constitution *Pastor Bonus* (promulgated June 28, 1988, and effective from March 1, 1989) regulate these visits. The CCEO (207) prescribes only a quinquennial report that the head of a *sui iuris* church sends to the Holy See. See *Bishop; Collegiality; Diocese; Eastern Catholic Churches, Four Ranks of; Holy See; Pope.*

Adoption as God's Children. A Pauline way of expressing the new relationship to God of those redeemed through Christ. No longer slaves to sin but adopted children who cry "Abba, Father" (Rom 8:15; Gal 4:5–7), believers have become heirs with Christ, the Son of God by natural right (Rom 8:17; Gal 4:7). Their adoption will be completed by the bodily resurrection (Rom 8:21–25). See *Deification; Grace, Habitual; Redemption; Regeneration; Resurrection.*

Adoptionism. An eighth-century Spanish heresy that held that, as God, Christ was by nature truly Son of God but, as man, only God's adopted son (see DH 595, 610–15; ND 638). Its chief proponents were Elipandus (ca. 718–802), archbishop of Toledo, and Felix (d. 818), bishop of Urgel. The Muslim domination of Toledo, at the time the capital of Spain, and Islamic theology, one of whose main tenets is that God cannot have a son, provide the background. This heresy had precedents in Ebionitism and dynamic Monarchianism, which became associated with Adoptionism through the work of Adolf von Harnack (1851–1930). See *Ebionites; Islam; Monarchianism; Nestorianism.*

Adoration. The highest reverence to be offered only to God (Exod 20:1–4; John 4:23), our creator, redeemer, and sanctifier, who alone should be "worshipped and glorified" (Nicene-Constantinopolitan Creed). Believers adore God through various images (e.g., the cross); they also adore Christ present in the Eucharist (see DH 600–601; ND 1251–52). See *Cross; Icon; Veneration of Saints; Worship.*

Advent. In Western Christianity, the four weeks that prepare for Christmas and form the beginning of the liturgical year. They are characterized by the curtailing of festivities: at Mass no *Gloria* is said (except on the feast of the Immaculate Conception), and the liturgical color is penitential violet (except for the third Sunday of Advent, when rose may be used). "Advent" also refers to Christ's "second coming" at the end of history. See *Calendar, Liturgical*; *Christmas Preparation*; *Gloria*; *Immaculate Conception*; *Parousia*.

Aesthetics. The principles for judging beautiful objects. Theology needs aesthetic criteria drawn from artistic, cultural, and contemplative experience so as to appreciate the material images that manifest and communicate the spiritual and divine realities (see GS 57, 62; IM 6; SC 122–23). See *Beauty, Theology of*.

Agape (Gr. "love"). The characteristic term used in the NT, especially in John's gospel and the letters of John and Paul, to designate the love of God (or Christ) for us and, derivatively, our love for God and one another (e.g., John 15:12–17; 1 John 4:16; 1 Cor 13). The word also applies to the common meal early Christians held in connection with the Eucharist. See *Eucharist*; *Love*.

Agnosticism (Gr. "not knowing"). The view that we cannot know anything with certainty about God, the "other" world, and the afterlife (see DH 3475–77; 3494–95; GS 57). In popular usage, the term covers various forms of religious skepticism. See *Atheism*.

Akathistos (Gr. "not sitting"). One of the oldest and most beautiful songs of praise to the Mother of God in the Byzantine East. Consisting of twenty-four strophes, it is usually sung standing (hence its name) during the Saturday vigil service of the fifth week in the Greek Lent. The first part of the text is based on the infancy narrative of St. Luke, interspersed with some apocryphal elements and the repetitive "Hail, Mary!" (literally, "Rejoice, Mary!"), whereas the second part contemplates Jesus' birth in its salvific impact on the whole cosmos. The *Akathistos* may be addressed to Christ, to the other two persons of the Trinity, and to saints, but it is directed above all to Mary the Mother of God. The fact that the *Akathistos* has been attributed to two patriarchs of Constantinople, Sergius (patriarch 610–38) and St. Germanus (patriarch 715–30), and especially to St. Romanos the Melodian (d. ca. 560) reflects its importance. See *Kondakion*; *Theotokos*.

Albigensianism. A medieval heresy named after its center, Albi, in southern France. It understood redemption as the soul's liberation from the flesh, dismissed matter as evil, and, hence, rejected Christ's Incarnation, the sacraments, and the resurrection of the body. Its adherents were divided into the perfect, who did not marry and lived an extremely austere existence, and ordinary believers, who led normal lives until they came to be in danger of death.

In 1215 the heresy was condemned at the Fourth Lateran Council (see DH 800–802; ND 19–21). See *Bogomils; Cathars; Dualism; Lateran Council, Fourth; Manichaeism.*

Alexandrian Theology. A theology that began in Alexandria as a catechetical school toward the end of the second century AD. It interpreted the scriptures with an allegorical bias and, as the classic Christology from above, focused on the Word becoming flesh and the divine nature of the incarnate Christ. The many famous thinkers of Alexandria include St. Pantaenus (d. ca. 190), Clement of Alexandria (ca. 150–ca. 215), Origen (ca. 185–ca. 254), St. Athanasius of Alexandria (d. 373), Didymus the Blind (ca. 313–98), and St. Cyril of Alexandria (d. 444). See *Antiochene Theology; Christology from Above; Christology from Below; Logos-Sarx Christology; Monophysitism; Origenism; Senses of Scripture.*

Allegory (Gr. "speaking under the guise of something else"). A point-by-point interpretation that goes beyond what a narrative says on the surface to find deeper and further links with reality (e.g., the allegory of the vine in Isa 5:1–7; Ps 80:8–13). In places, St. Paul follows Jewish exegesis of his time by interpreting the OT allegorically (e.g., Gal 4:21—5:1). Unlike the Antiochene writers, Origen (ca. 185–ca. 254) and the school of Alexandria sometimes favored an allegorical over a literal meaning of the OT narratives. Like other Latin fathers, St. Augustine (354–430) recognized both the literal and the allegorical meaning of the scripture. See *Alexandrian Theology; Antiochene Theology; Exegesis; Haggadah; Hermeneutics; Origenism; Parable; Senses of Scripture.*

Alleluia (Heb. "praise Yah [shortened form for Yahweh], praise the Lord"). In the Latin liturgy, an acclamation at the antiphonal verse before the gospel. It became connected with the joy of Easter and so was dropped from the penitential seasons of Advent and Lent. In Eastern liturgies, it has no festal connotations and is used much more frequently, even during funeral services. "Alleluia" is especially associated with the hymn *Cherubikon* or "hymn of the cherubim," which, when the Liturgy of the Word ends and the Liturgy of the Eucharist begins, accompanies the transfer of the gifts to the altar in the Great Entrance (as distinguished from the Small Entrance, which precedes the reading of the Gospel). Christians (see Rev 19:1–6) took the term *alleluia* (or *halleluia,* the form employed in Milan's Ambrosian rite until 1976) from the OT, where it occurs only in the psalms, with the exception of Tobit 13:17. The Jewish rabbis called Psalms 113–18 the "Great Hallel." At the end of their last Passover meal together, Jesus and his disciples sang the second half of the "Great Hallel," Psalms 115–18 (Mark 14:26). See *Advent; Cherubikon; Christmas Preparation; Entrances; Liturgy of the Eucharist; Liturgy of the Word; Passover.*

Altar (Lat. "elevated"). A raised platform on which sacrifice is offered. The identification of altar and table was questioned by Pius XII in order to stress the sacrificial value of the Mass (*Mediator Dei*, 62). With Vatican II (1962–65), the Mass was commonly understood to be both sacrifice and meal (SC 47). Since the Eucharist was celebrated in private homes, early altars were wooden tables. Stone altars came into use from celebrating on the tombs of martyrs. Hence relics became obligatory for consecrated altars in the Roman Catholic Church. Unlike the West, where one church can have many altars, the Orthodox churches have simply one altar on which only one eucharistic liturgy is celebrated on a given day. The sanctity of altars guaranteed safety to fugitives, often depicted as clutching their columns. In the absence of a consecrated altar, the Orthodox use an *antimension* (Gr. "instead of the table"), which is made of cloth or wood and generally depicts the image of Christ's burial. Necessary when iconoclasts desecrated altars, the *antimension* has come to be used on altars whether they are consecrated or not. After being used, the *antimension* is not washed but burned. See *Church, Dedication of; Consecration; Iconoclasm; Sacrifice of the Mass; Veneration of Saints.*

Ambo (Gr. "go up"). An elevated step in ancient churches (either in front of the altar or in the middle of the church), from which cantors (Lat. "singers") led singing, lectors (Lat. "readers") read scriptural texts, and preachers delivered sermons. Sometimes churches had two ambos: on the south side and on the north side, respectively; one for reading the OT lesson and the epistle, and the other for proclaiming the gospel. Among the most lavishly decorated ambos are one made by Justinian I (emperor 527–65) for Hagia Sophia in Constantinople (modern Istanbul) and another in the Basilica of St. Mark in Venice. Ambos were often superseded by lecterns (or portable bookstands) and an elevated pulpit (usually on the north side of the church). Today elevated pulpits outside the sanctuary have frequently become decorative and are used only on special occasions. In Greek Orthodox churches, the ambo is usually attached or at least close to the icon-wall or iconostasis. See *Epistle; Gospel; Iconostasis; Lectern; Lector; Liturgy of the Word.*

Amen (Heb. "support, stand firm"). Derived from Hebrew roots that could indicate (literally) a peg dug in the ground to keep a tent erect, (metaphorically) truth and faithfulness, and (in the setting of religious activity) "so it is" or "so be it." At the end of a doxology or other prayer, "amen" confirmed or approved what had been said (Ps 41:13; 1 Cor 14:16). Jewish assemblies responded to the teaching of priests with "Amen" (Deut 27:15–26). According to the gospels, Christ frequently introduced some solemn declaration with one "amen" (e.g., Matt 6:2) or a double amen (e.g., John 12:24)—a practice that strikingly diverged from the normal use of "amen" to conclude approvingly a prayer or statement (see also Rev 22:20). "Amen" occurs understandably as a title for the risen Jesus as "the faithful and true witness" (Rev 3:14). From NT times, Christians everywhere have ended prayers, hymns, and creeds with "amen," as we find in all their liturgies today. See *Doxology; Liturgy; Prayer.*

Americanism. An ill-defined nineteenth-century movement among Catholics in the United States who were open to the best ideals of American Puritanism, the Enlightenment, incipient ecumenism, and contemporary culture, and who were influenced by Fr. Theodore Isaac Hecker (1819–88), the founder of the Paulist Fathers. In 1899 Leo XIII censured a distorted version of Americanism (DH 3340–46; ND 2015–18). Some themes of Americanism, such as religious liberty, were later vindicated in Vatican II (1962–65) (see DHu 2–8). See *Ecumenism; Enlightenment; Liberty, Religious; Puritans; Vatican Council, Second.*

Anabaptists (Gr. "re-baptizers"). A sixteenth-century movement found mainly in Germany, Holland, and Switzerland that considered infant baptism invalid and so promoted the "re-baptism" of adults. There were several groups, the most famous of which was that headed by Thomas Münzer (ca. 1490–1525), who led the Peasants' Revolt (1522–25). Another group of Anabaptists tried to set up a theocratic type of government in Münster (1533–35) under Jan Mattys and John of Leyden. The heirs of the Anabaptists are the Mennonites, the followers of Menno Simons (1496–1561), who are mainly found in North America. See *Infant Baptism; Theocracy.*

Anachoretism (Gr. "withdrawing oneself"). Term applied to Eastern monks who live in solitude, as hermits do in the West. While Western hermits may be guided by the local bishop (CIC 603 §2), Eastern anchorites are attached to a monastery (CCEO 481–85, 570). An anchorite may also be known as a "recluse," as was the Russian bishop and spiritual writer St. Theophan the Recluse (1815–94). See *Athos, Mount; Cenobites; Monasticism.*

Anakephalaiosis (Gr. "recapitulation" or "summing up"). A term that in its verbal form refers to Christ bringing into unity everything in the universe (Eph 1:10). Along these lines, Church Fathers such as St. Irenaeus (ca. 130–ca. 200) presented Christ as the head of the church, who fulfills God's design in creation and salvation history.

Analogy (Gr. "proportion" or "correspondence"). The use of a common term to designate realities that are both similar and dissimilar with regard to the same point (e.g., "love" as predicated of God and human beings). Analogy is to be distinguished from (a) the case of equivocal terms, that is, terms that are the same but designate totally dissimilar realities (e.g., *pen* as an enclosure for cows and as a writing instrument); and (b) the case of univocal or perfectly synonymous terms, that is, different terms that refer to an identical reality (e.g., *king* and *sovereign* for the male hereditary ruler of an independent state). See *Equivocity; Univocity.*

Analogy of Being. The commonality underlying all reality. When we compare God with creatures, however, we should beware of violating the absolute mystery of God. As the Fourth Lateran Council points out, any similarity between the creator and creatures is characterized by an even greater dissimilarity (see DH 806; ND 320). There exists an infinite difference between saying "God is" and "creatures are." See *God; Lateran Council, Fourth; Mystery; Theologia Crucis; Thomism*.

Analogy of Faith. An expression drawn from Romans 12:6 and used in Catholic theology to recall that any passage of scripture or aspect of faith should be interpreted in the context of the one, whole, and indivisible faith of the church (DH 3016, 3283; ND 221). Karl Barth (1886–1968) used the expression to designate the similarity and dissimilarity that simultaneously exist between the human decision to believe and God's decision to bestow grace. See *Faith; Grace; Mystery; Theologia Crucis*.

Analysis of Faith. A study of the motives that lead to faith in God as freely revealed in Jesus Christ. The analysis of these motives shows that the *auctoritas Dei revelantis* (Lat. "the authority of God who reveals") is the decisive factor in believing. See *Experience, Religious; Faith; Mystery; Preambles of Faith*.

Anamnesis (Gr. "remembrance"). The effective bringing to mind of God's saving involvement in history, especially in Christ's passion, death, resurrection, and glorification. In the Eucharist, the Lord's command "do this in memory of me" (1 Cor 11:24, 25; Luke 22:19) invites the assembly to appropriate the salvation he has effected once and for all. See *Eucharist; Paschal Mystery; Salvation History*.

Anaphora (Gr. "offering"). The eucharistic prayer or canon of the Mass. Normally it includes an introductory dialogue, thanksgiving, the words of institution from the Last Supper, the *anamnesis*, the *epiclesis*, and the doxology. East Syrians call the anaphora *quddasha* (Syriac "hallowing"). In the East, it bears the name of an apostle or some other saint (e.g., the anaphora of St. John Chrysostom or that of Addai and Mari). While the anaphora of Addai and Mari does not explicitly include either the institution narrative as a continuous whole or the words of institution as such, the Pontifical Council for Promoting Christian Unity recognized it as valid form of the Eucharist on October 26, 2001 (after a decision by the Congregation for the Doctrine of the Faith earlier in 2001). See *Anamnesis; Doxology; Epiclesis; Eucharistic Prayer*.

Anathema (Gr. "curse" or "object that is accursed"). A solemn form of excommunication or exclusion from the community. St. Paul uses the term against anyone who preaches a false gospel (Gal 1:9) or refuses the love of Christ (1 Cor 16:22).

Anawim (Heb. "the afflicted"). Poor people, those unsupported by wealth and social position. Although poverty was sometimes considered the result of idleness (Prov 10:4) and the sign of God's displeasure, the prophets demanded justice for the oppressed (Isa 10:2). The term came to designate those who place their trust in God (Zeph 2:3). The messianic king will ride on a donkey like a poor man (Zech 9:9; Matt 21:5). According to the *Magnificat*, God endorses the cause of the poor (Luke 1:46–55), who come first in Jesus' Beatitudes (Matt 5:3; Luke 6:20). See *Beatitudes; Poverty*.

Angelology. That treatise in systematic theology that studies the function, nature, and hierarchies of angels as well as their cult and iconography. See *Icon*.

Angels (Gr. "messengers"). God's spiritual envoys, recognized, albeit differently by the Jewish, Christian, and Islamic faiths. In earlier OT traditions, angels are hardly distinguishable from God (Gen 16:7–13), their purpose being to mediate between God and human beings and to protect God's transcendence. Teaching about angels developed greatly in late Judaism, where the names Michael, Gabriel, and Raphael appear. In the NT, angels play prominent roles (e.g., Matt 1:20, 24; Luke 2:9–15; John 20:12–13). They serve humanity's salvation (Heb 1:14). Church teaching distinguishes between the spiritual reality of angels and that of material beings, and affirms their personal existence (see DH 3891). While angels are more agents of revelation than its object, both scripture and church teaching take their existence for granted (see DH 3320). See *Cherubikon; Choirs of Angels; Guardian Angels*.

Anglican Communion. A name used at least since the first Lambeth Conference of 1867 for the episcopally governed churches with autonomous provinces that arose from the reform of the English Church in the sixteenth century and that are in communion with the Archbishop of Canterbury. It understood itself as the church of the fathers and aimed at a middle road between papal authority and Lutheran reform (see DH 2885–88, 3315–19; ND 1722–28). After the Glorious Revolution of 1688, the Nonjurors or members of the Church of England (including nine bishops) who refused to swear allegiance to the new rulers (William and Mary) tried but failed to negotiate union with the Eastern Orthodox patriarchs and the Church of Russia (1716–25).

In 1973 an official dialogue began between Anglicans and the Orthodox. After a series of agreed statements (which also expressed an Anglican willingness to drop the *Filioque* from the creed), the dialogue was suspended in 1977 over the question of women's ordination. A second phase of bilateral conversations began in 1980; in 1989, with Bishop John Zizioulas as the new Orthodox chairman, a third phase began, now called the International Commission for

Anglican-Orthodox Dialogue. There is also an Anglican-Methodist International Commission.

Leo XIII's 1896 encyclical *Apostolicae Curae* (which rejected the validity of Anglican orders) did not prevent Anglican-Catholic dialogue reopening at the Malines Conversations (1921–25). When Archbishop Geoffrey Fisher (1887–1972) visited Blessed (Pope) John XXIII in 1960, he was not only the first Archbishop of Canterbury to visit Rome since 1397, but he also inaugurated a series of "summit" meetings between popes and archbishops of Canterbury. After Vatican II (1962–65) had referred to the "special place" of the Anglican Communion (UR 13) and Paul VI met with the Archbishop of Canterbury (Michael Ramsey) in 1966, a Joint Preparatory Commission convened in 1967 and was succeeded in 1970 by the Anglican-Roman Catholic International Commission (ARCIC I). This produced agreed statements and elucidations on the Eucharist, ministry and ordination, and authority in the church; all these documents were published together in the *Final Report* of 1982. Established in 1983, ARCIC II produced documents on salvation and the church and the church as communion. In 1999 it issued *The Gift of Authority* (Authority in the Church III). Since 1966 there has been an Anglican center in Rome; its director represents to the Holy See the Archbishop of Canterbury and the primates of the Anglican Communion. In a 2007 agreed statement, "Growing Together in Unity and Mission," the Joint Anglican-Catholic Commission proposed deepening the role of the Petrine office to consolidate the universal church. At a 2011 meeting in Bose Monastery (Northern Italy), the Commission raised the question at the level of the local churches.

The 1988 Meissen Agreement between the Church of England and the Evangelical (Lutheran) Churches of Germany involved a mutual recognition of Eucharist and ministry. The Poorvoo Agreement of 1992 between the Anglican Churches of England, Ireland, Scotland, and Wales and the Lutheran Churches of Nordic and Baltic countries, all of which are episcopal, went further—by inviting one another's bishops to take part in episcopal ordinations. Around the world there are at least eighty million members of the Anglican Communion. See *Bishop; Communicatio in Sacris; Eastern Churches; Episcopalians; Fathers of the Church; Filioque; Holy Orders; Lambeth Conferences; Lutheranism; Methodism; Puritans; Reformation, The; Thirty-Nine Articles; Validity.*

Anglo-Catholicism. A term first employed in the mid-nineteenth century to designate High Church Anglicans who shared Catholic doctrines, traditions, and sacramental practice. See *Ecumenism; Oxford Movement.*

Anhypostasia (Gr. "without a hypostasis"). A term used of Christ's human nature, which, while complete, does not subsist on its own as a human person or *hypostasis*, but rather in the divine Logos. See *Enhypostasia; Hypostasis; Logos; Nature; Neo-Chalcedonianism; Person.*

Animism (Lat. "soul," "spirit"). A term once widely applied to the belief of less developed peoples that certain plants and material objects have a spirit or soul of their own.

Annulment. A declaration of invalidity: that is, an official declaration by a church court that a sacrament, especially a marriage or ordination, all appearances to the contrary notwithstanding, never existed because of some impediment, a lack of consent, or some failure to observe the proper form or procedure in being married or ordained. If the nullity of marriage is established, both parties are free to remarry, but only after an appeals court has confirmed the verdict (see CIC 1671–85, 1708–12; CCEO 842, 1096, 1357–77). See *Canon Law; Holy Orders; Marriage; Marriage Impediments; Validity*.

Annunciation. The feast celebrating the message of Christ's conception brought to Mary by the angel Gabriel (Luke 1:26–38). Of Byzantine origin, the feast seems to have been observed in Rome from the seventh century. The date of March 25 comes nine months before Christmas, the traditional but not historically reliable date for the birth of Jesus. See *Advent; Christmas; Christmas Preparation; Virginal Conception of Jesus*.

Anointing. Smearing or pouring oil on persons (or sometimes on things) to change them and their relationship to God and the community. The OT speaks of kings, priests, and prophets being anointed and so endowed with God's Spirit (see Exod 30:25–31; 1 Sam 10:1; Ps 2:2; Isa 45:1; 61:1). Christians anoint with oil the sick and those being baptized, confirmed, ordained to ministry (in the West), or installed as kings. See *Chrism; Confirmation; Messiah*.

Anointing of the Sick. The new name for "extreme unction" after the reforms of the Second Vatican Council (1962–65) (SC 73). As a sacrament, it recalls the NT ministry to the sick (see Mark 6:13; Jas 5:13–15) and expresses the whole church's solidarity with the sick, the old, and the dying by enabling them to draw spiritual and physical healing from Christ's victory over sickness and death (DH 1694–1700, 1716–19; ND 1635–40, 1656–59). In the West, the sacrament is administered by one priest; in the East, by several. See *Sacrament*.

Anomoeans (Gr. "dissimilars"). The followers of Aetius (d. ca. 370) and Eunomius (d. 394) who held that the Son is only the first creature and unlike the Father in essence. Eunomius also taught that the Spirit was simply the first and highest creature produced by the Son. Hence his disciples baptized only "in the name of the Lord," and, therefore, those Anomoeans who accepted or returned to orthodox faith had to be baptized. See *Arianism; Cappadocian Fathers; Eunomianism; Filioque*.

Anonymous Christians. The term of Karl Rahner (1904–84) for those who are saved by Christ's grace, even if (through no fault of their own) they remain unbaptized and outside the Christian community (see LG 16 and GS 16). Rahner developed this term and thesis in the light of God's will to save all people (1 Tim 2:4). See *Church; Salvation.*

Anthropocentricism. An approach to theological questions that takes human experience as its point of departure and subsequent guide. When this approach degenerates into making human beings the center and sole measure of all things, anthropocentricism makes genuine theology impossible. See *Mystery; Theocentricism; Theology.*

Anthropology. The interpretation of human existence (in its origin, nature, and destiny) in the light of Christian faith. As a secular, academic discipline, anthropology involves the study of human societies and customs. See *Creation; Deification; Eschatology; Grace; Image of God; Original Sin; Protology.*

Anthropomorphism. The attribution to God of human characteristics, both physical (e.g., face, mouth, and hands) and emotional (e.g., sorrow, joy, and anger). See *Apophatic Theology; Negative Theology.*

Antichrist. Christ's supreme opponent, connected with the end of the world (1 John 2:18, 22; 4:3) and personified by those who deny the Incarnation (2 John 7). He has also been identified with "the man of sin" (2 Thess 2:3–10) and "the beast" (Rev 11:7; see DH 916, 1180). A recurrent theme in Russian religious thought and literature, the Antichrist was a name the Old Believers gave to Tsar Peter the Great (1672–1725). Vladimir Solov'iev (1853–1900) wrote the classic *Short Story of the Antichrist*; and Dmitri Merezhkovski (1865–1941), a trilogy, *Christ and Antichrist.* See *Messiah; Old Believers.*

Anticlericalism. An attitude that denies the right and duty of church leaders to speak out on issues of public morality and have any real influence on a country's political and sociocultural life. See *Church; Clergy; Clericalism; Political Theology.*

Antidoron (Gr. "in place of the gift"). See *Eulogy.*

Antimension (Gr. "instead of the table"). See *Altar; Veneration of Saints.*

Antinomianism (Gr. "against the law"). A disregard of or even contempt for law. In general this rejection may be supported by philosophical or theological reasons, spring from a psychological rejection of authority, or simply be dictated by economic greed. Since NT times, various sects have claimed that Christians are no longer bound by law. They have justified this attitude by misrepresenting Paul's teaching (see Rom 3:8, 21) or claiming a special guidance of the Holy Spirit that delivers them from ordinary moral obligations. See *Anabaptists; Gnosticism; Law.*

Antiochene Theology. An orientation in theology, connected with the Christian community of Antioch and emerging with a very distinct exegetical profile in the fourth century. It stressed the literal and historical interpretation of the Bible, but also looked for a *theoria* (Gr. "insight") that went beyond the mere letter of the text. While open to the danger of inadequate *dyophysism* (Gr. "two-natures") by not properly relating the divine and human natures in the one person of Jesus Christ, its emphasis on his full humanity partly anticipated modern Christology from below. Antiochene theology is generally thought to have been shaped by the martyr St. Lucian of Antioch (d. 312), who had studied at Edessa, and then developed by St. Eustathius of Antioch (d. ca. 336) and Diodore of Tarsus (d. ca. 390); it reached its high point with St. John Chrysostom (ca. 347–407), Theodore of Mopsuestia (ca. 350–428), and Theodoret of Cyrrhus (ca. 393–ca. 466). See *Alexandrian Theology; Christology from Above; Christology from Below; Edessa; Logos-Anthropos Christology; Nestorianism; Senses of Scripture; Three Chapters, The.*

Antiphon (Gr. "alternate response" or "refrain"). A verse often taken from the psalms or other scriptural books and sung by a choir alternating with the congregation or by one choir alternating with another. Common to all Christian liturgies, antiphons usually emphasize the liturgical feast being celebrated or the biblical readings being used. In the Byzantine liturgy, the *antiphanon* signifies either a group of three psalms or a group of verses sung between the first litanies of the Eucharist. See *Byzantine Christianity; Choir; Eucharist; Litany; Liturgy.*

Antisemitism. Hostility toward Jews on racial, religious, and political grounds. The Second Vatican Council (1962–65) rejected the charge against the Jews of collective guilt in the death of Jesus and deplored "the hatred, persecutions, and displays of antisemitism directed against the Jews at any time and from any source" (NA 4). A 1998 Vatican document, "We Remember: A Reflection on the *Shoah*," distinguishes "Anti-Judaism" (or mistrust of and hostility toward Jews on the part of Christians) from "Anti-Semitism," an evil ideology that has its roots outside Christianity and falsely rejects the dignity of all peoples in the unity of the one human race. See *Holocaust; Jew.*

Apatheia (Gr. "lack of passion or suffering"). A Stoic term sometimes used by the Church Fathers to indicate the serenity that comes through growing freedom from one's evil passions and deepening union with God. See *Asceticism; Deification; Hesychasm; Impassibility; Mortification; Stoicism.*

Aphthartodocetism (Gr. "incorruptibility" and "appearance"). A sixth-century Monophysite heresy, founded by Julian of Halicarnassus (d. after 518). It claimed that from the first moment of the Incarnation Christ's body was incorruptible and immortal, but he freely accepted suffering for our sake. See *Chalcedon, Council of; Docetism; Monophysitism.*

Apocalyptic Literature (Gr. "uncovering," "revealing"). A style of writing that ran from around 200 BC to AD 100 and claimed to reveal divine mysteries, above all the signs that will precede the (already determined) end of all history, the resurrection of the dead, and the general judgment, which will lead to the final transformation of the world. Apocalyptic writings include both non-canonical works (e.g., Enoch) and canonical works (e.g., Daniel, Revelation, and Mark 13). See *Eschatology; Parousia; Resurrection of the Dead; Revelation.*

Apocatastasis (Gr. "universal restoration"). A theory, ascribed falsely (it seems) to Origen (ca. 185–ca. 254), and later condemned as heretical, that all angels and human beings, even the demons and the damned, will ultimately be saved (see DH 409, 411). Mitigated forms of apocatastasis were held by some early writers such as St. Gregory of Nyssa (ca. 330–ca. 395) and St. Isaac of Nineveh (seventh century). See *Hell.*

Apocrypha (Gr. "hidden" or "not genuine"). OT books or sections of books written in or translated into Greek (from ca. 200 BC to possibly as late as AD 40), printed in Catholic Bibles but often omitted in Protestant Bibles. Some of these works (e.g., Judith, Wisdom, and 2 Maccabees) were composed in Greek; others (e.g., 1 Maccabees) were composed in Hebrew, but only the Greek translation is extant. Tobit was originally written in Hebrew or Aramaic, but apart from some fragments in those languages, only the Greek version remains. Composed in Hebrew before 180 BC, Sirach was rendered into Greek fifty years later; since 1900, two-thirds of the original Hebrew text has been recovered. (See DH 179, 213, 354; ND 202–3.) See *Bible; Canon of Scripture; Deuterocanonical Books; Old Testament; Vulgate.*

Apocryphal Gospels. Writings from the second to the fourth centuries that aim to supplement and revise what the canonical gospels tell us of Jesus' birth, life, teaching, death, and resurrection. These sometimes fanciful and Gnostic-tinged texts include "The Gospel of the Hebrews," "The Gospel of Judas," "The Gospel of Mary," "The Gospel of Peter," and "The Gospel of Thomas." See *Gnosticism; Gospel.*

Apollinarianism. A christological heresy coming from a bishop of Laodicea, Apollinarius (ca. 310–ca. 390). Intent on defending Christ's full divinity against the Arians, he undercut his full humanity by holding that Christ had no spirit or rational soul, this being replaced by the divine Logos (see DH 146,

149, 151; ND 13). His overriding concern was thus to establish a strict unity in Christ, as is shown in his formula, "the one incarnate nature of the Logos." See *Arianism; Christology; Logos; Monophysitism.*

Apologetics. The intellectual defense of Christian beliefs about God, Christ, the church, and our common human destiny. The arguments may be addressed to adherents of other religions, atheists and agnostics, members of separated Christian communities, wavering members of one's own church, or simply to believers who want to see how responsible their faith is (see 1 Pet 3:15). See *Dialogue; Fundamental Theology.*

Apologists. The name given to St. Justin Martyr (ca. 100–ca. 165), St. Theophilus of Antioch (late second century), Athenagoras (who ca. 177 addressed his *Apology* to Emperor Marcus Aurelius), Tatian (d. ca. 160), and other Christian writers who defended their faith against Jewish and pagan objections. Whereas some, such as Justin, became the first Christian authors to make serious use of philosophy, others, such as Tatian, were hostile to Greek philosophy. The apologists offered educated outsiders a case for the Christian religion. Latin apologetics came of age somewhat later with Minucius Felix (the second- or third-century author of *Octavius*) and Tertullian (ca. 160–ca. 220). See *Apostolic Fathers; Fathers of the Church; Philosophy; Platonism; Stoicism.*

Apophatic Theology (Gr. "prohibiting," "negative"). Central concept in Eastern theology, often translated as negative theology. It points out the inadequacy of all attempts to describe the absolute mystery of God. Any affirmation about God has to be qualified by a corresponding negation and the recognition that God surpasses in an infinite way our categories. Knowledge of God is never purely intellectual, but calls for an ascent to God through moral and religious purification, classically described in *The Life of Moses* by St. Gregory of Nyssa (ca. 330–ca. 395). See *Cataphatic Theology; Dark Night; Essence and Energies; Negative Theology.*

Apophthegmata Patrum (Gr./Lat. "sayings of the Fathers"). An anonymous (end of the fifth century) collection in Greek of anecdotes and sayings from the desert fathers of Egypt and elsewhere, who include St. Antony the Abbot (ca. 251–356), St. Syncletica (fourth century), and Poemen (fifth century). Some extravagances apart, the work is characterized by wisdom and discretion. It offers an invaluable source for the origins of monasticism and Christian spiritual life. Analogous collections, translated into Latin, go by the name of *Verba Seniorum* (Words of the Elders). See *Anachoretism; Cenobites; Monasticism.*

Apostasy (Gr. "standing apart"). A word occurring in the Greek OT (Jer 2:19) and Acts 21:21 to describe defection from the faith and the believing community. In its current usage, it means the deliberate and complete abandonment of the faith by a baptized Christian and is thus to be distinguished from mere heresy and schism. Julian the Apostate (Roman emperor, 361–63) is so known because he withdrew imperial support for Christianity and attempted to restore the cult of the pagan gods. See *Faith; Heresy; Schism*.

Apostle (Gr. "somebody sent," "ambassador"). In a narrower sense, the twelve disciples chosen by Christ (Matt 10:2; Luke 6:13–16) who were to witness to his ministry, death, and resurrection through the power of the Holy Spirit (Acts 1:5, 8). In a broader sense, the apostles include Paul (1 Cor 9:1; Gal 1:1, 17), Barnabas (Acts 14:4, 14), James (1 Cor 15:7), and others (Rom 16:7) who served as leaders in the original Christian mission and were invested with Christ's authority in founding the church (Eph 2:20). See *Apostolic Succession; Petrine Ministry*.

Apostolic Fathers. The name for the oldest nonbiblical and orthodox Christian writers, commonly adopted after Jean Baptiste Cotelier published in 1672 the so-called *Epistle of Barnabas* (first century), St. Clement of Rome (d. ca. 96), St. Ignatius of Antioch (ca. 35–ca. 107), the *Shepherd of Hermas* (second century), and St. Polycarp of Smyrna (ca. 69–ca. 155) as well as the acts of the martyrdom of Clement, Ignatius, and Polycarp. In 1765 Andrea Gallandi added the *Epistle to Diognetus*, a defense of Christianity, and Papias of Hierapolis (ca. 60–130). Philotheos Bryennios published in 1883 what may be the oldest work in this whole group, the anonymous *Didache* (Gr. "teaching"). These writings shed invaluable light on the passage from the NT church to post-apostolic Christianity. Some modern scholars wish to exclude those authors who were probably not directly connected with the apostles, or whose mentality is not so close to the NT. This suggests listing as apostolic fathers only St. Clement, St. Ignatius of Antioch, St. Polycarp, and Papias as well as St. Quadratus (second century), who around 124 addressed to Emperor Hadrian the oldest apology for Christian faith. See *Apologists; Didache; Fathers of the Church*.

Apostolic Succession. The unbroken continuity in essential belief and practice between the church today and the church founded by Christ through the apostles. This continuity is expressed by calling the bishops the successors of the apostles (LG 20). As a visible sign of this succession and of an individual bishop's union with his fellow bishops, the consecrating bishops lay hands on the bishop-elect. See *Apostle; Bishop; Petrine Ministry*.

Apostolicity. The identity in Christian faith and practice of the present church with the church of the apostles. Along with unity, holiness, and catholicity, the Nicene-Constantinopolitan Creed names apostolicity as one of the four marks of the church. See *Catholicity; Creed, Nicene; Holiness; Marks (Notes) of the Church.*

Appearances of the Risen Lord. A special series of encounters with the risen Jesus that were the primary ways the first Christians knew that he had risen from the dead. He appeared to such individuals as Mary Magdalene (Matt 28:9–10; John 20:11–18), Peter (1 Cor 15:5; Luke 24:34), and Paul (1 Cor 9:1; Gal 1:12, 16; Acts 9:1–19), and to groups, above all, "the eleven" (e.g., Mark 16:7; Matt 28:16–20; 1 Cor 15:5). As 1 Corinthians 15:8, John 20:29, and other NT texts (e.g., 1 Pet 1:8) indicate, the appearances of the risen Christ were experiences reserved to the original witnesses, whose preaching and ministry inaugurated the Christian mission and church. See *Apostle; Ascension; Resurrection.*

Appropriation (Lat. "to make one's own"). Assigning a divine action or attribute, which is actually common to all three persons of the Trinity, to only one of them. Thus creation is appropriated to the Father; redemption, to the Son; and sanctification, to the Holy Spirit. In fact, all *opera ad extra* (Lat. "outward actions") are common to the three persons (see DH 545–46, 1330; ND 325). See *Attributes, Divine; Immanent Trinity.*

Archbishop. Title used from the fourth or fifth century for bishops of particularly prominent sees, and later applied in the West to metropolitans or heads of an ecclesiastical region. In the Latin Church, *archbishop* can also be used as a purely honorific title. In the East, patriarchs were called archbishops, a title later extended to metropolitans. See *Bishop; Patriarch.*

Archdeacon. Originally, the head of the college of deacons, who helped the bishop with the administration and discipline of his diocese. The term came to designate a priest in charge of important functions in the diocese. See *Deacon; Diocese.*

Archimandrite (Gr. "ruler of a fold"). A title in the Byzantine East applied to the superior of a large monastery or group of monasteries, or used to honor certain celibate priests.

Arguments for the Existence of God. Philosophical ways of showing the ultimate reasonableness of belief in God by moving, for example, from design in the world to a divine Designer (see DH 3004, 3026; ND 113, 115). Far from replacing belief, these arguments come from a prior faith in and experience of God. See *Experience, Religious; Five Ways, The; God; Mystery; Natural Theology; Philosophical Theology; Teleological Argument.*

Arianism. A heresy condemned at Nicaea I (325) and derived from an Alexandrian priest Arius (ca. 270–ca. 336), who asserted that God's Son did not always exist and consequently was not divine by nature but only the first among creatures (see DH 125–26, 130; ND 7–8). After seriously disturbing church peace down to 381, Arianism survived in a mitigated form for several centuries among the Germanic tribes. See *Anomoeans; Filioque; Homoeans; Homoousios; Nicaea, First Council of; Semi-Arianism; Subordinationism*.

Aristotelianism. A philosophical orientation, originating with Aristotle (384–22 BC) and characterized by a greater realism than the earlier and often rival school of Platonism. After being neglected or opposed by some Fathers of the Church, Aristotelian ethics, logic, theory of causality (with efficient, final, formal, and material causes), and view of the human soul as the form of the body (not its prisoner, as in Platonism) came into their own in the Middle Ages through the support of Arab philosophers, Moses Maimonides (1135–1204), and St. Thomas Aquinas (ca. 1225–74). Aquinas elaborated his proofs for the existence of God on an Aristotelian basis, but championed the natural immortality of the soul apparently denied in Aristotelianism. See *Causality; Five Ways, The; Neoplatonism; Platonism; Soul; Thomism*.

Armenian Christianity. Since September 23, 1991, once again an independent country (even if some of its former territory still remains part of Turkey and Iran), Armenia claims to have been evangelized by the apostles Thaddaeus, Bartholomew, Simon, and Jude. Although Christianity had arrived by the end of the first century, the real credit for establishing Christianity belongs to St. Gregory the Illuminator (ca. 260–ca. 328). He converted the king, who made Christianity the state religion in 301—the first time this had happened in any country. Prevented by a war with the Persians from sending delegates to the Council of Chalcedon (451), Armenia remained united with Constantinople until 518, when the latter definitively accepted Chalcedon, after which Armenia stayed non-Chalcedonian. During the crusades (1198) and through the influence of the Council of Florence (1438–45), some Armenians reached a union with Rome (see DH 1006–20, 1310–28, 1344–45; ND 407, 1412–18, 1305–8, 2534). The Armenian Catholic patriarch resides in Beirut, Lebanon. The highest spiritual authority of Orthodox Armenians, the Supreme Patriarch and *Catholicos* of All Armenians, resides in Etchmiadzin, Armenia. See *Chalcedon, Council of; Eastern Catholic Churches, Four Ranks of; Eastern Churches; Florence, Council of; Monophysitism; Patriarchates, Orthodox*.

Ars Moriendi (Lat. "art of dying"). Late medieval teaching on the way Christians ought to face death. Books on this topic, for example, the work of Jean Gerson (1363–1429), enjoyed great popularity and influenced the portrayal of death in art. See *Death*.

Ascension. The risen Christ's "going up" into heaven to enter into full and final glory at "the right hand of the Father," where he intercedes for us and exercises his power over the whole universe (see DH 10–30, 189; ND 2–5). Marking the close of the post-resurrection appearances (except for the unique case of Paul), the ascension inaugurates Christ's new presence through his followers, on whom the Holy Spirit is now poured out. Hence the ascension was initially celebrated together with Pentecost, but toward the end of the fourth century the Feast of the Ascension was fixed at forty days after Easter (Acts 1:3), and became widespread in the fifth century. See *Pentecost; Resurrection*.

Asceticism (Gr. "exercise"). Ways and means adopted by Christians under the action of the Spirit to purify themselves from sin and remove obstacles in the way of freely following Christ. Genuine asceticism brings a growth in contemplation and the love of God, which not only is not detrimental to but also favors personal maturity and social responsibility. See *Abstinence; Contemplation; Fasting; Imitation of Christ; Monasticism; Mortification; Mysticism; Penance*.

Ash Wednesday. In the Roman rite followed generally in the West, the first day of Lent, characterized by a penitential service during which the faithful receive ashes on their foreheads or on the crown of their heads with the exhortation: "Turn away from sin and be faithful to the gospel," or "Remember, you are dust and to dust you will return." Ash Wednesday and Good Friday are the only obligatory abstinence and fasting days in current Roman Catholic practice. In the Ambrosian rite, still followed by the Archdiocese of Milan, Lent begins on the Monday of the first week after Ash Wednesday and the first Lenten fast occurs on the Friday of that week. The Roman rite added the five days from Ash Wednesday to the following Sunday inclusively, because the next six weeks up to Easter included only thirty-six days of fasting and not forty, since Sundays were excluded from the Lenten fast. See *Abstinence; Clean Monday; Fasting; Lent; Penance; Rite*.

Assent, Notional. A merely abstract assent to some truth without fully grasping or being touched by the reality of that truth. See *Theology*.

Assent of Faith. The confession of God's saving self-revelation in the crucified and risen Jesus (e.g., Rom 10:9) that involves a personal commitment to Christ as Lord (e.g., Rom 1:5; 1 Cor 12:3) and a hopeful confidence in the resurrection to come (Rom 6:8). This free and reasonable act, made possible through the power of the Holy Spirit, enables one to be baptized and enter the church. See *Baptism; Faith*.

Assent, Real. A full assent to truth, in particular, to concrete rather than abstract truths. Observing how many people accept only notionally the realities mediated by the concrete truths and language of Christian revelation, Blessed John Henry Newman (1801–90) popularized the distinction between real and merely notional assent. See *Faith*.

Assumption of the Blessed Virgin. The dogma defined in 1950 by Pope Pius XII that at the end of her earthly life Mary was taken up body and soul into eternal glory (see DH 3900–3904; ND 713–15). Where Christ "ascended" of his own power, Mary was "assumed" by divine power. From the fifth century, Eastern Christians celebrated the *koimesis* ("falling asleep") of Our Lady. "Assumption" replaced *dormition* ("falling asleep") when Rome adopted the feast in the seventh century. Out of deference to the Eastern tradition of Mary's "falling asleep," Martin Jugie (d. 1954), an expert on Eastern theology, persuaded Pius XII in the formulation of the dogma to speak of her assumption occurring "when her earthly life came to an end" (DH 3903; ND 715), rather than "when she died." See *Dogma; Mariology*.

Atheism (Gr. "godlessness"). The denial of God's existence, in theory or in practice. The many forms of atheism range from tolerant indifference to a militant rejection, which varies according to the particular concept of God being rejected and the socio-ecclesiastical setting for the conflict. For some, even a long, time it is possible to withhold assent to God, but to bracket off consistently the question of God's existence is irresponsible and blameworthy. Through his publications (e.g., *The God Delusion*) and speaking engagements (e.g., leading the Global Atheist Convention in Melbourne, April 2012), Richard Dawkins (b. 1941) has led militant atheists in the English-speaking world. See *Agnosticism; God; Mystery; Negative Theology*.

Athos, Mount. The famous Holy Mountain at the end of the most eastern promontory of the three-pronged Chalcidice peninsula in northern Greece. On this promontory there are twenty autonomous monasteries, the first one being founded by St. Athanasius the Athonite in 962. All types of Orthodox monks are to be found on Mount Athos: (a) the anchorite or hermit; (b) the semi-hermit or anchorite living in a colony of hermits under the spiritual guidance of an experienced monk; (c) the cenobite or monk living in community, with cenobitism predominating throughout the East, especially after St. Basil the Great (ca. 330–79) wrote his two rules (the rule St. Athanasius the Athonite adopted for Mount Athos followed closely those of St. Basil and St. Theodore the Studite [759–826], the great Eastern reformer of monasticism); and (d) a fourth type, the *idiorrhythmic* (Gr. "own style") monk, who enjoys some measure of financial independence, was introduced on Mount Athos in the fourteenth century. In general monks of the Holy Mountain enjoy a considerable degree of administrative autonomy; ecclesiastically, they are under the Patriarch of Constantinople. No women may set foot on the peninsula. See

Anachoretism; Cenobites; Hermit; Hesychasm; Monasticism; Palamism; Philocalia; Theocracy.

Atonement. Often used as a synonym for *redemption* (and sometimes carelessly used as a synonym for *expiation*), "at-one-ment" refers to the end effect of the process of redemption: being at one with God (from whom we were previously alienated) and so sharing in the divine life. The language of atonement may also point to means for removing guilt and reconciling sinners with God, in particular, various ceremonies in the OT (e.g., those prescribed for *Yom Kippur* or the annual Day of Expiation) and the death and resurrection of Christ in the NT. See *Deification; Expiation; Justification; Redemption; Salvation; Yom Kippur*.

Attributes, Divine. Properties predicated of God on the basis of philosophical thought (e.g., immutability) and/or biblical revelation (e.g., faithfulness), and expressing, within the limits of analogy, the ineffable essence of God, from which in the final analysis they are not really distinct. See *Analogy; Essence and Energies; Palamism*.

Attrition (Lat. "remorse"). A term coined in the twelfth century to designate that sorrow for sins produced by shame or fear of punishment rather than by love of God, and sometimes called imperfect contrition. The Council of Trent (1545–63) taught that attrition suffices for the fruitful reception of the sacrament of penance when it is animated by the hope of being forgiven and the resolution not to sin again (see DH 1678; ND 1624). See *Contrition; Penance, Sacrament of*.

Augsburg Confession. The first confessional statement of the Lutheran Church. Composed mainly by Philipp Melanchthon and presented to Charles V at the Diet of Augsburg in 1530, it consists of twenty-one articles summarizing essential Lutheran doctrines and seven articles directed against abuses in the Roman Church. In the 450th anniversary year (1980) Blessed (Pope) John Paul II (pope 1978–2005) joined the German bishops in recognizing that the *Augsburg Confession* expresses fundamental truths of our common Christian faith. See *Dialogue; Lutheranism*.

Augustinianism. The philosophical and theological system of St. Augustine of Hippo (354–430), a synthesis emphasizing (a) God's sovereign freedom in granting grace and (b) the primacy of God's illumination in human knowledge. Augustine's own views are sometimes called *Augustinism*, to distinguish them from the Augustinianism that was developed by Thomas Aquinas's pupil Aegidius Romanus of the Colonna family (= Giles of Rome, ca. 1243–1306) and that became dominant among the Hermits of St. Augustine. See *Grace; Semi-Pelagianism*.

Authority. The justified expectation that a command will be obeyed or that a statement will be accepted as true. In the church, all authority comes from Christ and is to be exercised under the guidance of the Holy Spirit as a service, not as an assertion of power (see Luke 22:24–27; LG 24). See *Analysis of Faith; Antinomianism; Autonomy; Charisms; Heteronomy; Jurisdiction; Magisterium; Obedience; Theonomy.*

Autocephalous (Gr. "having its own head"). A term mainly used of churches governed by their own synods and belonging to the communion of Eastern and Oriental Orthodox churches. All patriarchates are autocephalous, but not all autocephalous churches are patriarchates. For the Eastern Orthodox, the Patriarch of Constantinople enjoys a primacy of honor, and a general council could legislate for all autocephalous churches. See *Eastern Churches; Oriental Orthodox; Patriarch.*

Autonomy (Gr. "self-government"). A term often used since Immanuel Kant (1724–1804) of the right to be self-determining in the spheres of moral freedom and religious thought. As this independence is exercised in a universe created and conserved in being by God, our autonomy can only be relative. See *Enlightenment; Heteronomy; Theonomy.*

Azymes (Gr. "without yeast"). Thin bread baked without yeast (see Gen 19:3), eaten during a week-long OT feast commemorating the Exodus from Egypt (Exod 12:15; 23:15; 34:18). On account of its fermentation, leavened bread came to signify corruption (Matt 16:6; 1 Cor 5:7). Since the Synoptic Gospels report the Last Supper to have taken place on the first day of the feast of Azymes (Matt 26:17; Mark 14:12; Luke 22:7), unleavened bread is used in the Latin Mass. Most Eastern churches, however, follow St. John, who dates the Last Supper and crucifixion to just before the feast of Azymes began (John 13:1; 18:28; 19:14,31). This difference provided one of the immediate pretexts for the schism of 1054 between East and West. Archbishop Leo of Ohrid accused the Latins of being "azymites" or "infermentari," while the Easterners were nicknamed "prozymites" or "frumentari." The Council of Florence (1439) taught that both unleavened and leavened bread may be used for the Eucharist (see DH 1303; ND 1508). All Easterners, except the Armenians and the Maronites, use leavened bread. See *Armenian Christianity; Eucharist; Florence, Council of; Lord's Supper, The; Maronites; Passover.*

B

Baptism (Gr. "washing" or "dipping"). The basic sacrament of "rebirth" that makes one a member of the church and thus capable of receiving the other sacraments. Washed with water and consecrated by the Holy Spirit (John 3:5; Matt 28:19), with faith and repentance the baptized are cleansed from sin, share in the dying and rising of Christ, and begin a new life in him (Rom 6:3–11). In the first centuries, baptism was normally followed at once by confirmation and communion, a practice still maintained by the Orthodox and now standard practice in the Latin Church in the case of adults. Baptism is necessary for salvation, but its place can be taken by baptism of blood (martyrdom) or baptism of desire (the implicit or explicit wish to be baptized) (DH 1524; ND 1928). See *Catechumens; Character; Initiation; Sacrament; Sponsor.*

Baptism by Affusion (or infusion). A way of baptizing by pouring water three times on the head of the candidates. Introduced for the sick who could not be immersed or submerged, it became in the thirteenth century the standard Western way of baptizing. Often taken to have been invented later by the Latins, a very early Christian document and one written in Greek, the *Didache* (no. 7), attests the practice of baptism by "affusion." See *Apostolic Fathers.*

Baptism by Aspersion. A way of baptizing under emergency circumstances by sprinkling (instead of pouring) water three times on the candidates.

Baptism by Immersion. A way of baptizing, once popular but now found only among East and West Syrians, which consists in pouring water three times on candidates when they are already in the water or are going down into it. See *Syrian Orthodox Church.*

Baptism by Submersion. The normal way of baptizing among Eastern Orthodox and among many Baptists in the West. The candidates' whole body, or at least their head, is completely submerged three times in the water. See *Eastern Churches.*

Baptists. Members of a very large evangelical church who trace their immediate origins to the early seventeenth century when they broke with the Anglican Church. John Smyth (ca. 1554–1612), called the Se-Baptist because he baptized himself, founded the first Baptist Church in Amsterdam in 1609. Baptists reserve baptism for those who consciously profess repentance for their sins and faith in Christ, and maintain the relative autonomy of the local congregations. See *Anabaptists; Evangelicals; Infant Baptism.*

Basic (Base) Communities. A term coming from Latin America to describe the many local groups of Christians who strive to revitalize their church life by worshiping and studying the scriptures together, by using their personal gifts in the service of others, and by becoming involved in common social action. This movement has been encouraged by the general conferences of the Latin American bishops held at Medellín, Colombia (1968), and Puebla, Mexico

(1979). The texts of Puebla speak of "Basic Ecclesial Communities" to distinguish them from other groups that may have weaker links with church authority. See *Church; Liberation Theology; Option for the Poor.*

Basle, Council of (1431–49). Convoked by Martin V (pope 1417–31) and then by Eugenius IV (pope 1431–47), this council was still tainted by the conciliarism of the previous Council of Constance (1414–18). Partly for this reason and partly because the Greek Church agreed to attend a general council in Ferrara, Pope Eugenius ordered the council transferred there in 1437. A minority at Basle obeyed, but the majority stayed to elect an antipope, Felix V. This tried the patience of Western Christian nations, which gave their allegiance to Pope Eugenius when Basle became schismatic. Felix V abdicated in 1449. In spite of some unacceptable conciliarist teaching, Basle decreed a series of reforms for the church (see DH 1445). See *Conciliarism; Constance, Council of; Florence, Council of.*

Beatific Vision. That immediate and fulfilling vision of God in heaven that will constitute the core of eternal happiness for the redeemed (see DH 1000–1002, 1304–6; ND 2305–9). See *Heaven; Light of Glory; Palamism.*

Beatification. The solemn approval for the public veneration after death of a Christian of heroic virtue. In 1747 Benedict XIV reserved to the pope the right to beatify. Since Blessed John Paul II (pope 1978–2005), many beatifications have taken place outside Rome, sometimes with the pope presiding and sometimes with the local bishop (or someone else) presiding. See *Canonization.*

Beatitudes. The eight (or nine) blessings in Christ's Sermon on the Mount (Mt 5:3–11), which have partial parallels in the OT (e.g., Ps 1:1; Tob 13:15–16; Sir 14:20–27; 25:7–10) and sum up perfection for all Christians. In the parallel Sermon on the Plain (Luke 6:20–26), the four blessings, coupled with the four woes, are more specific in their demands. The beatitudes, which present the kingdom of God in its central requirements and promises, have proved inspiring to many non-Christians. See *Imitation of Christ; Kingdom of God.*

Beauty, Theology of. In aesthetics, beauty is that quality or combination of qualities that gives pleasure. The harmony of God's own perfections and the interplay of forces in the drama of salvation produce delight through their beauty. We can contemplate this beauty in the glory or splendor that Christ revealed as the only-begotten Son of the Father (John 1:14). In recent times Hans Urs von Balthasar (1905–88) in the West and Pavel Florenskij (1882–ca. 1943) and Paul Evdokimov (1901–70) in the East did much to develop the theology of beauty. See *Aesthetics; Glory of God; Transcendentals.*

Being. Anything that is or exists. As applicable to everything, "being" as such has a minimal conceptual content. Exodus 3:14 ("I am who I am"), interpreted in the light of Greek philosophy, led Christians to speak of God as the Supreme Being or Being itself.

Benediction. A eucharistic devotion that became common in the West from the sixteenth century. A consecrated host is placed in a monstrance on the altar and exposed for veneration. After hymns, prayers, and the use of incense, the celebrant blesses the congregation by making a sign of the cross with the monstrance. In the East, benediction is unknown, except among some Catholics influenced by the West. See *Blessing*.

Berakah (Heb. "blessing"). Jewish prayer of thanksgiving to God (e.g., Gen 24:27; Ps 28:6). The Christian term *Eucharist* is a translation of *berakah*.

Berith (Heb. "obligation" or "covenant"). Central Jewish concept that might have originally indicated simply an obligation imposed by God or (occasionally) a promise made by God. Later it denoted the reciprocal, covenantal relationship between God and the chosen people. See *Covenant*.

Bible. The sacred writings inspired by God and expressing the Jewish and Christian faith in a way that is normative for all time. See *Apocrypha; Canon of Scripture; Deuterocanonical Books; Hermeneutics; Inspiration, Biblical; Marcionism; New Testament; Old Testament*.

Biblical Criticism. That modern search for a richer understanding of the Bible that follows various scholarly approaches. Textual criticism seeks to establish as closely as possible the original wording of the scriptures. Historical criticism tries to clarify the date, first context, and intention of each biblical book, using evidence from the other scriptures and from such external sources as archeological remains and nonbiblical literature. Form criticism analyzes and classifies the styles of biblical speech and writing (e.g., parables and miracle stories). Tradition criticism investigates the handing down of the oral and written units that entered the books of the Bible as we now have them. Redaction criticism studies (a) the motivation and mindset of the biblical authors in editing, sometimes over various stages, their inherited traditions; and (b) the meaning and message they wished to convey to their particular audience. Literary criticism deals with the value and impact of the biblical texts as pieces of literature (see DH 3828–31; ND 235–36). See *Hermeneutics; Parable; Quelle; Redaktionsgeschichte; Senses of Scripture; Synoptic Gospels*.

Biblical Theology. Any theology that bases itself primarily on the scriptures. Particular biblical theologies develop such OT and NT themes as covenant, justification, promise, prophecy, and salvation history to draw from the scriptures a unified message for today. See *Hermeneutics; Theology.*

Binitarianism. A modern term for some brief NT confessions (e.g., 1 Tim 2:5–6; Rom 4:24; 2 Cor 4:14) that name only the Father and the Son and are found alongside trinitarian formulas (e.g., Matt 28:19; 2 Cor 13:13). Binitarianism may also denote the heretical denial of the Holy Spirit's divinity and belief that there are only two persons in God. See *Constantinople, First Council of; Creed; Trinity, Theology of.*

Birth Control. Using natural or artificial means to prevent sexual intercourse from being open to conception. Natural means include abstinence from sexual intercourse on days when the female is likely to conceive, and withdrawal. Among the artificial means, those that work after intercourse when conception may already have taken place are properly called *abortifacients* (Lat. "effecting abortion"). *Contraceptives* ("countering conception"), for example, pills and physical barriers, work beforehand to hinder the possibility of conception taking place. In his 1968 encyclical *Humanae Vitae*, Paul VI (pope 1963–78), while advocating the deep values of married love and responsible parenthood, taught that every sexual act must remain open to conception, condemned direct sterilization, and rejected artificial means for birth control as intrinsically disordered (DH 4470–79; ND 2220–25). While the encyclical is clear teaching and to be heard conscientiously, it was not proposed as an infallible statement. See *Abortion; Infallibility.*

Bishop (Anglo-Saxon corruption of Gr. *episcopos*, "overseer"). One who has been ordained to the fullness of the priesthood and is entitled to lead a particular church or diocese by his teaching, pastoral care, and liturgical ministry. As successor of the apostles and in communion with the bishop of Rome, he shares with the whole body or college of bishops a responsibility for the entire church (see LG 22–23). He confers holy orders and, in the West, is the ordinary minister of confirmation; the blessing of the sacred oils is also reserved to him (see CIC 375–430; CCEO 42, 45 §2, 46 §1, 693, 744, 871 §2). See *Apostolic Succession; Cathedra; Collegiality; Diocese; Enthronement; Episcopal Conference; Jurisdiction; Ordinary; Sacrament.*

Black Theology. North American theological school developed by black Christians in the aftermath of Martin Luther King's (1929–68) civil rights movement. It has opposed racist and exclusively white interpretations of the Christian faith, supported further struggles for social rights, and joined forces with such similar movements as feminist theology and Latin American liberation theology. See *Feminist Theology; Liberation Theology; Political Theology.*

Blasphemy (Gr. "damage to reputation"). Showing contempt for God and religious matters through one's words, thoughts, and actions (see Exod 22:28; Lev 24:10–23).

Blessed. In a narrower sense, all those who have been officially beatified; in a broader sense, all human beings in heaven. See *Beatification*.

Blessed Sacrament. A term employed for the bread and wine after their consecration in the Eucharist. See *Consecration; Eucharist; Transubstantiation*.

Blessing. In Christian usage, an authoritative declaration, invocation, or bestowal of divine approval and grace, usually accompanied by a sign of the cross. See *Berakah; Consecration; Sacramental*.

Blood of Christ. Understood against its OT background, the blood of Jesus expresses and effects deliverance from death to life (Exod 12:7, 13, 22–23; 1 Pet 1:18–19), cleansing from sin (Lev 16; Rom 3:25; Heb 9:12–14; 1 John 1:7; Rev 7:14), and a new loving relationship with God (Exod 24:3–8; Mark 14:24). See *Covenant; Expiation*.

Body of Christ. A term designating (a) the human body of Jesus, (b) the risen Christ present in the Eucharist, (c) the church (or the mystical body of Christ), made up of those incorporated into him through baptism and the Holy Spirit, and (d) the feast celebrated in the Latin rite after Trinity Sunday to honor the Blessed Sacrament. See *Blessed Sacrament; Church*.

Bogomils (Slavic "pleasing to God"). A dualistic, docetic, medieval sect that for a time enjoyed some support in Byzantium. Its founders were reputed to be a priest Jeremias (mid-tenth-century Bulgaria) and a certain Theophilus, who was active between 927 and 950. ("Bogomil" is the Slavic translation of Theophilus). Their abhorrence for matter led the Bogomils to reject (a) the OT (except for prophetic passages that point to Christ) and the psalms; and (b) various "material" practices such as veneration of images (including the crucifix), baptism by water, any kind of infant baptism, and marriage. The only prayer allowed was the Lord's Prayer. The sect spread rapidly through the Balkans, especially in Bulgaria, but with the coming of the Turks, many of its adherents became Muslims. Bogomils had an influence on the rise of Albigensianism. See *Albigensianism; Cathars; Docetism; Dualism; Gnosticism; Manichaeism; Marcionism; Priscillianism*.

Breaking of the Bread. A term drawn from daily life in the Near East, where the flat bread is more easily broken than cut. At the start of a meal, fathers of Jewish families broke the bread and shared it with those present while saying a prayer or singing a hymn of thanksgiving—a ceremony that corresponded to the later Christian grace before meals and that Jesus himself followed at the institution of the Eucharist. All three Synoptic Gospels recall that "he broke bread" (Matt 26:26; Mark 14:22; Luke 22:19), as does Paul (1 Cor 11:24). The two disciples at Emmaus recognized the risen Christ in the breaking of the bread (Luke 24:30–31, 35). In the Acts of the Apostles "the breaking of the bread" sometimes refers to the Eucharist (e.g., Acts 2:42, 46). This does not seem to be so before St. Paul's shipwreck on Malta (Acts 27:33–36). At Mass the consecrated bread is broken before the Our Father in the Ambrosian rite and afterward in the Latin rite. Originally part of the host was later distributed to those who could not be present—an expression of Christian unity that the sign of peace at this point in the Roman liturgy now recalls. In the Byzantine rite, the priest, shortly before communion, breaks the consecrated bread into four parts, which he then arranges in the form of a cross on the paten. The context in which St. Paul recalls Christ's "breaking of the bread" emphasizes its social implications in generous sharing and community building (e.g., 1 Cor 11:20–22). See *Eucharist; Kiss of Peace; Liturgy.*

Breviary. In the West, the book or books used for daily prayer by priests and others and containing all the psalms, a variety of hymns, readings from scripture, prayers, and lessons from the fathers and other spiritual writers, with variations adapted to the liturgical feasts and seasons (see SC 83–101; PO 5, 13). See *Calendar, Liturgical; Liturgy of the Hours.*

Buddhism (Sanskrit "enlightened one"). A world religion founded in India by Siddharta Gautama Buddha (ca. 563–ca. 483 BC). It exists in two forms: (a) *Hinayana* (Sanskrit "little vehicle") or *Theravada* (Pali "old doctrine") Buddhism (found in Burma, Sri Lanka, Thailand, and elsewhere), and (b) *Mahayana* (Sanskrit "great vehicle") Buddhism (found in China, Japan, Korea, Mongolia, Tibet, and elsewhere). Under the Bodhi tree (tree of enlightenment), the prince Gautama became enlightened about the four basic truths: (a) human existence is pain, (b) the cause of pain is desire, (c) pain ceases with the emancipation from every form of desire, and (d) the cessation of pain may be attained through the eightfold way of deliverance. This way involves right knowledge of these four truths: right intention, right speech, right action, right occupation, right effort, right control of sensations and ideas, and right concentration. This way promises to end suffering (which feeds on desire) and to lead to *nirvana* (Sanskrit "being extinguished") or a complete state of peace (see NA 2). The Buddhist scriptures exist in Pali (Sri Lanka) and Sanskrit (India). Two basic doctrines of Buddhism are (a) *karma* (Sanskrit "action, faith"), the belief that old deeds are rewarded or punished in this life or subsequent lives; and (b) rebirth or the transmigration of souls. *Mahayana* Buddhism, which arose around the time of Christ, teaches individuals not only to attain *nirvana* but also to become Buddhas themselves and so save others. This form of Buddhism includes the worship of gods and various syncretistic features. See *Reincarnation; Salvation; Syncretism; World Religions; Zen.*

Burial Rites. The ceremonial disposal of dead human bodies. In the Greek Orthodox Church the ceremonies that follow the commemoration of Christ's death on Good Friday (called "Great Friday") are popularly known as "the burial of Christ." A tomb-like piece of furniture called the *epitaphion* (Gr. "tomb") is the focus of these ceremonies. See *Cemetery; Death; Funeral Rite; Good Friday.*

Byzantine Christianity. A common name for Christians who belong to the Byzantine liturgical, canonical, spiritual, and theological tradition, deriving from the fact that in 330 Constantine the Great moved his capital from Rome to Byzantium on the Bosphorus and renamed the city Constantinople. (a) *Greek Byzantines.* Claiming from 381, and especially from 451, a position second only to Rome, Constantinople became the undisputed center for the majority of Christians in the East. In 1054 its patriarch and the pope's legates mutually excommunicated each other. After the Turks captured the city in 1453, the patriarchs have continued to enjoy a primacy of honor over all Eastern Orthodox. In 1965 Pope Paul VI and Patriarch Athenagoras of Constantinople mutually lifted the excommunication, which in any case had often been ignored. (b) *Byzantine-Slavonic Christians.* Those Christians of the Byzantine tradition who use Old Church Slavonic instead of Greek for their liturgy. There are churches in communion with Constantinople (e.g., Russians, Ukrainians, Serbians, Bulgarians, and Ruthenians), and their counterparts who are in communion with Rome. The mission of Sts. Cyril and Methodius in 863 began the conversion of the Slavic nations to Christianity. Cyril devised for Old Church Slavonic an alphabet, Glagolitic, later superseded by the Cyrillic alphabet, not created by the saint, but named after him and still in use today. With the baptism of Prince Vladimir of Kiev in 988, Christianity became the official religion of the Kievan Rus'. (c) *Other Byzantine Christians.* Besides Greek and Slavic-speaking Byzantines, there are several other ethnic groups, including the Georgians, some Arabs, and most importantly, the Romanians, who have the second-largest Orthodox Church today. See *Chalcedon, Council of; Constantinople, First Council of; Eastern Churches; Ruthenian.*

C

Caesaropapism. The state's practice of constantly interfering in church matters under the pretext of protecting the faithful's interests. The Roman emperors had been supreme pontiffs in the pagan state religion; after conversion to Christianity they often failed to respect the independence of church order. When the empire survived, primarily in the East, the Byzantine rulers dominated the patriarchs, especially in the period before the 1054 crisis between East and West. Many Byzantine scholars reject talk of Caesaropapism as misleading, since church and state were and are supposed to work hand in hand. See *Byzantine Christianity; Canon Law, Sources of Oriental; Church and State; Symphony.*

Calendar, Gregorian. The reform of the calendar that Pope Gregory XIII introduced by dropping the days from October 5 to October 14, 1582. In the earlier Julian calendar, created by Julius Caesar in 45 BC, a year was slightly more than the actual length of the time the earth takes to go round the sun. By the late sixteenth century, the calendar was running ten days late; these days were suppressed. To prevent the calendar from getting out of step with the seasons, a leap year of 366 days was inserted every four years, and century years were to count as leap years if divisible by 400. While the Gregorian reform had immediate effect in Catholic countries of Western Europe, England and the American colonies accepted it only in 1752. Most Eastern churches accepted a partly reformed Gregorian calendar after it was revised in 1923 and introduced in 1924. The Jerusalem, Russian, and Serbian Orthodox patriarchates, as well as the monks on Mount Athos, continue to follow the Julian calendar for Christmas and Easter; Greek Catholics in the Ukraine do likewise. Since the Julian calendar is now thirteen days behind, Christmas is celebrated on January 7. The Orthodox Church of Finland, however, follows the Gregorian calendar for both Christmas and Easter. Protestants always follow the Gregorian calendar. Once every four years, most Christians celebrate Easter on the same day. See *Athos, Mount; Calendar, Liturgical; Patriarch.*

Calendar, Liturgical. The calendar used in various Christian churches to regulate the weekly celebrations (above all, Sunday), movable feasts (especially Easter and Pentecost, whose dates vary), and immovable feasts such as Christmas, which always fall on the same date. See *Christmas; Easter Triduum; Liturgy; Liturgy of the Hours; Old Believers; Pentecost; Sunday; Twelve Feasts, The.*

Calvinism. That branch of Protestantism that traces its origin to the Swiss reformer John Calvin (1509–64). Within these churches, his theology (characterized by the unity of the OT and NT, an emphasis on God's sovereignty, the predestination of the elect to heaven and the reprobate to hell, and the church as a well-ordered community living in solidarity) exercises a decisive influence, even if his theory of double predestination has been modified. See *Congregational Theology; Predestination; Presbyterianism; Protestant; Puritans; Reformation, The; Theocracy; Westminster Confession; Zwinglianism.*

Candles. Cylinders or blocks of wax shaped around a wick and providing light when ignited. Church ceremonies are accompanied by lighted candles. Day and night a light, usually a candle, burns before the tabernacle containing the consecrated hosts. The life of Christians unfolds from the baptismal candle through the first communion candle to the candles used at burial. At the Easter Vigil, the Paschal Candle is lit and carried into the church by the celebrant. He sings three times "Lumen Christi!" (The Light of Christ) and shares the light with the congregation, who hold small candles. When the faithful visit a church, they often light a candle in front of a favorite saint. In the East, people light candles in front of icons. At the entrance or narthex (Gr. "antechamber") of Eastern churches, there are usually stands for votive candles. The *manoualia,* or large candlesticks in front of the iconostasis, are lit for the eucharistic liturgy, along with three candles for the Trinity (on the altar) or twelve candles (for the twelve apostles) on one (or several) candelabras. Candles from the Good Friday celebration are taken home and kept, much as Western Catholics take palms home on Palm Sunday. Candles symbolize complete dedication or "burning oneself out" in the service of the community. See *Blessed Sacrament; Communion; Easter Triduum; Eucharist; Icon; Iconostasis; Tabernacle.*

Canon. (a) In the Latin Church, a title often given to priests who help staff a cathedral or a collegiate church (see CIC 503–10). Under the direct jurisdiction of the local ordinary, they are obliged to celebrate together certain liturgical ceremonies and sometimes fulfill other duties, such as helping to select a new bishop when the see is vacant. (b) *Canon* is also a traditional Western term for the eucharistic prayer or anaphora of the Mass. See *Anaphora; Bishop; Cathedral; Eucharistic Prayer; Jurisdiction; Ordinary.*

Canonization. Church's solemn and final declaration that one of its dead and previously beatified members belongs among the saints in heaven and as such is to be publicly invoked and venerated (see CIC 1186–90; CCEO 201 §2, 884–85, 1057). This proclamation is reserved to the Holy See. See *Beatification; Communion of Saints; Holiness; Holy See; Saint.*

Canon Law. That body of codified law to be observed by Catholics, either individually or through various groups that they form within the church. In particular, it refers to the code promulgated by Blessed John Paul II (pope 1978–2005) in 1983 (superseding that of 1917), the Code of Canons of the Oriental Churches promulgated in 1990, and the apostolic constitution *Pastor Bonus* (effective from March 1, 1989) that regulates the Roman Curia. See *Code of Canon Law; Code of Canons of the Oriental Churches; Corpus Iuris Canonici; Nomocanon.*

Canon Law, Sources of Oriental. Prescriptions about the conduct of church members and ministers, usually coming from ecumenical councils and synods. Once the church was officially recognized by the state, church precepts automatically became law of the empire and entered the *Theodosian Code* and, even more, the *Justinian Code.* Under Emperor Theodosius II (reigned

408–50), all the general laws enacted since Constantine the Great (d. 337) were codified in one collection, officially in force from 439. In 529 Emperor Justinian I (reigned 527–65) published a new code, revised in 534. The *Justinian Code* aimed at procuring a *symphony* (Gr. "harmony") and *synalleleia* (Gr. "autonomous cooperation") between the imperial court and church leaders by making the emperor the executor of canonical legislation.

The *Justinian Code* helped canon law to emerge in the West during the later Middle Ages. The 102 canons enacted at the Quinisext Synod of 692 form what is often called the first draft of canon law. But any codification of Eastern canon law was long delayed. St. Nicodemus of Mount Athos (1749–1809) attempted such a compilation and added a commentary, called *Pedalion* (Gr. "rudder"), which was quickly recognized in the praxis of the patriarch of Constantinople. This rudder was meant to guide the ship of the universal church, with dogmas and traditions for its beams and planks, Jesus for its navigator, and the apostles and the clergy for the officers and crew. This image recalls the name for the chief code of Russian canon law, *Kormcaja Kniga* (Russ. "navigator's chart"), a collection of canons first printed in 1653. The work of St. Nicodemus reflects the close ties between law and spirituality and the interpenetration of law and dogma. Two terms summarize the spirit of Eastern canon law: not only *akribeia* (Gr. "rigor"), but also *oikonomia* (Gr. "house management"); that is, the strict measure of the law must be balanced with pastoral concern for the good of people. See *Church and State; Corpus Iuris Canonici; Economy; Nomocanon; Philocalia; Quinisext Synod; Symphony.*

Canon of Scripture (Gr. "rule, measuring rod"). List of biblical books authoritatively recognized by the church as inspired and normative for its teaching and practice. Among Christian denominations, the lists of OT books differ considerably. See *Apocrypha; Bible; New Testament; Old Testament.*

Cantor (Lat. "singer"). Someone who leads the singing in synagogue or church. Prior to the Second Vatican Council (1962–65), cantors were male and sang in alternation with the celebrant. In the East, where the liturgy is always sung, the cantor is one of the (lower) clergy and plays a significant part in the divine office and the Eucharist. See *Ambo; Chant; Clergy; Eucharist; Lauds; Lectern; Liturgy; Office, The Divine; Vatican Council, Second; Vespers.*

Cappadocian Fathers. Title used chiefly for three Cappadocian saints: Basil the Great (ca. 330–79), bishop of Caesarea in Cappadocia and organizer of monastic life in the East; his brother Gregory (ca. 335–ca. 395), bishop of Nyssa and a theologian of great mystical depth; and Gregory of Nazianzus (329–89), at first bishop of Sasima and then for a while bishop of Constantinople during the First Council of Constantinople. A cousin of Gregory of Nazianzus is sometimes listed among the Cappadocians: St. Amphilochius (ca. 340–ca. 394), bishop of Iconium. See *Constantinople, First*

Council of; Essence and Energies; Eunomianism; Fathers of the Church; Three Theologians, The.

Cardinal (Lat. "hinge"). The title of those who act as close advisors to the pope in governing the whole church, form the college of cardinals, gather with the pope for ordinary or extraordinary meetings called *consistories* (Lat. "standing together"), and serve as papal electors (CIC 349–59). Originally the cardinals comprised the bishops of seven dioceses near Rome, parish priests in Rome itself, and seven (later fourteen) deacons who staffed Roman centers of help for the poor and for pilgrims. In 1179 Pope Alexander III made the cardinals alone responsible for choosing the pope. Sixtus V (pope 1575–80) set the number of cardinals at seventy; Blessed John XXIII (pope 1958–63) abrogated this limit. In 1973 Pope Paul VI limited to 120 the number of cardinals eligible to elect the pope. Earlier he encountered difficulties over raising several Eastern patriarchs to the college of cardinals; for Eastern Christians, the highest dignity is that of a patriarch (CCEO 56). Active cardinals normally head important dioceses such as Buenos Aires, Chicago, Manila, Mexico City, Milan, Nairobi, New York, and Paris, or else run one of the Vatican offices by which the church is governed. Some prominent theologians, such as Yves Congar (1904–95) and Alois Grillmeier (1910–98), have been created cardinals when in their old age. In such circumstances, the episcopal ordination required for all cardinals by Blessed John XXIII is normally waived. All cardinals are addressed as "your eminence." See *Bishop; Conclave; Deacon; Parish; Patriarch; Pope.*

Cassock. A full-length garment worn by clergy and members of choirs. Different colors indicate varying status: white for the pope, red for cardinals, violet for bishops, black for priests, white for missionaries in hot climates. In the past, distinct cassocks indicated members of religious orders and seminaries. In Greece, the *rason* or black, loose-flowing, clerical cassock is worn with cylindrical headgear known as a *kamilafkion.* Other Orthodox churches have distinct head covering; for example, the cowl-like cap of the Armenian and the tight-fitting *tuque* of the Syrian clergy. St. Celestine I (pope 422–32) discouraged his clergy in Rome from wearing the cassock outdoors; they were to be distinguished rather by the holiness of their lives. The Synod of Braga of 572, however, enjoined the outdoor use of the cassock, as did Anglican canons of 1604. In wearing the cassock, many clerics now follow the customs of their country. See *Anglican Communion; Armenian Christianity; Bishop; Cardinal; Monasticism; Pope; Priests; Religious Life; Syrian Orthodox Church.*

Casuistry. The application of general moral principles to judge particular cases with their specific circumstances as one searches for God's will. See *Moral Theology; Probabilism.*

Catacombs (Gr. perhaps "at the ravine" or "under the tombs"). Ancient underground burial sites containing niches hewn in the rock (*loculi*) and found not only in Rome (around forty catacombs), but also in Asia Minor, Italy, Malta, North Africa, Paris, and Trier. With St. Damasus (pope 366–84), there was an attempt to list and set in order the relics in the Roman catacombs. Not limited to Christians; for Jews also buried their dead in catacombs. Catacombs were used for Christian burial and liturgical celebration even after the Roman persecutions ceased. They fell into disuse when their relics were transferred to churches. On December 10, 1593, the Maltese Antonio Bosio (ca. 1575–1627) initiated the rediscovery of catacombs by exploring the catacombs of St. Domitilla and almost failing to find his way back. Called "the Christopher Columbus of the catacombs," Bosio posthumously published in 1632 *Roma sotterranea*, a work superseded only by Gianbattista de Rossi's three-volume *Roma sotterranea cristiana* (1864–77). See *Martyr; Relics.*

Cataphatic Theology (Gr. "affirmative"). Sometimes called positive theology, it complements apophatic theology. Despite the radical inadequacy of our categories, we may nonetheless assert much that is true of God as revealed unsurpassably in Jesus Christ and known to us now through the Holy Spirit. However, apophatic theology insists that even after the divine self-revelation and self-gift in grace, God remains the primordial mystery. See *Apophatic Theology; Mystery; Positive Theology.*

Catechesis (Gr. "teaching"). In the early church, either the instruction given to those preparing for baptism or the books used for that purpose. Today the word is applied to any instruction meant to deepen Christian faith, even if given to those already baptized (CIC 773–80; CCEO 617–26). The ultimate responsibility for catechesis lies with the whole community. See *Catechumens; RCIA.*

Catechism. The instruction given to candidates for baptism as well as any book used for such purposes. Often the term refers to popular manuals explaining basic beliefs, moral teachings, and prayers.

Catechumenate. In the early church, the period of preparation for baptism, culminating in the scrutinies or prayers of healing on the third, fourth, and fifth Sundays of Lent and the actual reception of baptism during the Easter Vigil. From St. Cyril of Jerusalem (ca. 315–86), we have a series of homilies used for initiating catechumens and preached in the Church of the Holy Sepulchre. To a large extent this practice has been restored for adults (SC 64–66). See *Easter Triduum; Neocatechumenate; RCIA.*

Catechumens. In the early church, those preparing to receive the sacraments of initiation. They occupied a special place during the Liturgy of the Word.

Then the deacon solemnly dismissed them before the prayers of the faithful. See *Initiation; Liturgy of the Word.*

Catechumens, Mass of the. A common but outdated and misleading term for the Liturgy of the Word. All those present, and not just catechumens, have the serious duty of listening to God's word. See *Faithful, Mass of the; Liturgy of the Eucharist; Liturgy of the Word.*

Categorical Imperative. According to Immanuel Kant (1724–1804), an unconditional moral principle that binds in an absolute way—unlike a hypothetical imperative, which has binding force only in view of a chosen goal. See *Ethics.*

Cathars (Gr. "pure"). Name for several sects (mainly medieval sects in France, Germany, and Italy) that admitted to membership only the morally and doctrinally pure (see DH 127; 800–802; ND 1601). See *Albigensianism; Bogomils; Lateran Council, Fourth; Novatianism.*

Cathedra (Gr. "seat"). The bishop's throne in his cathedral and the oldest sign of his office, predating later (Western) episcopal emblems such as the miter and the ring. Flanked by lower chairs for concelebrating priests, the bishop's throne was placed behind the altar. From there he preached and presided over the Eucharist. The expression *ex cathedra* applies to solemn pronouncements about matters of revelation that can be made by the pope in virtue of his highest authority. The word *see* for a diocese indicates that it possesses its own episcopal *cathedra* or "seat" (Lat. *sedes*). See *Bishop; Diocese; Enthronement; Infallibility; Miter; Ordinary.*

Cathedral. The chief church of a diocese in which the bishop has his throne. See *Bishop; Cathedra; Diocese; Enthronement.*

Catholicism. That worldwide unity in belief and conduct, frequently identified with the Roman Catholic Church and also claimed by other Christians—in particular, the Anglicans and Orthodox. See *Churches; Ecumenism.*

Catholicity (Gr. "universality"). The all-embracing character of the true and undivided church that gathers into the one people of God those of different races, languages, and cultures (see LG 13). See *Inculturation; Marks (Notes) of the Church; Sobornost.*

Causality. The influence exercised by one being or partial being on another. An efficient cause produces effects in an already existing being or brings another being into existence. A material cause is the "stuff" out of which a being is made. A formal cause shapes and organizes something, making it to be what it is. A final cause is the purpose for which something is made. An exemplary cause serves as the model or pattern in producing a being. To show that human and divine activity are on different levels, God is called *causa prima* (Lat. "first cause"), inasmuch as all other things depend on God for their coming into being, continuing existence, and activity. Creatures are termed *causae secundae* (Lat. "secondary causes"), insofar as it is only in radical dependence on God that they influence each other. See *Analogy; Arguments for the Existence of God; Aristotelianism; Creation; Matter and Form; Ontologism.*

Celebrant. The bishop, priest, or deacon who leads a liturgical ceremony. Greater sensitivity to the active participation of the whole assembly means speaking today of "the president" of the assembly, especially when the Eucharist is concelebrated by two or more priests. The Second Vatican Council (1962–65) promoted concelebration of the Eucharist in the West. Stressing the communal character of all liturgy, Eastern Christians cherish concelebration. Even the sacrament of *euchelaion* (Gr. "holy oil") or anointing of the sick is preferably celebrated by seven, or at least several, priests. See *Anointing of the Sick; Bishop; Concelebration; Deacon; Priests; Vatican Council, Second.*

Celibacy. The renunciation of marriage for religious reasons. Nuns, monks, and other men and women in religious life express this commitment as a vow. In the Latin tradition, celibacy is required of candidates for the priesthood; permanent deacons are not permitted to marry after ordination. There is also a married clergy among Eastern Catholics (CCEO 373–76). Orthodox priests and deacons are generally married, but they may not marry or remarry after ordination. Priests of the Assyrian Church of the East may marry after ordination, but it is not usual for them to remarry if their wife dies. In the East, bishops must be celibate. Canon 3 of the First Council of Nicaea (325) prohibited clergy from living with any women except their mother, sister, aunt, or someone else above suspicion. As well as repeating this prohibition in its canon 5, the Quinisext Synod (691–92) in canon 13 allowed for clergy in the East to marry before the diaconate but not afterward. In the West, clerical celibacy is supposed to have been introduced at the Synod of Elvira (Granada) held around 306, but the relevant canon (33) is a later addition. Pope St. Gregory VII (Hildebrand) (pope 1073–85) reinforced celibacy for the clergy at synods held in 1074, 1075, and 1078. See *Church of the East (Assyrian); Deacon; Eastern Churches; Nicaea, First Council of; Priests; Quinisext Synod; Vow.*

Cemetery (Gr. "sleeping place"). A burial ground, especially one not in a churchyard. In some countries Christians who belonged to a minority of the population were often (and sometimes still are) buried in separate cemeteries or sections of cemeteries. The "Protestant Cemetery" in Rome is a case in point. Burial in Christian cemeteries has been (and still is occasionally) denied for various reasons. This happened at the death of the musician Nicolò

Paganini (1782–1840). He had claimed to have written "The Devil's Sonata" at the dictation of the devil himself and was rumored to be "in league with the devil." St. Ephraem the Syrian (ca. 306–73) opposed burial in a church—a privilege reserved today to a few state and church dignitaries. Canon law allows popes, bishops, and cardinals to be buried in their own church (CIC 1242; CCEO 874 § 3). See *Catacombs; Cremation; Funeral Rite*.

Cenobites (Gr. "living in community"). In the East, vowed religious, who live in community and observe the same spiritual rule. See *Athos, Mount; Monasticism; Religious Life*.

Censer. See *Incense; Thurible*.

Ceremony. Any religious function held in church, usually led by an ordained cleric if it is a liturgical service, and often led by a layperson if it is a paraliturgical function such as the recitation of the rosary. The Greeks speak of *akoluthia* ("church service"), a term indicating rites and gestures to follow on given occasions. See *Celebrant; Liturgy; Minister; Rosary*.

Chalcedon, Council of. Fourth ecumenical council, held in 451 at a city now called Kadi-Köy (Turkey) on the other side of the Bosphorus from Constantinople. The council was convoked to deal with the Monophysite heresy of Eutyches (ca. 378–454), whose strong opposition to those who divided Christ into two sons seems to have led him into the opposite error. This was to reduce Christ to one of his two natures, the divine, or to a third nature (that originated from both the divine and the human natures and was the only one to remain after the Incarnation). Condemned in 448 at a home synod held in Constantinople, Eutyches was rehabilitated the following year at a synod in Ephesus, summoned by Emperor Theodosius II (reigned 408–50) and, because of its violent and uncanonical procedure, branded by Leo I (pope 440–61) as an act of *latrocinium* (Lat. "brigandage"). After Theodosius II fell from his horse and died, Emperor Marcian, who had married the late emperor's sister St. Pulcheria (399–453) and come to the throne, in agreement with the pope, convoked a new council to be held at Chalcedon. This brought together between 500 and 600 bishops, all of them Easterners, except for three papal legates and two bishops from Africa. The council fathers condemned Eutyches, as also did Dioscorus of Alexandria, his former patron. Dioscorus (d. 454), however, was himself deposed for having dared to excommunicate Pope Leo. Drawing on various sources, including Leo's *Tomus ad Flavianum* (a letter to the patriarch of Constantinople, Flavian (d. 449)), the council affirmed the one person of Christ in his two natures, divine and human. It specified that "the one and the same Christ, Son, Lord, and Only begotten" was made known in these two natures, which, without detriment to their full qualities, continue to exist "without confusion or change, and without division or separation," while belonging to only one person and not two (DH 300–2; ND 613–15). Moreover, the council enacted twenty-seven canons concerning disciplinary matters. Jerusalem became a patriarchate, the fifth, but Pope Leo refused to recognize the twenty-eighth canon, which assigned Constantinople, "the new Rome," wide jurisdictional powers, second only to old Rome itself. See *Constantinople, First Council of; Constantinople, Second Council of; Ephesus, Council of; Eutychianism; Jerusalem; Monophysitism; Three Chapters, The; Trisagion.*

Chalcedonian Churches. Originally those churches that accepted the Council of Chalcedon. The term is still used for Orthodox churches that did not separate from Constantinople over this council. See *Eastern Churches; Oriental Orthodox.*

Chalice (Lat. "cup"). A goblet used to hold the wine to be consecrated at the Eucharist. In the West, chalices became smaller when the congregation no longer received communion under both kinds—a state of affairs ratified at the Council of Constance in 1415 (see DH 1198–1200; ND 1506). In the East, where the faithful have always received under both kinds, chalices have remained bigger. See *Ciborium.*

Chant (Lat. "song"). The singing or recitative proclamation of poetical or prose passages (often taken from the Bible) during liturgical ceremonies—a practice coming from our Jewish heritage. The NT includes Christian hymns (e.g., Luke 1:46–55; Phil 2:6–11; 1 Tim 3:16) that antedated the writing of the scripture. His hymns for church feasts and other liturgical occasions earned St. Ephraem the Syrian (ca. 306–73) the reputation of being "the harp of the Spirit." Through St. Hilary of Poitiers (ca. 310–67), chant seems to have spread from the East to the West. In the Eastern rites, the liturgy is always sung; and in most traditions, only percussion instruments, if any, are allowed. See *Gregorian Chant; Liturgy.*

Chaplain. A priest who is normally not in charge of a parish, but rather provides church services for the armed forces or in such institutions as schools, hospitals, and prisons (see CIC 564–72). The Eastern code does not speak of chaplains but of parochial vicars, who are priests, assist a parish priest, and live in a parish (CCEO 301–303; see CIC 545–52). See *Parish.*

Character (Gr. "seal"). An indelible and unrepeatable spiritual sign (DH 1313, 1609; ND 1308, 1319) marking those who become Christ's members (through baptism and confirmation) or his ministers (through ordination). Orthodox theologians speak simply of the unrepeatability of certain basic sacramental acts. See *Priests; Res et Sacramentum; Sacrament; Sphragis.*

Charismatic. In a general sense, every Christian who is called and graced by God. More specifically, the term refers to those who receive special gifts of the Holy Spirit, such as celibacy (1 Cor 7:7), miraculous powers, discernment, or the gift of tongues (1 Cor 12:10). See *Grace; Pentecostals.*

Charismatic Renewal. See *Pentecostals.*

Charisms (Gr. "gifts"). Special gifts of the Holy Spirit, over and above those strictly necessary for salvation. For the benefit of the church and the world, they are given to individuals or groups (see 1 Cor 12; LG 12) and are always to be exercised with charity (1 Cor 13:1). See *Glossolalia.*

Charity. Third theological virtue, which presupposes the other two (faith and hope) and gives life to all the virtues. Its primary object is God; secondarily, it is directed toward ourselves and other human beings (Deut 6:5; John 13:34; 1 John 4:7—5:4; 1 Cor 13:1). See *Agape; Faith; Hope; Love; Virtues, Theological.*

Chastity. That virtue which enables human beings to integrate sexuality within their whole personality according to their vocation in life: for the celibate, through complete abstention; for the married, through fidelity; and for single persons, through self-control. See *Marriage; Religious Life.*

Cherubikon or **Cherubic Hymn**. In the Byzantine liturgy, a hymn that accompanies the passage from the Liturgy of the Word to the Liturgy of the Eucharist. This hymn invites the assembly, compared with the Cherubim or highest of the nine orders of angels, to receive the King of the universe, who comes with hosts of angels. The hymn is intoned before a procession called the Great Entrance (to be distinguished from the Small Entrance that precedes the deacon's chanting of the gospel), in which the priest carries the bread and wine to be consecrated. Interrupted during the Great Entrance, the Cherubic Hymn is resumed at its completion. See *Angels; Byzantine Christianity; Celebrant; Deacon; Liturgy of the Eucharist; Liturgy of the Word.*

Chiliasm (Gr. "thousand"). A movement in Christianity that interprets Revelation 20:1–5 as promising that, before the end of the world, Christ will establish a kingdom of a thousand years with the saints who have already risen from the dead (see DH 3839). See *Millenarianism.*

Choir. A special part of a cathedral or church from which singers accompany liturgical ceremonies. Originally the choir was part of the sanctuary and was occupied by those who recited daily the Liturgy of the Hours. Today choirs often occupy a loft or some other part of the church that does not block the view of the ceremonies. The Second Vatican Council (1962–65) stressed the role of choirs in leading the congregation (SC 121)—a teaching hardly needed in the East, where all liturgical functions are sung. Prefaces of the eucharistic liturgy refer to choirs of angels that praise God in harmony. See *Angels; Cantor; Liturgy; Office, The Divine.*

Choirs of Angels. A way of classifying the angels in nine choirs (which goes beyond the limited data of the Bible) popularized by Pseudo-Dionysius the Areopagite, an anonymous Christian writer of the late fifth or early sixth century. His nine choirs were arranged in groups of three: Seraphim, Cherubim, and Thrones; Dominations, Virtues, and Powers; Principalities, Archangels, and Angels. See *Angels; Guardian Angels.*

Chrism (Gr. "oil for anointing"). In the Western church, the oil that the bishop consecrates (along with other oils) on Maundy or Holy Thursday during the Chrism Mass held in the morning. Normally a mixture of olive oil and balsam, it is used at baptism and confirmation, at the ordination of priests and bishops, and at the consecration of churches and altars. In the Eastern church, this oil is called *myron* (Gr. "oil for anointing"); *chrismation* refers to what the Latin church calls the sacrament of confirmation. See *Anointing.*

Christ. See *Messiah.*

Christendom. A collective name for Christians, Christian countries, and Christianity's cultural and religious influence.

Christening. Being named with a Christian name and received into the church. In the West, this is done by baptism; in the East, confirmation and communion are also administered. See *Baptism; Initiation.*

Christ Event. Christ's coming, life, death, and resurrection as the decisive fact of salvation history. See *Salvation History.*

Christ of Faith. An expression used to indicate the difference between a merely historical study of Jesus and the stance of faith, which accepts Jesus as Son of God and savior of the world. See *Historical Jesus; Son of God.*

Christianity. The religion of those who belong to Christian churches and communities.

Christians. Followers of Christ, a term first used in Syrian Antioch (Acts 11:26).

Christmas. The celebration of the birth of Jesus Christ on December 25, a feast of Western origin that replaced the pagan feast of the Unconquered Sun and eventually became common to all Christian churches except the

Armenian. The Roman liturgy allows for Mass to be said during the night (normally at midnight), at dawn, and during the day to celebrate the threefold birth of the Son—in the bosom of the Father, from the womb of Mary, and in the heart of the believer. See *Armenian Christianity; Epiphany.*

Christmas Preparation. Called Advent in the West. The East Syrians call their preparation, which covers four Sundays before Christmas, *subára* (Syriac "annunciation"), as do the West Syrians their six Sundays before Christmas. Both celebrate in this season the annunciation to Mary and the birth of St. John the Baptist. In the Byzantine tradition, this pre-Christmas season starts on November 15 and involves a forty-day fast, sometimes called Philip's fast, because it begins a day after the feast of St. Philip the Apostle. See *Advent; Annunciation; Calendar, Liturgical; Fasting; Liturgy.*

Christocentricism. A systematic focusing of all theology and devotional life on the person and work of Jesus Christ.

Christological Titles. Such NT designations for Jesus as Christ, Son of God, and Son of Man. They entail various approaches to understanding who Jesus was and is, and what he did and does. See *Kyrios; Messiah; Son of God; Son of Man.*

Christology. The theological interpretation of Jesus Christ, clarifying systematically who and what he is in himself for those who believe in him. In a less systematic way, the NT contains various christological approaches to Jesus. See *Functional Christology; Hypostatic Union; Soteriology.*

Christology from Above. A Christology developed from the theme of the pre-existent Logos or Son of God who descended into our world (John 1:14). See *Alexandrian Theology; Logos-Sarx Christology.*

Christology from Below. A Christology developed from an examination of Christ's human history, especially as presented in the Synoptic Gospels. As such, Christology from below and Christology from above are not mutually exclusive. See *Antiochene Theology; Logos-Anthropos Christology; Synoptic Gospels.*

Christophany (Gr. "manifestation of the Anointed One"). The revelation of Jesus as God's Anointed One or the Messiah. This happened not only at Jesus' baptism in the Jordan (Matt 4:16–17; Mark 1:9–11; Luke 3:21–22) and his transfiguration on Mount Tabor, but above all in the Easter appearances. See *Anointing; Appearances of the Risen Lord; Messiah; Transfiguration.*

Church (Gr. "belonging to the Lord"). The community founded by Jesus Christ and anointed by the Holy Spirit as the final sign of God's will to save the whole human family. God's abiding presence among men and women is expressed in the preaching, sacramental life, pastoral ministry, and organization of this community, which consists in a communion of local churches presided over by the church of Rome. Orthodox Christians typically call particular churches "local" or "sister" churches (UR 14). The Catholic Church distinguishes between "sister churches," which are the mainline Orthodox churches (UR 14–18), and "ecclesial communities," who came into existence through the Reformation. The latter maintain such basic ecclesial elements as baptism and devotion to Bible. See *Body of Christ; Eastern Churches; Marks (Notes) of the Church; People of God; Reformation, The.*

Church and State. The relationship between these two bodies that are independently competent in their own spheres, but should work together harmoniously to advance the comprehensive welfare of human society and maintain a proper civil and religious freedom. While church members as such have no right to control political matters, the state and its leaders should not pretend to be independent of the moral law that the church upholds (see DHu *passim*). See *Canon Law, Sources of Oriental; Church; Liberty, Religious; Symphony.*

Church, Dedication of. The solemn rite, reserved to the bishop or his delegate, whereby a building is set apart for Christian worship, and thus indicates a special presence of God and of the church in the world. In the West, the rite generally consists of the Eucharist and a ceremony during which the building is blessed and relics of saints fixed in the altar. In the East, before the first liturgy is celebrated, the altar is sprinkled with holy water and anointed as in the rites of initiation. See *Blessing; Consecration; Initiation; Sacramental.*

Churches. Various Christian communities that may differ, to an extent, in beliefs, liturgy, and discipline, but have some measure of union with one another by holding to "one Lord, one faith, one baptism" (Eph 4:5; see AG 19–22; LG 26; OE *passim*; and UR *passim*). See *Church; Ecumenism; Local Church.*

Church Militant. The visible, pilgrim church here on earth, to be distinguished from the Church Expectant (or Suffering) or the souls in purgatory and from the Church Triumphant or the saints already in heaven. See *Heaven; Purgatory.*

Church of the East, Assyrian. A Middle-Eastern Church, the oldest surviving church to have separated from undivided Christendom. This form of Christianity developed under less Greek influence, having been founded in very early Christian times apparently from Palestine and Edessa. In 410 at the Synod of Seleucia-Ctesiphon (Persia), it reorganized itself under its own "catholicos" or primate; and in 424 at the Synod of Markabta, it proclaimed its independence and established its center outside the Byzantine Empire—in Seleucia-Ctesiphon. The Church of the East regarded Theodore of Mopsuestia (ca. 350–428) as its chief theologian. His orientation in Christology was sharpened by like-minded theologians who were expelled from Edessa in 489 by Emperor Zeno and fled to Persia. This church goes by the name of Church of the East, because it lay east of the Roman Empire. Later on, because of its rejection of the Council of Ephesus (431), it was widely known in the West as the Nestorian Church. Today the Catholic heirs of this church are called Chaldeans, while those not in communion with Rome are called Assyrians. In November 1994 the patriarch of the Assyrian Church of the East, Mar Dinkha IV, along with Pope John Paul II, signed a common "Christological Declaration," which officially ended any doctrinal differences and promised close cooperation for the future (ND 683). See *Antiochene Theology; Eastern Catholic Churches, Four Ranks of; Eastern Churches; Edessa; Ephesus, Council of; Nestorianism; Malabar Christians; Patriarchates, Orthodox; Three Chapters, The.*

Ciborium (Gr. "seed-like cup obtained from water-lily"). A cup bigger than a chalice that holds the wafers to be consecrated for communion or for reservation in the tabernacle. The "baldacchino" or canopy over the altar in some old churches, such as St. Clement's in Rome, is also called a ciborium. See *Chalice.*

Circumcision. Cutting off the foreskin of male infants to symbolize their admission to the religious community. The Jews made this rite the hallmark of their alliance with God (Gen 17:10–14; Exod 12:48; Lev 12:3). The early church refused to impose circumcision on male converts, as baptism replaced it (Acts 15:5, 28–29; Gal 5:2–6; 6:15; Col 2:11–15). One of the events celebrated on January 1 is the Circumcision of Our Lord. Female circumcision, practiced by some Coptic and Ethiopian Christians, is being resisted. See *Baptism; Coptic Christianity; Ethiopian Christianity; Judaism.*

Circuminsessio (Lat. "sitting around"). See *Perichoresis, Trinitarian.*

Civil Religion. The use of religious traditions to support public activities in a country where there is no established religion. In the United States, a civil religion derived from a Jewish-Christian heritage expresses itself in various ways: for example, political leaders appeal to the nation's "manifest destiny," use the Bible on taking their oath of office, and echo the basic belief "in God we trust." See *Church and State; Religion.*

Classical Consciousness. Expression used by Bernard Lonergan (1904–84) to describe how culture conditions awareness in its progress from naive to philosophical knowledge. Classical consciousness is a developed form of awareness that believes one culture to be the normative and superior criterion by which to judge other cultural experiences and expressions. After centuries of domination in the West, classical consciousness has given way to a *pluralistic consciousness*, which is more descriptive than normative. In theology, this means that many classical answers, though not necessarily invalidated, can no longer be maintained as the exclusive interpretations of Christian faith. See *Pluralism; Postmodernism; Theology, Methods in.*

Clean Monday. The Monday the Greeks call *Kathara Deutera;* and the Russians, *Chistij Ponedilnik;* it opens the pre-Easter, forty-day period of fasting or Great Lent (so called because the Orthodox have other periods of fasting). Festivities are held on Clean Monday. The Greeks usually spend the day in the countryside and children fly kites. See *Ash Wednesday; Christmas Preparation; Fasting; Lent; Penance.*

Clergy (Gr. "lot, fate, portion"). Collective term for ordained deacons, priests, and bishops. See *Bishop; Deacon; Priests.*

Cleric (Gr. "one chosen by lot," "an inheritor"). Someone who has received an ecclesial ministry entailing precise obligations and rights over and above those of lay-persons, but different from those of religious (see CIC 232; CCEO 328). One becomes a cleric by receiving the diaconate. See *Laity; Religious Life; Tonsure.*

Clericalism. An effort by clergy to enhance their influence in non-ecclesial affairs; an approach to pastoral and theological problems that seeks to concentrate everything in the hands of the clergy. Clericalism is about power; priesthood is about service. See *Anticlericalism.*

Code of Canon Law (CIC). The highest code of law for the Latin Church. A revision was first announced by Pope John XXIII in 1959, in view of the forthcoming ecumenical council, Vatican II (1962–65). The code was drawn up after extensive collegial consultation with bishops and episcopal conferences. The CIC promulgated by John Paul II (pope 1978–2005) in 1983 contains 1,752 canons arranged in seven books (as compared with the first CIC promulgated by Benedict XV in 1917, which contained 2,414 canons in five books). The 1983 code aimed to express in juridical terms the teaching of Vatican II and its subsequent implementation. See *Canon Law; Corpus Iuris Canonici; Episcopal Conferences; Vatican Council, Second.*

Code of Canons of the Oriental Churches (CCEO). Scheme of canon law for the Eastern churches promulgated by Blessed John Paul II (pope 1978–2005) in 1990. As early as 1927—ten years after the promulgation of the *Codex Iuris Canonici* (CIC) by Pope Benedict XV—the Congregation for the Oriental Church (now Congregation for the Oriental Churches) proposed that these churches should have their own code of canon law, a suggestion accepted in 1929 by Pope Pius XI (1857–1939). Between 1944 and 1957, Pope Pius XII issued a series of canons (on such matters as marriage and church property) to help out until the code was completed. The first drafts included too much Roman centralism and Latin patterns of church life. After Vatican II (1962–65), which clearly acknowledged the special traditions, rights, privileges, and sacramental discipline of the Eastern churches (OE 5–23), Paul VI (1897–1978) set up the New Commission for the Code of Canon Law for the Eastern Churches. Despite inspiration from Oriental sources and consultation with the Catholic Eastern patriarchs, the main source for the Oriental code remained the Latin code promulgated in 1983. Historically important as the first code of canon law for the Oriental Churches, the CCEO was generally welcomed. The present patriarch of Constantinople, Bartholomaios I, studied canon law at the Pontifical Oriental Institute (Rome) and wrote his doctoral dissertation (on the need to organize the canons in the Byzantine Church) under the direction of Fr. Ivan Zuzek, S.J., who later became the secretary of the commission that prepared the CCEO. See *Eastern Churches; Local Church; Patriarch.*

Collect. First variable prayer in the Mass of the Latin rite after the *Kyrie* or, on Sundays and feast days, after the *Gloria*. It expresses what the congregation may have been silently praying, thus "collecting" their prayers and setting the tone for the particular feast or mystery being celebrated. See *Gloria; Kyrie Eleison.*

Collegiality. The responsibility for the whole church shared by the bishops in communion among themselves and with the head of the college of bishops, the pope (LG 22–23; CIC 336–41; CCEO 49–54). The primary place for the exercise of collegiality is an ecumenical council, but it is also expressed, to a lesser degree, through episcopal conferences and synods. See *Council, Ecumenical; Episcopal Conference; Sobornost; Synod.*

Communicatio Idiomatum (Lat./Gr. "interchange of properties"). Exchange of attributes because of the union of divinity and humanity in the one person of the Incarnate Son of God. This means that attributes of one of his natures may be predicated of him even when he is named with reference to the other nature: for example, "the Son of God died on the cross," and "the Son of Mary created the world" (see DH 251). This method of attribution calls for certain distinctions, so as not to confuse the two natures. The Son of God precisely as divine did not die on the cross, nor did the Son of Mary precisely as human create the universe. See *Chalcedon, Council of; Constantinople, Second Council of; Ephesus, Council of; Hypostatic Union; Monophysitism; Trisagion.*

Communicatio in Sacris. Participating in the liturgy, especially the sacraments, of a church other than one's own (CIC 1365; CCEO 908, 1440) and called eucharistic hospitality by some when it refers only to eucharistic sharing. Ecumenism encourages sharing the word of God, but sacraments, especially the Eucharist, normally express (and further) an ecclesial union already present (see UR 8). In case of necessity and in the absence of Catholic clergy, Catholics may confess, communicate, and receive the anointing of the sick from Orthodox priests (OE 26–27). Most Protestant churches are willing to extend eucharistic hospitality to any baptized Christian who believes in Jesus Christ as Lord and approaches the eucharistic table with proper dispositions, as a 1975 decision of the German Lutheran Churches expressed it. Anglicans are usually more open to Orthodox and Catholics, as they hold eucharistic views similar to their own. The Orthodox, however, see membership in their church to be implied when someone receives the Eucharist; hence, they tend to limit eucharistic hospitality to cases of pastoral emergency (e.g., danger of death), which are to be judged on the basis of the "economy." When Sergius Bulgakov (1871–1944), at a meeting between Orthodox and Anglicans in 1933, proposed occasional eucharistic hospitality between those who shared the same eucharistic doctrines, he met with much opposition. A 1984 agreement exists between the Roman Catholic and the Syrian Orthodox churches, signed by Pope John Paul II (pope 1978–2005) and Patriarch Ignatius Zakka I (patriarch 1980–present), allowing members of their respective churches to avail themselves of eucharistic hospitality when they are unable to communicate in their own church. See *Anglican Communion; Eastern Churches; Economy; Eucharist; Liturgy; Orthodoxy; Protestant; Sacrament.*

Communion. Sharing in the body of Christ by receiving the consecrated host during Mass and after due preparation (e.g., by fasting for one hour or abstaining from all food and drink, except water, and, where this is needed, by confessing grave sins). When communion is received on other occasions (e.g., at home by the sick), the link with the Mass should not be ignored. Church law prescribes that communion should be received at least once a year, but not necessarily under both species (see DH 1198–1200; ND 1506; CIC 912–23; CCEO 707–8, 713). See *Eucharist; Koinonia; Mass.*

Communion of Saints. The spiritual union between Christ and all Christians, whether already in heaven (or purgatory) or still living on earth (LG 49–50). See *Church Militant; Heaven; Koinonia; Purgatory.*

Communion, Spiritual. Receiving communion in desire when actual communion is not possible. Those who wish to partake spiritually in the body of Christ ought to prepare themselves as if they were attending Mass (e.g., by asking pardon for their sins, reading the scriptures, and expressing perfect love for God).

Community. Christians united for prayer, ministry, and life in common. See *Basic Communities; Church; Parish; Religious Life*.

Comparative Religion. That science which developed in the late nineteenth century and which studies the parallels and differences among the beliefs and practices of various religions. Comparative religion as such does not pronounce on the relative merits and ultimate truth of religions. See *Religion; World Religions*.

Compunction. The "pricking of conscience" occasioned by an awareness of one's sins. It should lead to a healthy sorrow and divine pardon rather than to a morbid scrupulosity over one's faults. In patristic spirituality, compunction (Gr. *penthos*) is a key to joy and spiritual maturity. See *Attrition; Contrition; Fathers of the Church; Penance, Virtue of*.

Concelebration. The joint celebration of the same sacrament by several ministers led by a main celebrant. This practice, found in the early church, continued in the East, whereas in the Latin rite it was limited to a few occasions such as ordination to the priesthood. By once more encouraging concelebration of the Eucharist in the West, the Second Vatican Council (1962–65) did not abolish "private" Masses or Masses celebrated without a congregation (but preferably with an altar server). Rather, the council acknowledged the social character of the Eucharist and the unity of ministerial priesthood, in particular, that of the bishop with the priests of his diocese (SC 57–58). In the Eastern churches, "private" Masses are unknown, and concelebration once a day at the same altar is the norm. See *Anointing of the Sick; Celebrant; Communicatio in Sacris*.

Conciliarism. A theory that flourished at the time of the Great Schism (1378–1417), when the West was divided in allegiance between two or even three popes. It held that supreme authority is vested in an ecumenical council independent of the pope, unlike the teaching of Vatican II (1962–65), which situates the college of bishops with and under the pope. See *Basle, Council of; Collegiality; Constance, Council of; Council, Ecumenical; Pentarchy; Pope; Vatican Council, Second*.

Conciliarity. See *Sobornost*.

Conclave (Lat. "under lock and key"). The election of the pope by the cardinals. During the first millennium, the popes were chosen by the clergy and the people of Rome. The reforms of St. Gregory VII (pope 1073–85) aimed to curb increasing corruption, since papal elections had often become struggles between powerful families in Rome. Under Alexander III (pope 1159–81), regulations became stricter; in particular, a two-thirds majority was required for the papal election. After it took more than two years to elect Blessed Gregory X (pope 1271–76), the Second Council of Lyons (1274) introduced laws to exclude outside influences on the cardinals in conclave. Present regulations prescribe that after the pope's death, cardinals of less than eighty years of age will meet in locked sections of the Vatican Palace to choose, usually by a secret ballot, the next pope. The votes from a successful ballot are burned without straw and produce white smoke to indicate at once to those outside the conclave that a new pope has been elected. See *Cardinal; Lyons, Second Council of; Pope.*

Concupiscence. In general, desire or covetousness. More specifically, it refers to the disordered desire that comes from original sin and remains after baptism (see DH 1515; ND 512). See *Original Sin; Trent, Council of.*

Concursus Divinus (Lat. "divine concurrence"). The constantly needed cooperation from God that enables creatures to initiate, continue, and complete their actions. The fact that rational creatures sometimes sin raises the question of accounting for God's collaboration in actions that deliberately run counter to the divine will. See *Freedom; Grace; Molinism; Omnipotence; Pelagianism; Synergism.*

Confession. The whole sacrament of penance or that part of it when penitents acknowledge their sins to the priest (CIC 959–91, see 916; CCEO 707, 711, 718–36). Confession usually takes place individually, but general absolution (or absolution of a group without previous confession) may be given under certain circumstances (see CIC 961; CCEO 720 §§2–3). Confession once a year is obligatory for all Catholics who have reached the age of reason (CIC 989; CCEO 719). Confession of venial sins is recommended, whereas "all grave sins" must be confessed (CIC 988; CCEO 719)—an example of how the new code speaks of "grave" rather than "mortal" sins. See *Absolution; Attrition; Compunction; Contrition; Lateran Council, Fourth; Penance, Sacrament of; Satisfaction; Sin.*

Confession of Dositheus. A profession of faith approved by the 1672 Synod of Jerusalem and recognized as authoritative in the Eastern Orthodox Church. It was mainly composed by Dositheus (1641–1707; Orthodox Patriarch of Jerusalem from 1669), who opposed Protestant influence in the Byzantine Church, and, in particular, the ideas of Cyril Lukaris. See *Eastern Churches; Orthodoxy.*

Confession of Lukaris. A profession of faith showing Calvinist tendencies and written by the Patriarch of Constantinople Cyril Lukaris (1572–1638), maybe the most gifted theologian of Eastern Orthodoxy since the fall of Constantinople (1453). Although repeatedly condemned in the Eastern church, the confession exercised an influence on subsequent Orthodox theology. See *Calvinism; Eastern Churches; Eastern Theology; Orthodoxy.*

Confession of Peter Moghila. A profession of faith composed by the Orthodox Metropolitan of Kiev, St. Peter Moghila (1596–1646), in reaction to Cyril Lukaris's Calvinist trends. Approved in a modified form by the Synod of Jassy (1642) in modern Romania, and the foremost Orthodox patriarchs in 1643, it remains the most pro-Latin document accepted by the Orthodox.

Confirmation. The Western name for one of the seven sacraments, the second of the sacraments of initiation. The minister imposes hands on the candidates and anoints their foreheads with chrism while saying: "Be sealed with the gifts of the Holy Spirit." In the East, confirmation (called *chrismation*) is administered by the priest immediately after the baptism of an infant. In the West, confirmation is administered by the bishop and for pastoral reasons comes later (e.g., at the age of reason or even during adolescence). Adult converts, however, are confirmed immediately after baptism and before receiving their first communion. The East recognizes the presence of the bishop by the fact that the chrism has been blessed by him. In the West, a simple priest may be the extraordinary minister of confirmation (see CIC 879–96; CCEO 692, 695–96). See *Baptism; Character; Charisms; Chrism; Holy Spirit; Initiation; RCIA; Sacrament; Sphragis.*

Confucianism. The beliefs and practices drawn from the ancient Chinese classics and transmitted in a special way by Confucius or K'ung Fu-tzu (ca. 550–478 b.c.). He may have authored the last of the five classical or "canonical" books: the *Shu King* (historical documents), *Shih King* (poems), *Li Ki* (ceremonies and institutions), *Yi King* or *Book of Changes*, and the *Annals of Lu.* Confucius approved the traditional religion of his time, emphasizing religious rituals and firmly believing in T'ien, a supreme cosmic power that assigns to human beings and all things their destinies. On that basis Confucius developed his ethical teaching. He insisted on sincerity, loyalty to principles, and the cultivation of kindness (*jēn*) and good character. He taught that inward goodness is fully expressed in all human relationships through decorum, propriety, and the observance of rites (*li*). The marks of true nobility are kindness, filial piety, loyalty, reciprocity, propriety, and a harmonious balance between extremes. From about 200 BC to AD 1912, Confucianism was the official state doctrine in China. See *Buddhism; Taoism; Zen.*

Congregational Theology. A form of Protestant Christianity that developed out of the Reformation and that maintains the right of local churches to regulate their own affairs in complete independence, a principle seen to be anchored in the Bible. See *Church; Protestant; Reformation.*

Conscience. The capacity to evaluate and choose a course of action according to the law God has written in our hearts (Rom 2:12–16; see GS 16; DHu 3). Conscience cannot simply be identified with God's law, because it may fail through scrupulosity and laxity or insensitivity to the guidance of the Holy Spirit. See *Heart; Moral Theology.*

Consecration. The solemn act whereby someone or something is set apart for God. Persons are consecrated for sacred office, buildings dedicated for worship, and bread and wine consecrated at the climax of the Eucharist. See *Blessing; Eucharist; Ordination.*

Consensus Fidelium. See *Sensus Fidelium.*

Constance, Council of (1414–18). Normally considered the sixteenth general council by Roman Catholics and convened to resolve the Great Schism (1378–1417), in the last phase of which three popes claimed the allegiance of Christians. These were John XXIII, who convoked the council at the instigation of the German emperor Sigismund and was deposed by the council; Gregory XII, who resigned; and Benedict XIII, who was deposed. In their place Martin V was elected. The council condemned John Wyclif (ca. 1329–84) and John Huss (ca. 1369–1415) (DH 1151–1195, 1201–79; ND 807–8, 1303, 1610), and also defined that in the Eucharist, Christ is wholly present under the appearance of either bread or wine (DH 1198–1200; ND 1506). See *Conciliarism; Hussites.*

Constantinople, First Council of (381). Convoked by Emperor Theodosius I to consolidate the unity of faith after the long Arian controversy, this council was attended, as planned, only by Eastern bishops (according to tradition 150 of them; in reality 146). Neither Pope St. Damasus I (pope 366–84) nor any other bishops from the West were officially represented. When the first president of the council, St. Melitius of Antioch, died, St. Gregory of Nazianzus (ca. 329–ca. 389) presided for some time before resigning; the council then chose St. Nectarius (d. 397) as its president and bishop of Constantinople. The council confirmed and expanded the Nicene Creed, proclaimed the divinity of the Holy Spirit against the Pneumatomachians, and upheld the full humanity of Christ against the Apollinarians. It gave the see of Constantinople the place of honor in Christendom after Rome. It was recognized later as the second ecumenical council—partly through Chalcedon, which promulgated the Nicene-Constantinopolitan Creed (see DH 150, 300; ND 12). See *Apollinarianism; Chalcedon, Council of; Creed, Nicene; Holy Spirit; Macedonians; Pentarchy; Pneumatomachians.*

Constantinople, Second Council of (553). The fifth general council, convened by Emperor Justinian I (reigned 527–65) to bring peace to the church in the East. In order to win over the Monophysites, Justinian encouraged the 165 bishops present (practically all Easterners) to condemn Theodore of Mopsuestia (ca. 350–428), Theodoret of Cyrrhus (ca. 393–ca. 458), and Ibas of Edessa (435–457) for Nestorianism. After considerable harassment, Pope Vigilius (pope 537–55) dropped his opposition to the proceedings and accepted the council (see DH 421–38; ND 620–23). See *Monophysitism; Neo-Chalcedonianism; Nestorianism; Quinisext Synod; Three Chapters, The.*

Constantinople, Third Council of (680–81). The sixth general council, convoked by Emperor Constantine IV (Pogonatus) (emperor 668–85) to resolve the issue of Monotheletism. Pope Agatho was represented through three delegates who, however, did not preside; the emperor did. The council reaffirmed the Chalcedonian profession of faith and taught, as a necessary corollary, that Christ has two distinct wills (divine and human) that nonetheless operate together in perfect moral harmony (see DH 550–59; ND 635–37). See *Chalcedon, Council of; Lateran Councils; Monoenergism; Monotheletism; Quinisext Synod.*

Constantinople, Fourth Council of (869–70). Considered by Roman Catholics the eighth general council, it asserted Rome's jurisdictional primacy, condemned iconoclasm, and tried to win over the supporters of Photius (ca. 810–ca. 895), the deposed patriarch of Constantinople. He is acknowledged as a saint by the Orthodox. In the twenty-first canon issued by the council, Pope Hadrian II (pope 867–72) acknowledged for the first time Constantinople's precedence over Alexandria (see DH 650–64; ND 1253). Basing themselves on the scholarship of Franz Dvornik (d. 1975), Daniel Stiernon and others have suggested considering Constantinople IV (which condemned Photius) and the Constantinople Synod (which ten years later rehabilitated Photius) part one and two of the same council. See *Iconoclasm; Patriarch; Primacy.*

Consubstantial. See *Homoousios.*

Consubstantiation (Lat. "along with the substance"). The view, condemned at Trent (1545–63), that after the words of eucharistic consecration, the substances of bread and wine continue to exist alongside the body and blood of the Lord (DH 1652; ND 1527). See *Transubstantiation.*

Contemplation. That form of silent prayer in which the mind and imagination are less active, and the believer looks with love at God and the divine mysteries. Eastern writers speak of such prayer as "the mind descending into the heart." When contemplation comes through diligent exercise, it is called acquired. When it is simply granted as a special gift of God, it is called infused. See *Meditation; Prayer.*

Contingency. The characteristic of beings and events that do not exist or occur by necessity but only in dependence—ultimately on God, the only Being that necessarily exists.

Contrition. A heartfelt sorrow for past sin accompanied by the intention not to sin again (see Ps 51; Luke 15:11–32; 18:9–14; DH 1676–78; ND 1622–24). Contrition is necessary for the sacrament of penance to be valid (see DH 1451–65, 1704; ND 1614/5–14, 1644). See *Attrition; Penance, Sacrament of.*

Convent (Lat. "assembly"). A house of male or female religious living according to an approved rule and under the guidance of competent authorities. Convents differ from monasteries (CIC 609, 614–16; CCEO 433), or houses of monks and nuns who belong to Western monastic orders and Eastern rite religious groups. Especially in the East, convents are understood to be everyone's home; that of Optino Pustin south of Moscow, for instance, was famous for welcoming and encouraging philosophers and other scholars. See *Athos, Mount; Monasticism; Religious Life.*

Conversion. A turning from sinful priorities to God in a way that enhances both personal integrity and the good of the Christian community. Conversion is required by the coming of God's kingdom (Mark 1:15; Matt 4:17). See *Metanoia.*

Coptic Christianity (Arabic *qubti*, from the Gr. for "Egyptian"). That church which claims to have originated with the evangelist Mark, supposedly martyred in Alexandria in AD 68. By the late second century, it had its own self-identity, and after the Council of Chalcedon (451), went its own way by maintaining a verbal kind of Monophysitism. Coptic, a late form of the old Egyptian language, is still used for the liturgy in monasteries and southern Egypt; in Alexandria, Cairo, and elsewhere, Arabic, the language of the country, has become the liturgical language. Through efforts at a wider communion, a Coptic Church recognizing Rome emerged in the late eighteenth century (see DH 1330–53; ND 208, 325–26, 408–9, 644–46, 810, 1003–5, 1419). The challenge facing all Copts is to show how their form of Christianity, rich in monasticism and literature, can contribute to a predominantly Islamic Egypt. In May 1973 the Coptic pope, Shenouda III of Egypt, joined Pope Paul VI in signing a common declaration that officially set at rest christological differences that had arisen after the Council of Chalcedon (ND 671a). See *Chalcedon, Council of; Eastern Churches; Melkites; Monophysitism; Oriental Orthodox; Syrian Orthodox Church.*

Co-Redemptrix. A problematic title sometimes applied to Our Lady in a desire to express her cooperation in the work of salvation. While remaining strictly subordinate to Christ, the sole source of grace, she collaborates in his

Incarnation (Lk 1:26–38) and redemptive death (John 19:25–27) (see DH 3370; ND 712). See *Atonement; Eve; Incarnation; New Eve; Redemption.*

Corpus Christi (Lat. "Body of Christ"). A feast in the Western church celebrated after Trinity Sunday and commemorating Christ's gift of the Eucharist. Its institution was largely due to Blessed Juliana of Liège (d. 1258). See *Blessed Sacrament; Eucharist.*

Corpus Iuris Canonici (Lat. "Body of Canon Law"). The main collection of laws of the Catholic Church until Pope Benedict XV promulgated the *Codex Iuris Canonici* in 1917. The *Corpus Iuris Canonici* emerged in six stages: (1) Gratian, a twelfth-century monk from Bologna, created the discipline of canon law by putting together in an organized way legal rulings from councils, popes, and Church Fathers in his *Concordia Discordantium Canonum* (Lat. "Concordance of Discordant Canons"), usually called *Decretum Gratiani* (Lat. "Decree of Gratian") (1141); (2) Pope Gregory IX (ca. 1148–1241) ordered the renowned canonist St. Raymond of Peñafort (1185–1275) to complete Gratian's *Decretum.* The result was the *Liber Decretalium Extravagantium* (Lat. "Book of Decretals not [yet] Included"), divided into five books and promulgated on the pope's authority; (3) Boniface VIII (ca. 1234–1303) added a sixth book in 1298, *Liber Sextus Decretalium;* (4) in connection with the Council of Vienne (1311–12), Clement V (1264–1314) added further legislation. These decretals were promulgated in 1317 and are known as the *Clementinae;* (5) the decrees of Pope John XXII (1249–1334) were collected and published as the *Extravagantes Ioannis XXII;* and (6) the *Extravagantes comunes,* or papal decrees enacted between 1261 and 1471, entered the *Corpus Iuris Canonici,* which was revised and promulgated in 1582 by Pope Gregory XIII (1502–85). See *Code of Canon Law.*

Cosmological Argument. See *Arguments for the Existence of God; Five Ways, The.*

Cosmology. A coherent interpretation of the universe in its ultimate origin, nature, order, and destiny. See *Creation; Eschatology; Protology.*

Cosmos (Gr. "world," "adornment"). The universe as an orderly whole. In the NT, *cosmos* can denote our wider environment (Gal 4:3) or else the world as hostile to Christ (John 1:10). In Eastern theology, *cosmos* refers to the beauty of creation as opposed to the repulsive chaos (see Gen 1:1—2:4). See *Beauty, Theology of; Doxa; World.*

Council, Ecumenical (General). An occasional assembly of the bishops of the whole church who, with and under the pope, teach and legislate as one college and may even pronounce infallibly on matters of revealed faith and morals. The Second Council of Nicaea (787), in rejecting the claims of the iconoclastic Synod of Hieria (753), laid down that the pope in Rome and four Eastern patriarchs (of Constantinople, Alexandria, Antioch, and Jerusalem) must agree if a council is to be considered ecumenical. On the basis of a list first drawn up by St. Robert Bellarmine (1542–1621), Roman Catholics usually accept twenty-one ecumenical councils, from Nicaea I (325) to Vatican II (1962–65). By current law, it belongs to the pope to call a council, preside over it personally or through his legates, determine its program, extend an invitation to those who are not strictly entitled to attend, and confirm the council's decrees. A council has to be re-convoked if the pope dies while it is still in session (CIC 337–41; CCEO 53–54). See *Conciliarism; Episcopal Conference; Nicaea, Second Council of; Oikoumene; Reception; Seven Ecumenical Councils, The; Synod of Bishops.*

Counter Reformation. The revival and reaction of the Catholic Church (from ca. 1520 to the end of the Thirty Years' War in 1648) to the forces of the Reformation. The term itself is problematic, because earnest efforts to reform the church had been undertaken long before Martin Luther's initial protest in 1517. Spain remained practically untouched by Protestantism, partly through the reforms already introduced by Cardinal Francisco Ximénez de Cisneros (1436–1517) and supported by the Spanish crown. In Italy, Girolamo Savonarola (1452–98) died in the cause of ecclesiastical reform. Lateran V (1511–17) decided to correct abuses. After the initial shock that Luther's protest triggered, reforming forces within the Catholic Church gained momentum. New religious orders came into being, such as the Theatines (founded by St. Cajetan [1480–1547] and Giovanni Pietro Caraffa, later Pope Paul IV [1476–1559]) and the Capuchins (founded by Matteo Serafini da Bascio [ca. 1495–1552]). Although every schoolbook used to say that St. Ignatius of Loyola (1491–1556) founded the Jesuit Order to combat Protestantism, this was still not a major objective when he received papal approbation (1540). He aimed rather at the reform of Catholic life within Europe and mission work abroad. Later, especially through St. Peter Canisius (1521–97), Jesuits became deeply involved in the struggle to save Germany, Austria, Poland, England, and other countries for the one Catholic Church. Further leading figures in the Counter Reformation included St. Philip Neri (1515–95), St. Charles Borromeo (1538–84), St. Francis de Sales (1567–1622), and Mary Ward (1585–1645). The Council of Trent (1545–63) was of immense importance through its careful restatement and/or reformation of a whole range of church beliefs and practices. Any full account of the Counter Reformation will also deal with the influence of Jesuit colleges; baroque culture; missions in the Americas, Asia, and Africa; and the reigns of Charles V (1500–1558) and Philip II (1527–98) of Spain. See *Calvinism; Inquisition; Lateran Council, Fifth; Lutheranism; Presbyterianism; Protestant; Puritans; Reformation, The; Trent, Council of; Tübingen and Its Schools.*

Covenant. God's alliance of friendship with humanity, represented by Noah (Gen 9:8–17), and Abraham and Sarah and their offspring (Gen 15:18; 17:1–22). At Sinai, God made a covenant through Moses (Exod 19:5–6; 24:7–8); the Ten Commandments summarized Israel's corresponding duties (Exod 20:1–17; Deut 5:6–21). The major prophets announced the interior holiness to be offered and effected by God (e.g., Jer 31:31–34). The new and eternal covenant was sealed by the blood of Christ (Luke 22:20; 1 Cor 11:25; Heb 7:22; 8:8–13). See *Berith; Decalogue*.

Creation. The act whereby in sovereign freedom and out of nothing God has brought about and constantly maintains in existence all that exists (DH 800, 3001–3, 3021; ND 19, 327, 412–14). The Bible is less interested in the starting point than in the end product of creation, the world created for God's glory (e.g., Isa 43:7; Ps 8; see DH 3025). See *Causality; Contingency; Deism; Evolution; Pantheism*.

Creationism. (a) The doctrine that each human soul is created directly by God (see DH 3896) and not generated by the parents, as some have claimed. (b) Creationism also refers to the anti-evolutionary view of those who interpret the Genesis accounts of creation in a fundamentalist way and argue that our universe came into being through a series of separate divine interventions "from the outside." See *Evolution; Fundamentalism; Soul*.

Creature. Whatever is not God and depends for existence on God. While all creatures share in the divine goodness (Gen 1:31), men and women have been created in the image and likeness of God (Gen 1:26–27), and fulfill their destiny by truly loving God and their fellow human beings. See *Image of God*.

Creed. A concise version of the chief points of Christian faith. As answers to questions about the Father, Son, and Holy Spirit, creeds developed in connection with baptism. Debates and heresies forced the church to clarify further the doctrines and express them in creedal form.

Creed, Apostles'. The creed promoted by the Emperor Charlemagne (ca. 742–814) and used at baptism in the Western church. It has a simple tripartite scheme, constructed around the Father, the Son, and the Holy Spirit (see DH 16; ND 4). Rufinus of Concordia (ca. 345–410) reports the legend that the twelve apostles composed it, each one being responsible for a phrase and so putting together this *symbol* (Gr. "something thrown together") of their common faith. In its oldest and shortest form (also known as the "Old Roman Creed"), the Apostles' Creed is reproduced by St Hippolytus (d. 235) in a question and answer form that preceded baptism. In a declaratory form Marcellus of Anycra (d. ca. 374) cited the creed to Julius I (pope 337–52) to prove his orthodoxy, apparently, however, omitting "Father" from the expression "God the Father almighty." In its definitive form, the Apostles' Creed is attested by St Pirmin (d. 753), bishop and abbot of Reichenau. See *Modalism*.

Creed, Athanasian. Profession of faith, also called *Quicumque vult* (Lat. "Whoever wants") after its opening words, falsely attributed to St. Athanasius of Alexandria (ca. 296–373) and probably originating in southern France in the fifth century. It has much to say about the Trinity, the Incarnation, and the redemption (see DH 75–76; ND 16–17).

Creed, Nicene. The creed ratified at Nicaea I (325). Against the Arians, it proclaimed the eternal divinity of the Son, who is "of the same substance" or "of one being" (*homoousios*) with the Father (DH 125–26; ND 7–8). Often, the term *Nicene Creed* refers to what is more precisely called the Nicene-Constantinopolitan Creed, ascribed to the First Council of Constantinople (381). This creed presupposes that of Nicaea but is more specific about the divinity of the Holy Spirit, who is to be "worshiped and glorified" with the Father and the Son (DH 150; ND 12). Widely used during the Eucharist and at baptism, this is the most commonly accepted creed among Christians. See *Constantinople, First Council of; Filioque; Homoousios; Nicaea, First Council of*.

Cremation (Gr. "burning"). Disposing of human corpses by burning them. The OT, far from accepting cremation, prescribed death by burning for certain heinous sins (Lev 20:14; 21:9). Christianity long resisted the practice of cremation. Today the Catholic Church allows cremation, provided it is not intended to deny the resurrection of the body (CIC 1176 §3; CCEO 876 §3). Many Christians, however, in particular, the Orthodox, strongly dislike the practice of cremation. See *Cemetery; Death; Funeral Rite; Resurrection of the Dead*.

Cross. The characteristic Christian sign, expressing Christ's death for our salvation and used by Paul to sum up his message (1 Cor 1:17–18). The sign of the cross, the feast of the Exaltation of the Cross (September 14), the veneration of the cross on Good Friday, and, in the Latin tradition, the stations of the cross are some of the many ways for recalling Christ's death. In any case, it is constantly remembered and re-presented through the church's sacraments. The sixth- or seventh-century Coonan Cross, found at the tomb of St. Thomas the Apostle in Mylapore, near Chennai (Madras), combines the cross with a lotus in an ancient act of inculturation. See *Icon; Inculturation; St Thomas Christians; Sign; Theologia Crucis*.

Crusades (Lat. "cross"). Military expeditions undertaken by Western Christians to liberate from Islamic domination the land where Jesus lived and died. Between 1096, when Peter the Hermit (ca. 1050–ca. 1115) preached the first crusade, until 1270, when what is usually considered the last crusade ended with the death of St. Louis IX, there were five major crusades. Christian

56

expeditions against the Turks continued in later centuries. The crusades have fired the imagination of writers and painters, but their evil effects included a radical hostility between Christians and Muslims, and a deeper rift between Eastern and Western Christianity. With the fourth crusade in 1204, when the crusaders sacked Constantinople and set up the Latin empire and patriarchate (1204–61), they practically sealed the schism between Rome and Constantinople. At the same time, however, the crusades increased cultural contacts; for instance, the crusaders brought back to the West books of Aristotle that Syriac-speaking Christians had preserved from loss. See *Aristotelianism; Byzantine Christianity; Islam; Maronites; Schism.*

Crypt (Gr. "hidden place"). An underground room that is situated beneath a church or its altar, and that often contains tombs of martyrs, saints, or others (for instance, founders or benefactors of the particular church). See *Catacombs.*

Cult. The religious homage due to God as creator, redeemer, and sanctifier. Christian cult stresses praise and thanksgiving more than petition. See *Adoration; Worship.*

Cultic Meal. The meal through which in the highest way worshipers acknowledge and identify themselves with their deity. In Christianity, the supreme act of worship is the Eucharist, the sacrificial and spiritual meal given to us by Jesus Christ in his death and resurrection (with the gift of the Holy Spirit), so that in anticipation of his final coming we may thank and unite ourselves with God. See *Epiclesis; Eucharist; Mass; Sacrifice of the Mass.*

D

Damnation (Lat. "condemnation"). The fate of those who die in unrepented grave sin. Having radically rejected God and their fellow human beings (Matt 25:31–46), they will suffer forever in hell. See *Hell; Last Judgment; Metanoia; Reprobation; Sin, Mortal and Venial.*

Dark Night. At night the visible world disappears, making way for the invisible world. For mystics, "night" becomes the privileged place to encounter God. "Dark" indicates that this privileged experience comes through trials that purify the soul from earthly attachments. With St. John of the Cross (1542–91), one may distinguish between the dark night of the senses, which weakens the grasp of sensual attractions, and that of the spirit, which detaches the soul from spiritual consolation. See *Mysticism; Spirituality.*

Deacon (Gr. "servant"). Inspired in part by the seven men chosen to care for the material needs of the Jerusalem community (Acts 6:1–6), deacons flourished in the early centuries of the church. Later their importance declined in the West, and the diaconate became simply a temporary stage before priesthood. The Second Vatican Council (1962–65) endorsed the restoration of the permanent diaconate for older, married men (LG 29), a decision implemented in 1967. Besides being entrusted with administrative and pastoral duties, a deacon in the West, when authorized, may as ordinary minister baptize (CIC 861 §1), solemnly preach, distribute the Eucharist, and officiate at marriages (CIC 1108 §1) and funerals. In Eastern Catholic churches, a deacon may baptize in cases of emergency (CCEO 677 §2); only the assisting priest can impart the marriage blessing (CCEO 828 §2). See *Clergy; Cleric; Ministry; Ordination.*

Deaconess. Woman in the early church holding an office similar to that of the deacon, so that some prefer to call her a woman deacon. Paul calls Phoebe (Rom 16:1) a "deacon," and 1 Timothy 3:11 may refer to women deacons (or to the wives of deacons). Canon 15 of the Council of Chalcedon (451) requires that a woman should not be ordained a deacon before the age of forty—an instruction repeated by canon 14 of the Quinisext Synod (692). Besides caring for the sick and the poor, deaconesses assisted in baptizing women. St. Olympia (d. 410), a noble collaborator of St. John Chrysostom (d. 407), features among the famous woman deacons in the Christian East. Up to the eleventh century, we find popes allowing Western bishops to ordain women as deacons. Partly due to the spread of infant baptism, the office of deaconess died out in the Middle Ages, but was revived in the nineteenth century by Anglicans and Protestants. In a 2003 document, the International Theological Commission, after examining the diaconate in history, theology, and official teaching, reached two conclusions with regard to the ordination of women to the diaconate: (a) in the ancient church there was a substantial (but incomplete) equivalence between the rites of institution and functions of deacons and deaconesses; and (b) in the unity of Holy Orders, there is a "clear distinction between the ministries of bishops and priests, on the one hand, and the diaconal ministry on the other." By a *Motu Proprio, Omnium in Mentem* (Lat. "To everyone's attention"), dated October 2, 2009, Pope Benedict XVI (pope 2005–13) changed some of the language used by the 1983 Code of Canon Law about deacons; in his words, "deacons receive the power to serve the people of God in the *diaconia* of liturgy, word and charity." This seemed to open the way to women being ordained deacons. There are women deacons among the Coptic Orthodox, and, in 2004, the Greek Holy Synod decided to restore women deacons. See *Anglican Communion; Bishop; Chalcedon, Council of; Deacon; Holy Orders; Priests; Protestant; Quinisext Synod.*

Dead Sea Scrolls. See *Qumran Scrolls.*

Death. The definitive end of our biological existence whereby the history of our life before God assumes its complete, irreversible shape (GS 18). The Bible sees death both as natural (e.g., Ps 49:11–12; Isa 40:6–7) and as the consequence of sin (Gen 3:19; Rom 5:12). Death will be the last enemy to be overcome (1 Cor 15:26) through our sharing in Christ's resurrection. See *Cemetery; Cremation; Funeral Rite; Resurrection; Soul.*

Death of God Theology. A theological movement of the 1960s, found chiefly in the United States, which at times merely entered into dialogue with contemporary atheism, but at other times represented the world as truly Godforsaken or even followed Friedrich Wilhelm Nietzsche (1844–1900) in proclaiming God's death at the hands of men. See *Postmodernism.*

Decalogue (Gr. "ten words"). The Ten Commandments, which sum up our religious and moral responsibilities. They are found in two versions (Exod 20:1–17 and Deut 5:6–21). Jesus did not abolish the Ten Commandments but, drawing on Deuteronomy 6:4–5 and Leviticus 19:18, summarized them in terms of love toward God, our neighbor, and ourselves (Mark 12:29–31). He also indicated that observance of the Decalogue may lead to perfect detachment and discipleship (Mark 10:17–21). See *Imitation of Christ; Love; Moral Theology; Perfection.*

De Fide (Lat. "pertaining to faith"). Theological statements possessing the highest degree of certitude coming from divine revelation and being proclaimed as such by the teaching authority of the church. See *Dogma; Magisterium; Qualification, Theological; Revelation.*

Deification. The purpose of the Incarnation, according to St. Irenaeus (ca. 130–ca. 200), St. Athanasius (ca. 296–373), and other Greek Fathers. Already created in God's image and likeness (Gen 1:26–27), human beings are called by grace to share in the divine life (2 Pet 1:3–4). See *Fathers of the Church; Grace; Incarnation.*

Deism. An umbrella term for the beliefs of many British, European, and American writers of the seventeenth and eighteenth centuries, who in various ways stressed the role of reason in religion and rejected revelation, miracles, and any providential involvement in nature and human history. By denying any special divine activity in the world, some contemporary theologians in Europe and North America make themselves latter-day deists. See *Enlightenment; Miracle; Providence.*

Demiurge (Gr. "artisan, craftsman"). A name used by Plato (427–347 BC) for the divine architect who fashioned the world according to the eternal ideas.

Gnostics reduced the demiurge to an inferior deity, responsible for the creation of the material universe, which they despised. See *Creation; Gnosticism.*

Demonology. The study of demons, their nature as fallen angels, and their role in tempting and harming human beings. See *Angelology; Angels; Exorcism.*

Demons. Spiritual beings that in the Jewish-Christian tradition correspond to devils, who are angels in revolt against God and bent on harming human beings. See *Devil, The.*

Demythologization. The attempt by Rudolf Bultmann (1884–1976) to translate what he called biblical mythology into contemporary language. Although the term suggests elimination, Bultmann's intention was positive: to interpret myths existentially. See *Existentialism; Hermeneutics; Myth.*

Denzinger. A collection of excerpts from church documents in chronological sequence, first published by Heinrich Joseph Denzinger in 1854. (Its forty-second edition, revised by Peter Hünermann, appeared in 2009.) His other works included a still useful collection of Eastern liturgical texts, *Ritus Orientalium, Coptorum, Syrorum et Armenorum* (Würzburg, 1863–64).

Deposit of Faith. All that God revealed through Christ for our salvation, considered as a treasure entrusted to the church to be preserved, interpreted, lived, and proclaimed faithfully to all people until the end of time (1 Tim 6:20; 2 Tim 1:12, 14; see DV 10; GS 62). See *Magisterium; Revelation; Tradition.*

Depravity, Total. A term used by Calvinists to express the view that human beings were radically corrupted by the fall into sin. See *Calvinism; Fall, The; Original Sin.*

Descent into Hell. A traditional term (mentioned in the Apostles' Creed but not in the Nicene Creed) for (a) Christ's stay among the dead after his death on the cross; and (b) his victory over death, often expressed in Byzantine iconography by his liberation of Adam, Eve, and other OT figures. This latter scene forms the characteristic icon for Easter and is also called the *anastasis* (Gr. "resurrection"). See *Creed, Apostles'; Creed, Nicene; Easter Triduum; Icon.*

Desert (Lat. "solitary place"). Waterless, barren land. By depriving human beings of their normal supports for living, deserts confront them more immediately with the forces of good and evil. Moses gathered his inner resources by a stint in the wilderness of Midian. He led God's people out of slavery, but forty years' wandering in the desert preceded their entry into the promised land. Jesus faced diabolic temptations during his forty days of prayer and fasting in the desert. Later, St. John Chrysostom (ca. 347–407), St. Benedict of Nursia (ca. 480–ca. 550), St. Palladius (ca. 365–425), and other outstanding Christians have found their spiritual energies transfigured when they took to the wilderness. In early times, God-thirsty monks fled en masse to the desert, as did many who wanted to avoid legal problems and martyrdom. Some modern spiritual movements and groups such as the Little Brothers and Sisters of Jesus, who draw their inspiration from Charles de Foucauld (1858–1916), foster ascetic contemplation through desert experiences. See *Apophthegmata Patrum; Asceticism; Monasticism.*

Determinism. An interpretation of the universe according to which all states of affairs and events come about inevitably and without any exercise of human freedom. According to genetic determinism, inherited genes predetermine human behavior (e.g., toward lives of crime and drug dependency). Our experience of choosing between alternatives contradicts this view of reality as rigidly predetermined. See *Foreknowledge; Freedom; Predestination.*

Deuterocanonical Books. A Catholic name for those seven books (plus further portions of other books) found in the Greek (Septuagint) version of the OT but not in the canon of Hebrew scriptures. The seven books are Baruch, Judith, 1 and 2 Maccabees, Sirach, Tobit, and Wisdom. See *Apocrypha; Septuagint.*

Development of Doctrine. Growth in the church's teaching since the apostolic age (DV 8). Authentic development requires identity-in-change between the new teaching and the original deposit of faith or revelation that reached its climax with Christ. St. Vincent of Lérins (d. before 450) compared doctrinal development to the identity-in-change between a child and the same person as an adult. When completing *An Essay on the Development of Christian Doctrine* (1845), Blessed John Henry Newman (1801–90) became a Catholic. He criticized St. Vincent's canon of ubiquity, universality, and unanimity, "*quod ubique, quod semper, quod ab omnibus creditum est*" (Lat. "what is believed everywhere, always, and by all") as too abstract, and elaborated seven notes or tests for distinguishing between faithful development and corruption. In grappling with the issue of development, much depends on one's view of revelation, understanding, and interpretation. See *Deposit of Faith; Doctrine; Revelation; Tradition.*

Devil, The (Gr. "accuser," "tempter"). Name used for Lucifer or Satan, chief of the fallen angels. Allusions to Satan and his followers are frequent in the Bible (e.g., Wis 2:24; Matt 25:41; Luke 10:18; Jude 6, 9; Rev 12:9–12; 16:14). See *Angels; Demons.*

Devotion. That prayerful and affective dedication that makes believers deeply responsive to God's will. See *Religion.*

Devotions. Paraliturgical prayers and practices, such as the Way of the Cross and the Rosary, that develop one's spiritual life and deepen one's religious convictions. See *Liturgy; Prayer; Rosary; Sacramental.*

Diaconia (Gr. "service"). NT term indicating that ministry and mission in the church are for the service of the community (Acts 1:17, 25; 21:19; Rom 11:13; 1 Tim 1:12). The Second Vatican Council (1962–65) describes the office of bishops in this way (LG 24). See *Ministry.*

Dialectical Theology. An important movement in Protestant theology during the 1920s that was led by Karl Barth (1886–1968) and radically dissented from the prevailing Liberal Protestantism. Emphasizing the infinite qualitative difference between God and human beings, dialectical theology reveled in paradoxes (e.g., eternity and time) that do not allow for an intellectual synthesis. See *Liberal Protestantism.*

Dialogue (Gr. "conversation"). Courteous discussion between individuals who hold different beliefs with a view to reaching or at least drawing closer to a consensus. Vatican II (1962–65) encouraged Catholics to dialogue with the world at large (GS 92), with members of non-Christian religions (AG 16), with other Christians, both those who belong to the churches of the East (UR 14–18) and those who belong to churches in the West that became separated from Rome during the Reformation (UR 19–23). Dialogue with non-Christian religions has been called interreligious or interfaith, whereas dialogue between Rome and other Christian churches has been called ecumenical or interconfessional. Various Vatican offices have issued guidelines for dialogue or directories. Thus the Secretariat for Promoting Christian Unity, founded by Blessed John XXIII (pope 1958–63) in 1960—and renamed in 1989 by Blessed John Paul II (pope 1978–2005) the Pontifical Council for Promoting Christian Unity—published a *Directory Concerning Ecumenical Matters*, Part One (1967) and Part Two (1970), followed by supplements and eventually by the *Directory for the Application of Principles and Norms on Ecumenism* (1993), a revision of the original directory of 1967 and 1970 (ND 932a–g).

In the case of the Eastern churches, one distinguishes between (a) the dialogue of charity, which consists in signs and gestures that express both the common faith already shared by all members of the dialogue and their desire to remove obstacles blocking full communion; and (b) official theological dialogue, sometimes called the dialogue of truth, in which through discussion representatives of various churches seek to reach full communion in faith and sacramental life. See *Eastern Churches; Ecumenism; Faith and Order; Vatican Council, Second; World Religions.*

Diaspora (Gr. "dispersion"). Initially applied to Jews deported under the Assyrian (722 BC) and Babylonian (597 BC) conquests, the term eventually designated all Jews living outside Palestine (John 7:35), of whom there may have been a million in Alexandria alone at the time of Jesus. To some Greek-speaking Jews of Alexandria, the church owes the Septuagint translation of the OT. The Christian proclamation outside the Holy Land first took place in Jewish synagogues (e.g., Acts 9:19–20; 11:19; 13:5, 14–44; 17:12). With the destruction of the Temple and the advance of Christianity, the Diaspora Jews became more isolated and their religion developed into the Talmudic Judaism of medieval and modern times. The NT, in places, uses *diaspora* to refer to Christians spread around the world and living in strange and sometimes hostile environments (Jas 1:1; 1 Pet 1:1). Modern persecution and emigration have brought a large-scale *diaspora* of Eastern Christians. In Germany, *diaspora* refers to confessional minorities, whether Catholic or Protestant. See *Church; Missions, Church; Septuagint; Talmud.*

Didache (Gr. "teaching"). A work from around the end of the first century, compiled from various sources by a Jewish-Christian author of western Syria or eastern Asia Minor. It presents the ways that lead to life or death as well as material concerning baptism, fasting, prayer, prophets, and the Eucharist. After the NT writings, the *Didache* and 1 Clement are our oldest documents on church order. See *Apostolic Fathers.*

Diocese (Gr. "house management," "administration"). (a) An administrative division of the Roman Empire, resulting from the reorganization initiated by Emperor Diocletian (ca. 245–316; ruled 284–305). By the beginning of the fifth century, there were fifteen such dioceses in the Roman Empire, by then divided into East and West. (b) When the term passed into the vocabulary of the church, its meaning varied greatly—from what we would call a parish right through to an eparchy or an ecclesiastical district including several provinces. (c) In current usage, *diocese* or *archdiocese* refers to a territory under the immediate jurisdiction of a bishop or an archbishop who governs in his own name and not as someone else's vicar. Hence he is called a *diocesan bishop* or *ordinary*. A diocese corresponds to an *eparchy* in the Eastern churches. The CIC defines a diocese (or see) as that portion of the people of God which is guided by its bishop as a pastor who with his priests gathers his faithful, in the Spirit, to hear the word of God and celebrate the Eucharist (CIC 369; see CCEO 177). See *Archbishop; Bishop; Eparchy; Exarch; Holy See; Ordinary; Patriarch.*

Diptychs (Gr. "twofold, double writing tablets"). The names of living and dead people, read during the Eucharist. These names were originally written on two tablets, joined together by hinges. Naming such persons expressed communion with them, whereas striking their names off the list signified excommunication. Diptychs of the living continue to be used on more solemn occasions in Byzantine liturgies. See *Eucharistic Prayer.*

Discernment of Spirits. The special gift of being able to distinguish divine charisms from merely natural or evil influences (1 Cor 12:10). To decide whether a particular state of affairs comes from the Spirit of God or from the spirit of evil and error (1 John 4:1–6), many Fathers of the Church and later authors have devised rules, such as those elaborated by St. Ignatius of Loyola (1491–1556) for people doing his spiritual exercises. Ideas on discernment owe much to Origen (ca. 185–ca. 254) and his teaching on five spiritual senses as well as to St. Diadochus of Photike (mid-fifth century), who spoke instead of a single spiritual sense, "a taste/feel for God." He stressed the need to make one's choices within the context of the church and its sacraments, especially baptism. See *Charisms; Experience, Religious; Prudence*.

Disciplina Arcani (Lat. "discipline of the secret"). The early church's practice of reticence about its most sacred rites and teachings in order to ensure that catechumens and pagans did not treat them with irreverence. See *Catechumenate*.

Divine Office. See *Breviary; Liturgy of the Hours; Office, The Divine*.

Divinization. See *Deification*.

Divorce. See *Marriage*.

Docetism (Gr. "appearance"). The early heresy that held that the Son of God merely seemed to be a human being. Christ's bodily reality was considered heavenly or else a body only in appearance, with someone else, such as Simon of Cyrene, suffering in his place. Against Docetic views, which were already rejected in the NT (1 John 4:1–3; 2 John 7), the church taught that Christ took from Mary a genuine body like ours and suffered in a really human way (DH 76, 292, 1338, 1340–41; ND 17, 645). See *Christology; Johannine Theology*.

Doctor of the Church. A title given to certain saints for their outstanding, orthodox teaching. From the eighth century, the West recognized four such doctors: Pope Gregory the Great (ca. 540–604), Ambrose of Milan (ca. 339–97), Augustine of Hippo (354–430), and Jerome (ca. 342–420). A century later in the East, Basil the Great (ca. 330–79), Gregory of Nazianzus (328–89), and John Chrysostom (ca. 347–407) came to be known as the Three Hierarchs and Ecumenical Teachers. Then Athanasius of Alexandria (ca. 296–373) was added, so as to have four Eastern doctors paralleling four Western doctors. Pope Benedict XIV (1675–1758) elaborated the norms for qualifying as a doctor of the church, above all, eminence of doctrine and sanctity of life. The last Eastern saint to become a doctor was Ephraem the Syrian (ca. 307–73), who was so proclaimed in 1920 by Benedict XV (pope 1914–21). In 1970 Pope Paul VI put two women saints on the list of doctors of the church: Catherine of Siena (ca. 1347–80) and Teresa of Avila (1515–82). In 1997 Pope John Paul II (pope 1978–2005) added St. Thérèse of Lisieux (1873–97), and in 2012 Benedict XVI (pope 2005–13) added St. John of Avila (1500-69) and St. Hildegard of Bingen (1098–1179), bringing the number of the doctors of the church to thirty-five. From ancient times, the Assyrian Church of the East has revered as saints and as "the Three Greek Doctors" Theodore of Mopsuestia (d. 328), Diodore of Tarsus (d. 390), and Nestorius (d. ca. 451). See *Church of the East (Assyrian); Cappadocian Fathers; Three Theologians, The.*

Doctrine. Church teaching in all its many forms, which is intended not only to communicate orthodox beliefs, but also to feed Christian life and worship. See *Magisterium; Orthodoxy.*

Dogma (Gr. "opinion" or "decree"). A divinely revealed truth, proclaimed as such by the infallible teaching authority of the church, and, hence, binding now and forever on all the faithful (DH 3011, 3073–75; ND 121, 839–40; LG 25). Despite their importance, dogmas are not ultimate norms. "The supreme rule of faith" is found rather in "the Scriptures, taken together with sacred Tradition" (DV 21), and celebrated in the church's worship. In the Eastern Orthodox Church, dogma denotes conciliar teaching (especially that of the first seven ecumenical councils), accepted by all the particular churches in communion with one another and nourishing the faithful in liturgy and life. See *Council, Ecumenical; Deposit of Faith; Hierarchy of Truths; Infallibility; Magisterium; Revelation; Regula Fidei; Seven Ecumenical Councils, The.*

Dogmatic Theology. The chief branch of theology, which, drawing on scripture and tradition for the data of revelation, examines and presents coherently all major Christian doctrines. Current attempts to renew this discipline reflect on the common faith in the light of the whole history of Christianity and the changing circumstances of our times (OT 16). See *Dogma; Systematic Theology; Theology.*

Donatism. A schism that arose ca. 311 over the episcopal consecration of Caecilian of Carthage by a bishop (Felix of Aptunga) who was accused of being a traitor during the persecution of the emperor Diocletian. The dissenting bishops chose instead Majorinus, later succeeded by Donatus—hence, the name of the schism. The Donatists seem to have denied the validity of sacraments administered by unworthy ministers, and to have required the rebaptism of Christians who lapsed back into sin (see DH 123, 705, 913). St. Augustine of Hippo (354–430) strongly opposed the Donatists; a conference organized at Carthage in 411 weakened them, and they finally disappeared when the Saracens destroyed the church in North Africa. See *Novatianism; Schism; Validity.*

Doubt. Uncertainty about or suspension of assent to particular Christian beliefs or even to the faith as a whole. Serious questions and the honest facing of difficulties do not amount to sinful doubt. See *Assent of Faith; Faith; Probabilism.*

Doxa (Gr. "glory"). The sublime majesty and radiant splendor of God revealed in Israel's history (especially in the Exodus [Exod 14:4, 17–18; 15:1–21]), through nature (Exod 24:15–17; Ps 104:31–32), and in the experience of the divine holiness (Isa 6:1–7). Luke associates God's glory with Jesus' birth (Luke 2:9), transfiguration (Luke 9:31–32), triumphal entry into Jerusalem (Luke 19:38), resurrection from the dead (Luke 24:26), and ascension (Acts 1:9, 11; 7:55). John's gospel begins with the contemplation of the divine glory (John 1:14), which is already revealed in Christ's life and especially through his miraculous signs (John 2:11). In Jesus Christ, the glory of God has been disclosed (2 Cor 4:4–6) and will be fully manifest at the end (Titus 2:11–13). *Doxa* is one of the key theological ideas in Eastern theology and exercises an increasing influence in the West. See *Beauty, Theology of; God; Revelation; Theologia Gloriae; Theology, Methods in; Transfiguration.*

Doxology. Giving glory to God. The psalms frequently glorify God (Pss 8; 66; 150), and so does the NT (Rom 16:27; 1 Tim 6:16; 1 Pet 4:11; Rev 4:11; 5:12). (a) The early church developed what came to be known as the subordinate doxology: "Glory be to the Father through the Son in the Holy Spirit." When the Arians abused it to argue that the Son was inferior to the Father and the Spirit inferior to the Son, St. Basil the Great (ca. 330–79) encouraged a coordinate doxology: "Glory be to the Father and to the Son and to the Holy Spirit." This latter doxology became dominant and is known as the short doxology, the long doxology being "Glory to God in the highest!" of the Latin Mass (see Luke 2:14). (b) A doxological style of theology, shaped by worship and the rule of prayer, has been developed in the West by Geoffrey Wainwright (b. 1939) and others. See *Eastern Theology; Gloria.*

Dualism. Any interpretation of reality that explains everything through two quite independent primordial principles. An example of dualism in philosophy is that of René Descartes (1596–1650), who interpreted the universe in terms of two irreducible principles, mind and matter (even though he held that God ultimately created both). Radical theological dualism normally proposes two antagonistic deities, a good one and an evil one: as did the Manichaeans and some Gnostics in the early church; and, in the Middle Ages, the Albigensians and the Cathars in the West and the Bogomils in the East. Christianity acknowledges a qualified dualism (between soul and body, and, above all, between God and the created universe), but proclaims that in Christ all things are reconciled to God (2 Cor 5:18–20; Col 1:20). See *Albigensianism; Bogomils; Cathars; Gnosticism; Manichaeism.*

Dyotheletism (Gr. "two wills"). The doctrine of the church that in Christ there are two wills, which belong to his two natures. Although separate, his divine and human wills work together in a perfect moral unity (see DH 556–58, 2531; ND 635–37). See *Constantinople, Third Council of; Monophysitism; Monotheletism.*

E

Easter. The earliest and most important feast of the Christian year, which recalls the rising from the dead of Jesus Christ. Initially it seems to have been celebrated every Sunday, while Jewish Christians still kept up the Jewish Passover. This was bound to create friction, since the Christian message proclaimed that Israel's deliverance from Egypt had been fulfilled by Christ's resurrection (1 Cor 5:7). Setting aside one special day each year to celebrate the resurrection led to controversy between the Christians of Asia Minor, who kept the feast on whichever day the Jewish Passover (14 Nisan) fell and were called *Quartodecimans* (Lat. "followers of the fourteenth"), and other Christian communities, which celebrated on the following Sunday. Such controversies continue. The Orthodox, even after accepting the Gregorian reform of the Julian calendar, still follow the Julian calendar for the Easter feast. Recent ecumenical development, however, has brought an agreement between Eastern Catholics and the Orthodox over celebrating Easter on the same day every four years (OE 20). In the Gregorian calendar, the dates for Easter vary between March 21 and April 25. See *Calendar, Gregorian; Passover; Resurrection.*

Eastern Catholic Churches, Four Ranks of. Among the twenty-two Eastern Catholic churches, which emerged from the traditions of Alexandria, Antioch, Armenia, Chaldea, and Constantinople, (a) the highest is a patriarchate, or a regional church led by a patriarch, a bishop with jurisdiction over other bishops in the patriarchate, including metropolitans, or bishops with responsibilities over other dioceses (CCEO 55–150). There are six Catholic patriarchates: the Coptic, the Melkite, the Syrian, the Maronite, the Chaldean, and the Armenian. Upon election. a patriarch does not seek the pope's confirmation, but asks for communion with him in a eucharistic liturgy, in which the *pallium* is no longer given to the patriarch as if he were only a metropolitan. (b) Major archiepiscopal churches are headed by a major archbishop with almost all the prerogatives of a patriarch but without the title and corresponding order of precedence (CCEO 151–54). There are four such churches: the Ukrainian, the Syro-Malabar, the Romanian, and the Syro-Malankara. A major archbishop, upon election, must seek confirmation from the pope. (c) There are eight autonomous (*sui iuris*) metropolitan churches: the Ethiopian, the Ruthenian Church in the United States, the Italo-Albanian (without a metropolitan), the

Bulgarian, the Greek, the Church of Krizewci (in former Yugoslavia), the Slovak, and the Hungarian (CCEO 155–73). (d) Finally, there are four examples of churches without a hierarchy: the Belarussians, Russians, Georgians, and Albanians. (In this entry, as in the next entry, we follow the order adopted by the (seventh) 2004 edition of Ron Roberson's *Eastern Christian Churches*.) See *Armenian Christianity; Bishop; Church; Coptic Christianity; Diocese; Eastern Churches; Eparchy; Ethiopian Christianity; Maronites; Melkites; Pallium; Patriarch; Pope; Rite; Ruthenian; St. Thomas Christians*.

Eastern Catholic Churches, Origins of. The twenty-two Eastern Catholic churches may be subdivided according to the way they originated. (a) Two churches, as they did not emerge from any Orthodox church, have no corresponding church among the Orthodox: the Maronite and the Italo-Albanian churches. (b) From what was known in antiquity as "the Church of the East" and is now called the Assyrian Church of the East, two churches are derived: the Chaldean Church and the Syro-Malabar Church, a church that had existed for centuries before it came under the Chaldean hierarchy. (c) Five churches originated from the Oriental Orthodox churches: the Armenian Catholic Church, the Coptic Catholic Church, the Ethiopian Catholic Church, the Syrian Catholic Church, and the Syro-Malankara Catholic Church. (d) Thirteen churches derive from the Orthodox Byzantine Church: the Melkite Catholic Church, the Ukrainian Catholic Church, the Ruthenian Catholic Church, the Romanian Catholic Church, the Greek Catholic Church, Byzantine Catholics in former Yugoslavia, the Bulgarian Catholic Church, the Slovak Catholic Church, and the Hungarian Catholic Church. A subsection in this group includes Eastern Catholic communities without hierarchies: Belarussians, Russians, Georgians, and Albanians. See *Armenian Christianity; Byzantine Christianity; Catholicism; Church of the East, Assyrian; Coptic Christianity; Eastern Catholic Churches, Four Ranks of; Eastern Churches; Ethiopian Christianity; Hierarchy; Malabar Christians; Maronites; Melkites; Proselytism; Ruthenian*.

Eastern Churches. Those churches that gradually evolved into independent communities after the death of Theodosius I (395), when the Roman Empire was divided into East and West. There are four groups: (1) The (Assyrian) Church of the East recognizes the first two general councils, but not Ephesus (431), which condemned Nestorius. Hence its members used to be called Nestorians. (2) The Oriental Orthodox churches recognize the first three general councils but not Chalcedon (451), and their adherents used to be called Monophysites. This group includes six independent churches: the Armenian Apostolic Church; the Coptic Orthodox Church; the Ethiopian Orthodox Church; the Syrian Orthodox Church; the Oriental Orthodox in India, who are evenly divided between the autocephalous Malankara Orthodox Syrian Church and an autonomous church under the supervision of the Syrian Orthodox Patriarch in Damascus; and the Eritrean Orthodox Church, which was recognized as independent from the Ethiopian Orthodox Church in 1993. (3) The (Eastern) Orthodox churches, whose break with Rome is conventionally dated to 1054, are all in communion with each other and recognize the patriarch of Constantinople as the first among equals. They include the old patriarchates of Constantinople, Alexandria, Antioch, and Jerusalem; the new patriarchates of Russia, Serbia, Romania, Bulgaria, and Georgia; the autocephalous churches of Cyprus, Greece, Poland, Albania, and Czechoslovakia; and the Orthodox Church of America, whose autocephaly is recognized by Moscow but not by Constantinople; the autonomous churches of St. Catherine's Monastery (Sinai); and the Orthodox churches of Finland, Japan, and China. (Constantinople does not recognize the autocephalous status granted by Moscow to the Orthodox Church in (former) Czechoslovakia, but it does recognize this church as autonomous. There is a similar problem regarding the autonomous Orthodox churches of Japan and China. Since they were made autonomous by Moscow without Constantinople's consent, Constantinople does not recognize them as such.) (4) The Eastern Catholic churches are in communion with Rome. Parallel to the Assyrian Church of the East there are the Chaldean and the Malabar Catholic churches. Parallel to the Oriental Orthodox churches there are the Armenian, the Coptic, the Ethiopian, the Syrian, and the Malankara Catholic churches. Parallel to the Eastern Orthodox churches we have the Melkite, the Ukrainian, the Ruthenian, the Romanian, the Greek, the Bulgarian, the Slovak, and the Hungarian Catholic churches; besides these are the Byzantine Catholics in ex-Yugoslavia. The Maronite and the Italo-Albanian Catholic churches do not correspond to any other church. See *Armenian Christianity; Autocephalous; Church of the East (Assyrian); Coptic Christianity; Eastern Catholic Churches, Four Ranks of; Eritrean Orthodox Church; Ethiopian Christianity; Malabar Christians; Maronites; Monophysitism; Nestorianism; Oriental Orthodox; Patriarch; Patriarchates, Orthodox; Rite; Ruthenian; Syrian Orthodox Church; Tradition; Ukrainian Catholic Church; Uniates.*

Eastern Theology. A theology developed by the Greek and Syrian Fathers of the Church. In general, Eastern theology is committed to preserving the whole of tradition, as guided by the Holy Spirit, recorded by the Bible, taught especially by early general councils, and celebrated in worship and icons. It is characterized by the primacy of the spiritual, spirituality being considered as lived dogma and dogma as that spirituality which has found official endorsement in its verbal expression. In uniting harmoniously church teaching, spirituality, and discipline, this theology is maintained and shaped by liturgy and monasticism. See *Alexandrian Theology; Antiochene Theology; Apophatic Theology; Council, Ecumenical; Doxa; Doxology; Fathers of the Church; Fools for Christ's Sake; Holy Spirit; Icon; Johannine Theology; Liturgy; Monasticism; Origenism; Seven Ecumenical Councils, The; Symbol, Theology of; Theology, Methods in; Three Theologians, The; Tradition; Worship.*

Easter Triduum (Lat. "three days"). The liturgical celebrations starting with evening Mass on Maundy Thursday and ending at vespers on Easter Sunday. The Thursday Mass recalls the Last Supper and Christ's institution of the Eucharist. On Good Friday, after the reading of the passion according to St. John, special prayers for the whole world, and the adoration of the cross, comes the Liturgy of the Presanctified, in which there is no consecration, but hosts already consecrated are distributed. After sunset on Holy Saturday, the Easter Vigil celebrates Christ's resurrection and our dying and rising with him in baptism. A service of light and the blessing of the paschal candle introduce a series of scriptural readings that recapitulate the whole history of salvation from creation to the resurrection. Then catechumens are baptized and the whole community renews its baptismal promises before the Eucharist is celebrated. In the Byzantine liturgy, Holy Week is called Great Week, Maundy Thursday Great Thursday, and Good Friday Great Friday. The Easter Vigil is particularly solemn, usually begins on Saturday evening, and finishes very late at night. See *Catechumens; Good Friday; Holy Week; Liturgy of the Presanctified; Lord's Supper, The; Paschal Mystery; Resurrection.*

Ebionites (Heb. "poor men"). An ascetic group of Jewish Christians in the first and second centuries that considered Jesus to be the human son of Mary and Joseph, a mere man on whom the Spirit descended at baptism. The group stressed adherence to the law of Moses, and for this reason rejected St. Paul. See *Christology; Encratites.*

Ecclesiology (Gr. "study of the church"). That branch of theology that systematically reflects on the origin, nature, distinguishing characteristics, and mission of the church. Although no articulated ecclesiology can be found in the Bible, the NT offers various images for the church, including: the spouse of Christ (Eph 5:25–32; Rev 21:2; 22:17), the body of Christ (Rom 12:4–5; 1 Cor 12:12–27; Eph 1:22–23; Col 1:18, 24), the people of God (1 Pet 2:10; Rom 9:25), the temple of the Holy Spirit (1 Cor 3:16; 6:19), the family and the household of God (Eph 2:19–22) (see LG 6–8). St. Irenaeus of Lyons (ca. 130–ca. 200), in his struggle with the Gnostics and their purported revelations accessible only to an elite, insisted on the local churches' visible apostolic succession, which could be recognized by everybody. St. Cyprian of Carthage (d. 258) wrote the first treatise on the unity of the church. Almost all breaches in the church's unity would be related, directly or indirectly, to different interpretations of its visibility and holiness. When the Donatists claimed that sacraments are valid only if performed by worthy ministers, St. Augustine of Hippo (354–430) explained that the church's holiness does not exclude sinners but presupposes them. As Karl Rahner (1904–84) put it centuries later, the church is the holy church of sinners. The *Summa de Ecclesia* by John of Torquemada (1388–1468), uncle of the Grand Inquisitor, signaled the development of ecclesiology as a distinct discipline, which then became more important through the Reformation controversies. The break between East and West led the Orthodox to develop a more pneumatological ecclesiology to account for the union of local churches in the same faith. Notable influences in the growth of Catholic ecclesiology were St. Robert Bellarmine (1542–1621) and the teaching of Vatican I (1869–70). In the twentieth century, the ecumenical movement, Vatican II (1962–65), and the work of theologians such as Yves Congar (1904–95), Avery Dulles (1918–2008), Karl Rahner (1904–84), Francis A. Sullivan (b. 1922), and Jean-Marie-Roger Tillard (1927–2000) contributed to the growth of the discipline. Orthodox theologians, such as Nikolai Afanas'ev (1893–1966) and Bishop John Zizioulas (b. 1931), have developed an ecclesiology centered on the Eucharist. Ecclesiology's major themes include the origins of the church in the OT; the ministry of Jesus, his resurrection from the dead, and the outpouring of the Holy Spirit; the relationship between the church and the kingdom of God; the variety of models for the church; the church's mission in and for the world; the church's pneumatological, charismatic, institutional, hierarchical, and eschatological nature; ministry and the sacraments; the Petrine ministry. Ecclesiology—and, especially, the church as tangible ministry—has been a main theme shaping the Roman Catholic/Eastern Orthodox meetings in Rhodes/Patmos (1980) and Balamand, Lebanon (1993), and the resumption of dialogue in Belgrade (2005). See *Augsburg Confession; Body of Christ; Charisms; Church; Communion of Saints; Conciliarism; Eschatology; Extra Ecclesiam Nulla Salus; Febronianism; Gallicanism; Gnosticism; Hierarchy; Holy Spirit; Magisterium; Marks (Notes) of the Church; Mission, Theology of; Petrine Ministry; Primacy; People of God; Reformation, The; Sobornost; Synod; Ultramontanism; Vatican Council, First; Vatican Council, Second; World Council of Churches.*

Ecology, Human (Gr. "study of the house"). The study of human beings in their interaction with their environment. As God's representatives, men and women were to be responsible stewards of creation (Gen 1:26–31; see Job 28:1–2, 9–11). The Messianic Age was to restore what nature lost through sin (Isa 11:6–8; see Ezek 47:1–12). The Christian hope is for the whole of creation to share in the risen glory (Rom 8:18–30) of "the new earth and the new heavens" (2 Pet 3:12–13). Such a hope encourages here and now a conscientious concern for and management of our environment—a theme developed in the teaching of Blessed John Paul II (pope 1978–2005) and the theology of creation coming from Jürgen Moltmann (b. 1926) and others. See *Creation; Messiah; Nature.*

Economy (Gr. "house management"). God's saving plan for the human race revealed through creation, and, above all, through the redemption effected in Jesus Christ (Eph 1:10; 3:9). In Eastern theology, economy also denotes concessions to human weaknesses made by the church, which, in particular cases, dispenses from its own canonical prescriptions. See *Canon Law, Sources of Oriental; Trinity, Theology of; Immanent Trinity; Salvation.*

Ecumenism (Gr. "inhabited world"). A worldwide movement among Christians who accept Jesus as Lord and savior and, inspired by the Holy Spirit, seek through prayer, dialogue, and other initiatives to eliminate barriers and move toward the unity Christ willed for his church (John 17:21; see Eph 4:4–5; UR 1–4). Christian communities separated over the Council of Ephesus (431), over the Council of Chalcedon (451), through the East-West schism conventionally dated 1054, at the Reformation in the sixteenth century, and later. Vatican II (1962–65) taught that the true church "subsists in" (that is to say, continues to exist fully in) but is not simply identified with the Catholic Church (LG 8). Belief in Christ and baptism establishes a real, if imperfect, union among all Christians (LG 15). In particular, the Orthodox share with Catholics very many elements of faith and sacramental life, including the Eucharist and apostolic succession (see OE 27–30). The Church Unity Octave, eight days of prayer for the religious unity of all Christians (celebrated each year from January 17 to 25), was started in 1908 by the founder of the Society of Atonement, Fr. Paul Wattson (1863–1940) when still a member of the Protestant Episcopal Church in the United States. The following year, with other friars, sisters, and laymen of his Graymoor community, he was received into the Catholic Church. From 1934, Abbé Paul Couturier (1881–1953) energetically promoted the Church Unity Octave (now named the Week of Prayer for Christian Unity), thus giving a strong impetus to what Vatican II called spiritual ecumenism (UR 8). See *Apostolic Succession; Communicatio in Sacris; Dialogue; Faith and Order; Hierarchy of Truths; Oikoumene; Schism; Vatican Council, Second; World Council of Churches.*

Edessa (now Urfa in Turkey). The most important center of Syriac Christianity, which, in spite of the Muslim invasion in 639, was active until the twelfth century. According to legend, Jesus sent a letter and his portrait to the king of Edessa, Abgar V Ukkama (4 BC–AD 50). Christianity was certainly known there from the second century. Its most significant writer was St. Ephraem the Syrian (ca. 306–73) who started the School of the Persians in Edessa after his native Nisibis was abandoned by the Romans in 363. Emperor Zeno closed the school in 489 because of acute conflicts between Nestorians and Monophysites. Edessa served as headquarters for the Syrian Orthodox Church. See *Antiochene Theology; Church of the East, Assyrian; Eastern Churches; Monophysitism; Nestorianism; Syrian Orthodox Church.*

Elders. Men having responsibility in Jewish synagogues (Luke 7:3), the Jerusalem Sanhedrin (Mark 14:43, 53; 15:1), and in early Christian communities (Acts 11:30; 14:23; 15:22). At times in the NT, *elders* (or *presbyters*) seem synonymous with "overseers" (or "bishops") (Phil 1:1; Titus 1:5, 7). John Calvin (1509–64) distinguished between teaching elders (ordained pastors) and ruling elders (laymen), a division still found in Reformed and Presbyterian churches. See *Bishop; Laity; Presbyter.*

Election. God's free choice of individuals and groups. In the OT, Israel was conscious of being God's "chosen people" (Deut 4:32–40; Isa 41:8–16). A new community of believers gathered through Christ's choice (John 15:1–17). In spiritual theology, *election* refers to the choice of one's state in life or the improvement of one's lifestyle, especially according to rules found in the *Spiritual Exercises* of St. Ignatius of Loyola (1491–1556). Canon law uses *election* to mean the choice made by the authorized voters for appointment to an office in the church, for example, the election of the pope by cardinals in conclave (see CIC 349). See *Predestination*.

Elevation. The raising of the consecrated host and chalice at Mass to invite adoration of Christ now eucharistically present and to express our offering to God. In the Ambrosian, Latin, and Mozarabic rites, the canon or eucharistic prayer ends with a second or minor elevation when the priest holds up both the host and the chalice. See *Adoration; Canon; Real Presence*.

Emanation. A reality that issues from a source (God) as light comes from the sun. This language, which goes back to the Neoplatonism of Plotinus (205–70) and was used by St. Thomas Aquinas (ca. 1225–74), has been opposed by many Christians because it seemed to make the world necessary and even identical with God, instead of being freely created by God (see DH 3024; ND 331). See *Gnosticism; Neoplatonism; Pantheism*.

Ember Days. Four periods of fasting and abstinence that originally may have been linked with crop festivals, and, subsequently, formed a preparation for ordination. The Ember Days were the Wednesday, Friday, and Saturday after Ash Wednesday, Pentecost Sunday, the Exaltation of the Cross (September 14), and the feast of St. Lucy (December 13). See *Abstinence; Cross; Fasting; Pentecost*.

Emmanuel (Heb. "God is with us"). The symbolic name for a child announced by Isaiah to King Ahaz (Isa 7:14). Matthew interprets this sign as a prophecy of Jesus' birth (Matt 1:23) and concludes his gospel with the related promise "I am with you always" (Matt 28:20). See *Christology; Virginal Conception of Jesus*.

Encratites (Gr. "abstainers"). A name used for various early Christian extremists who commonly abstained from meat, wine, and even marriage. It was among such fringe groups that some of the apocryphal gospels were written. See *Apocryphal Gospels; Asceticism; Docetism; Ebionites; Gnosticism*.

Encyclical (Gr. "circular letter"). A bishop's letter intended for wide circulation. From the eighteenth century, Western Catholics have applied the term to letters addressed by the pope to the whole church or a part of it. Papal encyclicals are not infallible pronouncements, but rather authoritative statements of the ordinary magisterium (see DH 3884–85; ND 858). Eastern Christians still call authoritative letters from their patriarchs *encyclicals*, a term also used by Anglicans since the first Lambeth Conference (1867) for the message issued at the end of those conferences. See *Lambeth Conferences; Magisterium*.

Enhypostasia (Gr. "in the person"). The doctrine of Christ's fully human nature, personalized through being assumed by the *hypostasis* or person of the Logos. Christ's humanity subsists in the *hypostasis* of the divine Word (hence, *enhypostasia*). To clarify the teaching of Chalcedon (451) on Christ's one person in two natures, the neo-Chalcedonian Leontius of Jerusalem (sixth century), rather than his contemporary and namesake Leontius of Byzantium, seems to have coined the term "enhypostasia" and developed the doctrine later supported by St. John of Damascus (ca. 650–ca. 750). Once widely considered to be an Origenist, Leontius of Byzantium was described by Cardinal Alois Grillmeier (1910–98) as "the key witness to the doctrine of the Council of Chalcedon." See *Anhypostasia; Chalcedon, Council of; Hypostasis; Logos; Neo-Chalcedonianism; Origenism*.

Enlightenment. A movement starting in seventeenth-century Europe (and spreading to North America) that resisted authority and tradition, defended freedom and human rights, encouraged empirical methods in scientific research, and aimed at deciding issues through the use of reason. In religious matters, many representatives of the movement supported biblical criticism, rejected special divine revelation and miracles, and could be strongly opposed to mainline Christianity. The prominent figures of the Enlightenment include Denis Diderot (1713–84), Benjamin Franklin (1706–90), David Hume (1711–76), Immanuel Kant (1724–1804), Gotthold Ephraim Lessing (1729–81), John Locke (1632–1704), Moses Mendelssohn (1729–86), Jean-Jacques Rousseau (1712–78), and François-Marie Arouet (Voltaire) (1694–1778). Although the Enlightenment fostered some false hopes for social progress and encouraged an anti-doctrinal rationalism, it did hand on a healthy respect for human reason and religious freedom. See *Authority; Autonomy; Deism; Liberty, Religious; Miracle; Postmodernism; Rationalism; Revelation*.

Entelechy (Gr. "bearing its own perfection"). The realization of what is potential, the actualization of the goal for which something exists. See *Aristotelianism; Causality*.

Enthronement. A bishop's being seated after ordination on the *cathedra* in his own cathedral, symbolizing the beginning of his teaching and pastoral government of his diocese. See *Cathedra; Cathedral; Diocese*.

Enthusiasm (Gr. "possession by God"). Ecstatic or emotional behavior attributed to the special influence of the Spirit of God. St. Paul warns against stifling the Spirit at work in prophecy and other unusual gifts (1 Thess 5:19–22), yet recognizes love as the highest gift (1 Cor 12:13—13:13). In the history of Christianity religious enthusiasm, when directed with discernment, has often produced lasting benefits. Misguided claims to the special influence of the Spirit can cause considerable harm (see DH 803–8; ND 317–20). See *Charisms; Discernment of Spirits; Experience, Religious; Prophet.*

Entrances. Some movements of celebrants at important moments in the eucharistic liturgy. In the Latin liturgy, entrance antiphons (introits) or hymns accompany the movement of the celebrant(s) from sacristy to altar. Solemn entrance processions stress the importance of a feast. In Eastern liturgies, at the Little Entrance, the deacon carries the gospel; at the Great Entrance, the priest brings the bread and wine to be offered on the altar. See *Cherubikon; Deacon; Introit; Liturgy; Priests.*

Eparchy (Gr. "province"). A word frequently occurring in the canons of general councils in the East to designate an ecclesiastical province governed by a metropolitan. Today it means "diocese." See *Diocese; Exarch.*

Ephesus, Council of. Third ecumenical council and the first of which we possess the conciliar acts. It was convoked by the Eastern emperor Theodosius II (reigned 408–50) to settle the debate provoked by Nestorius (d. ca. 451), patriarch of Constantinople, who had expressed reservations about *Theotokos* (Gr. "Mother of God"), a popular title for Mary. Without waiting for the papal legates or the Syrian bishops headed by John of Antioch (d. 441), St. Cyril of Alexandria (d. 444) on June 22, 431, opened the council, which condemned Nestorius's teaching and excommunicated him. Ephesus coined no new dogmatic formula, but rather proclaimed St. Cyril's second letter to Nestorius to be consonant with the faith of Nicaea I (325) (see DH 250–68; ND 604–6). By declaring Mary to be Mother of God, the council acknowledged Jesus Christ to be "one and the same" divine person. This primarily christological teaching paved the way for the formula of Chalcedon (451). The eighth canon of Ephesus recognized the church of Cyprus to be autocephalous. See *Apollinarianism; Chalcedon, Council of; Church of the East, Assyrian; Constantinople, Second Council of; Nestorianism; Theotokos; Three Chapters, The.*

Epiclesis (Gr. "invocation"). In general, any invocation of God to bless and sanctify material creation (see 1 Tim 4:1–5). In the anaphora or canon of the Mass, the epiclesis is the prayer asking that the Spirit or the Logos descend upon the gifts to change them into the body and blood of Christ for the spiritual profit of those who receive them. In the Middle Ages, there was a controversy as to whether the consecration was complete with the words of institution, as the Latins maintained, or only with the subsequent prayer of epiclesis, as in most Greek and Oriental anaphoras (see DH 1017, 2718, and 3556). The reform of the liturgy after the Second Vatican Council (1962–65) put into the new canons an epiclesis before the consecration (praying that the gifts be changed) and after the consecration (praying that the communicants be changed). The debate as to whether the prayer *quam oblationem* before the consecration, and the *supra quae* and *supplices te* after the consecration in the old Roman canon (the first eucharistic prayer) are prayers of epiclesis seems settled in favor of the anaphora being epicletic. See *Anaphora; Canon; Consecration; Eucharistic Prayer; Holy Spirit.*

Epiphany (Gr. "manifestation"). In general, any appearance of the divine in space and time (Exod 3:12; 19:18; Acts 2:3–4). The Johannine literature sees the Incarnation and the whole of Christ's life as an epiphany (John 1:14; 1 John 1:1–3). As a major feast, held on January 6 in the East from at least the fourth century, the Epiphany celebrated the entire cycle of Christ's appearance in his birth, adoration by the Magi, baptism, and first miracle at Cana (John 2:1–11). Gradually, Christmas came to be observed almost everywhere on December 25, with the Armenian tradition still commemorating Christ's birth on January 6. In the East, where baptism is also called *photismos* (Gr. "enlightenment"), the Epiphany is celebrated with lights, and the waters of rivers and other bodies of water (representing the Jordan) are blessed by plunging a cross into them. An icon of Christ's baptism is used for the feast, called the *Theophany* (Gr. "manifestation of God"), since the baptism of Christ revealed the three persons of the Trinity. In the West, the feast of the Epiphany celebrates the coming of the Magi and the revelation of Christ to the Gentiles; the following Sunday is invariably dedicated to the baptism of the Lord, while, in cycle C, the next Sunday (the Second Sunday of the Year) recalls the marriage at Cana. The *Magnificat* antiphon for the second vespers of the Epiphany retains, however, the original, inclusive character of the feast: "Three wonders mark this day we celebrate: today the star led the Magi to the manger; today water was changed into wine at the marriage feast; today Christ desired to be baptized by John in the River Jordan to bring us salvation." See *Christmas; Doxa; Johannine Theology; Theophany.*

Episcopacy (from Gr. "bishop," "overseer"). Church government by bishops who together, as the successors to the collegiate system of apostles found in the NT, form the present college of bishops responsible for that government. See *Apostolic Succession; Bishop; Collegiality; Diocese; Ordinary; Pope.*

Episcopal Conference. The assembly of Catholic bishops of a certain country or region held at least every year to plan collective pastoral initiatives for the good of the church in the whole territory. Episcopal conferences were encouraged by Vatican II (1962–65) (CD 37–38; LG 23) and entered the 1983 Code of Canon Law (CIC 447–59; 753). In a *Motu proprio* of May 1998, *Apostolos suos*, Pope John Paul II (pope 1978–2005) clarified their theological and juridical nature. For a conference's doctrinal statements to constitute authentic magisterial teaching they require unanimous agreement. Those statements supported by a two-thirds majority of the bishops require approval from the Holy See. See *Bishop; Collegiality; Magisterium; Motu proprio.*

Episcopalians. Members of a church led by bishops, and, in particular, those Christians in the United States who are in communion with the archbishop of Canterbury. See *Anglican Communion.*

Epistemology (Gr. "theory of knowledge"). That branch of philosophy which investigates human knowledge, its nature, sources, criteria, possibilities, and limits. See *Philosophy.*

Epistle (Gr. "letter"). Term traditionally used for the twenty-one letters of the NT and for the second reading at the Sunday Eucharist that precedes the gospel.

Equivocity (Lat. "using the same word"). The use of words with more than one meaning (e.g., *star* for a heavenly body and for an outstanding actor). This will make arguments fallacious when some claim is valid only for one of the meanings. See *Analogy; Univocity.*

Eritrean Orthodox Church. The recently formed autocephalous Church of Eritrea, which belongs among those Oriental Orthodox churches that do not recognize the Council of Chalcedon (451), and, thus, are not in communion with the patriarch of Constantinople. Headed by a patriarch, who lives in Asmara, the capital of Eritrea; this church has about 1,470,000 faithful. Eritrea formed the ancient Kingdom of Aksum, whose capital, Aksum, was also considered to be the holy city of Ethiopian Christianity. After centuries under Ethiopian, Ottoman, and Italian rule, Eritrea obtained independence on May 24, 1993. Negotiations with Pope Shenouda III of Egypt and the Coptic Synod enabled Patriarch Paulos of Ethiopia and Archbishop Philippos of Eritrea to separate in September 1993 and still agree to continue close collaboration. Archbishop Philippos was chosen and enthroned as the first patriarch for the Eritrean Orthodox Church in 1998; he died on September 18, 2002. See *Chalcedon, Council of; Coptic Christianity; Ethiopian Christianity; Oriental Orthodox.*

Eros (Gr. "love of desire"). Love that seeks self-fulfillment. It is distinguished both from *agape*, which is God's self-giving love in Christ that calls for a human response (1 John 4:7–12), and from *philia*, the love between friends and relatives. In his first encyclical, *Deus Caritas est* (2006), Pope Benedict XVI (pope 2005–13) has taught that, far from being reducible to sex, *eros* or the love of desire joins *agape* in leading us to God. See *Agape; Love.*

Error. False belief or incorrect conduct. People held to be in error should, however, be treated with courtesy and love, and their religious liberty should be respected (GS 28; DHu 14). See *Heresy*.

Eschata (Gr. "the last things"). The current term for what used to be called *novissima* (Lat. "the latest things"): death, judgment (both the particular judgment of the individual and the universal judgment of all humanity), heaven, and hell. These elements of our destiny, necessarily shrouded in mystery during this life, find their focus in Christ himself, who is the Alpha and the Omega, the beginning and the end (Rev 22:13). Without taking an explicit position about modern debates over purification at the moment of death and the possibility of all humans being finally saved through God's infinite mercy, a 1979 letter of the Congregation for the Doctrine of the Faith drew attention to church teaching on resurrection for the whole person, purgatorial purification, and our two final possibilities, heaven or hell (DH 4650–59; ND 2317). See *Apocatastasis; Beatific Vision; Death; Heaven; Hell; Last Judgment; Mystery; Purgatory.*

Eschatology (Gr. "knowledge of the last things"). That branch of systematic theology which studies God's final kingdom as expressed by its OT preparation (e.g., the messianic hopes), the preaching of Jesus, and the teaching of the NT church. According to Albert Schweitzer (1875–1965), Jesus mistakenly expected the imminent coming of the kingdom. According to the opposite thesis of realized eschatology, proposed by Charles Harold Dodd (1884–1973), Jesus announced that with his ministry the essential elements of the kingdom had already come. Mediating positions argue for a kingdom already inaugurated with the ministry, death, and resurrection of Jesus (see Luke 11:20; 1 Cor 10:11), but still to be consummated (see Mark 13; Luke 11:2; 1 Cor 15:20–28) when Christ comes in glory to judge the living and the dead (see Matt 25:31–46; Rev 22:12–13). More than a mere branch of theology, eschatology denotes that future-directedness of our entire present existence. See *Apocalyptic Literature; Hope; Johannine Theology; Kingdom of God; Messiah; Millenarianism; Parousia; Resurrection.*

Eschaton. See *Parousia.*

Essence and Energies. A key distinction in the theology of St. Gregory Palamas (ca. 1296–1359), according to which the divine essence remains unknowable, but not God's self-disclosing and life-giving energies or activities. This differentiation in God was meant to safeguard both our deification and the inaccessible otherness of God. Energies correspond to what Western theology calls the divine attributes. See *Attributes, Divine; Apophatic Theology; Deification; Eunomianism; Hesychasm; Palamism.*

Essence and Existence. In the philosophy of St. Thomas Aquinas (ca. 1225–74), the basic, real distinction between the two principles of being that account for the ultimate composition of whatever exists in the created world. The act of existence actualizes the potentiality of essence and thus enjoys a primacy over essence. In God, essence and existence coincide. See *Being; Thomism*.

Essenes. An ascetic and highly organized Jewish group mentioned by Philo (ca. 20 BC–ca. AD 50), the elder Pliny (ca. 23–79), and Flavius Josephus (ca. 37–ca. 100). They seem to have originated in the second century BC and were probably identical with the Qumran community. See *Qumran Scrolls*.

Eternity (Lat. "endless duration"). Having neither beginning nor end, but being unchangeably full of life. Eternity is a divine attribute, but through grace God lets us share in eternal life (John 11:25–26). See *Attributes, Divine; Grace; Heaven; Hell; Resurrection*.

Ethics (Gr. "custom, ethos"). That branch of philosophy which studies moral principles to clarify what is right and wrong, or what human beings should freely do or refrain from doing. *Deontological ethics*, represented by Immanuel Kant (1724–1804), considers human conduct morally good when, guided by a sense of duty, it fulfills its obligations independently of their consequences and respects human beings as ends-in-themselves. *Utilitarian ethics*, represented by Jeremy Bentham (1748–1832) and modified by John Stuart Mill (1806–73), takes consequences to be the ultimate norm of morality and tries to effect "the greatest happiness of the greatest number." Situation ethics, developed by Joseph Fletcher (1905–91), finds the context for ethics in "the situation," and waives the demands of moral law, if this would better serve love, which is the justification of that law. See *Freedom; Moral Theology*.

Ethiopian Christianity. Founded by two Syrian saints, Frumentius and Edesius, the Ethiopian Church came under the patriarch of Alexandria when Frumentius was consecrated bishop (ca. 350) by St. Athanasius of Alexandria. Christianity soon became the state religion, with the religious capital at Aksum and a metropolitan or *abuna* (Arab. "our father"). Through the Egyptian connection and the Nine Saints (probably Syrian monks who had came to Ethiopia because they were opposed to the Council of Chalcedon [451]), the Ethiopian Church became non-Chalcedonian without a struggle. The union reached with Rome at the Council of Florence (1442) proved short-lived (see DH 1330–53; ND 208, 325–26, 408–9, 644–46, 810, 1003–5, 1419). The emperor's conversion to Catholicism in 1621 ended with his abdication in 1632. In the twentieth century, Emperor Haile Selassie reformed the church and promoted the establishment of an independent Ethiopian Patriarchate in 1959. The Oriental Orthodox Patriarchate of Alexandria retains a primacy of honor over the Ethiopian and the Eritrean Orthodox churches. Ethiopian

Oriental Christianity is characterized by certain Jewish elements, such as the practice of circumcision and the observance of the Sabbath. The language used for the liturgy is the classical Ge'ez, whereas the spoken language is Amharic. A small group of Ethiopian Christians in communion with Rome makes up the Ethiopian Catholic Church, uses the Ethiopian rite, and. since 1961, has its metropolitan see in Addis Ababa. See *Autocephalous; Chalcedon, Council of; Coptic Christianity; Eastern Churches; Eritrean Orthodox Church; Monophysitism; Oriental Orthodox.*

Etiology (Gr. "account of causes"). A story "explaining" how something came into existence by recounting a particular event supposed to have originally caused it. Thus an act of Lot's wife accounts for a strange geological formation (Gen 19:26). Etiological explanations are offered for names of persons, such as Abraham (Gen 17:5) and Moses (Exod 2:10); Israel, the new name given to Jacob (Gen 32:28); and such places as Beersheba (Gen 21:31). Hermann Gunkel (1862–1932) did important work in analyzing and classifying biblical etiologies. Following Karl Rahner (1904–84), some call Genesis 1—11 a historical etiology or a collection of stories to explain our present situation before God. The OT writers experienced, on the one hand, the goodness of God as savior and creator, and, on the other hand, the reality of sin and its consequences. They explained the tension between grace and sin in present reality by referring it to the origins of the human race. This is not to say that the opening chapters of the Bible offer us a historical report. But it is to say that real, primordial events account for the present human condition. See *Biblical Criticism; Creation; Original Sin; Protology.*

Eucharist (Gr. "thanksgiving"). Word used for the whole service of the Mass and especially for the second part, which follows the celebration of the word of God, reaches its highpoint with the consecration of the bread and wine into the body and blood of Christ, and ends with communion. *Eucharist* refers besides to Christ's real presence under the appearances of bread and wine (DH 1640, 1651; ND 1517, 1526). The greatest of the sacraments and the center of church life, the Eucharist was instituted by Christ at the Last Supper (DH 1637, 1727; ND 1514, 1537). A sacrifice of praise and thanksgiving, in which Christ is present as priest and victim, the Eucharist (a) re-presents the new covenant (1 Cor 11:25; Luke 22:20) effected through his death and resurrection that reconciled us with God (DH 1740, 1742; ND 1546, 1547), and (b) anticipates the consummation of the divine kingdom. As a meal, the Eucharist (Acts 2:46; DH 847) makes us guests at God's own banquet and expresses our deepest unity in the church. As sacrifice and meal, the Eucharist efficaciously symbolizes the self-sacrificing service to others to which Christians are called. See *Agape; Anaphora; Blessed Sacrament; Breaking of the Bread; Church; Communion; Covenant; Ecclesiology; Epiclesis; Liturgy; Lord's Supper, The; Mass; Sacrament; Sacrifice; Transubstantiation.*

Eucharistic Prayer. The prayer at the heart of the Eucharist, called the canon in the Roman liturgy. Some later forms seem to be variants of the first fully developed eucharistic prayer, found in the *Apostolic Tradition* (apparently ca. 215), which is often attributed to St. Hippolytus of Rome. With some variations in order, a eucharistic prayer contains the following elements: an introductory dialogue between the priest and the congregation, a prayer of praise and thanksgiving, the narration of the institution of the Eucharist, the *anamnesis* recalling God's salvific actions, the *epiclesis* inviting the descent of the Spirit both on the eucharistic elements and on the faithful to make them one in Christ, the commemorations or intercessions, and the final doxology. See *Anamnesis; Anaphora; Canon; Doxology; Epiclesis; Intercession.*

Euchologion (Gr. "prayer book"). A text used by bishops, priests, and deacons for divine services in the Byzantine and Coptic traditions. The *Great Euchologion* contains the liturgies of St. Basil (ca. 330–79) and St. John Chrysostom (ca. 347–407), the Liturgy of the Presanctified, and blessings for various occasions. The *Small Euchologion* contains the formulas used for administering the sacraments. See *Bishop; Byzantine Christianity; Coptic Christianity; Deacon; Liturgy; Priests.*

Eulogy (Gr. "blessing," "thing blessed"). In the latter sense, the blessed but not consecrated bread distributed to the faithful at the end of the Eucharist. As *pain bénit,* or blessed bread, the practice has survived in some French-speaking areas. Its counterpart in Eastern liturgies is *antidoron* (Gr. "instead of the gift"), distributed in practice to all present at the service. See *Blessing.*

Eunomianism. Heresy propagated by a bishop of Cyzicus, Eunomius (d. 395). He asserted that God is an ungenerated, utterly simple, and absolutely knowable substance. The Son is the first being created by the Father, with the Holy Spirit then being created by the Son. Against such pronounced rationalism both in method and content, St. Basil the Great (ca. 330–79), St. Gregory of Nazianzus (329–89), and St. Gregory of Nyssa (ca. 335–ca. 395) reasserted orthodox teaching on the Trinity and a proper sense of Christian faith that respects mystery and "gives fullness to our reasoning" (Gregory of Nazianzus, "29th Theological Oration"). They thereby distinguished the unknowable and ineffable essence of God from the energies whereby God communicates himself to us—a distinction St. Gregory Palamas (1296–1359) made central in Orthodox theology. See *Anomoeans; Apophatic Theology; Cappadocian Fathers; Essence and Energies; Nicaea, First Council of; Palamism; Pneumatomachians; Rationalism; Trinity, Theology of.*

Euthanasia (Gr. "easy death"). An action (or omission) which of and by itself is deliberately intended to cause the death of a patient. This is to be distinguished from decisions to forego disproportionately expensive and burdensome means for prolonging life. Euthanasia has been condemned as morally unacceptable by Christian tradition, the Second Vatican Council (1962–65) (GS 27), and the papal magisterium, for example, by John Paul II's 1995 encyclical *Evangelium vitae* (64–66). Those who accept euthanasia generally do so because they dismiss suffering as senseless; judge the incurably ill, the handicapped, and elderly persons to be an economic burden on society; and hold that human beings have autonomous control over life and death. See *Autonomy; Death; Suffering of God.*

Eutychianism. Heresy associated with Eutyches (ca. 378–454), head of a large monastery in Constantinople. He was accused of acknowledging only one (divine) nature or *physis* in Christ after the Incarnation—a Monophysite view which denies that Christ also has a human nature like ours. Condemned in 448 at a home synod in Constantinople, through the influence of the emperor and the patriarch/archbishop of Alexandria he was rehabilitated the following year at a synod held in Ephesus and dubbed by Pope St. Leo the Great the *Latrocinium* (Lat. "brigandage"). However, at the Council of Chalcedon (451), Eutyches was condemned and disowned by all parties (see DH 290–303; ND 609–16). See *Chalcedon, Council of; Monophysitism.*

Evangelical Counsels. Three radical ideals for Christian discipleship that involve freely embracing a life of poverty, chastity, and obedience for the sake of the coming kingdom of God (see DH 1087–94, 1810, 3911; ND 1817; LG 44; PC passim; CIC 573). See *Celibacy; Kingdom of God; Obedience; Perfection; Poverty; Religious Life.*

Evangelicals (from Gr. "Gospel"). In general, Protestant Christians who stress justification through faith and the supreme authority of the Bible. Evangelical is also the name for the main Protestant Church in Germany, and for Anglicans who (a) highlight personal conversion, the authority of the scriptures, and atonement through Christ's death; and (b) do not fully share High Church views about grace, the Eucharist, and other sacraments. See *Anglican Communion; Episcopalians; Justification; Protestant.*

Evangelization. The proclamation to all peoples (Matt 28:19–20; Rom 10:12–18) and cultures of the good news about Jesus Christ (Mark 1:1). Through the power of the Holy Spirit (Acts 1:8), the gospel message goes out both to Christians alienated from the church (evangelism) and to non-Christians (missions). The church's divine mission obliges it to spread the good news of salvation (CIC 781, 782 §1; CCEO 584–85). See *Gospel; Inculturation; Missions, Church; Proselytism.*

Eve (Heb. "living"). In the creation story the first woman, the mother of all the living, and wife of Adam (Gen 3:20; 4:1; Tob 8:6), who followed her into sin (Gen 3:1–7; 2 Cor 11:3; 1 Tim 2:13–14). See *Adam; New Eve.*

Evil, Mystery of. The mystery of God who, while being infinitely good and powerful, allows so much sin, pain, and other suffering in our world. Only partial solutions are available; they appeal to (a) the divine respect for our created freedom, (b) Christ's enduring the mystery of evil through his death on the cross, and (c) the glorious consummation of our world (Rom 8:18–23) when the forces of evil will be definitively overcome (1 Cor 15:24–28). See *Apophatic Theology; Mystery; Theodicy.*

Evolution. A theory launched by Charles Darwin (1809–82) that claims that, through natural selection, present living beings developed gradually from less complex forms. Some fundamentalists wrongly hold that the theory of biological evolution conflicts with the Genesis account of creation, and fail to appreciate the admirable picture evolution offers of God working with wisdom and power "from the inside" to bring about higher forms of life and eventually the emergence of human beings. See *Creationism; Fundamentalism; Polygenism.*

Exarch (Gr. "ruler"). A civil title for the ruler of a province in the Byzantine Empire. In Eastern canon law, it refers to the head of a portion of God's people (CCEO 984 §2) that has not yet fully become an eparchy (CCEO 311–313) or diocese. The equivalent in the West is an apostolic vicariate or prefecture. See *Eastern Churches; Eparchy.*

Ex Cathedra Definition (Lat. "from the throne"). Solemn and binding definition made by the pope with his full apostolic authority as the pastor and teacher of all Christians (DH 3073–75; ND 839–40) in revealed matters concerning faith and morals. See *Cathedra; Enthronement; Infallibility; Magisterium; Pope.*

Excommunication (Lat. "exclusion from communion"). Exclusion from the reception of the sacraments and the exercise of full rights in the church (CIC 1331; CCEO 1434). Excommunication either follows automatically from certain acts or is pronounced by a church tribunal or authority. See *Anathema; Ferendae Sententiae; Latae Sententiae.*

Exegesis (Gr. "bringing out the sense"). Interpreting the meaning of sacred texts, usually biblical texts (DV 12, 23; OT 16). As well as trying to establish what the authors of the Bible intended to say in their original contexts (or what the text meant), exegetes also interpret the message of the text for today (or what it means). See *Alexandrian Theology; Antiochene Theology; Biblical Criticism; Hermeneutics; Senses of Scripture.*

Exemplarism. Any theory that highlights exemplary causality in explaining reality. Thus the value of Christ's saving action on our behalf has been understood to consist largely or even solely in the example he gave of self-sacrificing love—a theory that goes back to Peter Abelard (1079–1142; see DH 721–39). See *Atonement; Causality; Love; Redemption.*

Existentialism. A philosophical, religious, and literary trend exemplified by writers such as Søren Kierkegaard (1813–55), Fyodor Dostoyevsky (1821–81), Miguel de Unamuno (1864–1936), Karl Jaspers (1883–1969), and Martin Heidegger (1889–1976), and which has enjoyed considerable influence on Catholic and Protestant theology. In general, existentialists highlight individual persons in their freedom and search for authentic existence. They vary from avowed atheists such as Jean-Paul Sartre (1905–80) and Simone de Beauvoir (1908–86) to Christian believers such as Rudolf Bultmann (1884–1976) and Gabriel Marcel (1889–1973). See *Dialectical Theology.*

Ex Opere Operantis (Lat. "on the basis of the one acting"). The subjective dispositions for receiving a sacrament, which function not as a cause but rather as the condition for the full effectiveness of God's grace (see DH 781, 1451, 1601–13; ND 1309, 1311–23, 1410). See *Sacraments.*

Ex Opere Operato (Lat. "on the basis of the act performed"). The objective efficacy and fruitfulness of sacraments, which do not primarily depend on the attitudes or merits of those receiving or administering the sacraments. See *Donatism.*

Exorcism (Gr. "adjuring under oath"). Expelling evil spirits (or even the devil himself) from persons possessed by them or at least affected by their power. A form of exorcism is found in the prayers preceding baptism. In the case of a person possessed by the devil, an exorcist appointed by the bishop performs a rite consisting of prayers, sprinkling with holy water, and the laying on of hands (CIC 1172; nothing in CCEO). The practice of exorcism imitates what Christ and his disciples did in similar cases (Matt 10:1; Mark 1:21–28; Luke 4:31–37; 11:14–23; Acts 19:11–12). In January 1999 the Vatican published a new rite of exorcism; the last revision had been in 1614. See *Demons; Devil, The; Possession, Diabolical; Sacramental.*

Experience, Religious. Immediate, personal contact with God and the things of God (Exod 24:2, 15–18; 33:11; DH 3033, 3484; ND 127; DV 8, 14). In the second annotation of his *Spiritual Exercises,* St. Ignatius of Loyola (ca. 1491–1556) followed a tradition that goes back to Origen (ca. 185–ca. 254) and ultimately to St. John (John 1:39; 13:23; 1 John 1:1–3; see Ps 34:9) in expecting that prayer will bring us to "feel and taste interiorly" the things of God. Whether intense or ordinary, religious experiences need to be tested and interpreted in the church and under the guidance of the Holy Spirit (1 Thess 5:21)—especially dramatic, mystical experiences. The ancient Messalians, for instance, confused the feeling (psychology) of grace with grace itself. See *Contemplation; Discernment of Spirits; Holy Spirit; Messalians; Modernism; Mysticism; Prayer.*

Expiation (Lat. "atone," "purify"). Making amends for sin and repairing the damage caused in the moral order and in one's personal relationship to God. The need for their sins to be expiated was institutionalized by the Jews in the day of expiation, *Yom Kippur.* The NT, in a particular way the Letter to the Hebrews, understands Christ to be the priest and victim who has representatively expiated our sins and cleansed a contaminated world (Heb 2:17–18; 9:6—10:18; see Rom 3:24–25; Titus 2:13–14). See *Atonement; Heart, Sacred; Penance, Sacrament of; Priests; Redemption; Sacrifice; Salvation; Satisfaction; Sin; Yom Kippur.*

External Forum. See *Forum Internum.*

Extra Ecclesiam Nulla Salus (Lat. "no salvation outside the Church"). An adage that goes back to St. Cyprian of Carthage (d. 258) and highlights the necessity of belonging to Christ's church in order to be saved (Mark 16:16; LG 14). This is not, however, to deny salvation to those who in good faith do not belong to the church and follow their consciences in living by truths they know (LG 16). See *Anonymous Christians; Church; Salvation; Supernatural.*

Extreme Unction. See *Anointing of the Sick.*

F

Faith (Lat. "belief"). The objective, revealed truth believed in (*fides quae*) or the subjective, personal commitment to God (*fides qua*). Made possible through the help of the Holy Spirit (Acts 16:14; 2 Cor 3:16–18), faith is a free, reasonable, and total response (DV 5) through which we confess the truth about the divine self-disclosure definitively made in Christ (John 20:31; Rom 10:9), obediently commit ourselves (Rom 1:5; 16:26), and entrust our future to God (Rom 6:8; Heb 11:1). See *Analogy of Faith; Analysis of Faith; Deposit of Faith; Fideism; Justification; Rationalism; Revelation; Semi-Pelagianism; Sola Fides; Truth.*

Faith and Order. An ecumenical body founded to study theological problems (especially about creeds and constitutions) underlying the divisions of Christians. It organized world conferences at Lausanne (1927), Edinburgh (1937), Lund (1952), Montreal (1963), Santiago de Compostela (1993), and it is now a subunit within the World Council of Churches. See *Ecumenism; World Council of Churches.*

Faith and Works. A question already raised in the NT (e.g., Jas 2:14–26) that was vigorously debated at the time of the Reformation. While not being opposed to doing good works, Martin Luther (1483–1546) argued that human beings could not claim any merit for them. St. Paul insists that justification comes by grace through faith and not by the works of the law (Rom 3:20–26; Gal 2:16; 3:2, 5, 10). Nevertheless, God works in believers (Phil 2:12–13) to produce the fruits (Gal 5:22–23) of a faith that issues in love (Gal 5:6). See *Decalogue; Faith; Grace; Imputation; Justification; Law; Lutheranism; Merit; Reformation, The; Sola Fides; Torah.*

Faith Development. A growth in living and understanding Christian faith that follows the stages of human maturation. St. Paul notes that he has outgrown the ways of a child (1 Cor 13:11), and interprets the life of faith as our being steadily "changed" into Christ's "likeness from one degree of glory to another" (2 Cor 3:18). Trials test and perfect faith (Jas 1:2–12), and "discipline" brings growth in holiness (Heb 12:5–13). Maturing in faith requires not only a full sacramental life, constancy in prayer, and practical love toward the neighbor in need, but also a regular study of Christian revelation that keeps pace with one's intellectual growth. See *Catechesis; Moral Development; Mystagogy; Neocatechumenate; Perfection; Sanctification.*

Faithful, Mass of the. An outdated term for the second part of the Mass, which follows the Liturgy of the Word. The term belonged to a situation when many catechumens (adults preparing for baptism) were instructed to leave before the creed was recited and the second part of the Mass was begun. The correct expression used today for the second part of the Mass is Liturgy of the Eucharist. See *Catechumens, Mass of the; Liturgy of the Eucharist; Liturgy of the Word.*

Fall, The. The vivid story of how Adam and Eve freely disobeyed God and so lost their innocent, ideal existence (Gen 3:1–24; see Wis 2:23–24; Rom 5:12–18). The doctrine of the fall teaches that it was the earliest human beings (not God) who brought moral evil into our world—a sinful condition that affected all subsequent generations and from which Christ has redeemed us. See *Adam; Eve; Original Sin; Redemption.*

Fasting. Abstention from food motivated by religious reasons such as repentance (Joel 1:14; Jonah 3:7) or the preparation for a special mission (Matt 4:2; Acts 13:2–3) and normally accompanied by prayer (Acts 14:23). Fasting may be quantitative (when the amount of food to be consumed is limited) or qualitative (when certain kinds of food such as meat are not taken [abstinence]).

After fasting in the desert (Luke 4:2), during his ministry Christ was criticized for not fasting like the Pharisees (Matt 11:18–19), and he, in turn, criticized those who made a self-righteous practice out of fasting (Matt 6:16–18; Luke 18:12). In the Latin tradition, Catholics observe Ash Wednesday and Good Friday as obligatory fast days, whereas the Eastern Christians prepare not only for Easter, but also for Christmas by a forty-day fast. In addition, they fast from the Sunday after Pentecost to the vigil of Sts. Peter and Paul and for a fortnight before August 15, the *koimesis* of Our Lady (see CCEO 882). Before receiving holy communion, the faithful should normally abstain for at least an hour from food and drink except for water and medicine (CIC 919; see CCEO 707 §1, 713 §2). See *Abstinence; Ash Wednesday; Assumption of the Blessed Virgin; Christmas Preparation; Ember Days; Good Friday; Holy Week; Lent.*

Father, God as. A way of speaking of God's relationship to the whole people (and less commonly to individuals such as the Davidic king) already found in the OT (Isa 63:16; 64:6–8), but much less common than God as king and as lover/husband. Driven by his unique filial consciousness, Jesus taught his followers to address God as "Father" (Luke 11:2; Rom 8:15; Gal 4:6). Paul distinguished between Jesus as the Son of God and the baptized and justified as adopted sons and daughters (Rom 8:14–17; Gal 4:5–7). John distinguished between the only-begotten Son of God and our new life as God's "children" (John 1:12). Against Marcion, St. Irenaeus (d. ca. 200) and later the Nicene-Constantinopolitan Creed identified the OT God (YHWH) with the Father of our Lord Jesus Christ. Its "genetic" approach confessed the *monarchy* (Gr. "one, sole principle") of the Father, who is the unoriginated origin of the Son and the Holy Spirit as well as of all created reality. This "monarchy" is to be distinguished from modalist Monarchianism, which denied personal distinctions within God. The OT (Isa 49:15; 66:13) and such official teaching as John Paul II's 1980 encyclical *Dives in Misericordia* (Rich in Mercy) (4, n.52) offer maternal images for God. No dominant "male," God the Father transcends sexuality and gender, and should be characterized by all that is imaginably best in human fathers and mothers, as Jesus' parable of the prodigal son (better called the parable of the merciful father) insists (Luke 15:11–32). See *Abba; Adoption as God's Children; God; Monarchianism; Patripassianism; Son of God; Trinity, Theology of.*

Fathers of the Church. A popular title for certain early Christians who wrote in Greek, Latin, Syriac, and Armenian, and whose doctrine and personal holiness won general approval in the church. "Each in a different way and to a different degree," they remain "classics of Christian culture" (1989 *Instruction on the Fathers* by the Congregation for Catholic Education). In theological controversy, it became customary to appeal to the Eastern and Western Fathers, their unanimous consent being considered a decisive argument (see DH 271, 510–20, 2856, 3541; ND 627/10–16). In the West, the era of the Church fathers is understood to have ended with St. Isidore of Seville (ca. 560–636); in the East, with St. John of Damascus (ca. 675–ca. 749). See *Cappadocian Fathers; Patristics; Patrology.*

Fear of God. In the OT, that deep sense of religion and filial piety, which summarizes our proper attitude toward God (Job 28:28; Prov 1:7; 9:10; Sir 1:11–20), and which is not to be taken as slavish terror. See *Hesed; Holiness; Love; Religion.*

Feast. A day of special celebration in the church's liturgical calendar. Sunday commemorates Christ's resurrection from the dead, and, in the East, is often called the eighth day or the first day of the new creation brought about by Christ. Movable feasts (e.g., Easter and Pentecost) are celebrated on dates that vary from year to year; immovable feasts (e.g., Christmas and feasts of saints) are always celebrated on the same day. See *Calendar, Liturgical; Resurrection; Sabbath; Sunday; Twelve Feasts, The.*

Febronianism. A German theory of church-state relations that rejected certain papal powers as medieval accretions. The movement was named after Johann Nikolaus von Hontheim (1701–90), coadjutor bishop of Trier, who in 1763, under the pseudonym Justinus Febronius, published *On the State of the Church and the Legitimate Authority of the Roman Pontiff.* The book recognized the pope as head of the church, but denied his jurisdiction on most issues beyond the diocese of Rome (see DH 2592–97). See *Church and State; Gallicanism; Pope.*

Feminist Theology. An approach to theology (developed largely in the United States since 1968) that protests against the long-standing, masculine bias in Christian theology, exegesis, and church life. Its demands include the ordination of women and the use of an inclusive language that does not reflect and support a male power structure. See *Black Theology; Liberation Theology; Political Theology.*

Ferendae Sententiae (Lat. "by imposed sentence"). An ecclesiastical penalty that is binding only if formally imposed by a church judge (see CIC 1314, 1318; CCEO 1402). Because of the complexity of individual cases and the subtlety of the law, most penalties in the Western church and all in the Eastern Catholic churches are of this nature. See *Latae Sententiae.*

Fideism. The tendency (a) to undervalue the role of reason in examining religious claims, and (b) to overemphasize the free decision of faith. At best fideism rightly challenges attempts to demonstrate scientifically the truth of Christianity. At worst it represents faith as a blind leap in the dark. See *Analysis of Faith; Modernism; Natural Theology; Preambles of Faith; Rationalism; Traditionalism.*

Fides Fiducialis (Lat. "faith as trust"). The major element of faith according to Martin Luther (1483–1546). While maintaining the priority of this confident trust (*fiducia*) in the salvation effected by Christ, later Lutheran theologians included the role of knowledge and assent in their account of faith. See *Faith; Lutheranism.*

Fides Quaerens Intellectum (Lat. "faith seeking understanding"). The title St. Anselm of Canterbury (ca. 1033–1109) originally gave to one of his works (later renamed *Proslogion*). The title, a variant on the Augustinian *credo ut intelligam* (Lat. "I believe in order to understand"), indicates that in theology, faith inspires and guides intellectual understanding rather than the reverse. In his October 1998 encyclical *Fides et Ratio*, Blessed John Paul II (pope 1978–2005) pleaded for an end to the modern separation of faith and reason. See *Augustinianism; Ontological Argument.*

Filioque (Lat. "and [from] the Son"). A phrase added to the Nicene-Constantinopolitan Creed at the Fourth Synod of Braga (in today's Portugal) (675)—its use in the creed used at the Third Council of Toledo in 589 seems to be an interpolation (see DH 470)—indicating (a) that the Holy Spirit proceeds from the Father and the Son, and (b) that the three persons of the Trinity are perfectly equal. Emperor Charlemagne (ruled 771–814) promoted the addition; in 1013 St. Henry II (ruled 995–1024) ordered the whole Latin Church to add the Filioque to the creed. The Greek Orthodox Church objected strongly to this insertion, since it jeopardized the "monarchy" of the Father (the single, unoriginated principle) by introducing a second principle for the procession of the Spirit—a view expressly rejected by the Catholic Church (DH 850, 1300–1302). After the time of Patriarch Photius of Constantinople (ca. 810–95), the Filioque has often been considered the greatest point of difference separating East and West. The Council of Florence (1438–45) did not insist that the Greeks accept the Filioque addition, provided they acknowledge the truth behind it (DH 1301–2; ND 323–24), as they did. While many Orthodox continue to reject the Filioque as heretical, some follow Vasilij V. Bolotov (d. 1900), a Russian patristic scholar who understood it to be a free opinion of St. Augustine (354–430), or join with modern followers of St. Gregory Palamas (1296–1359), such as Vladimir Lossky (1903–58), in seeking to mediate between East and West on this point. See *Arianism; Creed, Nicene; Florence, Council of; God as Father; Holy Spirit; Lyons, Second Council of; Neo-Palamism; Processions; Theologoumenon; Trinity, Theology of.*

Finality. A principle in Scholastic philosophy according to which beings act always for a purpose or end, even if this principle applies in a different way to intelligent and nonintelligent agents. See *Scholasticism.*

Five Ways, The. Five arguments for the existence of God found in the *Summa Theologiae* of St. Thomas Aquinas (ca. 1225–74). From the fact of change (motion) in the world, the First Way infers the existence of a first Unmoved Mover. The Second Way argues from our experience of causes producing effects to an ultimate Uncaused Cause. The Third Way moves from the observed contingency of our world to a first Necessary Cause. The Fourth Way begins with the limited grades of perfection found in the universe to arrive at a first Unlimited Cause. The Fifth Way observes the world's orderly design, which can only be explained through the purposeful activity of a divine Designer. The Five Ways have been radically challenged by the work of David Hume (1711–76), Immanuel Kant (1724–1804), and other philosophers, but they still offer valuable perspectives on our (limited) knowledge of God. See *Arguments for the Existence of God; Causality; Finality; Teleological Argument.*

Florence, Council of (1438–45). Reckoned the seventeenth ecumenical council of the Roman Catholic Church and sometimes dated from 1431 because the first part of the Council of Basle was a preparation for Florence. Principally convened to achieve reunion with the Greek Church, it met at Ferrara (1438–39) when the Greek prelates arrived, and was transferred first to Florence in 1439 and then to Rome in 1443. On July 6, 1439, the bull of union was signed with the Greeks; on November 22, 1439, the union with the Armenians (DH 1310–28; ND 1305–08, 1412–18, 1509–11). The council achieved reunion with the Copts and Ethiopians (February 4, 1442) (DH 1330–54; ND 208, 325–26, 408–09, 644–46, 1003–05, 1419) and some other Eastern Christians. Florence insisted on the doctrine of the Filioque (without imposing it on the Greeks, as far as the recital of the creed is concerned), the immediate vision of God after death for those who have not committed or have been purified from post-baptismal sin, the primacy of the pope (in somewhat general terms), and the seven sacraments (DH 1300–08; ND 322–24, 809, 1508, 2308–9). Motivated partly by the fear of Turkish conquest, the unions achieved at Florence did not prove long-lasting. But with the Council of Florence as a precedent and through the Union of Brest (1595–96), millions of Slavs joined the Catholic Church—as other Eastern groups were to do. See *Basle, Council of; Conciliarism; Eastern Churches; Filioque; Primacy; Processions; Sacrament; Schism.*

Fools for Christ's Sake. A category of saints consisting of those who are particularly but not exclusively cherished in Eastern Christianity, and who have taken seriously St. Paul's words: "We are fools for Christ's sake" (1 Cor 4:10; see 1 Cor 1:18–19, 25; 3:18–19; 2 Cor 6:8; Matt 5:11). This type of sanctity is found already in the *Apophthegmata Patrum*. Among the Greeks, the fool for Christ's sake is known as *salos* (probably from the Syriac rendering of 1 Corinthians 4:10 as "sakla"). Perhaps the most beloved of such saints is the legendary St. Andrew of Constantinople (tenth century), whose life is associated with the great Eastern feast of the *Pokrov Bogomateri* (Russ. "Protection of the Theotokos") that is connected with Mary's sheltering cloak. The land of holy fools par excellence is Russia, where the fool for Christ's sake is called *jurodivij*; examples are St. Isaac Zatvornik (d. 1090) and St. Basil the Blessed (d. 1552). By what can seem a mere caricature of real holiness, such fools for Christ's sake prophetically challenge the pseudo-values of society and the superficiality of many Christians. In the West, saints known for their holy folly include St. Francis of Assisi (ca. 1181–1226), St. Philip Neri (1515–95), and St. Benedict-Joseph Labré (1748–83). The theme of holy folly has inspired classical works such as Blessed Ramon Lull's (ca. 1233–ca. 1315) *Blanquerna*, Miguel de Cervantes' (1547–1616) *Don Quixote*, and Fyodor Dostoyevsky's (1821–81) *The Idiot*, as well as various figures in the works of Alexander Pushkin (1799–1837) and Leo Tolstoy (1828–1910). See *Apatheia*; *Apophthegmata Patrum*; *Cross*; *Eschatology*; *Holiness*; *Saint*; *Theologia Crucis*; *Wisdom Literature*.

Foreknowledge. God's knowledge of all future events. Since some future events depend partly on human choice, there exists the problem of reconciling the divine foreknowledge with human freedom. See *Freedom*; *Grace, Systems of*; *Predestination*; *Prophet*; *Scientia Media*.

Forgiveness of Sins. A central belief in the Jewish-Christian understanding of God's merciful dealings with us (Ezek 18:21–28; Mark 1:4; Luke 15). Jesus forgave sins (Mark 2:1–12; Luke 7:36–50) and empowered his church to do the same (Luke 24:47; John 20:22–23). The forgiveness of sins through baptism (Acts 2:38) and in other ways requires repentance from us and the willingness to forgive those who sin against us (Matt 5:23–24; 6:12, 14–15; 18:21–35). See *Baptism*; *Penance, Sacrament of*.

Fortitude (Lat. "strength"). The virtue that enables us to do what is good but difficult, and is one of the four "cardinal" virtues, on which hinge the whole structure of the moral life. As doing good and fulfilling one's responsibilities inevitably involve overcoming unpleasant and even dangerous moments, fortitude characterizes moral life as a whole and is not just one virtue among others. It enables us to face with forthright determination difficult situations that threaten our moral, physical, psychological and spiritual well-being. In the garden of Gethsemane, Christ refused to be dominated by fear and showed fortitude in clinging to the mission entrusted to him. Paul Tillich (1886–1965) described fortitude as "the courage to be." See *Moral Development*; *Moral Theology*; *Virtues, Cardinal*.

Forum Internum (Lat. "internal forum"). An image taken from Roman cities, wherein the forum functioned as the center not only for politics and commerce, but also for religion and justice. Applied to our inner life, it means the private arena of the personal conscience to which only God has adequate access. Church tribunals deal with the *forum externum* (Lat. "external forum"), or the public arena, and document their proceedings and judgments in writing (CIC 37; CCEO 1514; see also CIC 74, 130, 144, 1074, 1081–82, 1123, 1126, 1145, 1319, 1340, 1361, 1732; CCEO 791, 796, 798–99, 813, 815, 856, 996, 1420, 1422, 1514). Private and confidential matters, and, above all, what penitents say (as strictly protected by the seal of confession) in the sacrament of reconciliation belong to the internal forum (see CIC 64, 74, 130, 142, 144, 508, 596, 1079, 1082, 1355, 1357; CCEO 980, 992, 994–95, 1527 §2). See *Penance, Sacrament of*.

Founder. One who creates a movement or institution and shapes it by laying down at least some principles or guidelines. Thus Christ is the founder of Christianity; and St. Dominic (1170–1221), the founder of the Order of Preachers, popularly known as Dominicans. See *Christianity; Religious Life*.

Frankfurt School. A group of scholars associated with the University of Frankfurt whose critical theory has uncovered various links between our understanding and interests, and aims to produce a more rational society by freeing knowledge from domination and manipulation. Important members of this school (which has had a considerable influence on contemporary theology) include Theodor Adorno (1903–69), Jürgen Habermas (b. 1929), Max Horkheimer (1895–1973), and Herbert Marcuse (1888–1979). See *Hermeneutics; Liberation Theology; Political Theology; Postmodernism*.

Freedom. The power of self-determination, that is, of deliberately choosing and following a course of action. Created in the likeness of God, human persons have this capacity, which has been impaired but not destroyed by sin (DH 1965–67; ND 1986/67, 1987/66). Through redemption, Christ has set us free (Gal 5:13; 1 Pet 2:16), and this freedom is the foretaste of our future freedom in glory (Rom 8:18–25). See *Anthropology; Concupiscence; Image of God; Liberty, Religious; Sin; Torah*.

Friends, Society of. A body of Christians founded by George Fox (1624–91) that branched off from the Anglican Church. They describe themselves as "friends of truth," but are popularly known as Quakers, because when listening to the word of God they were supposed to quake or shiver. Their doctrine stresses the inner light of the living Christ and a church order based on the priesthood of all the faithful, both men and women, with a consequent rejection of the sacraments and the ordained ministry. There are, however, elders to lead the congregation in prayer and overseers to watch over the observance of church order. Quakers are also known for their opposition to war. See *Anglican Communion*.

Functional Christology. A Christology that focuses on the saving activity of Christ and thus largely coincides with soteriology. It necessarily implies, however, an ontological Christology that focuses on who and what Christ is in himself. See *Christology; Soteriology*.

Fundamental Option (Lat. "basic choice"). The general orientation of life or a particular, very serious decision that, for good or evil, determines our essential moral and religious situation. Reflections on the fundamental option have developed in reaction to a legalism that considered moral acts in isolation from the whole context of one's life and growth. In a 1993 encyclical, *Veritatis splendor*, Blessed John Paul II (pope 1978–2005) criticized an interpretation of the fundamental option that separates it from particular personal acts. Karl Rahner (1904–84), who occasionally used (in French) the expression "fundamental option," defended the connection between option and acts on which the pope insisted. See *Conversion; Freedom; Moral Theology; Person; Sin*.

Fundamental Theology. That branch of Western theology which studies foundational issues such as the divine revelation in the history of Israel and Jesus Christ, the conditions that open up human beings to this self-communication of God, the signs that make faith in and through Jesus Christ a reasonable option, the transmission (through the church's tradition and the inspired scriptures) of the experience of God's self-communication, and theological method. See *Apologetics; Dogmatic Theology; Faith; Inspiration, Biblical; Method, Theological; Preambles of Faith; Revelation; Systematic Theology; Tradition*.

Fundamentalism. A movement in twentieth-century Protestantism, especially in the United States, that generally defends such fundamental beliefs as the divinity of Christ and his bodily resurrection, but interprets the Bible with little attention to its historical formation, various literary forms, and original meaning. This neglect of good exegesis has led to false problems about OT stories such as the creation, the flood, and the story of Jonah. See *Biblical Criticism; Creationism; Evolution; Inerrancy*.

Funeral Rite. The ceremonies for taking leave of deceased Christians from the time of death until the burial or cremation of the body (see CIC 1176–85; CCEO 278 § 3, 874–79). Reverence for the body, prayers for the dead, and hope for resurrection characterize the various ceremonies: at home, in the church, and at the graveside or in the crematorium. In accord with the Second Vatican Council (1962–65) (SC 81), the Requiem (Lat. "rest") Mass strongly expresses joyful faith in the resurrection of Christ. The vestments worn by the priest are no longer black, but violet or white. Normally the great Easter candle is lit and placed at the head of the coffin. In Byzantine Christianity, the rites differ considerably, depending on whether a child of not more than seven years, a layperson, or a priest is being buried; bishops are buried with the rite for priests; and deacons, with that for laypeople. Then a special office for the dead person, called *Pannychida*, is often celebrated on the third, ninth, and thirtieth day after his or her death. See *Burial Rites; Candles; Cemetery; Cremation; Death; Easter; Resurrection; Vatican Council, Second; Vigil.*

G

Gallicanism. A long-standing movement in France, with parallels in other countries, claiming considerable independence from the papacy. It was classically expressed in the Four Gallican Articles, which (a) were drawn up by the Bishop of Meaux, Jacques Bénigne Bossuet (1627–1704), and approved by a Paris assembly of the clergy in 1682; and (b) among other things, asserted the authority of general councils over the pope (DH 2281–85). Though revoked by King Louis XIV and the clergy in 1693, the influence of these articles continued into the nineteenth century until a strong papacy and the teaching of Vatican I (1869–70) put an end to Gallicanism. A form of eastern Gallicanism, ethnophyletism (Gr. "nation" and "tribe"), can promote the nation and the national church at the expense of wider Christian unity; it was condemned in 1872 at a synod held in Constantinople. See *Conciliarism; Constance, Council of; Febronianism; Vatican Council, First.*

Generation. The teaching of Nicaea I (325) ("begotten, not made") about the way the Son eternally originates from the Father without being created by the Father (see DH 125; ND 7). See *Arianism; Homoousios; Nicaea, First Council of.*

Genre, Literary. A particular style or form of writing. It may be shorter (like a psalm of lamentation or a parable within the gospels) or longer (like a gospel or a homily from a Father of the Church). A literary genre is to be interpreted according to the common norms that govern this style of writing and set it apart from other styles. See *Exegesis; Hermeneutics.*

Gifts of the Holy Spirit. Ways in which the Spirit of God is manifested in human beings. To a list in the Hebrew text of Isaiah 11:2 (wisdom, understanding, counsel, fortitude, knowledge, and fear of God), the Septuagint and the Vulgate added piety. Originally meant as a poetic description of God's abundant blessings for the messianic king, the seven gifts were interpreted as graces given to Christians through the indwelling of the Holy Spirit. See *Charisms; Glossolalia; Grace; Messiah; Septuagint; Vulgate.*

Gloria (Lat. "glory"). Very ancient hymn inspired by the angelic praise when Christ was born (Luke 2:14). In the Latin Mass, it is recited or sung on Sunday (except during Advent and Lent) and on feast days. In the East, it is used at morning prayers. See *Advent; Feast; Lent; Sunday.*

Glory of God. In the OT, the majestic radiance manifesting God's presence (Exod 33:18–23). Through the Incarnation, the glory of the Son of God was already revealed in this life (John 1:14), a glory consummated in his death and resurrection (John 17:1, 4–5). Like the angels (Luke 2:14), human beings are called to give glory and praise to God (Luke 17:18; Acts 12:23). See *Cherubikon; Doxa; Doxology; Epiphany; Grace.*

Glossolalia (Gr. "speaking in tongues"). Broken and unintelligible utterances of those gifted by the Spirit in praising and petitioning God (1 Cor 12:10, 28, 30; 13:1, 8; 14:1–40; see Rom 8:26). Prophetic inspiration, a higher and more useful charism, can express for others the meaning of these utterances. While interpreting the phenomenon of tongues as miraculously speaking foreign languages (Acts 2:4; see Mark 16:17), St. Luke also refers to glossolalia (Acts 10:46; 19:6) in a way that resembles what we learn from St. Paul in 1 Corinthians. See *Charisms; Holy Spirit; Pentecost; Pentecostals; Prophet.*

Gnosis (Gr. "knowledge"). A way of describing eternal life (Jn 17:3). No mere intellectual grasp of things, this life-giving knowledge of Father and Son springs from a deep personal relationship (John 10:14–15; 14:9). For St. Paul, knowledge is imperfect, even useless, if it is not animated by love (1 Cor 13:2, 9, 12).

Gnosticism. A dualistic religious movement that clearly emerged in the second century. It drew on Jewish, Christian, and pagan sources and presented salvation as spiritual elements being freed from an evil, material environment. Christian Gnostics denied Christ's real Incarnation and the *salus carnis* (Lat. "salvation of the flesh") he effected. They rejected (or modified) the tradition and scriptures of mainline Christianity, claiming a privileged knowledge (of God and our human destiny) from secret traditions and revelations. Orthodox Christian writers, especially St. Irenaeus (ca. 130–ca. 200), provide much information about Gnosticism. Extensive direct knowledge of the movement became available after 1945 when fifty-two separate Gnostic tractates from the fourth century AD, written in Coptic, were found at Nag Hammadi (Egypt). See *Albigensianism; Bogomils; Demiurge; Dualism; Manichaeism; Regula Fidei; Valentinians.*

God. The supreme being who is to be worshiped and served (Deut 6:4–5), and who, in the monotheistic tradition, is acknowledged as the personal, eternal, immutable, all-knowing, and all-powerful creator. According to the OT, the unique and holy God of Israel transcends our material world and is not to be represented in images (Exod 20:4; Lev 19:4; Deut 4:12, 15–24). At the same time, God is ever close to the chosen people, cherishing them with covenanted love and the merciful fidelity of a parent (Josh 24; Isa 46:1–13; Hos 2:14–23). At the Incarnation, God's self-communication within history reaches its climax with the revelation of the Trinity. In the Son and through the indwelling Spirit, human beings are adopted (Gal 4:4–6) and can come to the Father (John 14:6–7). Although the OT had already indicated the divine concern for other nations (e.g., Jonah), God in the NT is revealed as the God of love (1 John 4:7–10, 16) for all peoples (Matt 28:19–20; Rom 3:29–30; 9:1—11:36). See *Attributes, Divine; Covenant; Creation; Father, God as; Incarnation; Monotheism; Polytheism; Transcendence; Trinity, Theology of.*

God of the Gaps. A phrase associated with Dietrich Bonhoeffer (1906–45), and used against those who look for God in phenomena that science has not yet been able to explain and who forget that God is actively present within all processes of the created world.

Godparent. See *Sponsor.*

God's Wrath. The anger ascribed to God (Exod 4:14; Deut 11:17; 2 Sam 24:1; Rom 1:18; 2:5–8). Besides being anthropomorphic, such talk (e.g., that about creation, incarnation, and other mysteries) also raises the question of the divine immutability, as when God threatens to destroy sinful Nineveh and then "repents" (Jonah 3:1–10). God's anger should be interpreted in an analogical way as indicating the utter incompatibility between the divine holiness and human sin. Hans Urs von Balthasar (1905–88) gave God's wrath a place in the drama of salvation to recall that salvation involves both divine and human freedom. See *Analogy; Anthropomorphism; Immutability.*

Good Friday. The feast which recalls that day (probably April 7, AD 30) when Christ died on a cross to redeem sinful humanity. A day of fast and abstinence for Catholics, its Western liturgy begins with the proclamation of the passion according to John. Then it follows intercessions for many classes of people; the unveiling and veneration of the cross; and a communion service in which hosts consecrated on Holy Thursday are distributed. Special Good Friday processions and plays are still held in various parts of the world, for instance, Spain, the Philippines, and Italy. Greek-, Russian-, and Arabic-speaking Christians call Good Friday "Great Friday." See *Communion; Easter Triduum; Liturgy of the Presanctified; Theologia Crucis.*

Good Works. Actions inspired by faith and the Holy Spirit; they include prayer, fasting, almsgiving, protecting the weak, visiting the sick, building community, teaching, and practicing hospitality (Matt 7:12; Rom 12:1—15:13; Jas 1:26—2:17). See *Faith and Works.*

Gospel (Old English "good news"). The message or proclamation that the kingdom of God is at hand (Mark 1:14–15) and that Jesus is effectively revealed as God's Son and our Lord through his resurrection from the dead (Rom 1:3–4; 1 Cor 15:1–11). This good news brings salvation to everyone who believes (Rom 1:16), sums up St. Paul's message (Gal 1:11), and calls for personal sacrifice (Mark 8:34–35; 10:29). In the second century, *gospel* became a title for the four NT books dealing with the teaching, activity, death, and resurrection of Jesus: the Gospel According to Matthew, the Gospel According to Mark, the Gospel According to Luke, and the Gospel According to John. See *Apocryphal Gospels*.

Grace (Lat. "favor"). Any undeserved gift or help freely and lovingly provided by God, but above all the utterly basic gift of being saved in Christ through faith (Rom 3:21–26; 4:13–16, 25; Eph 2:5–8), a grace that God wishes to give all human beings (1 Tim 2:4–6). The fullness of Christ's grace (John 1:16–17) brings us new birth (John 1:13; 3:3; 1 Pet 1:3–5) and the gift of the Holy Spirit (Rom 5:5), making us adopted children of God (Rom 8:14–16) and members of Christ's body (1 Cor 12:27). The self-communication of God (often called *uncreated grace*) means the deification of human life (2 Pet 1:4) and lifts to a new and undeserved level the relationship of creature to creator, thereby transforming human nature (*created grace*) and anticipating the future life of heaven. From the beginning, Christians have recognized the special role of the sacraments in the life of grace. It is through the grace of baptism, for example, that our sins are forgiven and that we are justified and sanctified (1 Cor 6:9–11). See *Adoption as God's Children; Beatific Vision; Deification; Faith; Gifts of the Holy Spirit; Heaven; Justification; Pelagianism; Sacrament; Sanctification; Supernatural Existential.*

Grace, Efficacious. Any grace offered by God that is freely accepted. Where human beings fail to accept such an offer, grace is called (merely) *sufficient*.

Grace, Habitual. A term for the new, ongoing life in Christ brought about by (uncreated) grace. It is often called *sanctifying grace* because it is the state of being fundamentally sanctified or made holy by the Holy Spirit. As distinguished from habitual grace, *actual grace* is the effect of the Holy Spirit in meeting a particular need or supporting a specific action. See *Habit; Holiness; Holy Spirit.*

Grace, Systems of. Speculative attempts to explain how God's absolute freedom in granting grace and anticipating human decisions does not rule out human collaboration and responsibility. See *Apophatic Theology; Molinism; Predestination; Semi-Pelagianism; Synergism.*

Gregorian Chant. The music of the Latin rite traditionally attributed to Pope St. Gregory I, the Great (ca. 540–604), who may have contributed to its development in Rome. Called plainchant or plainsong because it does not have a complicated rhythm, Gregorian chant is characterized by an austere beauty and discipline that favor an atmosphere of prayer (SC 116–17). Its modern revival owes much to the abbot of Solesmes, the Benedictine Dom Prosper Guéranger (1805–75). See *Chant*.

Guardian Angels. Intelligent, nonmaterial spirits charged by God to care for human beings (see Matt 18:10; Acts 12:15). In the OT, angels protect individuals (Tob 5:1—12:22; Ps 91:11–12), small groups of people (Dan 3:24–28), and even whole nations (Dan 10:13–21). See *Angels*.

Guilt. The fact and/or awareness of having done wrong and so being culpable. Legal guilt comes from committing a crime (to which penalties are attached); ethical guilt, from violating moral norms; and religious guilt, from offending God through sin. Scrupulous people can feel guilty even when they have not, in fact, sinned against God. At the other extreme, lax people can claim to be innocent even when they offend God and do real harm to their fellow human beings. See *Conscience; Metanoia; Sin*.

Guilt, Collective. The guilt attributed to a whole nation, family, or some other group. At times we can truly speak of sins in which the overwhelming majority or almost a whole society shares. Nevertheless, only a personal decision makes one participate in such collective guilt, which is not transferred automatically to the innocent (see Deut 24:16; Jer 31:29–30; Ezek 18:2–4). See *Original Sin*.

H

Habit (Lat. "dress"). The distinctive clothes worn by men and women who belong to religious orders and congregations. In the dress of Byzantine monasticism, a *rasophore* ("wearer of the *rason* or cassock") corresponds to a Western novice; a *mikroscheme* ("small habit") or *staurophore* ("cross carrier") corresponds to those who have made a simple profession; a *makroscheme* ("big habit") constitutes the highest grade to be attained late in life by a monk who hardly ever leaves his monastery. In Western philosophy and theology, habits mean modifications within us that produce regular patterns of good or bad behavior. Virtues such as courage are good habits, while vices such as cowardice are bad habits. Western scholasticism called sanctifying grace a created, supernatural habit because it both transforms our soul and its merely natural capacities, and supports the three theological virtues that go beyond our natural powers. See *Anachoretism; Cassock; Cenobites; Grace, Habitual; Monasticism; Religious Life; Scholasticism; Supernatural; Virtue; Virtues, Theological.*

Habit, Infused. A good habit suddenly provided by God, as distinct from an acquired habit that grows and matures gradually.

Haggadah (Heb. "narrative"). Jewish interpretation of the scriptures by narrating legends, folklore, parables, and other nonlegal material. Together with *Halacha* (Aramaic "law"), it forms the *Talmud*. See *Talmud.*

Hagiography (Gr. "saints," "writing"). Written works on the lives of saints. While such writing goes back to early Christianity, as a scholarly enterprise hagiography received a great impulse from John van Bolland, S.J. (1596–1665). His work has been continued by the Jesuit Bollandists, who have included notable scholars such as Hippolyte Delehaye, S.J. (1859–1941). See *Martyr; Saint.*

Hagios (Gr. "holy"). A Greek anthem acclaiming God three times to show the fullness of the divine holiness (see Isa 6:3), and, hence, better known as *Trisagion* (Gr. "threefold holy"): "Holy God, Holy and Mighty, Holy and Immortal, have mercy on us!" Whereas in the Latin liturgy, this refrain is used only on Good Friday; it is regularly chanted in Eastern liturgies. See *Good Friday; Holiness; Theopaschite Controversy; Trisagion.*

Hallel (Heb. "praise"). The name given by the Jews to Psalms 113–18, which were sung at such festivals as the Passover (see Matt 26:30), Pentecost, and the feast of the Tabernacles (see John 7:2). *Hallelujah* (Heb. "praise to the Lord"), a word that occurs frequently in these psalms, is used by all Christian liturgies, especially during the Easter cycle. See *Liturgy; Passover; Pentecost.*

Hamartology (Gr. "study of sin"). That section of theology which studies sin and its effects on human beings. See *Sin.*

Hanukkah. See *Temple, The.*

Hatred. Intense, irrational, and destructive ill will toward other individuals, groups of persons, or even whole nations. The opposition between love (and light) and hatred (and darkness) plays a key role in the theology of St. John. Unlike St. Thomas Aquinas (ca. 1225–74), whose supreme appreciation for love did not deter him from also exploring hatred, many modern theologians have failed to think about hatred. Unlike those who take hatred to be the opposite of love, George Bernard Shaw (1856–1950) argued that indifference, which simply ignores those who are ethnically, politically, and religiously "other," is the opposite of love; hatred at least is taken up emotionally with those "others." See *Charity; Love; Person.*

Heart. For the Bible, the innermost place for a human being's knowledge, feelings, and decisions (Isa 65:14; Jer 24:7; Luke 2:19). The heart is the principle of good and evil thoughts (Mark 7:21; Luke 6:45) and can be the seat of wisdom (1 Kgs 3:12) and the instrument of faith (Rom 10:10). The Holy Spirit dwells in the hearts of the justified (Rom 5:5)—a theme maintained by the Fathers of the church and still a central concept for Eastern anthropology. Western Scholasticism, while appreciating its biblical worth, found *heart* somewhat too unspecific and preferred to think in terms of the faculties of the soul (intellect, will, and emotions). For many Fathers, the piercing of Christ's heart symbolized the birth hour of the church, sprung from his opened side like the New Eve coming from the New Adam who had fallen asleep in death (see Gen 2:21–23). The blood and water that came from the side of Christ (John 19:33–37) signified the church and the sacraments (in particular, baptism and the Eucharist)—a teaching that became common from the Council of Vienne in 312 (DH 901) down to Vatican II (1962–65) (LG 3; SC 5). See *Anthropology; Hesychasm; Jesus Prayer; Kardiognosis; Scholasticism.*

Heart, Hardening of. A sinful refusal to see God's hand at work, as happened to Pharaoh (Ex 11:10), or to face up to painful human situations by helping those in need (Deut 15:7). The NT uses similar language of those who refuse to open themselves in faith to Christ and his message (Matt 13:13–15; Mark 16:14). See *Depravity, Total.*

Heart, Prayer of the. See *Hesychasm; Jesus Prayer.*

Heart, Sacred. The wounded heart of Jesus symbolizing his self-sacrificing love for all human beings (see John 7:37–39; 19:34). While present in the Middle Ages, devotion to Jesus' wounded heart became much more popular through the visions of St. Margaret Mary Alacoque (1647–90), which encouraged, for example, acts of reparation and the practice of receiving holy communion on the first Friday of every month. Although concrete forms of the devotion prevalent around 1950 have declined, the Sacred Heart remains an efficacious symbol of redemption, as pointed out by Karl Rahner (1904–84). See *Devotions; Love; Reparation; Symbol.*

Heaven. According to primitive religious understanding, the place in or beyond the sky where the gods live. The Bible reflects an early cosmology about the vault of heaven resting on pillars (Job 26:11). It speaks of heaven as the place where God is enthroned (Pss 11:4; 115:16) and from which God descends (Exod 19:18–20), but recognizes that "heaven and earth" cannot contain God (see Gen 1:1; 1 Kgs 8:27). At the end, new heavens and a new earth will be created (Isa 65:17; 2 Pet 3:13; Rev 21:1—22:5), heaven being the "place" or state where the blessed will dwell forever with God through Christ's glorified humanity (see 1 Thess 4:17; John 14:3; 1 Pet 1:4). Heaven begins wherever one accepts in Christ a stable relationship with God. See *Beatific Vision; Eschatology; Life after Death; Paradise; Resurrection.*

Hebrews (etymology uncertain). The people who under Moses entered the land promised to Abraham and who preferred to call themselves Israelites, or sons of Israel, the name God gave to Jacob (Gen 32:28; 35:10). They were called Hebrews mainly by others, sometimes in contempt (see Gen 43:32). An ancient term (Gen 14:13), *Hebrew* pointed to the core qualities of an authentic Jew (see 2 Cor 11:22; Phil 3:5). Hebrew is also the older, classical language in which most of the OT books were written. It was supplanted by Aramaic after the Babylonian Captivity (587–539) and ceased to be commonly spoken around the fourth century BC. Since 1948, as "Ivrit," it has been revived as the official language for the modern state of Israel, with, however, changes over against biblical Hebrew and even ancient Hebrew in general. The innovations include not only new terms for social and geographical data and items of modern technology, but also grammatical changes drawn from various stages in the history of Hebrew. See *Israel; Judaism; Old Testament.*

Heilsgeschichte. See *Salvation History.*

Hell. The place or state where devils and unrepentant sinners suffer forever (DH 1002; ND 2307). This eternal punishment, which varies according to the gravity of the sins committed (see DH 1306; ND 2309), consists in exclusion from God's presence (*poena damni,* i.e., pain of loss or damnation proper) and in suffering from an inextinguishable but unspecified "fire" (*poena sensus;* see DH 443, 780; ND 1409). Church teaching follows the NT (Matt 13:36–43; 25:31–46) by insisting on the possibility of hell for those who through free malice refuse to love God and their neighbors. But it makes no claims about the number of the damned. God's saving love for all remains a fundamental and effective force (1 Cor 15:28; 1 Tim 2:3–6). See *Apocatastasis; Eschatology; Heart, Hardening of.*

Henotheism. See *Monotheism.*

Heresy (Gr. "choice"). In the NT, a sectarian group (Acts 5:17) or a disruptive faction and opinion (1 Cor 11:19; Gal 5:20; 2 Pet 2:1). Heresy came to mean a baptized person's willful and persistent dissent from orthodox doctrines of faith (see CIC 751, 1364; CCEO 1436–37). At times, the challenge of heresy has encouraged the solemn definition of church teaching. See *Apostasy; Faith; Orthodoxy; Orthopraxis; Revelation; Schism.*

Hermeneutical Circle. A notion developed, at times differently, by Martin Heidegger (1889–1976), Rudolf Bultmann (1884–1976), Hans-Georg Gadamer (1900–2002), and others, apropos of the interpreter's search for meaning. In a particular historical situation and with some prior understanding of what a given text is about, the interpreter begins a "dialogue." The text will modify questions put to it, challenge expectations, and even radically correct our presuppositions. In the dialogue with the interpreter, the text and its message retain their priority. A 1989 document of the International Theological Commission ("The Interpretation of Dogmas") proposed a "metaphysical hermeneutics" to avoid the risk of relativism involved in the hermeneutical circle.

Hermeneutics (Gr. "interpretation," from Hermes, the messenger of the gods). The theory and practice of understanding and interpreting texts, biblical or otherwise. Hermeneutics, while seeking to establish the original meaning of a text in its historical context and to express that meaning today, recognizes that a text can contain and convey meaning which goes beyond the original author's explicit intention. Besides drawing help from such disciplines as philology, history, literary criticism, and sociology, interpreters need also to reflect philosophically on the human condition and its role in creating and reading texts. Despite the distance between individual minds and cultures, our common humanity bridges the gap to allow texts to be understood and interpreted. See *Allegory; Analogy of Faith; Biblical Criticism; Dogma; Exegesis; Haggadah; Magisterium; Scripture and Tradition; Senses of Scripture.*

Hermit (from Gr. "desert"). A person who retires from society to spend a solitary life dedicated to prayer and penance. The place where such recluses live is called a hermitage. Although the number of hermits fell after the Reformation, much of their tradition has passed into such monastic orders as the Camaldolese, Carmelites, and Carthusians. The Latin Church still recognizes the life of solitaries as long as they take vows before the local bishops and remain under their ultimate guidance (see CIC 603; CCEO 481, 570). In the Eastern Church, hermits flourish and are known as anchorites. See *Anachoretism; Athos, Mount; Monasticism; Religious Life.*

Heroic Virtue. The practice of Christian virtues to an unusual degree. Such heroism is characterized by charity, humility, and endurance through long periods of difficulty. Before being beatified and canonized, a candidate's practice of Christian virtues must be shown to be above average in this sense. Martyrs form the only exception, because the heroic nature of their death puts their whole life in a new perspective. Sergius Bulgakov (1871–1944) and Paul Evdokimov (1901–70) spoke for the Christian East in valuing saints for being "illuminated" through the indwelling of the Holy Spirit rather than stressing their practical achievements or moral holiness. See *Beatification; Canonization; Holiness; Martyr; Virtue.*

Hesed (Heb. "loving kindness"). A word characterizing God that occurs 254 times in the OT, including 127 times in the psalms. God is even addressed as "my *hesed*" (Ps 144:2). *Hesed* indicates God's merciful fidelity in keeping the covenant promises despite the fickleness of the human partners. See *Berith; Covenant.*

Hesperinos. See *Vespers.*

Hesychasm (Gr. "quiet"). A style of unremitting prayer and ascetical life that is characteristic of Eastern Christianity and enables the practitioner to remain tranquilly recollected in God. In its inspiration and general approach, hesychasm coincides with the origins of monasticism itself. Its founder is held to be St. Arsenius the Great (d. ca. 449), who, after hearing the words "flee, be silent and be quiet," abandoned a brilliant career as imperial preceptor to live in the desert. With St. Simeon the New Theologian (949–1022), the mystical approach of this spirituality was deepened. St. Gregory of Sinai (1265–1346) and St. Nicephorus the Hesychast (thirteenth/fourteenth century) both contributed much to its propagation; the latter added an intricate psychosomatic technique involving the repetition of the Jesus Prayer. With St. Gregory Palamas (ca. 1296–1359), hesychasm attained fully fledged dogmatic status. But the claim that one could see the uncreated light of the divinity as the three disciples did on Mount Tabor touched off controversy. This light, while held to be truly divine, was considered one of God's energies rather than the divine essence itself. When St. Nicodemus of Mount Athos (ca. 1749–1809) published the anthology of patristic and hesychast spiritual writings known as *Philocalia*, the movement experienced a new popularity. Hesychasm aims at human integration through the constant remembrance of God, which we can attain by "guarding" our hearts. Hesychasm can therefore be summed up as the prayer of the heart. See *Essence and Energies; Jesus Prayer; Palamism; Philocalia.*

Heterodox (Gr. "of different belief"). Opinions that deviate from the normative teaching of the church. See *Orthodoxy.*

Heteronomy (Gr. "alien law"). A term used since Immanuel Kant (1724–1804) to describe the state of those who are not autonomous or self-determining but rather live subject to some external law. Since God's supreme authority is mediated through our created consciousness and freedom, theonomy (Gr. "divine law"), when rightly understood, delivers us from unreal alternatives: either an absolute autonomy or a slavish heteronomy. See *Autonomy; Ethics; Freedom; Theonomy.*

Hierarchy (Gr. "holy origin," "order"). The principle of order organizing the universe, angels, human society, and the church. Pseudo-Dionysius the Areopagite (late fifth/early sixth century) popularized the notion of a hierarchy among the angels. Through holy orders (*hierarchia ordinis*), the church has the classes of bishops, priests, and deacons (see CIC 330–572; CCEO 42–310). In the *hierarchia jurisdictionis,* jurisdiction belongs to the pope and bishops, other forms of church government being derivative from them (see CIC 330–67; CCEO 323 §1; 325, 743–53). The hierarchical union between pope and bishops and between a bishop and his priests is expressed through collegiality (see DH 1767–70; ND 1710–13; LG 18–29). The notion of hierarchy as the three classes of bishops, priests, and deacons, who do not derive their authority from the people, distinguishes the Roman Catholic and Orthodox churches from Protestants (see DH 2595). In a popular sense, the hierarchy simply refers to the pope and the bishops. See *Bishop; Choirs of Angels; Collegiality; Episcopacy; Holy Orders; Jurisdiction; Ordination; Sobornost.*

Hierarchy of Truths. A principle for interpreting (not selecting) truths of faith by their proximity to the central mystery of faith, the revelation of the Trinity that Christ brought and through which we are saved in the Spirit. Clearly enunciated by the Second Vatican Council (1962–65) (UR 11), this principle has biblical precedents, in particular, when the NT states briefly the essentials of faith (e.g., Rom 1:3–4; 1 Cor 15:3–5). While all truths should be believed, classifying and interpreting these truths according to their relative importance can eliminate false emphases and facilitate ecumenical dialogue (see DH 3016; ND 132). See *Analogy of Faith; Creed; Dialogue; Dogma; Ecumenism; Faith; Revelation.*

High Christology. As distinguished from a "low Christology," which makes little or no room for the divine identity of Christ, a high Christology highlights his divinity. This distinction differs from the distinction between an explicit (clearly stated) and an implicit (but understood) Christology. See *Christology from Above; Christology from Below.*

Hinduism. One of the world's main religions and the principal religion of the Indian subcontinent. Not founded by one person at a given point in history and not holding a clear-cut ensemble of truths, Hinduism accepts many gods, notably Brahma, who creates the Universe; Vishnu, who preserves it; and Siva, who destroys it. Yet these gods are understood to be only different manifestations of one Supreme God (either Siva for Saivism or Vishnu for Vaishnavism) in the theist current of thought, or of an impersonal, divine Absolute (Brahman) in the non-dualist current of thought. The sacred writings of Hinduism include the *Vedas, Upanishads* (later, more mystical treatises), and the most popular religious work, the *Bhagavad-gita.* Hinduism has been transmitted through the tradition of spiritual masters and teachers in different castes and sociocultural contexts. Its ascetical practices and meditation (*dhyana*) through yoga aim at freeing people from passion and restlessness in order to be united with God in love and surrender (theist trend) or absorbed into the ultimate divine Absolute (non-dualist trend)—a freedom believed to come normally after a series of reincarnations (see NA 2). Key Hindu thinkers of recent times include Ramakrishna (1836–86), Swami Vivekananda (1863–1902), Mohandas (Mahatma) Gandhi (1869–1948), and Sri Aurobindo (1872–1950). See *Religion; World Religions*.

Historical Criticism. See *Biblical Criticism*.

Historical Jesus. The earthly Jesus as known through historical research without recourse to faith. Often the "historical Jesus" has been contrasted with the "kerygmatic Christ" or the "Christ of faith" (or the Christ believed in and preached by the church). Today it is generally agreed that it is impossible to write a genuine "life" of Jesus. Nevertheless, a soundly based consensus maintains many historical conclusions about Jesus: for instance, his Jewishness, his proclamation of the kingdom, his miraculous activity, his parables, and his crucifixion at Jerusalem under Pontius Pilate. The deep challenge to the quest for the historical Jesus comes, however, from the question: Is it either possible or desirable to attempt a merely critical study of Jesus that looks only to "facts" and refuses to evaluate them theologically? See *Christ of Faith; Christology*.

History (Gr. "inquiry, narrative"). The record and study of important events in human affairs at the local, national, international, or world level. Modern historians, while developing the careful use of evidence from the datable past, have come to recognize how presuppositions, methods, and the inevitable role of interpretation show the aim of writing purely objective, "scientific" history to be a fallacy. Many have also abandoned any hope of producing a coherent system that would describe and explain the meaning, direction, and unity of all history. As a historical religion, Christianity is tied to a series of specific events and persons—above all, to Jesus and the events in which he was involved. He came at "the fullness of time" (Gal 4:4), bringing God's self-revelation to its complete climax (DV 4). The church lives now in the expectation of the end (LG 48–51), when Christ's parousia or second coming will terminate and consummate world history (1 Cor 15:20–28; Titus 3:1–7). Like the Israelites (Exod 20:1–2; Deut 26:5–9), Christians accept a saving revelation of God mediated through human history. They experience their own history as founded in and nourished by Jesus' own history. While not being simply validated by historical inquiry, their faith is supported by historical signs and inspires them to be active protagonists in history. This faith accepts the divinely guided direction, meaning, and unity of all human history, even though we cannot yet recognize many clear features in this total story. From the individual to the global level, it remains true that "God writes straight on crooked lines." See *Eschatology; Historical Jesus; Liberation Theology; Parousia; Salvation History.*

History of Religions School. A largely German group of scholars that included Wilhelm Bousset (1865–1920), Hermann Gunkel (1862–1932), and Richard Reitzenstein (1861–1931). When interpreting Judaism, Christianity, and their origins, they argued for many parallels and sources in other religious traditions of the Near East. See *Comparative Religion.*

Holiness (Old German "whole"). The attribute of a being that entirely fulfills the purpose of its existence, and is, thus, at one with itself. Strictly speaking, only God is holy, as being "the awesome and fascinating mystery (*mysterium tremendum et fascinans*)," "utterly other" than human beings and indescribably holy (see Isa 6:3, 5), and yet the source of all our spiritual and moral perfection. In the OT, a Holiness Code (Lev 17–26) invites the Israelites to be holy because their God is holy (Lev 19:2; 20:26). Paul understands both the whole church and individual Christians to be the temple of the Holy Spirit (1 Cor 3:16–17; 6:19). Things, places, ceremonies, scriptures, law, and a covenant may also be said to be holy, inasmuch as they are sanctified and consecrated to God. See *Consecration; Covenant; Doxa; Grace; Hagios; Perfection; Saint; Sanctification; Trisagion.*

Holiness of the Church. One of the main marks characterizing the church and its members, and an article of faith found in the earliest creeds (e.g., DH 1–2, 4, 5, 10–39, 41–43; ND 1–5, 9–10). Through Christ's sacrifice, the Holy Spirit, and baptism, the whole church has been sanctified (Rom 5:5; 1 Cor 6:11; Eph 5:25–27). Paul addresses Christian communities as the "holy ones" (2 Cor 1:1) or "called to be holy ones" (Rom 1:7; 1 Cor 1:2). At times, Donatists and others have exaggerated the holiness of the church here and now. The truth is that for its present pilgrimage the church has been made holy by God's Spirit, is always supported by the witness of some heroically dedicated members, and yet (because of the many sins of Christians) constantly needs purification (LG 8). At the end the heavenly church, the new Jerusalem, will shine with radiant holiness (Rev 21:2, 10–11; 22:19). See *Canonization; Communion of Saints; Donatism; Marks (Notes) of the Church; Saint; Sanctification.*

Holocaust (Gr. "something completely burnt up"). An OT sacrifice in which the victim was entirely consumed by fire. God was understood to be manifested in fire (Exod 3:2; 19:18; 1 Kgs 18:36–39). On the human side, burning symbolized that nothing was kept back by those making the offering. Prophets and others insisted that such sacrifices were superficial or even useless unless accompanied by a right relationship to God and neighbor (Isa 1:11; Jer 7:21–26; Ps 51:18–19; Mark 12:33). According to the NT, Christ's self-sacrificing obedience fulfilled and went beyond all holocausts (Heb 10:1–10). Since World War II, *Holocaust* has been applied to the six million Jews murdered by the

Nazis in an attempt to exterminate the whole Jewish race. The Jewish term for the Holocaust, *Shoah*, was used both in the Vatican's document of March 1998, "We Remember: A Reflection on the *Shoah*," and in what Blessed John Paul II (pope 1978–2005) said on the occasion of its publication ("the unspeakable iniquity of the *Shoah*"). The pope had already made his visit to the synagogue in Rome on April 13, 1986, the occasion for an examination of conscience that he encouraged among all Catholics. Visiting Auschwitz on May 26, 2006, Pope Benedict XVI (pope 2005–13) has called the *Shoah* a crime against God himself. See *Antisemitism; Judaism; Sacrifice.*

Holy Orders. A sacrament imparting a special character and empowering the recipient to share in Christ's priestly ministry by teaching, governing, and officiating at worship as bishop, priest, or deacon. In each of these cases, the rite of ordination shows that the candidate has been called and chosen, invokes the Holy Spirit for the effective exercise of the new ministry, and, along with various prayers, includes an imposition of hands by the ordaining bishop. The Anglican, Roman Catholic, and Orthodox churches hold that holy orders are of divine institution and qualify those ordained to represent Christ in certain ministries that the non-ordained cannot perform. See *Anointing; Bishop; Character; Clergy; Deacon; Ministry; Ordination; Priests; Sacrament.*

Holy Saturday. The day before the greatest feast of the Christian calendar, Easter Sunday. The Latin liturgy offers nothing on this day of preparation. The altar remains bare; and the tabernacle, empty. In the Byzantine rite, the liturgy of St. Basil is celebrated on Holy Saturday morning; the priest announces the resurrection and sprinkles on the people laurel leaves as a prelude to the Easter Vigil, which will begin in the evening. See *Altar; Calendar, Liturgical; Easter Triduum; Liturgy of the Presanctified; Tabernacle.*

Holy See (Lat. "holy seat"). The government of the pope, whose authority is symbolized by his throne as bishop of Rome. While the Holy See recognizes the apostolic origin of other sees (e.g., Jerusalem), "Apostolic See" without any further specification denotes the Holy See. In canon law, "Holy See" and "Apostolic See" refer not only to the pope himself, but also, when the context so indicates, to his Secretariat of State and other offices in the papal government (CIC 361; CCEO 48). See *Cathedra; Enthronement; Pope.*

Holy Spirit. The third person of the Trinity, adored and glorified together with the Father and the Son as one in nature, and equal in personal dignity with the Father and the Son. The Council of Braga (675) added to the Nicene-Constantinopolitan Creed that the Spirit proceeded from the Father "and the Son" (or *Filioque*). The earlier Eastern formulations agreed that the Spirit was not begotten like the Son, but proceeded from the Father "through the Son" (or *per Filium*). The work of sanctification, common to all three persons, is appropriated to the Spirit, because it entails the self-gift of the Spirit (John 20:22; Rom 5:5). Both St. Athanasius of Alexandria (ca. 296–373) and St. Cyril of Alexandria (d. 444) argued for the divinity of the Spirit precisely because the Spirit makes us similar to God by divinizing or sanctifying us. The divinity of the Spirit was proclaimed at the First Council of Constantinople in 381. See *Appropriation; Charisms; Constantinople, First Council of; Epiclesis; Filioque; Florence, Council of; Pneumatology; Trinity, Theology of.*

Holy Week. The most important week in the church's calendar, which starts with the blessing of the palms and the procession on Palm Sunday, recalls the institution of the Eucharist on Holy Thursday, also known as Maundy Thursday (Lat. "command," for the Lord's injunction to love one another as he loved us [John 13:34]), and culminates in the Easter Vigil on Holy Saturday. In the East, it is known as the Week of Salvation; Greek-, Russian-, and Arab-speaking Christians call it the Great Week. The *Festal Letters* of St. Athanasius of Alexandria (ca. 296–373) offer the first clear documentary evidence of Holy Week celebrations. When Egeria made her pilgrimage from Spain to Jerusalem in the late fourth century, she found a highly developed Holy Week liturgy in the city where Christ spent the last few days of his earthly life. See *Easter Triduum; Good Friday; Holy Saturday; Liturgy of the Presanctified; Palm Sunday.*

Homiletics. The branch of pastoral theology dedicated to the art and science of effective preaching. See *Pastoral Theology.*

Homily (Gr. "company, conversation, spontaneous speech"). Originally a reflection on scripture during Christian worship—a custom derived from a similar practice in Jewish synagogues (see Luke 4:16–22; Acts 13:15). The term came to mean the sermons bishops preach to their flocks. *Homilaries* were collections of homilies from the Fathers to be used during the Liturgy of the Hours. In current usage, a homily is the sermon given during the Eucharist after the gospel; it aims to develop Christian faith and life by explaining the texts of scripture that have just been read. On Sundays and important feast days, the homily should not be omitted; it is recommended for weekday Masses, especially during Advent and Lent (CIC 767; CCEO 614). The homilist at Mass is normally a bishop, priest, or deacon. Since Christ is present not only in the sacraments, but also in the word of God (DV 24), Vatican II (1962–65) encouraged homilies whenever sacraments are administered. They require a deep familiarity with scripture and should encourage listening to the word of God. See *Bible; Pastoral Theology; Preaching.*

Homoeans (Gr. "similar"). A group of Arians led by Bishop Acacius of Caesarea (d. ca. 366), who tried to mediate between the Semi-Arians and those who accepted Nicaea I. With the support of Emperor Constantius II, their formula ("the Son was similar in all things to the Father, according to the scripture") was endorsed at the Council of Sirmium (359). Subsequently weakened to "similar to the Father," the formula of the Homoeans failed as soon as the emperor died. See *Homoousios; Nicaea, First Council of; Semi-Arianism.*

Homoousios (Gr. "one in being," "consubstantial"). Word referring to Christ and inserted into the creed by the Council of Nicaea (325) to combat Arianism. Although previously used in a doubtful or even heretical sense by Gnostics and condemned at the Synod of Antioch of 268, at Nicaea the term expressed the identity of essence between the Father and the Son, implying a corresponding equality in dignity. Fifty years of dispute followed. St. Athanasius (ca. 296–373) in the East and St. Hilary of Poitiers (ca. 315–67) in the West championed *homoousios*, whereas such opponents as Basil of Ancyra (now Ankara) and George of Laodicea added an i to the term and called Christ *homo-i-ousios*, that is, "similar in being/substance" to the Father. See *Arianism; Constantinople, First Council of; Nicaea, First Council of; Semi-Arianism.*

Hope. The active expectation of future blessings (1 Cor 15) based on faith and expressing itself through love (1 Cor 13:13). Hope responds to God's promises communicated through the history of the OT and NT—in particular, through the Exodus from Egypt, Christ's resurrection from the dead (1 Pet 1:3; 2 Cor 1:9–11; Heb 6:19–20), and the gift of the Holy Spirit. In hope, we go beyond our present incomplete existence to anticipate the full future of God's final kingdom and the liberating resurrection of all creation (Rom 8:18–25). Far from encouraging mere passive waiting for God's definitive intervention, authentic hope obliges Christians to be responsible for the world and to work for more justice and peace here and now (GS 21, 34, 39, 43). Benedict XVI (pope 2005–13) in his 2007 encyclical *Spe Salvi* ("saved by hope") spelled out the true shape of Christian hope as well as settings for learning and practicing it. See *Eschatology; Virtues, Theological.*

House Churches. A post–Second World War movement to relive the early Christians' experience of common prayers and Eucharist in their homes (see Acts 1:12–14; 2:42, 46). In some cases, the movement has led to groups breaking away from institutional churches. This has hardly happened in the Catholic Church, in which many regular or spontaneous groups enjoy the Mass celebrated at home. See *Charismatic; Pentecostals; Worship.*

Humanae Vitae. See *Birth Control.*

Humanism. Any movement that values the intellect, freedom, and dignity of human beings and their capacity to learn and improve their whole cultural situation. The rediscovery of classical culture inspired the Renaissance humanism. Its typical leaders, while often critical of church and society, could be devout and religious: Blessed Ramon Lull (ca. 1233–ca. 1315), Lorenzo Valla (ca. 1406–57), Pico della Mirandola (1463–94), Erasmus of Rotterdam (1469–1536), and St. Thomas More (1478–1535). Recent humanists have often been nonbelievers (GS 7, 56), who regard human beings as the absolutely autonomous measure of all things. Nevertheless, a new humanism that responsibly seeks to build a better world based on truth and justice (GS 55) is quite compatible with and even required by Christian faith. See *Anthropology; Atheism; Autonomy; Reformation, The.*

Hussites. Followers of John Huss (ca. 1369–1415), a priest from Bohemia who taught philosophy and theology at the University of Prague. He came to know and spread the reforming ideas of John Wyclif (ca. 1330–84). Huss was tried and burned at the stake during the Council of Constance (see DH 1201–30, 1247–79; ND 808; 1254; 1304; 1507/16–17; 1611/20–21, 25; 1684/26–27), thus becoming a national Czech hero. The Hussites adopted his positions, which included predestination and scripture as the only norm of faith. Their legacy is continued somewhat in various Moravian churches around the world. In 1920 the Czechoslovak Hussite Church, which claimed to represent this legacy, broke off from the Catholic Church, after its demands for a vernacular liturgy, optional celibacy for the clergy, and lay participation in church government were not met. Huss himself wrongly rejected the validity of sacraments administered by a simoniacal priest. The primacy he accorded to scripture as the sole norm of faith made him a precursor of the reformers (see DH 1480). His view that the laity should receive from the chalice was accepted at the Second Vatican Council (1962–65) (see DH 1257, 1725; ND 1507/17; SC 55). See *Celibacy; Constance, Council of; Donatism; Predestination; Reformation, The; Simony; Sola Scriptura; Vernacular.*

Hylomorphism. See *Matter and Form.*

Hyperdoulia (Gr. "more than just veneration"). The special devotion paid to Mary as the Mother of God. It is more than the *doulia* (Gr. "servitude") or honor shown to other saints, but less than the *latreia* (Gr. "worship") or adoration due to God alone. See *Adoration; Theotokos; Veneration of Saints.*

Hypopante (Gr. "encounter"). The Greek name for the feast of our Lord's presentation in the Temple and the meeting that followed with Simeon and Anna (Luke 2:22–38). In the West during the Middle Ages, the feast was known as *occursus Domini* (Lat. "the Lord's encounter"). Celebrated in Jerusalem from at least the fourth century, the feast became universal in the seventh century. See *Twelve Feasts, The.*

Hypostasis (Gr. "substance," "that which stands or is set under"). The substantial nature or reality underlying something (see Heb 1:3). The term created problems in christological and trinitarian controversies of the fourth and fifth centuries, when it came to mean "concrete, individual reality" or "distinct personal existence." Eventually official church teaching spoke of God as three "*hypostaseis*," sharing one substance or nature; and of Christ as one "*hypostasis*," or person in two natures (see DH 125–26, 300–303, 421; ND 7–8, 613–16, 620/1). See *Chalcedon, Council of; Monophysitism; Neo-Chalcedonianism; Nicaea, First Council of.*

Hypostatic Union. The union between full divinity and humanity in the one (divine) person of Jesus Christ, which occurred when "the Word became flesh" (John 1:14; see DH 252–63, 301–2; ND 606/1–12, 614–15). See *Apollinarianism; Arianism; Monophysitism; Nestorianism.*

I

I and Thou. The name of a short work by a Jewish religious thinker, Martin Buber (1878–1965). Published first in 1923 in Germany, it exercised a great influence on subsequent philosophy and theology. Buber argued for a qualitative difference between relating to and using a thing (I–it) and relating to a person. In dealing with persons who address me and respond, authentic I–Thou interrelationships are possible. I–Thou interaction is the way to become one with oneself—a self-identity ultimately made possible through an integrating relationship to God. See *Mysticism.*

Icon (Gr. "image"). A sacred image painted on wood or formed by a mosaic. Icons are usually flat pictures, even if sometimes the outlines of clothes jut out from the icon itself. Rather than realistically representing persons and scenes, icons present them symbolically and have an integral function for public and private worship in Eastern churches. Some makers of icons have become world famous: the Mount Athos iconographer Manuel Panselinos (ca. 1300), Theophanes the Greek (d. ca. 1410), St. Andrei Rublev (d. 1430), Master Dionysius (d. 1510), and Photios Kontoglou (d. 1965). But most icon makers remain anonymous, because devout faithfulness to tradition rather than originality is central. Artists create these works as a religious activity, preparing themselves by prayer and fasting. According to St. Basil the Great (ca. 330–79), the reverence shown to icons does not refer to the images in themselves but to the sacred persons they represent: the living God, Our Lady, the angels, or the saints. See *Adoration; Eastern Theology; Veneration of Saints; Worship.*

Iconoclasm (Gr. "smashing of images"). A movement that opposed the use of images in Christian worship and disturbed the Byzantine Empire from ca. 725 to 843. In a first phase, icons were destroyed as being pagan idols that were incompatible with Christian faith and a scandal to Jews and Muslims. From the monastery of St. Sabas near Jerusalem, St. John Damascene (ca. 675–ca. 749) argued that using images to represent Christ and other sacred persons was a necessary consequence of the Incarnation. After iconoclasm was accepted by the heretical synod of Hieria (753), the ecumenical council of Nicaea II (787) restored images and their veneration (DH 600–603, 2532; ND 1251–52). In a second phase of the crisis (814–43), icons, while tolerated for teaching purposes, were considered unsuitable for public worship and so were removed from churches or otherwise made unavailable for veneration by the public. From the beginning, monks were persecuted and sometimes killed by the iconoclasts. A notable defender of images, St. Theodore the Studite (759–826) was a leading monastic reformer. To mark the end of the controversy, the feast of Orthodoxy was established, and it is still celebrated on the first Sunday in Lent by the Eastern churches. See *Image of God; Islam; Nicaea, Second Council of; Orthodoxy.*

Iconostasis (Gr. "image wall"). In Oriental churches, a screen or wall that is covered with icons and separates the nave from the sanctuary. The sanctuary symbolizes heaven; and the nave, earth. Both are found under the same roof to show that in the liturgy on earth we are united with heaven. The iconostasis has three doors: in the center, the so-called "royal door" (by way of analogy to the front door through which the emperor entered the church) is reserved for the main celebrant, bishop, or priest and leads directly to the altar; the door on the right leads to the *diakonikon,* a kind of sacristy for the deacons who assist the celebrant; the door on the left leads to the *prothesis,* or chamber reserved for the preparation of gifts.

Idealism. Any comprehensive interpretation of reality and history in which ideas and ideals predominate over concrete experience and the objects of external perception. More specifically, idealism refers to any philosophical system that subsumes everything under consciousness, mind, and reason. In this sense, idealism is opposed to common-sense realism as well as to naturalism and materialism, which interpret the real as being constituted, respectively, by nature and matter. Idealism has varied from Plato (427–347 BC), who considered the world of changing sense experience unreliable and found true knowledge in the higher realm of eternal ideas, to Georg Wilhelm Friedrich Hegel (1770–1831), for whom all history is the evolutionary manifestation of the Absolute. In between are such variants as René Descartes (1596–1650), who anchored certainty in the individual's act of knowing, and Immanuel Kant (1724–1804), who showed to what extent the human mind constructs what we call external reality. Church teaching has condemned idealism in those extreme forms (DH 3878, 3882; ND 147), which exclude God's absolute freedom and our limited freedom, rejecting in particular the rationalistic attempt by Anton Günther (1783–1863) to adapt theology to Hegelianism (see DH 2828–31, 2914, 3025). See *Philosophy; Rationalism.*

Idolatry (Gr. "adoration of images"). The worship of false, nonexistent gods. The OT rigorously condemns adoring idols or the images of false gods (Exod 20:3–5; Deut 5:7–9; Ps 115:4–8). The NT not only denounces idolatry (1 Cor 5:10; Rrv 21:8; 22:15), but also, developing an extension of the notion (see Iss 2:6–11), rejects the cult of money as idolatry (Eph 5:5; Col 3:5). See *Adoration; Icon; Iconoclasm; Judaism; Worship.*

Image of God. The doctrine according to which human beings, male and female, were created in the divine image and likeness (Gen 1:26–27). Some Fathers of the Church and later theologians distinguished between (a) the "image" of God that belongs to human beings as creatures of reason and free will and that can only be obscured by sin; and (b) the "likeness" to God, which, if lost by sin, can be restored through grace by baptism and a life of faith. The NT recognizes Christ as God's true image (Col 1:15), the model according to whom men and women are to be shaped (Rom 8:29). The doctrine of the image of God has helped to develop a sense of human dignity and rights. See *Creation; Deification; Depravity, Total; Fall, The; Grace; Original Sin.*

Imagination. The creative capacity to go beyond the immediate data, so as to form, recall, and relate ideas and objects presented here and now by the senses. Although some major philosophers and theologians have rejected the imagination for its dangerous and distorting influence, more and more contemporaries have seen the positive role of the imagination in religious life, thought, and worship. It is essential for the communication of faith. The disciplined exercise of the imagination leads to knowledge and helps us to perceive, interpret, and integrate the truth. See *Aesthetics; Beauty, Theology of; Icon.*

Imitation of Christ. A very influential manual on seeking spiritual perfection through following Christ as model. Usually ascribed to Thomas à Kempis (ca. 1380–1471), the book classically expresses the *devotio moderna* (Lat. "modern devotion"), a form of deeply prayerful and personal piety that in the late fourteenth century spread from Holland to the rest of Europe. See *Devotion.*

Imitation of Christ. The ideal and practice of following Jesus Christ that is found in the earliest Christian document (1 Thess 1:6), and that is associated with imitating the apostle himself (1 Cor 4:16; 11:1; 2 Thess 3:7). For Paul, the imitation of Christ means a deliverance from sin and a self-abnegation that conform believers to the pattern of the crucifixion and resurrection (Rom 6:1–11), a readiness to be shaped by the indwelling Holy Spirit (see Rom 8:4, 11), and a self-giving service of love toward others (1 Cor 13; Gal 5:13). The gospels characteristically speak of a personal discipleship that is ready to serve the neighbor in need (Luke 10:29–37) and to follow the Son of man on the road through suffering to glory (Mark 8:31–38). While the theme of the imitation of Christ is found in all phases of Byzantine theology, as noted by Irénée Hausherr (1891–1978), some Eastern theologians prefer to speak of "life in Christ" (see John 15:1–17; 1 John 2:1–6), a theme found in many Eastern treatises on the spiritual life (see *The Life in Christ* by Nicholas Cabasilas [ca. 1332–ca. 1396] and St. John of Cronstadt's [1829–1908] *My Life in Christ*).

Immaculate Conception. A Western feast held on December 8. By a unique privilege and in view of her Son's merits, Mary of Nazareth was free of all sin, even original sin, from her very conception (see DH 2800–04; ND 709). Several passages from scripture have been constantly understood to point in this direction (Gen 3:15; Luke 1:28). Although the dogma itself was defined by Pius IX only in 1854, the feast is known to go back at least to the seventh century. Partly because of differences over the notion of original sin, the Orthodox do not honor the Mother of God as immaculately conceived, but as *achrantos* (Gr. "immaculate") and *panagia* (Gr. "all-holy"). See *Original Sin; Theotokos*.

Immanence, Divine (Lat. "remaining in"). God's presence everywhere and in everything (see Ps 139). Unless complemented by a sense of the divine transcendence, which means that God also exists apart from and beyond the whole universe, the notion of immanence can lapse into pantheism. See *Omnipresence; Panentheism; Pantheism; Transcendence*.

Immanent Trinity. The ultimate mystery of the universe: the communion of three divine persons *within* their eternal life together. The revelation of the Father, Son, and Holy Spirit came through the *economy*, or history of salvation, which culminated with the Incarnation of the Son and sending of the Spirit. Thus from the economic Trinity, we come to know the immanent Trinity. In terms of the famous axiom from Karl Rahner (1904–84), the economic Trinity is the immanent Trinity and vice versa. See *Economy; Trinity, Theology of*.

Immensity of God. The divine attribute of being unmeasured and unmeasurable. Being beyond measure, God is the measure for everyone and everything else. This theme is developed in a particularly dramatic way in Job 38—42 (see DH 800, 3001; ND 19, 327). See *Attributes, Divine; God*.

Immolation (Lat. "sprinkling the sacrificial victim with meal"). A sacrifice involving victim, priest, and people in an offering to God. In the Eucharist, Christ's sacrifice, which was ritually expressed at the Last Supper and consummated on Calvary, is re-presented (not repeated) and its effects made available today (see 1 Cor 11:23–26; DH 1739–41; ND 1546). See *Eucharist; Sacrifice*.

Immortality. See *Death; Life after Death; Resurrection; Soul.*

Immutability. Freedom from change and the possibility of change. Strictly speaking, only the all-perfect God is completely immutable (see Mal 3:6; Ps 102:27; DH 285, 294, 800, 3001; ND 19, 327, 612). As man, Christ was subject to change and death. See *Incarnation.*

Impassibility (Lat. for "being exempt from suffering"). Freedom from the possibility of pain and of being changed by an outside cause. Only the all-perfect and immutable God is impassible (see DH 16, 166, 293, 300, 358–59; ND 4, 603/14, 611, 613), but this does not mean that God is indifferent and unconcerned. The divine love brought about the Incarnation (John 3:16). By assuming a human nature, the Son of God could suffer and die. See *Apatheia; Immutability; Passion; Theopaschite Controversy.*

Impetratory Prayer (Lat. "obtain by asking"). Praying to God for our own needs and those of others. Such prayer is legitimate so long as we ask God to bring about what is according to the divine will and for our own real good (Gen 18:22–33; Matt 6:9–13; 7:7–11; Luke 11:1–13; see DH 957–59). See *Intercession; Prayer.*

Imposition of Hands. A way of blessing found in the OT (Gen 48), adopted by Jesus in working miracles (e.g., Mark 1:41; 5:41), and used by his followers (Acts 13:3; 1 Tim 4:14; 5:22), in particular, to communicate the Holy Spirit (Acts 8:17–18; 19:6). By publishing the proceedings of the Council of Florence, the Pontifical Oriental Institute (Rome) showed that the council's 1439 decree enjoining the Armenians to keep the Latin ordination custom of handing over the "instruments" (e.g., the chalice and the book of the gospels) to the priest or deacon was only a disciplinary measure (DH 1326; ND 1705). In 1947 Pope Pius XII reverted to the Oriental practice by declaring the laying on of hands to be the "matter" for conferring the sacrament of orders in Western Catholicism, the "form" being the words signifying the effects of the sacrament (see DH 3858–60; ND 1737). The rites of baptism and confirmation include a laying on of hands, which is also recommended in the new rite of penance. See *Florence, Council of; Holy Orders; Penance, Sacrament of.*

Imputation. Legally ascribing to someone the guilt or righteousness of another. This notion is central to the Protestant view of justification as Christ's righteousness being ascribed (rather than imparted) to us sinners. Recent discussions, however, have tended to mitigate any sharp distinction between the Protestant view (God merely declares sinners to be just) and the Catholic view (God truly makes sinners just). See *Deification; Justification; Lutheranism; Protestant.*

Incarnation (Lat. "enfleshing"). The belief that, for the salvation of the world, the Son of God, while remaining truly and fully divine, became truly and fully human (John 1:14; Gal 4:4–5). At a particular place and time in history, he was born of the Virgin Mary, died on a cross under Pontius Pilate, and rose from the dead with a glorified humanity (Rom 1:3–4). From Nicaea I (325) to Constantinople III (680/81), church councils have rejected various attempts to tamper with or deny the full humanity and the full divinity of Jesus Christ. See *Chalcedon, Council of; Constantinople, Third Council of; Docetism; Hypostatic Union; Nicaea, First Council of.*

Incense (Lat. "burned"). Sweet-smelling gum or spice burned upon coals in a brazier or thurible. It is burned during processions or to honor the altar, the book of the gospels, the bread and wine to be used for the Eucharist, and the bodies of living and dead Christians. Incense accompanies prayers of praise and petition that rise up to God; this image, which occurs in Psalm 141:2, opens the first vespers of the first week in the divine office. The Book of Revelation pictures a heavenly altar of incense (Rev 8:3–5), such as the altar of incense in the Temple at Jerusalem (Exod 30:1, 27; Luke 1:11). From around AD 500, incense regularly accompanied Christian worship. See *Altar; Liturgy of the Hours; Thurible; Worship.*

Incomprehensibility. That which puts God as the absolute mystery beyond the reach of human understanding. What we know through revelation enables us to realize even more deeply that we do not really know God (see DH 800, 3001; ND 19, 327). See *Apophatic Theology; Mystery; Negative Theology.*

Inculturation. A new term for the old obligation to contextualize and indigenize the Christian message and way of life in the various cultures and peoples of our world. St. Paul and other early missionaries met the challenge of adapting to the masses of non-Jewish believers (see Acts 15:1–29; 17:16–34; Gal 2:1–10). After Christianity struck deep roots in Europe, it became too closely identified with European culture. Vatican II (1962–65) taught that the gospel does not make one culture normative, but should be incarnated in every culture for the salvation of all peoples (see LG 13, 17, 23; GS 39, 55, 58; AG 9–11, 21–22). In the encyclical *Slavorum Apostoli* (1985), Blessed John Paul II (pope 1978–2005) applied the term "inculturation" to the work of Sts. Cyril (d. 869) and Methodius (d. 885) in translating the Bible and the liturgy into the language of the people they evangelized. A decade later, John Paul II's apostolic letter *Orientale Lumen* (1995) and encyclical *Ut Unum Sint* (1995) reflected on cultural differences when expressing the one faith in new contexts. See *Catholicity; Evangelization; Mission, Theology of.*

Indefectibility (Lat. "freedom from being liable to failure, decay, and death"). The gift Christ gave to his church whereby it will last until the end of the world (see Matt 16:18; 28:18–20; John 14:16–17). Through the risen Lord's presence and the guidance of the Spirit, the church taken as a whole cannot fail in its central qualities and witness to revealed truth (see DH 3050–52; ND 818; LG 12). Infallibility is one aspect of this general guidance by the Holy Spirit. See *Infallibility; Marks (Notes) of the Church.*

Indifference. The lack of interest in religious matters that comes from secularism, the absence of a proper religious education, or a personal failure to practice one's faith in God (see DH 2915–18). *Indifference* can also mean a detachment from all creatures and experiences that allows the divine will to guide our choices. In this sense, indifference characterizes the spirituality of St. Ignatius of Loyola (1491–1556). See *Apatheia; Hesychasm; Secularism.*

Indulgences. The remittance of temporal punishment due to sin for which sorrow has already been expressed and forgiveness received. This canceling of punishment comes from the treasury of Christ's infinite merits and the saints' participation in his passion and glory. In the early church, the intercession of those awaiting martyrdom could reduce the severe penance imposed on repentant sinners. In the sixteenth century, the scandalous misuse of indulgences helped to trigger the Reformation. The right to grant indulgences is in principle reserved to the Holy See. Unlike partial indulgences, plenary indulgences are held to remove the whole debt of punishment, if the full conditions for their reception are met. Both kinds may be applied to the dead in purgatory. In his apostolic constitution *Indulgentiarum Doctrina* (1967), Paul VI restricted plenary indulgences and emphasized the need for personal conversion of heart (see DH 1467; ND 1685/17; CIC 992–97). See *Merit; Penance; Reformation, The; Sacrament of; Purgatory; Sin.*

Ineffability (Lat. "being inexpressible or indescribable"). God's being unutterably mysterious and, despite the divine names, ultimately unnamable (Exod 3:14; John 1:18; 1 Tim 1:17; Rom 11:33–36). While known, God remains indescribable or can be described only negatively (see DH 800, 3001; ND 19, 327). In the synagogue, when the name of God occurs in the reading, it is not pronounced but replaced by *Adonai* (Heb. "Lord"). See *Apophatic Theology; Incomprehensibility; Yahweh.*

Inerrancy. As a major consequence of biblical inspiration, the saving truth of the scriptures (DV 11). This truth emerges progressively from the inspired record, is centered on Christ, and is to be found in the whole of the Bible. To appreciate the truth conveyed by particular books of the Bible, we need to examine the intentions, presuppositions, context, and modes of expression of the authors as well as the traditions behind them (DV 12). Inerrancy also characterizes the sensitivity to the truth displayed by the whole people of God. Guided by the Spirit, the church cannot err in matters of belief (see 1 John

2:20, 27; LG 12). See *Bible; Exegesis; Inspiration, Biblical; Senses of Scripture; Sensus Fidelium; Truth.*

Infallibility. The freedom from the possibility of error in matters of revealed faith and morals that Christ bestowed on the whole church through the Spirit (John 16:12–15; LG 12) and, in particular, on the whole college of bishops in union with Peter's successor, the pope (see Acts 15:1–29; 1 Cor 15:3–11; LG 25). Infallible definitions have normally come from ecumenical councils (see DH 265, 363–64) and rarely from the pope. Vatican I (1869–70) taught that the pope is infallible when, as pastor of all Christians and successor of Peter (see Matt 16:18–19; Luke 22:31–32; John 21:15–17), he solemnly teaches some revealed truth concerning faith and morals *ex cathedra* (DH 3065–75; ND 831–40). In their ordinary magisterium, the whole college of bishops in union with the pope teaches infallibly when they agree about some revealed truth "to be held definitively and absolutely" (LG 25). When interpreting infallible statements, one must distinguish the point of the definition from its formulation, which will be conditioned by the historical circumstances of the time. See *Collegiality; Council, Ecumenical; Ex Cathedra Definition; Magisterium; Truth; Vatican Council, First.*

Infancy Gospels. Such apocryphal works as the *Protoevangelium of James* and the *Infancy Gospel of Thomas*, which invent miracles and further material in order to relate, often in a fantastic way, the story of Jesus' birth and childhood. These noncanonical works are to be distinguished from the infancy narratives of the gospels according to Matthew (1:1—2:23) and Luke (1:5—2:52). Although they are not to be harmonized in detail, Matthew and Luke agree that after being virginally conceived through the power of the Holy Spirit, Jesus was born of Mary in Bethlehem. His coming fulfilled the OT preparation and was to bring saving revelation to all the peoples on earth (Matt 2:1–12; Luke 2:30–32). See *Apocrypha; Protoevangelium; Virginal Conception of Jesus.*

Infant Baptism. The baptism of babies born to Christian parents. The NT hints at the practice of infant baptism when it reports that whole families embraced the faith and were baptized (see Acts 10:1–48; 16:15, 33; 18:8; 1 Cor 1:16). By the third century, we find St. Cyprian (d. 258) and Origen (ca. 185–ca. 254) explicitly referring to infant baptism, and Tertullian (ca. 160–ca. 225) polemicizing against it. By the early fifth century, infant baptism seems to have become a widespread, even universal, practice. With the arrival of the Reformation, first Anabaptists and later Baptists and other groups abolished infant baptism as opposed to the conscious and personal choice for Christ that they always require from the one being baptized. However, since all human beings are called to eternal salvation, the church asserts its right and duty to baptize the children of Christians (see DH 2552–62; 3296), provided that at least one of the parents agrees and there is hope that the child will be educated in a Christian manner (see CIC 867–68; CCEO 68,686). The baptism of infants may be postponed if this will prepare the parents to fulfill better their Christian responsibilities. In Orthodox Eastern churches, infant baptism is followed at once by confirmation and reception of the Eucharist; in Catholic Eastern churches, there is a movement to restore this practice. The new Catholic rite for adult baptism follows this practice. Infants, however, receive baptism alone. Communion and confirmation (in this order) are postponed until the children reach at least the age of reason. See *Anabaptists; Baptism; Baptists; Confirmation; Pelagianism; RCIA; Sacrament.*

Infinity (Lat. "boundlessness"). The quality of being unlimited and endless. Strictly speaking, only God is fully and perfectly infinite, being unlimited by space and time, and immeasurably superior to all creatures. In Aristotelian philosophy, prime matter, or pure potency "prior" to any determination, is indefinite in the sense of lacking any specification or quality that would make it concrete and limited. See *Aristotelianism; Eternity; Immensity of God.*

Infused Knowledge. Knowledge freely given through the Holy Spirit for some special task in the church and also given, according to a long tradition, to Christ and the OT prophets. It is opposed to acquired knowledge, which is the result of experience, normal study, and effort. See *Charisms; Prophet.*

Initiation. Introduction in stages to the mysteries of a religion. When Christianity began, it faced competition from Middle-Eastern religions characterized by esoteric doctrines and cults, into which the neophytes were gradually introduced. Like these religions, Christian initiation practiced a *disciplina arcani*. The creed was fully explained only shortly before the reception of baptism. Detailed instruction in the faith usually followed baptism. See *Baptism; Catechumenate; Disciplina Arcani; RCIA.*

Inquisition (Lat. "investigation"). A special ecclesiastical tribunal for tracking down, examining, and punishing heretics. This procedure spread from the time of Pope Innocent III (1160–1216) and fed on the conviction that heresy, as a threat to the social order, had to be suppressed. In 1479, with the approval of Pope Sixtus IV, Ferdinand V and Isabella introduced the Spanish Inquisition to deal with relapsed converts from Judaism and Islam, known, respectively, as Marranos and Moriscos. Those found guilty by inquisitors were usually handed over to the state for punishment. In 1542 Pope Paul III founded the Holy Office as the final court of appeal in heresy trials. In 1967 Paul VI not only changed its name to the Congregation for the Doctrine of the Faith, but also gave it the more positive role of encouraging as well as safeguarding sound doctrine in faith and morals. See *Heresy.*

Inspiration, Biblical. The special impulse and guidance of the Holy Spirit through which the books of scripture were composed and so can be called the word of God (see John 20:31; 2 Tim 3:16; 2 Pet 1:19–21; 3:15–16; and also Jer 18:18; Neh 8:1). What God had to say is found in what was said by the human writers, who were genuine authors and not mere stenographers copying down what God dictated (see DV 11; DH 3006, 3629; ND 216). The inspiration of the seventy-two books of the OT and NT was part of God's action in bringing the church into full existence. Hence the Bible can also be called the Book of the Church. In his apostolic exhortation *Verbum Domini* (2010), Pope Benedict XVI (pope 2005–13) has emphasized that the word of God proclaimed by the church receives a fresh hearing in every generation and accounts for an ever new evangelization. See *Bible; Biblical Criticism; Evangelization; Hermeneutics; Inerrancy; Senses of Scripture.*

Intention. The purpose for which one acts. Purity of intention comes from acting from completely worthy motives. The valid administration of the sacraments requires from the minister at least the intention to do what the church does (DH 1611; ND 1321). Besides expressing our willed purpose, *intention* and *intentionality* also refer in various ways to human concepts, knowledge, and consciousness. See *Epistemology; Ethics; Moral Theology; Sacrament.*

Intercession (Lat. "passing between"). Prayer of petition for others. Primarily intercession refers to the risen Christ's continuing mediation on our behalf in heaven (see 1 Tim 2:5; Heb 7:25; 9:24; DH 1523; ND 1927). His mother Mary also intercedes for us (DH 1400, 3274–75, 3370, 3916; ND 704, 712), as do the angels and saints (DH 3320–21). Intercession forms an integral part of all Christian worship. See *Impetratory Prayer; Liturgy; Mediation; Prayer.*

Intercommunion. See *Communicatio in Sacris.*

Interdict (Lat. "prohibition by decree"). A rarely used ecclesiastical punishment, called minor excommunication in CCEO 1431, which for a time deprives offenders of certain spiritual rights and functions, but does not cut them off from the church. Generally interdiction suspends the right to celebrate the sacraments (in the case of the clergy) and to receive them (in the case of the laity)—a prohibition that is automatically lifted in danger of death. Interdicts may affect individuals and individuals who make up a group, but no longer, as in older canon law, affects cities and whole countries (see CIC 915, 1109, 1331–32, 1370, 1373–74; for minor excommunication [interdict] in CCEO, see 450.2, 517.1, 559.1, 568, 685.6, 712, 1172.2). See *Excommunication.*

Interfaith and **Interreligious**. See *Dialogue; World Religions.*

Interpretation. See *Hermeneutics*.

Intinction (Lat. "dip in"). The dipping of the consecrated bread in the consecrated wine at the distribution of communion. One of the main ways in which communion under both kinds is administered. This is standard practice in the Eastern churches. See *Communion*.

Introit (Lat. "entry"). Known also as the entrance antiphon; this is the verse sung or recited as the priest enters to say Mass. Often taken from a psalm, it sets the tone for the day. Its opening words sometimes provide the name for a feast: for example, *Gaudete* for the third Sunday in Advent and *Laetare* for the fourth Sunday in Lent. See *Chant; Entrances*.

Intuition (Lat. "looking at attentively"). An immediate grasp of reality by the mind or the senses. Immediate intellectual apprehension is usually attributed to angels; as pure spirits, they do not need to reason by inference. In a lesser sense, the power of intuition also belongs to human beings. In theology, Thomism denies that we can enjoy here on earth an immediate insight into ourselves or God without this being mediated by the senses—a possibility accepted by Augustinianism. This latter view runs the risk of claiming a kind of *illuminism,* or direct access to God free from the mediation of creatures and of the church itself. Our intuitive vision of God in heaven, however, has been officially taught (see DH 990–91, 1000–01; ND 2305–06). See *Augustinianism; Beatific Vision; Thomism*.

Invincible Ignorance. A lack of knowledge that remains even after serious efforts to be appropriately informed and that excuses from any guilt before God. Thus, despite their conscientious concern and through no fault of their own, people may be unable to accept the church and its teachings. They can be prevented from doing so by their upbringing, social prejudices, or sheer lack of contact with the message of Christianity (see DH 2865–67; LG 16; GS 16). Invincible ignorance is physical, as in the case of children and the mentally sick; it is moral in other cases. See *Error; Tolerance*.

Irenicism (from Gr. "peace"). A peaceful or conciliatory approach to problems of church unity that may try to water down real differences between Christians or promote understanding at the expense of truth, an attitude which has rightly been condemned (see DH 3880; UR 11). But irenicism may also mean the serenity with which controversial issues are analyzed with hopes for further unity, in which case it is practically indistinguishable from true ecumenism. See *Dialogue; Ecumenism*.

Islam (Arab. "submission," namely to God's will). The world religion that recognizes Mohammed (ca. 570–632) as God's last prophet (*rasul*, or messenger) in a line that started with Abraham and continued through Jesus. Mohammed blamed the Jews for refusing to accept Jesus and the Christians for relapsing into polytheism by their teaching on the Trinity. Islam's absolute monotheism denies the possibility of God or Allah having a Son. Jesus is revered as a prophet; his death on the cross is denied and held to be only apparent. It is absolutely forbidden to represent God in images. Islamic art, in general, does not portray even human beings, since they are made in the image of God. Mohammed is believed to have received the revelation that later was written down in the *Qur'an* (Arab. "recital"), which reflects some OT and NT traditions and is divided in 114 sections, or *suras*, all accepted as divinely inspired word by word.

Islam involves five chief obligations: (1) the confession of God's unity and of Mohammed as God's last messenger or prophet; (2) ritual prayer five times a day, Friday being the special day for common noon-prayer at the mosque; (3) almsgiving to support the poor; (4) fasting during the whole month of Ramadan, which entails complete abstention from food, drink, and sex from sunrise to sunset; (5) the pilgrimage to Mecca, at least once in a lifetime. Besides the *shariah* (Arab. "path of law"), Islam developed a mystical tradition, *sufism* (Arab. "ascetic woolen garment"), which through self-renunciation seeks unity with God. While professing the same faith, Muslims have divided into various groups, above all the *Sunnites* (the orthodox) and the *Shiites*. The former follow the *sunna*, or authoritative traditions established by Mohammed and his first four successors or caliphs but not written down in the *Qur'an*. The Shiites, found chiefly in Iran, hold that Mohammed named only his cousin Ali to be his successor and rejected the other three caliphs.

While granting freedom of religion to the "people of the Scripture" (i.e., the Jews and Christians), Islam aims at winning the whole world to its message. Muslims consider themselves to be the heirs of Abraham's faith (see Gen 16:1–16; 21:1–21). The Second Vatican Council (1962–65) stressed Abraham's faith and the expectation of the judgment as elements Christians have in common with Muslims (see LG 16; NA 3). See *Docetism; Monotheism; Polytheism; Prophet; Religion; Trinity, Theology of; World Religions.*

Israel (Heb. "God rules"). The Hebrew or Jewish nation, descended from Jacob, received this new name as "he that struggles with God" (Gen 32:28–29). The twelve tribes of Israel (Gen 49:1–28) split after the death of Solomon (ca. 933 BC) into a Southern kingdom (Judah) with Jerusalem as capital, and a Northern kingdom with Samaria as capital. The latter was known as Israel because of its closer connections with the Jacob heritage (e.g., Jacob's well at Shechem). After this kingdom fell in 722 BC, the Southern kingdom was at times called Israel (e.g., Isa 1:3–4; 30:11–12; Ezek 2:3; 6:2–3). The NT applies the term to descendants of Jacob (Matt 10:6; 15:24; Luke 1:16) and the Jewish nation (Mark 12:29; Luke 1:54). The church understands itself as the new or true Israel (Gal 6:16). From late eighteenth century, hopes for emancipation led many Jews to speak of Israel rather than of Judaism. See *Hebrews; Jew; Judaism.*

J

Jacobites. See *Syrian Orthodox Church.*

Jansenism. A theological and spiritual movement, characterized by moral rigidity and pessimism about the human condition. It is named after Cornelius Otto Jansen (1585–1638), who in 1636 was consecrated bishop of Ypres, Belgium. With his friend Jean Duvergier de Hauranne, abbot of Saint-Cyran (1581–1643), Jansen wanted to encourage a true reformation of Catholic doctrine and morals. Since Protestantism frequently appealed to St. Augustine of Hippo (354–430), Jansen thoroughly studied his writings, especially those directed against Pelagius. In his posthumous *Augustinus* (1640), among other points, Jansen argued that God's grace irresistibly determines our free choices and that without special grace we cannot keep the commandments. Five propositions taken from Jansen's *Augustinus* were officially condemned in 1653 (DH 2001–5; ND 1989), in 1656 (DH 2010–13), and in 1690 (DH 2301–32; ND 2009/2–3). Despite their stress on the power of God's grace, Jansenists preached and practiced a strict morality and a scrupulous approach to the reception of the sacraments. The attacks made on Jesuits by Blaise Pascal (1623–62) in the eighteen *Lettres Provinciales* were influenced by his friendship with Port-Royal, a convent with strong Jansenistic leanings. See *Augustinianism; Determinism; Freedom; Grace; Pelagianism; Reformation, The.*

Jehovah. A hybrid name for God created at the time of the Renaissance. It was formed by fusing two Hebrew words for God, the consonants coming from the sacred name JHVH or YHWH, and vowels from *Adonai* ("Lord"), with the initial "a" being changed for euphonic reasons into an "e." See *Yahweh.*

Jehovah's Witnesses. A sect that started in the United States with Charles Taze Russell (1852–1916) and was first called the International Bible Students Association. Russell held Christ's second coming to be imminent and propagated his ideas in *The Watch Tower*. Hostile toward the mainline churches and subversive of civil authority, his followers often clashed with the law and were defended by Joseph Franklin Rutherford (1869–1941). Rutherford became the second head of the sect, which came to be called Jehovah's Witnesses. They have become less aggressive in their missionary methods, but continue to interpret the Bible and world history in a fanciful way. See *Fundamentalism; Millenarianism; Parousia.*

Jerusalem (Heb. "city of peace"). The city of the king and priest Melchizedek, who blessed Abraham (Gen 14:18–20). Strategically placed on Mount Zion and adjacent hills, Jerusalem was a stronghold of Jebusite resistance against the invading Israelites. Around 1000 BC, David conquered the city and made it the capital of Judah (2 Sam 5:6–7). Solomon built a "magnificent temple" there (1 Kgs 6:1–38), and Jerusalem was praised as the city of God (Pss 48; 87). But Solomon possibly did no more than to transform an already existing Jebusite sanctuary into a kind of royal chapel. After its fall in 586 BC (2 Kgs 24—25), Jerusalem became the home that the exiles yearned for (Ps 137). When they returned, the Temple was rebuilt (see Ezra 3:1–13; 4:24—6:22). After the Romans captured the city in 64 BC, Herod the Great (who ruled 37–34 BC) built a more majestic Temple. From childhood Jesus visited Jerusalem and its Temple (Luke 2:22–38, 41–50). He wept over the city (Luke 19:41–44) where he died by crucifixion. The Romans destroyed Jerusalem in AD 70. At the time of the Bar-Cochba revolt (AD 132–35), they rebuilt the city, naming it Aelia Capitolina, and under pain of death forbade Jews to return there. The mother church and most special place of pilgrimage for all Christians, Jerusalem was recognized as a patriarchate at the Council of Chalcedon (451). In Jerusalem, the Church of the Holy Sepulchre, which covers both the tomb of Christ and the site of Calvary, expresses the divisions in Christianity, as it is occupied by six separate groups of Christians: Armenians, Copts, Ethiopians, Greek Orthodox, Latin Catholics, and Syrians. There are at present three patriarchs in Jerusalem: the Armenian Orthodox, the Greek Orthodox, and the Latin. The "new" and "holy" city of Jerusalem will be the final home of all the blessed (Gal 4:25–26; Rev 3:12; 21:2, 10). See *Eastern Churches; Temple, The.*

Jesus Christ (Heb. "God saves" and Gr. "the anointed one"). Born 4/6 BC and crucified ca. AD 30, the founder of Christianity is confessed as one divine person (the Son of God) in two natures (being truly and fully both divine and human). After Albert Schweitzer (1875–1965) showed how modern "lives" of Christ repeatedly project onto him the values and personalities of the authors, many abandoned the attempt to write such full-scale biographies. A modest history of Jesus, however, would include at least the following items. He was a Galilean Jew of the house of David, the son of a woman called Mary, who was married to Joseph, a carpenter. After being baptized by John, Jesus proclaimed the kingdom of God, associated in a special way with public sinners and other outcasts, called disciples to follow him, chose a core group of twelve, worked miracles, and taught some memorable parables. His challenge to given forms of piety (Matt 6:1–18), his desire to correct certain traditions (Mark 7:1–23), his violation of some Sabbath observances (Mark 2:23–28), his attitude toward the Temple in Jerusalem (Mark 14:58; 15:29), his claim to divine authority in changing the law (Mark 10:2–12; Matt 5:21–48) and forgiving sins (Mark 2:5–10; Luke 7:48), and his attitude of extraordinary familiarity with God aroused the antagonism of some Jewish leaders and teachers. In Jerusalem (where he instituted a new covenant with God in the context of the Passover celebration), he was betrayed, arrested, interrogated by members of the Sanhedrin, condemned by Pontius Pilate, executed on a cross (which bore an inscription giving the charge against Jesus as a messianic pretender), and buried later the same day. Shortly thereafter he appeared gloriously alive to a number of individuals (e.g., Mary Magdalene, Peter, and James) and groups (e.g., "the eleven"). Mary Magdalene (John 20:1–2), probably accompanied by other women (Mark 16:1–8), found his tomb to be open and empty. Empowered by his Spirit, a community of disciples gathered around Peter and the Twelve to acknowledge and proclaim the risen and exalted Jesus as Christ (or Messiah), savior, divine Lord, and Son of God. See *Abba; Chalcedon, Council of; Christology; Communicatio Idiomatum; Enhypostasia; Historical Jesus; Hypostatic Union; Kyrios; Logos; Messiah; Passover; Son of God; Son of Man; Soteriology; Trinity, Theology of.*

Jesus Prayer. A popular Eastern prayer that consists in the repetition of the name of Jesus within a short formula, "Lord Jesus Christ, Son of God, have mercy on me." There are several variants, including the Russian addition of "a sinner" at the end. The Jesus Prayer, which echoes appeals (Mark 10:47–48; Luke 23:42) and acclamations (1 Cor 12:3) already found in the NT, came from a monastic spirituality with its desire to pray always (see Luke 18:1; Eph 6:18; 1 Thess 5:17). Since the thirteenth century, it has often been accompanied by a breathing technique, which may be helpful but is secondary. See *Hesychasm; Philocalia.*

Jew, Jewish. Those of Hebrew descent and/or whose religion is Judaism. According to a law passed in 1962 by the state of Israel, a Jew is someone who is born of a Jewish mother or is a convert to Judaism. See *Hebrews; Judaism.*

Johannine Theology. The theology drawn from the fourth gospel and 1 John, and, to a lesser degree, from 2 and 3 John and Revelation. John's gospel uses symbols (e.g., bread, water, and shepherd), contrasting images (e.g., truth/lies and love/hatred), and, in general, a prayerful, experiential, and trinitarian language to encourage faith in Jesus as the Christ and Son of God (John 20:31). This gospel is rich in the language of revelation (e.g., glory, signs, truth, and witness), without, however, neglecting what Christ, the true vine to whom we are to be joined (John 15:1–8), does in sharing life (*passim*) and empowering believers to become children of God (John 1:12–13). The prologue to the gospel (John 1:1–18) announces a struggle between light and darkness. An initial favorable reaction to Jesus, who comes as the divine "light of the world" (John 8:12; 9:5; 12:46), leads to a division between (a) those who remain spiritually blind, hate the light (John 1:5; 3:19; 9:39–41), and go into the night (John 13:30), and (b) those who are healed and see the truth (John 1:39;

9:1–38; 20:29). After Jesus' final words to his closest followers, the promise of the Holy Spirit and high-priestly prayer (John 13:1—17:26), the powers of darkness seem to prevail during the passion but give way to the dazzling victory of the resurrection. To offset docetic misunderstandings of the truth that the Logos did become flesh (John 1:14), 1 John insists again on the reality of the Incarnation (1 John 4:2–3), which revealed God as love (1 John 4:7–12). The Eastern church reveres St. John as *the* theologian. Patmos, the place where he is supposed to have written the Book of Revelation, is a place of pilgrimage. See *Docetism; Doxa; Revelation; Son of God; Three Theologians, The.*

Josephinism. An attempt by the state to become sovereign in church matters, inspired by the Enlightenment and adopted by Joseph II of Austria (Holy Roman Emperor 1765–90), who, for his interference in ecclesiastical matters, was nicknamed "the Emperor Sacristan." By his Edict of Toleration in 1781, contemplative religious orders were suppressed, pilgrimages were curtailed, and jurisdiction over church benefices and property was transferred from the pope to the state. Although Joseph II repealed part of the legislation on his deathbed, Josephinism was officially abolished only in 1850. See *Church and State; Enlightenment; Febronianism; Gallicanism.*

Jubilee (Heb. "ram's-horn trumpet"). A Jewish custom of celebrating every fiftieth year by freeing slaves, remitting mortgage debts, and allowing land to lie fallow (Lev 25:8–12). Since Boniface VIII (pope 1294–1303) declared 1300 a year of spiritual benefits for those who came on pilgrimage to Rome and performed other religious exercises (e.g., confession and visiting certain basilicas), *jubilee* has been applied to such holy years. In his *Divine Comedy,* Dante Alighieri (1265–1321) recorded his week in Rome during that first holy year. Sometimes jubilees have been celebrated every fifty or even every twenty-five years. In 1987 a special holy year recalled the birth of Jesus' mother. A jubilee starts with the first vespers of Christmas Day, when the holy doors of four major basilicas in Rome (St. Peter's, St. Paul's-Outside-the-Walls, St. John Lateran's, and St. Mary Major's) are opened simultaneously. For the Great Jubilee of 2000, the Vatican and the Italian state collaborated closely to care for the enormous number of pilgrims who came. See *Indulgences; Pilgrimage.*

Judaism. Religion of the Jews, a people descended from Abraham, delivered from Egypt, and uniquely chosen by God (Rom 9—11), who became strictly and clearly monotheistic at the time of the Babylonian Exile (587–538 BC). After surviving centuries of foreign domination and the destruction of Jerusalem in AD 70, they lost their land with the revolt of Bar-Cochba (132–35) and regained it only in 1948 with the foundation of the state of Israel. The religious and cultural identity of Judaism has been maintained through the Jewish Bible, the Sabbath, circumcision, faithful observance of the Mosaic Law, and traditional teaching. Encouraged by the work of Cardinal

Augustine Bea (1881–1968) and Blessed John XXIII (pope 1958–63), the Second Vatican Council (1962–65) stressed the common religious history that binds Jews and Christians together and that is recorded in the OT (see NA 4; LG 9). See *Diaspora; Haggadah; Hebrews; Holocaust; Monotheism; Old Testament; Sabbath; Shema; Synagogue; Torah.*

Jurisdiction (Lat. "judgment concerning what is lawful"). The legal authority to judge what is right and wrong and to act accordingly. In canon law, jurisdiction means the right and duty to govern within the church, an authority understood as being properly pastoral and to be exercised with loving humility (John 21:15–17; 1 Pet 5:1–4). Although ordained, clerics generally need to receive faculties (authorization from their ordinary) before exercising their ministry, for example, before hearing confessions (see CIC 966, 969; CCEO 722 §3; 724). Parish priests have ordinary delegated authority from their bishop and may delegate the right to baptize and officiate at marriages to other priests and to deacons. Those in holy orders may receive the power of jurisdiction; laypersons can cooperate in exercising this same power, for example, as judges in tribunals (CIC 129, 274). See *Clergy; Holy Orders; Ordinary.*

Just War. A war that might be considered morally right. Although building on ideas coming from Cicero (106–43 BC), St. Augustine of Hippo (354–430) came to be considered the author of the just-war theory. He understood war to be a lesser evil when compared with the raw cruelty of some armies and governments for whom might could be right. By the twentieth century, the conditions justifying a war were established as follows: (1) the war must be defensive and a response to unjust aggression; (2) there must be a realistic chance of success to justify all the wartime sacrifices; (3) there must be some proportion between the moral and physical costs of the hostilities and the peace and better social order sought after; (4) only military targets, not unarmed civilians, can be the targets of military strikes; and (5) force may never be used as a means in itself or to brutalize the social order and the military personnel. Since some of these conditions can hardly be met in a nuclear war, that kind of war is ruled out by most moralists, but the problem of nuclear deterrence is still debated (GS 79–82). See *Peace.*

Justice. The fairness and uprightness characteristic of a good judge. In the OT, God's justice is often synonymous with the divine fidelity and steadfast love (Mic 7:8–20) and is closely linked with mercy (Sir 35:11–24). The messianic king will show justice and wisdom (Isa 11:3–5; Acts 7:52). God's justice is revealed in the salvation bestowed on those who believe in Jesus Christ (Rom 3:21–26) and who dedicate themselves to a blameless life (Matt 5:6). The Christian tradition calls justice, along with prudence, temperance, and fortitude, one of the four *cardinal* (Lat. "hinge") *virtues*, because right human conduct revolves on them. Blessed John Paul II (pope 1978–2005) in his three social encyclicals highlighted the collective evil and structures of sin that hinder the realization of social justice, both nationally and internationally. In *Laborem Exercens* (1981), he shifted the emphasis from work to the worker (ND 2175–80); in *Sollicitudo Rei Socialis* (1987), he blamed both unbridled socialism and capitalism for the sufferings of workers (ND 1446a, 1592, 2187–91). In *Centesimus Annus* (1991), issued on the first century of Pope Leo XIII's ground-breaking encyclical *Rerum Novarum*, he chastised consumerism, while seeing in the fall of the communist system in Europe a new chance for the working class to listen to the church's message (ND 900Aa–b, 2193–97c). See *Liberation Theology; Option for the Poor; Social Teaching; Virtues, Cardinal.*

Justification. The saving gift of righteousness that makes human beings acceptable to God. Righteousness comes through faith in Christ (Rom 1:17; 9:30–31) and not through the works of the law (Rom 3:28; Gal 2:16). Lutherans have stressed the justifying verdict passed by God on those who have sinned (Rom 3:9–12, 23), whereas Catholics (and Orthodox) have highlighted the grace received that actually transforms sinners through the Holy Spirit (Rom 5:5; 6:4; 2 Cor 5:17; DH 1561; ND 1961). Although often seen as mutually exclusive, the two approaches can be interpreted as complementing rather than contradicting each other. In 1967 the international Catholic-Lutheran theological dialogue began; its 1999 "Joint Declaration on the Doctrine of Justification," which contains forty-four common statements covering basic truths regarding justification, was accepted by the Catholic Church and the Lutheran World Federation. Some differences still remain about the nature of justification, for example, God's grace and freedom. See *Deification; Faith and Works; Good Works; Grace; Imputation; Lutheranism; Sanctification; Simul Justus et Peccator; Sola Fides.*

Justinian Code. See *Canon Law, Sources of Oriental; Nomocanon.*

K

Kairos (Gr. "right time"). A word used not only like *chronos* (Gr. "time") to indicate the historical sequence of events (2 Tim 4:3), but also to point to God's special interventions at turning points in the history of salvation (Mark 1:15). In particular, *kairos* (in the singular and plural) denotes God's final dealings with human beings through Christ in the fullness of time (Eph 1:10; 1 Thess 5:1–2; Rev 1:3; 22:10). See *Eschatology; Parousia; Salvation History; Time.*

Kardiognosis or **Cardiognosis** (Gr. "knowledge of the heart"). A word from Eastern Christianity for the insights of and into the human heart in its yearning for God, who sees the heart and does not judge on outward appearances (e.g., 1 Sam 16:7; Jer 20:12). Jesus himself knew the secrets of the human heart (Mark 2:6–8; John 2:25). Insight into the "hidden person of the heart" (1 Pet 3:4) is what one expects from a spiritual director, known in Russian as *staretz* and in Greek as *geron*. See *Discernment of Spirits; Heart*.

Kenosis (Gr. "emptying"). The self-abasement that the second person of the Trinity underwent in the Incarnation (Phil 2:5–11; see 2 Cor 8:9). This did not (and could not) mean abandoning the divine nature or any of its essential properties. Rather, it entailed accepting the limitations of a human existence that ended with the utter humiliation of death by crucifixion. In modern times a number of Anglican, Catholic, Orthodox, and Protestant theologians have adopted kenosis as a central theme for their Christology. See *Christology; Cross; Glory of God; Incarnation; Preexistence; Suffering of God*.

Kerygma (Gr. "the act of proclaiming" or "the message proclaimed"). The core message that announces God's decisive act and offer of salvation in the death and resurrection of Jesus (Rom 16:25; 1 Cor 1:21; 15:3–5) and that precedes detailed instruction about Christ and Christianity. In the Septuagint, *kerygma* can be an official announcement by a priest (see Exod 32:5) or the inspired word of a prophet (see Isa 61:1). The gospels are eminently *kerygmatic*, because they set out to announce the good news (e.g., Mark 1:1, 14). See *Homily; Preaching; Septuagint*.

Kerygmatic Theology. A theology oriented toward proclaiming the decisive events of salvation history. In the 1930s at the theology faculty in Innsbruck, Franz Lakner (1900–74) developed a kerygmatic theology centered on Christ as he is to be preached. This experiment did not fully succeed. Nevertheless, through the work of Hugo Rahner (1900–64), Josef Jungmann (1990–75), and others, a more kerygmatic approach to theology has widely replaced the abstract speculations of Scholasticism. See *Neo-Scholasticism; Scholasticism; Schools of Theology; Theology*.

Kiddush. The name given to the very old way Jews observe the Sabbath and other feasts of obligation. At supper on the eve of a feast (e.g., for the sabbath, on Friday evening), the head of the family offers a cup of wine to all present and pronounces a blessing. See *Sabbath*.

Kingdom of God. Jesus' central message about the climactic reign of God (Mark 1:15), that divine act of salvation which is coming not as a reward for human merits but as sheer gift from God's kindness. Jesus invited his hearers to "enter" this kingdom or receive it as a child does a gift. Jesus gave himself totally to the service of the present (Matt 12:28; Luke 11:20; 17:21) and future (Matt 8:11) divine rule. This final saving intervention of God was already operative through Jesus' preaching, teaching, and miracles (Matt 4:23; 9:35).

His parables, in particular, indicated that the kingdom of God was an eschatological reality that had begun to take shape in the present. For Jesus to proclaim that "the reign of God is near" was to say "God and divine salvation are near." While the NT did not identify God's kingdom with the church, from the time of St. Augustine of Hippo (354–430) this has often been done. See *Church; Eschatology; Heaven; Parousia; Salvation.*

Kiss of Peace. Greeting exchanged during the eucharistic liturgy as a sign of love and unity. In the East and in some Western rites (for instance, the Anglican liturgy), the kiss of peace is exchanged when the gifts of bread and wine are brought to the altar (see Matt 5:23–24). Among the Orthodox, the kiss of peace occurs immediately before the recitation of the creed; and in the Latin Mass, before the *Agnus Dei* and communion. See *Communion; Liturgy; Peace.*

Koinonia (Gr. "communion," "fellowship"). A term used in the NT for sharing in Christ's sufferings (Phil 3:10), subsidizing those in need (Rom 15:26), participation in the Eucharist (1 Cor 10:16), the fellowship with (or brought about by) the Holy Spirit (2 Cor 13:13), and (as an adjective) of believers sharing in the very life of God (2 Pet 1:3–4). Today *koinonia* often expresses the union that exists and should exist among churches, linked by the love of Jesus Christ present through his Spirit. See *Church; Deification; Sobornost.*

Kondakion (from Gr. "short"). One of the oldest and most important forms of liturgical hymns in the Eastern church, going back to the fifth or sixth century and probably so named because of the short wooden stick around which the text was wrapped. The name, however, may have come from the fact that the composition succinctly sets the tone for the liturgical celebration that follows. A *kondakion* may contain from eighteen to thirty (or more) strophes. The composition has a title, followed by a poignant *proiomion,* or introduction, that summarizes the spirit of the feast and climaxes in the *ephymnion* or refrain. Then follows a series of *oikoi* (houses), or stanzas, the first of which is called *hirmos,* each ending with the refrain. The *oikoi* are often linked acrostically, each strophe beginning with a different letter of the alphabet. St. Romanos the Melodian, who was born in Homs near Edessa toward the end of the fifth century and served as deacon in Constantinople, is the most famous composer of *kondakia.* The best-known *kondakion* is the hymn *Akathistos.* See *Akathistos; Chant.*

Kyrie Eleison (Gr. "Lord, have mercy"). The triple prayer for mercy, originally addressed to Christ the Lord (though subsequently interpreted as addressed to the three persons of the Trinity), intoned by the celebrant (or the choir), and repeated by the congregation. In the Latin Mass, it comes after the introit and the penitential rite (if not incorporated in the latter) and before the *Gloria* and the collect. In Eastern liturgies, it is the most common response in the litanies. The *Kyrie* is found in the Antioch-Jerusalem liturgy, at least as early as 350. See *Collect; Gloria; Introit; Jesus Prayer.*

Kyrios (Gr. "Lord," "Sir"). (a) One who has sovereign rights and full control over someone or something, (b) a polite form of address, and (c) a whole range of intermediate meanings. In the OT, God is called Lord, and, especially in the prophetic books, Lord of hosts. When Jesus receives the title of Lord (Mark 12:36; Luke 19:31; John 20:18; 1 Cor 12:3; Phil 2:11; 2 Pet 2:20; Rev 22:20–21), he is clearly acknowledged as more than merely human. Whether this christological title has an OT and Jewish origin or a Hellenistic-pagan origin (where the ruler, considered to be divine, was so addressed) has been debated, but the evidence strongly supports the title's Jewish roots and very early application to Jesus in Christianity. See *Christology; Jehovah.*

L

Laicization. The legal process whereby a cleric is dispensed from his obligations and returns to the lay state. This change of status is relative because sacred orders, once validly received, can never be canceled. The process of laicization is reserved to the Holy See, whose sentence does not allow for any appeal. Laicization can be granted to deacons for grave reasons and to priests only on very serious grounds (CIC 290–93; CCEO 394–98). Except when the cleric's ordination is proved to have been invalid, laicization as such does not dispense from celibacy. A laicized cleric may not exercise his ministry except when somebody is in danger of death (see CIC 976). See *Annulment; Clergy; Cleric; Laity; Validity.*

Laity (Gr. "people"). The faithful who have been fully incorporated into the church through baptism, confirmation, and communion (1 Pet 2:9–10), but who have not received holy orders and become clerics. To designate Israel as God's chosen people, the Hebrew OT uses *am,* a word translated in the Septuagint by *laos* (see Exod 19:3–7; Deut 7:6; 14:2). The same Hebrew and Greek words can also refer to the people as contrasted with their leaders: priests, prophets, or princes (see Isa 24:2; Jer 26:11). The NT recognizes different offices, ministries, and gifts of the Spirit as given to be exercised in harmonious collaboration for the good of the whole church (see 1 Cor 12:4–31; Rom 12:3–8). A later sharp distinction between clergy and laity sometimes involved an emphasis on the former as if they alone were the real church (see DH 3050–75; ND 818–40). This one-sidedness was counterbalanced by the Second Vatican Council (1962–65), which not only insisted that the church consists of the entire people of God and not just the hierarchy (see LG 9), but also reminded the laity of their common call to holiness and wide responsibility in the life of the church and the world (AA *passim*; AG 41; LG 30–38; 39–42; GS *passim*; also CIC 224–31). See *Basic Communities; Clergy; Cleric; Hierarchy; Holy Orders; Ministry; Priests.*

Lambeth Conferences. The assemblies of Anglican bishops that began in 1867 and are now held about every ten years, generally at the London residence of the archbishop of Canterbury. He convokes these conferences, takes first place among Anglican metropolitans, but has only moral authority outside Great Britain. The resolutions of these conferences as such are not juridically binding, but have enjoyed a worldwide influence within the Anglican community. The 739 bishops (including 11 women bishops) and around 600 spouses made the 1998 Lambeth Conference, held at Kent University in Canterbury under the leadership of Archbishop George Carey (b. 1935), the biggest in history. The use of Swahili as well as English at worship expressed the importance of the Anglican Communion in Africa. Various controversies overshadowed the 2008 Lambeth Conference. See *Anglican Communion.*

Last Judgment. The coming of Christ at the end of time to judge the living and the dead (see DH 10, 13–14, 76, 150; ND 2–3, 12, 17). The OT prophets announce the coming of "the day of the Lord," when God's will shall be manifested, the nations judged, and an abundance of blessings granted (Isa 2:6–22; Jer 17:16–18; Joel 2:28—3:21; Amos 5:18–20). Often developing OT images of judgment, the Synoptic Gospels speak of wheat and chaff being separated at the end (Luke 3:17), weeds being burned when the wheat is harvested (Matt 13:24–30, 36–43), and the sorting out of good and bad fish (Matt 13:47–50). While retaining a future judgment (John 5:28–29), John's gospel also points to the present occurrence of judgment when people here and now believe or refuse to believe in Christ (John 3:18–19). The Council of Florence taught that besides a general judgment at the end of time there is also a particular judgment for the individual immediately after death (see DH 1304–6; ND 2308–9). Nevertheless, given the social nature of human beings and their redemption, the collective general judgment at the end remains paramount. Christos Androutsos (1867–1935), a Greek Orthodox theologian, objected to the Catholic belief in particular judgment as making the last judgment superfluous; like other Orthodox, he insisted that it is only with the last judgment that the fate of the universe becomes final. See *Advent; Eschata; Johannine Theology; Parousia.*

Last Supper. See *Lord's Supper, The.*

Latae Sententiae (Lat. "by imposed sentence"). An ecclesiastical penalty automatically incurred by somebody who commits a particular offense (see CIC 1314, 1318). The 1983 code reduced the number of such penalties. Examples that remain are the excommunications automatically incurred for desecrating the Blessed Sacrament (CIC 1367) or bringing about an abortion (CIC 1398). There are no *latae sententiae* penalties in the CCEO. See *Abortion; Blessed Sacrament; Excommunication; Ferendae Sententiae.*

Lateran Councils. A series of synods and councils held in the Lateran palace, which adjoins St. John Lateran, the cathedral of the bishop of Rome. In the first millennium, all the ecumenical councils met in the East, yet some synods at the Lateran enjoyed a certain importance. The first was convoked by Constantine the Great against the Donatists and held in 313 under Pope Miltiades. To combat Monotheletism, another famous synod met in 649 under St. Martin I (pope 649–55) and was run by a great Eastern theologian, St. Maximus the Confessor (d. 662). Five councils held at the Lateran in the Middle Ages came to be considered ecumenical by the Latin church. See *Council, Ecumenical; Donatism; Monotheletism; Synod.*

Lateran Council, First (1123). Convoked by Callistus II (pope 1119–24) to ratify the Concordat of Worms, which settled the long-standing *investiture* conflict between church and state. The question at issue was the right of emperors and princes to deliver to bishops the insignia of office and receive from them a pledge of loyalty. The council ruled against investiture by lay authorities, and, through twenty canons, tried to reform the clergy (see DH 710–12). It is considered the ninth ecumenical council by the Catholic Church.

Lateran Council, Second (1139). Called by Innocent II (pope 1130–43), whose election had provoked a schism, to condemn the antipope Anacletus II (d. 1138) and his followers. This council also promulgated canons against usury and simony (see DH 715–16) and condemned those who tamper with the sacraments or reject them outright (see DH 717–18). There was some representation from the East. Catholics consider it the tenth ecumenical council.

Lateran Council, Third (1179). A council summoned by Alexander III (pope 1159–81) to secure freedom in the church after Frederick I (Barbarossa) (Holy Roman Emperor 1152–90) had supported three antipopes. Its most significant decree required from the cardinals a two-thirds majority for the election of the pope. This council also issued decrees on the bond of marriage and the form of baptism (see DH 751–58). Catholics count it as the eleventh ecumenical council.

Lateran Council, Fourth (1215). The most important medieval council in the West, called by Innocent III (pope 1198–1216) at the height of the temporal power of the church. Its legislation aimed to secure a universal Christian society, a dream fed by the recent foundation of a Latin empire and patriarchate in

Constantinople (1204–63). Presupposing that the schism between East and West had ended, Lateran IV formally and solemnly ranked the patriarchates as follows: Constantinople, Alexandria, Antioch, and Jerusalem. Adopting measures against the Albigensians, Cathars, and the Waldensians, the council also condemned some of the views of Joachim of Fiore (d. 1202). Preachers were required to have a special license or *missio canonica* from their bishop. The word *transubstantiation* was used to describe the change effected by the consecration during the Eucharist. The council prohibited new religious orders, forcing the Dominicans to adopt an existing rule. Yearly confessions were required from those who had fallen into mortal sin (see DH 800–820; ND 19–21, 317–20, 1103, 1201–2, 1608–9). Catholics consider Lateran IV to be the twelfth ecumenical council. See *Albigensianism; Cathars; Crusades; Inquisition; Jurisdiction; Missio Canonica; Transubstantiation; Waldensians.*

Lateran Council, Fifth (1512–17). Convened by Pope Julius II (1443–1513) to combat resurgent forms of conciliarism and some views that seemed to deny the individuality and immortality of the soul. After Julius's death Leo X (1475–1521) took over. Some very useful reforms were agreed upon, but little was done to implement them. The church was thus caught unprepared for the real challenge that emerged in the year it closed: the ninety-five theses published by Martin Luther in 1517 (see DH 1451–92; ND 1309, 1923). Catholics consider Lateran V the eighteenth ecumenical council. See *Conciliarism; Lutheranism; Reformation, The.*

Latreia (Gr. "adoration," "worship"). See *Hyperdoulia; Worship.*

Lauds (Lat. "praise"). The ancient and official morning prayer of the Western church, called *laudes matutinae* or dawn praises. Matins referred to the early morning prayers in monasteries, whereas the cathedral services were called lauds. The two have coalesced into the morning prayer that, in the reform after the Second Vatican Council (1962–65), has the following structure: an invitatory prayer, a hymn, three psalms (one of which may be a canticle), a reading from scripture, a short responsory, the *Benedictus*, the intercessions, the Our Father, the collect for the day, and a final blessing. In the Byzantine rite, the *Orthros* (Gr. "dawn"), or morning prayer, is longer. See *Collect; Liturgy of the Hours.*

Law. A recurrent pattern in the way human beings and other creatures operate (as seen, for example, in the laws of history and physical laws). In a normative sense, law recognizes and regulates the rights and duties of citizens or believers, so as to make possible and enhance the common good in human society and the church. "The law" could designate the Jewish religion (Acts 23:29), just as "the holy commandment" was a way of referring to Christianity (2 Pet 2:21). The law of love (Matt 22:36–40) was taken from the OT, but given new force by being personified in Christ (John 13:34; 15:12–13). See *Antinomianism; Autonomy; Canon Law; Decalogue; Heteronomy; Law and Gospel; Natural Law; Torah.*

Law and Gospel. The contrast stressed by Martin Luther (1483–1546) between (a) fruitless attempts to be redeemed through one's own religious achievements, and (b) the justification that comes by faith alone, the gospel that is "the saving power of God for all who believe" (Rom 1:16). In this scheme law, even the God-given Law of Moses, makes us more conscious of a radical bondage to sin. The word of God announces that we are set free through the merits of Christ being graciously imputed to us and that we thus participate by faith in Christ's justice. Although intended as a principle for interpreting the whole of scripture and life itself, at times the notion of "Law and Gospel" has led to an exaggerated contrast between the OT and the NT. See *Faith and Works; Imputation; Justification; Law; Lutheranism; Reformation, The; Sola Fides; Torah; Trent, Council of.*

Laws of the Church. Particular commandments binding on all members of the Catholic Church. They include attending Mass on Sundays and feasts of obligation (CIC 1246; CCEO 880 §3), confessing grave sins and receiving holy communion at least once a year (CIC 920, 989; CCEO 708, 719, 881 §3), keeping the laws of fast and abstinence, and contributing to the work of the church and the welfare of the poor (CIC 222; CCEO 25). See *Canon Law; Marriage.*

Laxism (Lat. "slackness"). A seventeenth-century development in moral theology that excused Christians from their obligations on slight and insufficient grounds. In his *Lettres Provinciales* (1657), Blaise Pascal (1623–62) attacked Jesuit casuistry, wrongly interpreting it as a form of laxism. Laxism was condemned by Alexander VII (pope 1655–67) in 1665 (DH 2021–65; ND 2005) and by Innocent XI (pope 1676–89) in 1679 (DH 2101–65; ND 2006). See *Casuistry; Probabilism; Rigorism.*

Lectern (from Lat. "read"). A stand or raised platform from which to read or sing. For a long time, the lectern had practically disappeared as an official piece of liturgical furniture—the available space being monopolized by the altar, the pulpit, and, in the case of the cathedral, the bishop's throne. The Second Vatican Council (1962–65) helped to restore the lectern by teaching that it is Christ who speaks when scriptures are read in church (SC 7). See *Ambo.*

Lectionary. A liturgical book containing the official readings for the various feasts and seasons of the year. See *Calendar, Liturgical; Feast.*

Lector (Lat. "reader"). Someone who reads the scriptures during church services. The Eastern churches have retained this ancient office as one of the minor orders. A 1972 reform in the (Western) Catholic Church preserved as two ministries the office of acolyte and that of lector. During the Mass, laypersons may read the scriptures, except for the gospel, which is reserved for clerics. See *Ambo; Cleric; Holy Orders; Lectern; Liturgy.*

Lent. The forty days before Easter, which through prayer, fasting, almsgiving, and conversion prepare Christians for the greatest feast of the year. Obviously imitating the forty-day fasts of Moses (Exod 34:28), Elijah (1 Kgs 19:8), and, above all, Jesus himself (Mark 1:13), the present length of Lent was established in the seventh century, when in Rome the fast began on Ash Wednesday instead of after the first Sunday of Lent. In the Ambrosian rite of Milan, these extra days have never been added. The same holds true of the East, where the Lenten period extends over seven weeks, but as no fast is observed on Saturday or Sunday, the total number of fasting days is thirty-six. Originally the Lenten fast was very strict and allowed for only one meal toward evening, with meat, fish, and generally also dairy products being forbidden. Eastern Christians have maintained something of this severe discipline. Lent is the special season for catechumens to be prepared for baptism. It used to be forbidden to celebrate marriage during this time. In Rome, special Masses are celebrated each day in a particular church or "station." In the Byzantine tradition, the first Sunday of Lent is the feast of Orthodoxy, marking the victory over iconoclasts and other heretics; the second Sunday is the feast of St. Gregory Palamas (1296–1359); on the third, the cross is venerated; and on the Friday of the fifth week. the *Akathistos* is sung. See *Abstinence; Akathistos; Ash Wednesday; Catechumenate; Clean Monday; Fasting; Holy Week; Palamism.*

Lesson (Lat. "read"). The passages chosen (primarily from the Bible) for reading during liturgical services—a practice that goes back to the synagogue readings from the Law and the prophets. At the Eucharist, the OT reading precedes the epistle and the gospel. For the divine office in the Liturgy of the Hours, the lessons are taken not only from the Bible, but also from the fathers, saints, and other spiritual authors. See *Epistle; Gospel; Liturgy of the Hours.*

Lex Orandi—Lex Credendi (Lat. "the law of prayer is the law of belief"). An axiom whose fuller form is "legem credendi lex statuat supplicandi" ("let the law of prayer establish the law of belief"); it goes back to St. Prosper of Aquitaine (ca. 390–ca. 463). A secretary to St. Celestine I (pope 422–32), he composed the *Indiculus,* a dossier on grace drawn from St. Augustine of Hippo (354–430) (DH 246; ND 1913). From the need to pray for everybody (1 Tim 2:1–4), Prosper concluded the universal need for grace. Prayer, especially liturgical prayer, plays an essential role in the interpretation of Christian faith, as Eastern theology has always recognized. Western theology has often paid mere lip service to this principle, and, at times, not even that. In his classic work on theological sources and arguments, Melchior Cano (1509–60) did not list liturgy as a *locus theologicus* (Lat. "theological place/source"), and many have followed him in that omission. See *Development of Doctrine; Liturgy; Locus Theologicus; Theology, Methods in.*

Liberal Protestantism. A movement in nineteenth- and twentieth-century Protestant theology, heavily influenced by the philosophy of the Enlightenment, often opposed to church dogmas and intent on developing a scientific approach to the Bible. Generally considered the founder of this movement, Friedrich Schleiermacher (1768–1834) took religious experience and inner awareness of God to be normative in matters of faith. Various successors aimed to strip away from the scriptures legendary and mythical accretions so as to lay bare the original history. A strong ethical concern (that downplayed eschatology) highlighted the religion of the historical Jesus expressed through the Sermon on the Mount and summarized as human solidarity under God. Some, such as Ernst Troeltsch (1865–1923), underplayed the uniqueness of Christian revelation and understood Christianity as little more than a striking phenomenon in the history of religion. Faith in modern science, philosophy, and progress encouraged theologians to ally themselves deeply with European bourgeois culture and its political leaders, a stance strikingly exemplified by Adolf von Harnack (1851–1930). World War I and the emergence of dialectical theology checked for a time Liberal Protestantism. It has enjoyed a certain revival since the 1960s. See *Dialectical Theology; Enlightenment; Eschatology; Historical Jesus; Modernism; Protestant.*

Liberalism. A broad tendency in politics and religion that followed the Enlightenment in supporting freedom and progress and in welcoming new ideas from the science and culture of the day. At its best, liberalism has promoted open-minded education and social justice. At its worst, it has become a form of secular humanism that rejects religious authority, judges Christianity by the spirit of the age, and is incompatible with orthodox belief. See *Enlightenment; Humanism; Liberal Protestantism; Modernism; Secularism.*

Liberation Theology. A largely Latin-American movement that (a) is inspired by the Exodus, prophetic calls for justice, and Jesus' proclamation of the kingdom; (b) reads the Bible in the key of integral liberation; and (c) has struck deep roots where structures of injustice and economic dependence oppress great masses of poor people. Its better exponents include Juan Luis Segundo (1925–96), Jon Sobrino (b. 1938), and, above all, Gustavo Gutiérrez (b. 1928), whose book *A Theology of Liberation* (original edition 1972) launched the movement. Deeply concerned with the public function of theology in encouraging social change, the leaders of this movement have developed a spirituality of liberation. In his 1987 encyclical *Sollicitudo Rei Socialis,* Pope

John Paul II (pope 1978–2005) called for a worldwide process of "development and liberation" that expresses itself in a "love and service" of our neighbors, "especially the poorest" (no. 46). A 1984 "instruction" from the Congregation for the Doctrine of the Faith judged that some forms of liberation theology could be insufficiently critical in borrowing concepts from Marxist thought and could misread such biblical events as the exodus (ND 261–62). A subsequent instruction from 1986 took a more positive approach, and understood theologians to play the role of spokespersons for the poor. See *Black Theology; Feminist Theology; Option for the Poor; Political Theology; Theology, Methods in.*

Liberty, Religious. The right of all human persons and groups to practice their religion without interference from other groups. After centuries of persecution, the church gained its freedom with the so-called Edict of Milan in 313, enjoying toleration and support from Constantine the Great (d. 337), who is revered as a saint by the Orthodox. At a time when Christianity dominated European life, St. Thomas Aquinas (ca. 1225–74) maintained that, as their defection threatened the social fabric, lapsed Catholics should be regained even by force, but held that such interference with non-Christians sinned against natural justice. Centuries of religious wars, persecution, and discrimination in the name of established religions have illustrated repeatedly the evil of such intolerance. Provided the adherents of a particular religion do not infringe on the right of others, their freedom should be respected and protected. The Second Vatican Council (1962–65) emphasized the right to freedom in religious practice, in particular, for minority groups (see DHu 2–8, 15; NA 4–5). The world remembers with gratitude such modern defenders of religious freedom as Roger Williams (ca. 1604–84), Thomas Jefferson (1743–1826), Mohandas Gandhi (1869–1948), and John Courtney Murray (1904–67). See *Church and State; Freedom; Rights, Human; Tolerance.*

Life after Death. The conscious, personal existence of human beings that through God's power continues after they die biologically. While teaching that the definitive fate of all men and women is either heaven or hell, official Christian faith cannot specify in detail what life after death will be like. Reports from those revived after being thought to be dead cannot provide reliable information about life after death. Such persons were close to death, but did not return to life after being truly dead and genuinely experiencing the life to come. See *Beatific Vision; Death; Eternity; Heaven; Hell; Last Judgment; Limbo; Purgatory; Resurrection; Soul.*

Light of Glory. The light needed by those in heaven to see God in the beatific vision. Psalm 36:9 says that in God's light we see light, and Revelation speaks of the divine light replacing normal light in the new Jerusalem (Rev 21:23; 22:5). Against errors attributed to the Beghards and the Beguines, official teaching defined that without the special light of glory the human intellect cannot see God (see DH 895). The West has tended to interpret this light as a created, supernatural habit that transforms our intellect. The East has identified the light with God, while allowing for a distinction between the inaccessible divine essence and the transforming energy of God. See *Beatific Vision*; *Essence and Energies*; *Habit*; *Hesychasm*; *Palamism*.

Limbo (Lat. "hem of garment"). The supposed abode for unbaptized infants who die in original sin, but with no personal guilt (*limbus puerorum* or children's limbo). The souls of righteous persons who died before Christ were held to have waited for his coming in the *limbus patrum* or limbo of the fathers. Theologians have normally believed that limbo involves no punishment, but a natural happiness that, however, falls short of the full blessedness of the beatific vision. The 1992 *Catechism of the Catholic Church* made no mention of the *limbus puerorum*, and, in 2007, the International Theological Commission endorsed dropping it. Limbo presumes a restrictive view of salvation and can hardly be squared with God's will to save everyone. See *Beatific Vision*; *Descent into Hell*; *Life after Death*; *Original Sin*.

Litany (Gr. "petition," "religious procession"). Prayer in dialogue during which a priest, deacon, or cantor recites a series of petitions or, in the West, titles of Jesus or names of saints, and the congregation repeats a fixed response. Rooted in the repeated acclamations found in some psalms (e.g., Pss 118; 136), Christian litanies, at first associated with processions, seem to have originated in late-fourth-century Antioch. The Byzantine rite frequently uses such litanies as the *ektenai* (Gr. "extended, lengthy") and the *synapté* (Gr. "joined"). The most frequent response is *Kyrie eleison* (Gr. "Lord, have mercy"). In the West, litanies have a significant place in the Easter Vigil; at the canonization of saints; and during the ordination of bishops, priests, and deacons. The litany to Our Lady, which has a special link with the shrine of Loreto in Italy, may have been modeled on the *Akathistos*. See *Akathistos*; *Kyrie Eleison*.

Liturgical Movement. A modern movement that started among Catholics, but soon spread to other denominations. It encourages all members of the church to participate actively in official worship and to let the Eucharist become the real center of their community life. The movement was initiated by Abbot Prosper Guéranger (1805–75) and the Benedictine Abbey of Solesmes. Official encouragement came in 1903 when St. Pius X legislated measures encouraging frequent communion and effecting the reform of church music. Across Europe, Benedictines, such as Lambert Beauduin (1873–1960) and Odo Casel (1896–1948) with others such as Pius Parsch (1884–1954), Romano Guardini (1885–1968), and Joseph Jungmann (1889–1975), promoted not only scholarly studies of the liturgy, but also its pastoral development. Pius XII's 1947 encyclical *Mediator Dei* brought some reforms, which culminated in the restoration of the Holy Week ceremonies. Then the work of the Second Vatican Council (1962–65) introduced the full use of the vernacular and reformed the rites. For the Orthodox, liturgy has always remained central. Such minor reforms as the adoption of the Gregorian calendar have at times led to protests and even schisms. The Russian Orthodox St. John of Cronstadt (1829–1908), famous for his *Life in Christ*, favored lowering or even abolishing the *iconostasis*, so as to make the liturgy more accessible and communion more frequent. Protestantism was born as a reform movement that included a change to the vernacular and a stress on the Liturgy of the Word at the expense of the Eucharist. In the last century, many Anglicans and some Protestant churches began to reform and encourage sacramental worship. In recent decades, the ecumenical movement has helped to promote the reform of the liturgy in many denominations. See *Calendar, Gregorian; Gregorian Chant; Holy Week; Iconostasis; Old Believers; Oxford Movement; Rite; Vernacular; Worship.*

Liturgy (Gr. "public service"). In the NT, cultic priestly activity (Luke 1:23; Heb 8:6) or wider acts of Christian service (Phil 2:17, 30). In Byzantine Christianity, since the ninth century *liturgy* refers to community worship, with many calling the Mass "the divine liturgy." Originally the Latin church spoke of *divina officia* or divine offices, but from the sixteenth century adopted the Byzantine term. The first document promulgated by the Second Vatican Council (1962–65) was dedicated to the liturgy (see SC 5–13). See *Eucharist; Lex Orandi—Lex Credendi; Sacrament; Worship.*

Liturgy of St. John Chrysostom. A liturgy ascribed to the patriarch of Constantinople, St. John Chrysostom (ca. 347–407). This is the normal liturgy in the Byzantine rite, that of St. Basil taking its place on January 1, on the Sundays of Lent (except Palm Sunday), on Holy Thursday, Holy Saturday, on the vigil of Christmas and Epiphany (unless they fall on a Saturday or a Sunday), and on both feasts themselves if they fall on a Sunday or a Monday. The liturgies of St. Chrysostom, St. Basil, and St. James have the following structure: *prothesis*, or the private preparation of bread and wine; *enarxis*, or the opening service of three antiphons; *synaxis*, or the readings from scripture (in the Liturgy of the Word); and Liturgy of the Eucharist (or pre-anaphora, anaphora, communion, thanksgiving, and dismissal). See *Anaphora; Antiphon; Eastern Churches; Eucharist; Mass; Rite.*

Liturgy of the Eucharist. Term for the second part of the Mass, which follows the Liturgy of the Word. It consists in the offering of the bread and wine, which are changed into the body and blood of Christ. This celebration re-presents sacramentally the sacrificial death and resurrection of Christ, and ends with participation in the sacrificial meal at communion. See *Communion; Eucharist; Faithful, Mass of The; Liturgy of the Word; Mass; Sacrifice; Transubstantiation.*

Liturgy of the Hours. The official worship of the community, gathered at different times of day or night to hear passages from scripture (and other sources) and recite or sing together psalms and other prayers. The participants give praise to God, fulfill Christ's priestly office, and intercede for the salvation of the whole world (CIC 1173–75; CCEO 377). All Eastern Catholic clerics are obliged to share in the Liturgy of the Hours according to the law of their particular church. The Jews recalled the divine blessings through morning and evening sacrifice in the Temple (see Exod 29:38–42; Num 28:3–8), while those in exile practiced fixed times of prayer (Dan 6:10; see Ps 55:17 on prayer, morning, evening, and at noon). Christian communities, both secular and monastic, developed a daily program of common prayer. When clerics often could not be present for the common services, the West developed the *breviary* (Lat. "abridgment") or short version of the canonical hours for private recital. In the West, the canonical hours of the divine office became matins (or night prayer), lauds, prime (or first prayer), terce (or prayer at nine o'clock), sext (or prayer at twelve o'clock), none (or prayer at three o'clock), vespers, and compline (or final prayer at night). See *Breviary; Lauds; Monasticism; Secularism; Vespers*.

Liturgy of the Presanctified. Liturgy in which there is no consecration of bread and wine, but hosts, consecrated at a previous Mass, are distributed: hence, the unfortunate term "Mass of the presanctified." In the Byzantine rite, a liturgy of the presanctified is celebrated on Wednesdays and Fridays during Lent, the normal Eucharist being limited to Saturdays, Sundays, and the feast of the Annunciation (i.e., the festive days free from fasting and abstinence). In the Latin rite, the liturgy of the presanctified is celebrated only on Good Friday. See *Abstinence; Communion; Fasting; Good Friday; Lent*.

Liturgy of the Word. The first part of the Eucharist, which consists in the opening prayers of the assembly gathered to worship and readings from the Bible, with the last reading always from the gospels and followed ideally by a homily, and on some days by the creed and the prayers of the faithful. See *Catechumens, Mass of the; Collect; Creed; Epistle; Eucharist; Gospel; Homily; Word of God*.

Local Church. The community gathered around its bishop may be called church in the full sense, as long as it is in communion with the other local churches. The NT applies *church* both to the local congregations (Acts 8:1; Rom 16:1; 1 Cor 1:2) and to the whole body of Christians (Matt 16:18; Eph 1:22). The Second Vatican Council (1962–65) teaches that, through the bishop of the diocese presiding at the liturgy, the people of God are more visibly manifested (see SC 41–42; LG 26; AG 19–22). While the term "local church" is found in Vatican II (1962–65) documents (e.g., AG 19), it belongs more typically to Orthodox usage. Catholics call the particular church (e.g.,

141

LG 27; AG 20) the diocese (CIC 369, 373) or eparchy (CCEO 177.1). In a 1992 letter to Catholic bishops, "On Some Aspects of the Church Understood as Communion," the Congregation for the Doctrine of the Faith warned against setting over against each other the local and universal aspects of the church and insisted on the ontological and temporal priority of the universal church over the particular church (ND 900Ba–c). See *Catholicity; Church; Diocese; Ecclesiology; Eparchy; Eucharist; Rite.*

Locus Theologicus (Lat. "place/source of theology"). The main themes of Christian faith (*loci communes,* or common topics), or else fundamental principles and sources for medieval, baroque, and Neoscholastic theology (and Renaissance humanism) in systematically presenting doctrines. In a posthumous work *De locis theologicis* (1563), Melchior Cano (1509–60) displayed the impact of the new humanism. He enumerated seven *loci* that depend, directly or indirectly, on divine authority and revelation: (a) God's word in scripture, (b) the tradition of the apostles, (c) the universal church, (d) councils, (e) papal teaching, (f) the Fathers of the Church, and (g) theologians and canonists. As additional helps, Cano named natural reason, philosophers and jurists, and history and tradition. Cano's method has exercised a great influence but needs to allow more for mystery and to incorporate the themes of salvation history and liturgy. See *Deposit of Faith; Dogma; Doxology; Lex Orandi—Lex Credendi; Liturgy; Neo-Scholasticism; Revelation; Theology, Methods in; Tradition.*

Logos (Gr. "word," "message," "discourse," "reason"). In Greek philosophy, the reason that permeates and rules the cosmos. The OT spoke of the Logos as the creative power and personified self-revelation of God (Isa 55:10–11; Pss 33:6, 9; 107:20). The Jewish philosopher Philo (ca. 20 BC–ca. AD 50) linked Greek philosophy and OT wisdom literature to represent the Logos as the divine pattern and purpose active in creation. In Johannine thought, the Logos is the preexistent divine Word through whom "all things were made" and who "became flesh and dwelt among us" (John 1:1–14; 1 John 1:1–2; Rev 19:11–16). The "verbal" character of this christological title suggests that the divine self-revelation reached its climax with the historical Incarnation of the Logos. After Nicaea, "Logos" and "Son of God" were used interchangeably for the second person of the Trinity. See *Apollinarianism; Appropriation; Arianism; Christological Titles; Johannine Theology; Nicaea, First Council of; Wisdom Literature; Word of God.*

Logos-Anthropos Christology (Gr. "Word-human being"). A Christology from below, characteristic of Theodore of Mopsuestia (ca. 350–428) and the school of Antioch, and concerned to maintain the full humanity of Jesus Christ. Since the Antiochenes began with the duality of natures (the full human nature of Christ and his true divine nature), they had to face the question: How are Christ's divinity and humanity united in one acting subject?

Their Christology could go astray by abandoning the real unity of Christ and ending up with two subjects: the assuming Word and the man Jesus who is assumed. Recent dialogue has shown a complete convergence between the Christology of the two natures in one person of the Council of Chalcedon (451) and the Logos-Anthropos Christology of the Assyrian Church of the East. On November 11, 1994, Blessed John Paul II (pope 1978–2005) and Mar Dinkha IV (patriarch 1976–present), the patriarch of the Assyrian Church of the East, signed a joint declaration affirming that convergence. See *Alexandrian Theology; Antiochene Theology; Chalcedon, Council of; Christology from Below; Church of the East, Assyrian; Nestorianism.*

Logos-Sarx Christology (Gr. "Word-flesh"). A Christology from above, characteristic of Origen (ca. 185–ca. 254) and St. Cyril of Alexandria (d. 444), and centered on the eternally preexistent Logos who descends into the world. The Alexandrian school normally did well in maintaining the genuine divinity and true unity of Christ as an acting subject. For some Alexandrians, the most serious challenge came in showing his real humanity and facing the question: How could the eternal word of God take on a genuinely and fully human way of acting? As for Logos-Sarx Christology in its relationship to Logos-Anthropos Christology, Alois Grillmeier (1910–98) pointed out that they cannot simply be identified with Alexandria and Antioch, respectively, since there are important counter-examples. Recent dialogue between Eastern and Oriental Orthodox has shown a complete convergence between Logos-Sarx Christology and the Christology of two natures in one person of the Council of Chalcedon (451). See *Alexandrian Theology; Chalcedon, Council of; Christology from Above; Eastern Churches; Ephesus, Council of; Logos; Neo-Chalcedonianism; Oriental Orthodox; Sarx.*

Lord. See *Kyrios.*

Lord's Prayer, The. A prayer often known as the Our Father, which Jesus taught his disciples and which is found in a shorter, probably more original, version (Luke 11:2–4) and a longer version (Matt 6:9–13). At the end of the first century, the *Didache* prescribes that the Lord's Prayer (in its Matthean form) be said three times a day (8.2.3). After praying that God make the divine kingdom and will a present reality, the Lord's Prayer asks for physical sustenance, reconciliation with God and our neighbor, and deliverance from overwhelming trials and evils. This prayer, to be distinguished from the Jesus Prayer (addressed to Jesus and not to the Father), is important for the Mass, the Rosary, and other Catholic devotions. See *Abba; Didache; Father, God as; Jesus Prayer; Prayer.*

Lord's Supper, The. A name used by some Fathers of the Church and current among Protestants for the eucharistic meal instituted by Christ at the Last

Supper. In its one NT appearance (1 Cor 11:20), the Lord's Supper includes both the eucharistic sacrifice and the *agape* or fraternal meal that followed. Eastern Christians call it the Mystical Supper (to recall its sacramental nature, since *mysterion* means "sacrament") and the Eucharistic Liturgy, a term that has gained ground everywhere. See *Agape; Eucharist; Holy Week; Liturgy; Mass.*

Love. That free, self-transcending, life-giving, and unifying approval that has its source and standard within the life of the blessed Trinity and that justifies saying "God is love" (1 John 4:8, 16). The OT repeatedly acknowledges God as the faithful and tender covenant partner of the chosen people, who are called to respond by loving God (Deut 6:5) and neighbor (Lev 19:18). Jesus joined together these two basic commandments (Mark 12:29–31) and taught that our love should reach out in a particular way to enemies and those in special need (Matt 5:43–48; 25:31–46; Luke 10:29–37). As the greatest and "new" commandment (John 13:34; see 1 Cor 12:31—13:13), love can even entail dying for others as Jesus did (John 15:13; 1 John 3:16). It is God's initiative of love toward us sinners that makes possible our response of love (Luke 15:3–32; John 3:16; Rom 5:6–8; 8:31–39; 1 John 4:19). We are given the Spirit of love (Rom 5:5), called into the new community of love (Eph 5:25–26, 29), and invited to share in the divine love that is the inner life of the Trinity (John 17:26). See *Agape; Charity; Covenant; Virtues, Theological.*

Lumen Gloriae. See *Light of Glory.*

Lutheranism. That form of Christianity inspired by Martin Luther (1483–1546), initiator of the German Reformation. After joining the Augustinian Hermits in 1505, he eventually became professor of scripture at Wittenberg, where in 1517 he produced his famous ninety-five theses in protest against the scandalous sale of indulgences. He was excommunicated by Pope Leo X in 1521. Lutheranism spread over a large part of Germany as well as over the Scandinavian countries and Finland. Along with communities in the United States and elsewhere, nearly all these churches now form the Lutheran World Federation, which was established in 1948 and has its head-quarters in Geneva. In 2011 the LWF comprised 140 member churches in 78 countries representing 66.7 million of the world's 70.2 million Lutherans. The typical doctrines of Lutheranism can be found in the Lutheran confessional writings, especially the *Augsburg Confession* (1530), the *Apology of the Augsburg Confession* (1531), the *Smalkald Articles* (1536), and Luther's catechisms. They may be summarized as follows: *sola fide*, or justification by faith alone (not by good works); *sola gratia*, or justification through God's grace alone; and *sola scriptura*, or the Bible (not human traditions) as the only authoritative rule of faith. Lutheranism emphasizes Christ's cross and human bondage to the rule of sin. It accepts only baptism and the Eucharist as sacraments truly instituted by the Lord. See *Augsburg Confession; Faith and Works; Imputation; Indulgences;*

Justification; Law and Gospel; Protestant; Reformation, The; Sola Fide; Sola Gratia; Sola Scriptura; Tradition; Trent, Council of.

Lyons, First Council of (1245). Convoked by Innocent IV (pope 1243–54) to deal with what he called in his opening homily "the five wounds of the Church": (1) the scandalous lifestyle of many clerics and laypersons; (2) the capture of Jerusalem by the Saracens; (3) the Greek threat to the Latin Empire in Constantinople; (4) the invasion of Hungary by the Mongols; and (5) the conflict between the church and Frederick II (Holy Roman Emperor 1215–50). Besides ordering the Greeks to conform more to the Latin rite and clarifying some points concerning the sacraments and purgatory (see DH 830–39), the council deposed the emperor for heresy and encroaching on the rights of the church. Catholics consider it to be the thirteenth ecumenical council. See *Crusades; Lateran Council, Fourth.*

Lyons, Second Council of (1274). Convoked by Blessed Gregory X (pope 1271–76), who wanted a crusade (to free the Holy Land from the Saracens), an agreement with the Greeks, and a reformation of the church. It was attended by great theologians, including St. Albert the Great (ca. 1200–1280) and St. Bonaventure (ca. 1217–74), whose funeral was held on the last day of the council. St. Thomas Aquinas (ca. 1225–74) had been invited, but he died on the way, after having finished a preliminary study, "Concerning the Errors of the Greeks." In spite of a tax imposed on the income of clerics to finance it, the crusade never materialized. The legates of Michael VIII Paleologus (Greek Emperor 1259–82) signed an agreement of union, which was celebrated on July 6 with the *Filioque* being sung three times. The union, which partly aimed at calming fears that Charles of Anjou (1220–85) would try to restore the Latin Empire in Constantinople, proved ephemeral. Legislation for the reform of the church included suppression of some new orders and strict rules to be followed when cardinals gathered to elect a new pope. These rules were seen to be needed, since the Holy See had been vacant for three years (1268–71). Catholics have normally considered Lyons II to be the fourteenth ecumenical council, but in 1974 Paul VI (pope 1963–78) spoke of it as "a general council of the West." See *Conclave; Crusades; Filioque; Holy See.*

M

Macedonians. A sect that took its name from Macedonius, bishop of Constantinople from 342 until he was deposed by the Arian Council of Constantinople in 360. He himself had Semi-Arian tendencies (see DH 156, 2527). At Constantinople I (381), he was condemned with those who denied the divinity of the Holy Spirit (see DH 151; ND 13), but it is doubtful whether he really subscribed to that heresy. See *Arianism; Constantinople, First Council of; Holy Spirit; Pneumatomachians; Semi-Arianism.*

Magisterium (Lat. "office of teacher"). The office of authoritatively teaching the gospel in the name of Jesus Christ, yet as "serving" and not "superior to" the word of God (DV 10). All baptized believers are anointed and guided by the Spirit (John 14:26; 16:13; Rom 8:14; 1 John 2:27), and, in some degree, have a prophetic responsibility for announcing the good news about Christ. Those who have the authority to proclaim and teach officially share in the church's magisterium. Catholics believe that this magisterial authority belongs to the whole college of bishops (as successors to the college of apostolic witnesses) and to individual bishops united with the bishop of Rome (LG 20–25; DV 10). The bishops generally fulfill this magisterium on a day-to-day basis (various kinds of "ordinary" magisterium). When assembled in an ecumenical council or represented by the pope, they may teach some revealed truth to be held definitively (the "extraordinary" magisterium). As a specific service on behalf of the whole community, the magisterium recalls Christ's saving truth, so as to clarify and apply it to the new challenges and questions of each age and situation. The office of the magisterium comes from Christ himself, is guided by (and does not supplant) the Holy Spirit, and is exercised within the whole community of the faithful, who were and remain the primary recipients of God's self-revelation. The intersubjective nature of truth lends credibility to the existence of such a magisterium. Truth, including revealed truth, is experienced and maintained by human beings in community. This makes it more plausible that the church should be equipped with an institution (the magisterium) that functions to help people experience and abide in the truth of revelation. In the Middle Ages, theologians and the theological faculties of great universities were also credited with exercising a certain magisterium. Such authority derived from the quality of their personal gifts, just as apparently there was a similar charismatic basis for the role of "teachers" in the NT church (1 Cor 12:28; Acts 13:1). Among Orthodox Christians, synods enjoy a special importance for teaching; yet, whatever has not been defined by the seven ecumenical councils (325–787) does not enjoy infallible certitude and remains matter for discussion. See *Apostolic Succession; Authority; Bishop; Collegiality; Council, Ecumenical; Deposit of Faith; Ex Cathedra Definition; Hierarchy; Infallibility; Pope; Seven Ecumenical Councils, The; Sobornost; Synod; Theology, History of.*

Mandate. An attestation from the competent ecclesiastical authority recognizing that someone who teaches a theological discipline at a Catholic university or similar institute of higher learning is in good standing with the church and is teaching Catholic doctrine in communion with the bishops (CIC 812; CCEO 644). In this context, mandate replaces the term previously used: canonical mission. See *Magisterium; Missio Canonica; Theology.*

Manichaeism. The doctrine of Mani, born in Persia ca. AD 215 and skinned alive by order of the Persian emperor in 275. Borrowing elements from Zoroastrianism, Buddhism, Gnosticism, and Christianity, Mani saw himself as following the OT prophets, Zarathustra, Buddha, and Jesus to free the spark of light in human beings and so deliver them from matter and darkness. A strict asceticism and vigorous missionary activity spread this teaching to India, China, Italy, North Africa, and other parts of the Roman Empire. For nine years prior to his conversion, St. Augustine of Hippo (354–430) subscribed to Manichaeism. Manichee was often used synonymously with heretic, especially in the context of similar dualistic movements (see DH 435, 444–45, 455, 457, 461–64, 718, 1336, 1340, 3246; ND 402/5, 7, 11–13; 409; 621). See *Albigensianism; Cathars; Dualism; Gnosticism; Priscillianism.*

Manna (Gr. "small grain"). Food that through God's special providence (Ps 78:24–25) the Jews ate on their flight from Egypt and for forty years before they entered the promised land (Exod 16:12–36). The popular etymology of Exodus 16:15, according to which the word derives from the Hebrew "what is this?", is meant to underline God's intervention. Manna seems to have been a resinous, white substance that some desert trees and shrubs produce and that falls on the ground like frost. The plain taste of manna (Num 11:4–9) was one reason for the people complaining in the desert and incurring the divine displeasure (Num 11:1–35). John's gospel presents Jesus as the bread of eternal life, incomparably superior to the manna eaten in the desert (John 6:25–58; see Rev 2:17). See *Eucharist; Israel; Typology.*

Maranatha. An Aramaic word used in 1 Corinthians 16:22. As *Marana-tha*, it means "Our Lord, come!" As *Maran-atha*, it means "Our Lord has come." The first meaning is probably the one intended (see Rev 22:20). See *Advent; Eschatology; Kyrios; Parousia.*

Marcionism. A dualistic, ascetic movement founded by Marcion, a native of Pontus in Asia Minor, who came to Rome around 140 and was excommunicated in 144. In his *Antitheses*, he maintained that the creator (or demiurge) and OT law were quite incompatible with the God of love and grace preached by Jesus. Hence he rejected completely the Hebrew scriptures, retaining only the Pauline letters and a truncated version of Luke's gospel. He interpreted the person and work of Christ along docetic lines. For some time, Marcion had many followers, and major theologians such as St. Irenaeus of Lyons (ca. 130–ca. 200) and Tertullian (ca. 160–ca. 220) felt obliged to refute him. The formation of the canon came, in part, as a response to his erroneous teaching. By the end of the third century, his followers had largely become Manichees, but a Marcionite rejection or downplaying of the OT remains a recurrent temptation for Christians. See *Canon of Scripture; Demiurge; Docetism; Dualism; Manichaeism.*

Mariology. The systematic study of the person of Mary and her role in salvation history. Luke's infancy narrative (Luke 1—2) presents her as model believer, representative of the church, and mother of the Savior, whom she has conceived virginally. In John's gospel, she stands by the cross (John 19:25–27), and Acts reports that she was present with the community before Pentecost (Acts 1:14). For centuries, theological, pastoral, and popular reflection on these and other scriptural passages rightly associated Mary with Christ, the Holy Spirit, the church, and human redemption. When the Council of Ephesus (431), for example, declared Mary to be the Mother of God, it did so to defend the personal unity of Christ and to reject any teaching that in Christ there were two different persons: one divine and the other a merely human person born of Mary. In the West, devotion to Mary at times presented her apart from the proper christological, pneumatological, or ecclesiological context and indulged in exaggerations summarized by the adage *de Maria nunquam satis* (Lat. "one can never say enough about Mary"). The Second Vatican Council, while warning against abuses and purposely avoiding the title "co-redemptrix," was the first ecumenical council to offer a systematic treatment of the role and importance of Mary (LG 52–69). Rather than risk letting mariology become an independent field, Eastern Christians study theotokology, or Mary the Theotokos (Gr. "God-bearer"), and so hold together mariology and Christology. See *Assumption of the Blessed Virgin; Christology; Co-Redemptrix; Ecclesiology; Ephesus, Council of; Immaculate Conception; Nestorianism; New Eve; Pneumatology; Theotokos.*

Marks (Notes) of the Church. The essential qualities of Christ's church: unity, holiness, catholicity, and apostolicity (Nicene-Constantinopolitan Creed). After John Wyclif (ca. 1330–84) and John Huss (ca. 1372–1415) stressed the "spiritual" side of the church, in 1431 the Dominican cardinal John de Torquemada (an uncle of the future Grand Inquisitor) wrote a treatise about the church based on its four visible marks. During the Reformation, such Catholic apologists as Cardinal Stanislaus Hosius (1504–79) and St. Robert Bellarmine (1542–1621) emphasized these marks in response to those such as Martin Luther (1483–1546), who held that the unadulterated teaching of the gospel characterized the true church of Jesus Christ. In recent years, prophetic denunciation of and action against injustice have assumed a larger role as a visible sign of the church's holiness in the world; see Blessed John Paul II, *Sollicitudo Rei Socialis (1987)*. See *Apostolicity; Catholicity; Church; Holiness; Holiness of the Church; Hussites; Reformation, The.*

Maronites. Members of an Eastern Catholic church who trace their origin back to St. Maron, friend of St. John Chrysostom (ca. 347–407). The Maronite Church, which remained faithful to the Council of Chalcedon, probably achieved its organizational independence in the seventh century, at the time of the Monothelite dispute. Whether the Maronites endorsed this teaching, at least verbally, is a matter of controversy. In the eighth century, at a time when the patriarchal see of Antioch was empty, the title of "patriarch" was given to the superior of the Maronite monastery on the Orontes in Syria. With the arrival of the crusaders, communion with the Catholic Church, never renounced, was resumed without formality, and there have been only Catholic Maronites ever since. The Maronite Jeremias II attended the Fourth Lateran Council and was recognized as patriarch of Antioch a year later (1216). In 1584 Gregory XIII (pope 1572–85) founded a Maronite college in Rome, where important liturgical and other texts were published during the eighteenth century. The Maronite rite, one of the seven major extant rites, once considered simply a Latinized variant of the West-Syrian rite, is now recognized to be an independent tradition related to both the West-Syrian and East-Syrian liturgies. It underwent superficial Latinization in the seventeenth and eighteenth centuries, much of which has been purged in recent reforms. Maronites are found in Lebanon, Syria, Israel, Cyprus, the United States, and elsewhere. Given its origin around St. Maron's monastery, the Maronite Church was structured around monasteries rather than dioceses—at least until the eighteenth century. See *Crusades; Eastern Churches; Monothelitism; Rite.*

Marriage. A covenanted communion for life between one man and one woman through which they become husband and wife, mutually share their complete selves, promote each other's fullest welfare, and, in love, beget and raise children (GS 47–52). The OT speaks of man and woman as both being created in the image of God to rule over the earth, procreate children, and complete each other's being (Gen 1:27–28; 2:18–25). Jesus emphasized the dignity of married life in various ways—for instance, by comparing the divine kingdom to a wedding feast (Matt 22:1–14; 25:1–13). His love for the church is likened to the marriage bond (Eph 5:22–33), which is a sacrament for baptized Christians (LG 11, 35). The two partners are themselves the ministers of this sacrament, the priest (or deacon) serving only as an official, if necessary, witness (CIC 1108–11, 1115–16). Non-Catholic Eastern churches consider the priest to be the minister of marriage. Among Eastern Catholics, marriage is not valid without the blessing of the priest except in emergency situations, and, even then, the priest's blessing is required at the earliest convenience (CCEO 828–32). The bond of marriage is indissoluble as long as both partners remain alive. See *Deacon; Priests; Sacrament.*

Marriage Form. The way of performing the marriage ceremony established by the Council of Trent in 1563 and prescribed in canon law (CIC 1108–23; CCEO 828–42). For a marriage to be valid, it must be celebrated before the local bishop, the parish priest, or a priest or deacon legitimately delegated for the celebration. Where priests or deacons are not available, laypersons may be delegated, if this is granted by the episcopal conference. Two other witnesses must be present. For just reasons, the local bishop may dispense from the form prescribed by the law. See *Trent, Council of; Validity.*

Marriage Impediments. Qualities or personal circumstances that stand in the way of contracting a marriage are called diriment impediments and rule out a valid marriage. Diriment impediments include insufficient age, impotency, an already existing marriage, holy orders, public perpetual religious vows, and close blood-relationships (see CIC 1073–94; CCEO 790–812). See *Ratum et Consummatum; Validity*.

Martyr (Gr. "witness"). Somebody who, because of his or her faith in and love for Christ, undergoes suffering and death (LG 50). In St. John's gospel the term is used of the Father's witness in favor of the Son (John 5:37), and the witness given by Jesus (John 3:1–12) or by John the Baptist (John 1:6–8, 15, 19–36; 5:33). The apostles and other Christians witnessed to the truth (Luke 24:48; Acts 1:8, 22). In due course, martyrs designated those who suffered and died for their testimony (Acts 22:20; Rev 12:11), the death of Jesus himself being considered the prime example of martyrdom (see Acts 3:14). Isolated episodes of persecution became large-scale and systematic under the emperors Septimius Severus (202–3), Decius (249–50), and Valerian (257–58). The Roman persecution reached its climax under Diocletian and Galerius from 303 onward, ending with the victory in 312 of Constantine the Great over Maxentius. The first Christians to be venerated as saints were the martyrs. A chapel built on their tombs was known as a martyrion, being visited particularly on the *dies natalis* (Lat. "birthday, anniversary") or the day of their heavenly birth through martyrdom. From the beginning, the church has considered martyrdom as a "baptism of blood" that can replace sacramental baptism. The martyrology is a liturgical book containing the names of martyrs and other saints, listed according to the day of their death. In modern times, there have been numerous martyrs in and outside Europe—in Africa, the Americas, Asia, and Oceania. Many Christians have endured suffering and martyrdom because of their commitment to and solidarity with those who suffer (see John 15:13). See *Baptism; Holiness; Veneration of Saints*.

Marxism. The social, economic, political, and philosophical doctrine developed by Karl Marx (1818–83) and his collaborator Friedrich Engels (1820–95), and actualized in its most powerful way by Vladimir Ilyich Lenin (1870–1924) and Mao Tse-Tung (1893–1976). Outraged by massive social injustices, they argued that private property and capitalistic society had alienated human beings from themselves, their work, their products, and one another. A class struggle, led by the industrial proletariat, was expected to end this radical alienation, go beyond capitalism, and bring in a classless society of self-emancipated people. In that future society, the question of God would simply disappear. The atheistic materialism of official Marxism has opposed all religions, which were dismissed as ideologies favoring the prosperous and powerful, and encouraging the poor to suffer patiently and look for rewards after death. While condemning atheistic Marxism, church teaching has also criticized capitalistic materialism (DH 2786, 3773, 3865, 3930, 3939; Blessed John Paul II (pope 1978–2005), *Sollicitudo Rei Socialis* 20–21). Hard-line Marxism did not achieve either the true emancipation of humanity or economic prosperity for everyone. In a dramatic way, the governments of nearly all communist countries, around 1989–90, allowed and even initiated reforms that make the old, official Marxism, and, in many former strongholds, even communism, a thing of the past. See *Atheism; Frankfurt School; Materialism; Political Theology; Social Teaching.*

Mary, Mother of God. See *Mariology; Theotokos.*

Mass (Lat. perhaps "dismissal"). A word commonly used in the Roman Church, where the regular form of dismissal at the end of the liturgy is "Ite missa est" (Lat. "Go, the Mass is ended"). See *Eucharist; Liturgy.*

Mass of the Presanctified. See *Liturgy of the Presanctified.*

Materialism. Any belief that denies spiritual entities such as God and the human soul, and accepts the existence only of perceptible, extended reality. A classical form of materialism was articulated by the Greek philosopher Epicurus (341–270 BC) and expressed in verse by the Roman poet Lucretius (ca. 99–55 BC). Modern versions of materialism have come from Ludwig Feuerbach (1804–72), Karl Marx (1818–83), and Friedrich Engels (1820–95). See *Atheism; Marxism; Pantheism.*

Matter and Form. The Aristotelian analysis of all material reality into two complementary principles: the underlying stuff or pure potentiality, which is actualized by the form that determines the nature of things. This theory of hylomorphism (Gr. "matter," "form") enjoyed great popularity among Scholastic philosophers and theologians. See *Aristotelianism; Causality; Sacrament; Scholasticism.*

Mediation (Lat. "going between"). The intervention of a third party to reconcile two parties in conflict with each other and so promote, through a new understanding, some common goal or good. In the OT, Abraham (Gen 18:16–33), Moses (Exod 32:7–14), and various prophets, priests, judges, and kings mediated between the people and God. Being both divine and human, Jesus Christ is, fully, and, finally, the Mediator, that is, the only ultimate Mediator between God and sinful humanity (1 Tim 2:5; Heb 8:6; 9:15; 12:24)—a central Christian belief thematized by Pius XII (pope 1939–1958) in such encyclicals as *Mystici Corporis* (1943) and *Mediator Dei* (1947) (see DH 1526, 3370, 3820; ND 712, 1215). See *Redeemer; Redemption; Salvation.*

Mediatrix. A title for Our Lady that originated in the East and for which the first certain documentary evidence comes from St. Andrew of Crete (d. 740). Being so close to her Son, Mary can intercede for her other children (John 19:26), an intercession that relies on her Son's infinite merits. Angels, saints, and human beings alive today also intercede for others (1 Tim 2:1), and, in their own way, mediate God's blessings. Such subordinate mediators are sometimes called mediators in a relative sense; relative, that is, to the merits of Jesus Christ (see DH 3320–21, 3370, 3916; ND 712). The *deesis* (Gr. "prayer"), a common iconographic composition at the center of the iconostasis, shows the Mother of God and St. John the Forerunner (as John the Baptist is frequently called in the East) interceding with Christ, who is portrayed as the Pantocrator. See *Guardian Angels; Iconostasis; Intercession; Mariology; Pantocrator; Veneration of Saints.*

Meditation (Lat. "reflection"). As opposed to vocal (spoken) prayer, mental prayer is an interior prayer that aims at union with God and so with oneself. Here mental refers to (a) the "discursive" character of reflecting point by point on themes from scripture or other texts; and (b) the integration of one's faculties of intellect, memory, and will. The exercise of step-by-step meditation should lead to the higher and simpler stage of contemplation. Eastern Christians highlight (b), calling interior prayer "the descending of the mind into the heart." See *Contemplation; Jesus Prayer.*

Melkites (more common today) or **Melchites** (Syrian "king"). Those Christians in the Byzantine Empire, especially in Egypt and Syria, who supported the emperor and orthodox faith against the Monophysites (= those who dissented from the Council of Chalcedon [451]). When Constantinople broke with Rome in 1054, the Melkites sided with Constantinople, but after 1724 a Melkite Church united with Rome came into being. Today Melkite most often refers to Catholics of the Byzantine rite who belong to the patriarchates of Alexandria, Antioch, and Jerusalem. See *Chalcedon, Council of; Eastern Churches; Monophysitism; Rite; Schism.*

Mercy. God's loving care for all creatures, especially human beings, which invites us, in turn, to empathize with and alleviate the misery of others. The OT employs three words for mercy: *Hesed* (Heb. "goodness") is faithful kindness founded on a bond or covenant, such as marriage (Gen 20:13) or on a close relationship (1 Sam 20:8, 14–15). *Rahamin* (Heb. "womb") is visceral sympathy or compassion, such as that of a mother for her child (Isa 49:15). *Hen* (Heb. "grace") expresses the way God's favor is bestowed gratuitously and independently of the recipient's merits (Exod 33:12–17). Human beings call for mercy, and God is more than willing to grant it (see Pss 51; 113; 117). The NT celebrates God's mercy (Luke 1:50, 54, 72, 78), revealed and expressed above all through Jesus' words and deeds (Matt 9:10–13; 18:21–35; Luke

10:29–37). The blind man's plea to Jesus for mercy (Mark 10:47–48) has become part of Christian prayer life, especially in the East. One should aim at imitating the heavenly Father in one's mercy, and, in turn, God will be merciful with those who exercise mercy (see Matt 6:12; 25:31–46; Luke 11:4). See *Grace; Hesed; Jesus Prayer; Love.*

Merit (Lat. "reward, recompense"). The goodness of some deed that entitles one to a reward. After Tertullian (ca. 160–ca. 220) introduced the term, medieval theologians distinguished between *meritum de condigno*, or merit based on a strict claim in justice, and our situation before God, *meritum de congruo*, where it is appropriate to reward good actions of the justified (or the not yet justified). Behind this teaching were many scriptural passages indicating that God rewards good deeds and punishes evil ones (Exod 23:20–22; Matt 5:3–12; 6:4; 19:21; 25:31–46; 1 Cor 3:8; Rev 22:12). At the same time, St. Augustine of Hippo (354–430) pointed out that any "claims" before God are based only on what God has previously given freely: "God does not crown your merits as your merits, but as his own gifts" (see DH 248, 388; ND 1914). The Council of Trent, with reference to Romans 11:6, taught that we cannot merit the initial grace of justification and the eternal reward accompanying it (DH 1532; ND 1935). Nevertheless justification through Christ's infinite merits brings an intrinsic change through which the justified can produce the fruits of the Spirit (Gal 5:22–23). The Reformation controversy over merit hardly touched the Eastern churches. Their liturgies not only pray to the angels and saints, but also for them, indicating that the grandeur of any creature is always due to God's mercy. See *Deification; Good Works; Grace; Imputation; Justification; Sanctification; Trent, Council of.*

Messalians (Syrian "praying people"). A sect found in the Middle East, Greece, and Egypt that was condemned at the Council of Ephesus (431). Messalians held that, through Adam's sin, a devil was united to every soul and could be expelled only by sustained prayer and asceticism. They argued that, since temptations continued after baptism by water, they needed constant prayer or "baptism by fire." Such prayer and asceticism would automatically bring a vision of the Trinity. In the ancient world, their emphasis on prayer led them to be called Euchites (Gr. "praying people"). The Jesuit scholar Irénée Hausherr (1891–1978) wrote of Messalianism as the "Pelagianism of the East," since it taught that sustained human effort was all that was needed to attain the highest spiritual gifts. Much of the sect's literature was apparently attributed to St. Macarius of Egypt (ca. 300– ca. 390). See *Asceticism; Experience, Religious; Pelagianism; Prayer.*

Messiah (Heb. "anointed one"). God's promised deliverer for a suffering people. The Hebrew adjective *mashiach* ("anointed") was used of an anointed king (1 Sam 10:1; 24:6; 2 Sam 2:4), priest (Lev 4:3, 5), and prophet (Isa

61:1–4), in all three cases, indicating a person invested by God with special powers and functions. Through Nathan's promise to David (2 Sam 7:12–16), other influences (Isa 9:6–7; Ezek 34:23–24; 37:24–25), and the messianic psalms (e.g., Pss 2; 45; 72; 89; 110), the Messiah (or in Greek "the Christ") eventually came to indicate the promised king from the line of David, who would finally deliver the people. The NT recognizes Jesus as the kingly Messiah now reigning in heaven (Acts 2:36; 5:31) and to come in power and glory (Acts 3:20–21). But he was already invested with such functions during his ministry (Luke 4:17–21; Mark 8:29) and even in his infancy (Luke 1:32–33; 2:11; Matt 1:23; 2:6). As a comprehensive designation for Jesus, his powers, and his identity, Messiah or Christ (John 1:41; 4:25–26) became so frequent that by the time of Paul's first letter it had already become a (second) proper name (1 Thess 1:1), as is usually the case today when people speak of "Jesus Christ." See *Anointing*; *Christological Titles*.

Metanoia (Gr. "change of mind"). The biblical term for that repentance or complete change of heart which turns one away from sin to serve the living God. OT prophets called for a conversion that would turn people away from idolatry and from a merely superficial practice of religion to live in fidelity to God's law and their social responsibilities (Isa 1:10–20; Ezek 18:1–32). John the Baptist and then Jesus preached a radical change of heart as demanded by the coming of God's kingdom (Matt 3:1–12; Mark 1:15). John's baptism was for repentance (Mark 1:4; Acts 13:24; 19:4). In the name of Jesus, the apostles invited people to be converted and baptized and so begin a new life in the Spirit (Acts 2:38). The gift of authentic metanoia (see Ps 51:14) is so special that whoever jeopardizes it by subsequent sin may lose it forever (see Heb 6:4–6). See *Conversion*; *Faith*; *Penance, Virtue of*.

Metaphysics (Gr. "after the physics"). The study of the ultimate causes and constituents of reality. In the order in which his works were edited, Aristotle's Metaphysics came after the Physics (which studied natural things subject to change, as opposed to the permanent and all-pervasive features of reality examined by metaphysics). Since René Descartes (1596–1650) and Immanuel Kant (1724–1804), the tradition of Aristotelian metaphysics has been modified by an awareness of the extent to which "objective" reality is constructed by the knowing subject. Joseph Maréchal (1878–1944), Karl Rahner (1904–84), and Bernard Lonergan (1904–84) developed a moderate realism that allows for the role of subjectivity. Classical metaphysics has been opposed by those who reject as meaningless any statements that are not empirically verifiable. However as that principle itself is empirically unverifiable, its challenge to classical metaphysics has had to be substantially modified. See *Analogy*; *Aristotelianism*; *Augustinianism*; *Causality*; *Philosophy*; *Positivism*; *Thomism*.

Metempsychosis. See *Reincarnation*.

Method, Theological (Gr. "on the way toward"; "pursuit of"). Way of examining, classifying, and coherently teaching Christian doctrines. Theology finds its subject matter in the divine revelation narrated, communicated, and interpreted by scripture and tradition (DV 24; OT 16). Method covers (a) one's presuppositions; (b) use of biblical and historical data; (c) approaches to questions of meaning and truth; (d) reflection on the ecclesial, social, and cultural context in which one operates as a theologian; (e) one's particular aim and audience; and (f) the degree of systematic generalization desired. In the East, proper recognition of the divine mystery is guaranteed by the method of apophatic theology. The centrality of the liturgy accounts for the doxological character of Eastern theology. See *Analogy*; *Analogy of Faith*; *Apophatic Theology*; *Deposit of Faith*; *Dogmatic Theology*; *Doxology*; *Exegesis*; *Feminist Theology*; *Fundamental Theology*; *Hermeneutics*; *Kerygmatic Theology*; *Liberation Theology*; *Locus Theologicus*; *Mystery*; *Negative Theology*; *Orthopraxis*; *Political Theology*; *Theology, Methods in*; *Tradition*.

Methodism (Gr. "following a way"). That form of Christian practice that started as a revival movement in Great Britain under the leadership of John Wesley (1703–93) and his brother Charles (1707–88). It led to the establishment in 1784 of free associations (later churches), independent from the episcopal structure of the Church of England, but in communion among themselves and now members of the World Federation of Methodist Churches. Methodism imitated German Pietism and has cherished the conversion experience of the Wesley brothers in preferring a theology of the heart over a rigid and rationalist orthodoxy. Methodists stress evangelism, the priesthood of all the faithful, and social welfare. Their theology has tended to be largely Arminian; that is, it favors the anti-Calvinistic teaching of the Dutch Reformed theologian Jacob Arminius (1560–1609), who taught that Christ did not die just for the predestined few but for all, and that God's sovereign freedom does not exclude true freedom in human beings. Geoffrey Wainwright (b.1939) is a prominent Methodist theologian today. See *Calvinism*; *Evangelization*; *Protestant*.

Middle Knowledge. See *Scientia Media*.

Midrash (Heb. "investigation, research"). A method of Jewish exegesis developed after the return from the Babylonian Captivity. It aimed to edify by eliciting from a scriptural text associations and applications that went beyond its literal meaning. The Jews distinguished two kinds of midrash: *midrash halachah* (Heb. "conduct"), which was concerned with the oral law; and *midrash haggadah* (Heb. "narrative"), which aimed to elucidate nonlegal sections of the Bible. See *Exegesis*; *Haggadah*.

Migne. The summary title for the publications of Jacques Paul Migne (1800–75), who after nine years as a parish priest in the country, moved to

Paris and edited an immense number of theological texts. His main work was the *Patrologia Cursus Completus*. The 217 volumes of its *Patrologia Latina* (PL) include all Latin ecclesiastical authors up to Pope Innocent III (1160–1216). The 161 volumes of the *Patrologia Graeca* (PG) include the Greek writers (with a Latin translation) up to 1439. Where recent and more critical editions are not available, Migne's patrology is invaluable and remains a standard work of reference. See *Patrology*.

Millenarianism (Lat. "thousand"). The belief, influenced by apocalyptic writings and based on a literalistic interpretation of Revelation 20:1–7, that Christ will reign on earth for a thousand years with his saints until the final defeat of Satan and a definitive entry in glory. In the early centuries, even some mainline Christians such as St. Justin Martyr (ca. 100–ca. 165) and St. Irenaeus of Lyons (ca. 130–ca. 200) accepted this belief. After St. Augustine of Hippo (354–430), only some sectarian groups (e.g., around the year AD 1000) have at times revived Millenarianism. See *Chiliasm*; *Eschatology*; *Fundamentalism*; *Jehovah's Witnesses*.

Minister (Lat. "servant"). A person authorized to exercise spiritual functions in the church. A term for the clergy in nonepiscopal communities, it is increasingly used in the Catholic Church. Sacred ministers are clerics ordained to administer the sacraments (CIC 276; CCEO 369). Ministers of the word (see Acts 6:4; Col 1:23) preach the gospel, a responsibility not only of the pope and bishops (CIC 756), but also of priests, deacons, and others commissioned to preach and teach (CIC 757–61; CCEO 608). Ordinary ministers of holy communion are bishops, priests, and deacons; extraordinary ministers of communion are those laypersons commissioned to do so (CIC 910). In case of necessity, laypersons may be authorized to minister by baptizing, distributing communion, preaching, and presiding at the Liturgy of the Word (CIC 230). See *Bishop*; *Celebrant*; *Clergy*; *Cleric*; *Deacon*; *Laity*; *Priests*.

Ministry. A sharing in Christ's roles as prophet, priest, and king. All the faithful participate in these functions in virtue of their baptism and confirmation, clerics in a particular way through the sacrament of orders (see DH 1326; ND 1705; PO 1; AA 10). Particular and special gifts should be exercised through ministries that help the whole church (Rom 12:6–8; 1 Cor 12:1–31; 1 Pet 4:10–11). See *Charisms*; *Holy Orders*; *Ordination*.

Miracle. An event caused by a special divine action that does not follow the normal laws of nature and carries a religious message for people now and later. Far from being mere astonishing prodigies, miracles are saving and revealing signs from God (John 2:11, 18, 23; 12:18, 37). The Synoptic Gospels (Matt 4:23; 8:5–17; 11:5, 21; Mark 8:22–26; Luke 13:32) and Acts (e.g., Acts 2:22) witness to Jesus' miracles, which were tied in with his powerful proclamation of God's final kingdom. Acts reports various miraculous deeds of Peter and Paul. Without going into detail, Paul testifies to the same gift from God (Rom 15:19; 2 Cor 12:12). Miracles are normally required for the beatification and canonization of servants of God. See *Determinism*; *Doxa*; *Johannine Theology*; *Kingdom of God*; *Nature*; *Signs*.

Mishnah (Heb. "repetition"). Jewish collection of tractates interpreting and teaching scripture and Law. This work was probably compiled by Rabbi Judah ha-Nasi (ca. 135–ca. 220) and served as the basis for both the Palestinian and the Babylonian versions of the Talmud. The Mishnah still determines how a pious Jew ought to behave in many circumstances. See *Judaism*; *Talmud*.

Missio Canonica. Official authorization to participate in some way in the church's teaching, sanctifying, and pastoral ministry to the world. See *Cleric*; *Deacon*; *Lateran Council, Fourth*; *Mandate*; *Preaching*.

Mission, Theology of. Systematic reflection on the way that the whole church and individual Christians are sent by Christ. For all his courage and nobility, St. Francis Xavier (1506–52) imposed Latin customs on the Malabar coast, whereas a later Jesuit, Fr. Robert de Nobili (1577–1656), embraced Indian customs. In China, another Jesuit missionary, Matteo Ricci (1552–1610), adapted Christian ceremonies to the local culture, which gave rise to a violent controversy over "the Chinese rites." Clement XI (pope 1700–21) condemned such adaptations, and Benedict XIV (pope 1740–58) even required missionaries to take an oath against them. In 1939 Pius XII (pope 1939–1958) abolished this oath and rehabilitated the Jesuit missionaries. In the twentieth century, four papal encyclicals expressed changed views about missionary activity: Benedict XV's *Maximum Illud* (1919), Pius XI's *Rerum Ecclesiae* (1926), Pius XII's *Evangelii Praecones* (1951), and Blessed John XXIII's *Princeps Pastorum* (1959). While confirming the church's commitment to spread the gospel everywhere, these popes indicated the need to build up the local churches (Benedict XV), to develop an indigenous clergy (Pius XI), to encourage the laity in renewing the social fabric (Pius XII), and to adapt to the local culture (Blessed John XXIII). Vatican II (1962–65) saw the church's mission to be rooted in Christ's sending the apostles just as he himself had been sent by the Father (LG 17). By its very nature, the church is on mission to the whole world (AG 2, 10). In the past, some missionary activity suffered from the scandal of Christian divisions; tolerated much political, economic, racial, and cultural injustice; and could be partly a form of spiritual colonialism. Almost all mission theology today recognizes that integral development and liberation belong to the full missionary task of the church. For Catholics, Pope Paul VI's *Evangelii Nuntiandi* (1975) offers excellent guidelines on the nature of evangelization in the modern world. See *Anonymous Christians*; *Inculturation*; *Local Church*; *Proselytes*; *St Thomas Christians*.

Missions, Church. The church's response to being sent by Christ to continue his work for the whole world. All such Christian activity, and not merely "foreign" missionary work, is rightly characterized as mission. The prophetic books of the OT indicate that Jerusalem and the chosen people have a missionary role for the salvation of the nations (see Isa 2:2–5; 42:6–7; 49:6, 22–23; 56:1–8; 60:1–22; Jonah). Of universal significance (Luke 2:29–32), the good news of Christ is to be preached everywhere and to everyone (Matt 28:18–20; Mark 16:15–20; Luke 24:47; John 20:21; Acts 1:8). Led by Peter, Paul, and others (Gal 2:7–8; Rom 1:5; 16:3), the apostolic church spread the Christian faith through the Roman Empire. In the early centuries, Christianity reached Abyssinia, India, and (through the Nestorian or Assyrian Church of the East) even China. Great missionaries and their followers, at times supported by powerful rulers, had converted almost all Europe to Christianity by the year 1000. St. Patrick (ca. 390–ca. 460) helped to evangelize Ireland; St. Augustine of Canterbury (d. 604), England; St. Boniface (680–754), Germany; St. Anskar (801–65), the Scandinavian countries; and Sts. Cyril (826–69) and Methodius (ca. 805–85), the Slavic countries. With the discovery of America in 1492 and the opening up of new routes to Asia, a heroic missionary activity began in the Americas, China, India, Japan, and elsewhere. The foundation of the Congregation for the Propagation of the Faith by Pope Gregory XV in 1622 encouraged and helped to organize this development. From the early nineteenth century, Anglican and Protestant missionary societies, led and inspired by figures such as David Livingstone (1813–73), became very active outside Europe. In the late twentieth century, the need for Europe itself to be re-evangelized became more and more apparent as well as the need to develop a mission policy that is less Europe-centered than has been the case. See *Apostle*; *Church of the East (Assyrian)*; *Evangelization*.

Missions, Divine. The sending (or "procession") of the second and third persons of the Trinity by the Father in eternity and time (see John 14:26; 20:21; Gal 4:4–6). See *Appropriation*; *Filioque*; *Processions*; *Trinity, Theology of*.

Miter. A tall, cleft headdress worn by bishops when carrying their crozier or pastoral staff during processions and the liturgy, although never during the eucharistic prayer. This symbol of episcopal authority goes back to eleventh-century Rome. In the East, the Byzantine miter, which the ecumenical patriarch, and, subsequently, all bishops, borrowed from the emperor's crown, is worn only when fully vested. After the Great Entrance, when the eucharistic prayer begins, the bishop doffs his miter and dons it again for the final blessing. In the West, cardinals, abbots, and sometimes monsignors wear a miter, as do archimandrites or archpriests in the East. See *Anaphora*; *Archimandrite*; *Bishop*; *Byzantine Christianity*; *Canon*; *Cardinal*; *Cathedra*; *Entrances*; *Eucharistic Prayer*; *Patriarch, Ecumenical*; *Tiara, Papal*.

Modalism (Lat. "aspect, facet"). The heresy that so stressed the divine unity as to assert that Father, Son, and Spirit are only distinctions made by the human mind and are not personally distinct. They are merely manifestations or ways in which the one God is revealed and acts in creation and redemption. Starting in Asia Minor with Noetus (ca. 200), the heresy was propagated in the West by Praxeas (ca. 200), Sabellius (early third century), Photinus (fourth century), and, to a certain degree, by Marcellus of Ancyra (Ankara) (d. ca. 374) (see DH 151, 284; ND 13). See *Patripassianism*; *Trinity, Theology of*.

Modernism. An umbrella term for a rather diffuse Catholic theological movement of the late nineteenth and early twentieth centuries, found in England, France, Italy, and, to some extent, Germany. Among its main representatives were Alfred Loisy (1857–1940), George Tyrrell (1861–1909), and, perhaps, Baron Friedrich von Hügel (1852–1925). Modernists endorsed contemporary biblical criticism, accepted historical developments in Christianity, strongly opposed Neo-Scholasticism, and were thoroughly receptive to progress in science and philosophy. At times they went astray, for example, by overemphasizing religious experience and reducing the value of common statements of faith. In 1907 through the decree *Lamentabili* and the encyclical *Pascendi,* the Holy See condemned modernism in a way that failed to make careful distinctions. There was a subsequent campaign against those suspected of modernist tendencies. Pius XII's 1943 encyclical on biblical criticism (*Divino Afflante Spiritu*), the Second Vatican Council, and later developments in church teaching and theology have vindicated some, but not all, of the concerns and insights of the modernists. See *Biblical Criticism*; *Development of Doctrine*; *Doctrine*; *Experience, Religious*; *Immanence, Divine*; *Neo-Scholasticism*.

Molinism. The doctrine developed by the Spanish Jesuit Louis de Molina (1535–1600) about the relationship between free will and grace. God gives grace, arranges circumstances to bring about the proper result, and foresees our future actions. But since this foresight "depends" upon our free decisions, Molina called it *scientia conditionata* or *scientia media*: knowledge relative to future human decisions and actions. This system was opposed by the Dominicans, especially by Domingo Bañez (1528–1604). In emphasizing God's sovereign freedom, Bañez spoke of the divine concurrence in human action as *praemotio physica* (Lat. "physical pre-motion"), an idea that does not seem to do full justice to human freedom. Between 1598 and 1607, a commission, De Auxiliis, met in Rome but failed to resolve the issue. It ended by forbidding Jesuits to brand the Dominicans Calvinists and the Dominicans to call Jesuits Pelagians (see DH 1997, 2008). This debate indicates that the deepest theological questions cannot finally be answered adequately. The divine mystery has the first and the last word. See *Calvinism*; *Foreknowledge*; *Freedom*; *Grace*; *Mystery*; *Negative Theology*; *Pelagianism*; *Scientia Media*; *Semi-Pelagianism*.

Monarchianism (Gr. "of one principle"). A term coined by Tertullian (ca. 160–ca. 220) for the heretical belief that so stressed the unity of God as to deny a truly divine Son with a distinct personal existence. Some Monarchians held that Jesus was divine only in the sense of God's *dynamis* (Gr. "power") coming upon him and adopting him. Modalist Monarchians reduced the Trinity to the different ways in which God is manifested and acts. See *Adoptionism*; *Modalism*; *Patripassianism*; *Trinity, Theology of.*

Monastery. See *Convent.*

Monasticism (Gr. "life alone"). A movement among baptized believers who respond to Christ's call for perfection (Matt 5:48; 19:16–26) by giving themselves through poverty, celibacy, and obedience to a life of prayer, common worship, and service. Toward the end of the third century, numerous Christians went into the Egyptian desert in search of perfection. When the Roman persecution ceased in the early fourth century, many came to see in monasticism a "bloodless martyrdom" or alternative to martyrdom. Syrian anachoretism, located in Mesopotamia, was roughly contemporaneous with its Egyptian counterpart, while in some ways more advanced. Two Copts helped create monasticism: St. Antony the Abbot (ca. 251–356), who wrote no rule, and St. Pachomius (ca. 290–346), to whom the first (cenobitic) rule was attributed. Attracting many followers, Antony and Pachomius helped organize them, by means of spiritual direction, into the two standard forms of monasticism: anachoretism, or the life of hermits (and semi-hermits), and cenobitism, or life in common. Deeply influenced by St. Basil the Great (ca. 330–79), who wrote a rule, Eastern monasticism helped to promote Western monasticism through such writings as the *Life of St. Antony* by St. Athanasius of Alexandria (ca. 296–373) and the *Conferences* of St. John Cassian (ca. 360–435). After St. Martin of Tours (d. 397) and St. Augustine of Hippo (354–430), St. Benedict of Nursia (ca. 480–ca. 550) and his rule essentially shaped the future of monasticism in the West. Dominicans, Franciscans, and other active religious orders have offered an alternative to a strictly contemplative monastic life (see UR 15; PC 9). In the East, however, religious are mainly monks, although Latin influence has encouraged some Western type congregations. See *Acoemetae*; *Anachoretism*; *Athos, Mount*; *Cenobites*; *Hesychasm*; *Liturgy of the Hours*; *Religious Life.*

Monism (Gr. "one"). A term coined by Christian Wolff (1679–1754) for all attempts to interpret reality by eliminating diversity and distinctions (e.g., between body and soul or between the visible created world and the invisible God) and reducing everything to a single principle. This solipsism allows only for the existence of oneself and denies the ideas, experiences, and existence of other subjects. Or else the difference between mind and matter is denied by asserting that everything is only a modality of mind (idealism) or of matter (materialism). Pantheism rejects any real distinction between God and the created world. Greek philosophers prior to Socrates tended to interpret all reality through one primordial principle; for example, Thales of Miletus (ca. 624–ca. 545 BC) considered water to be the primeval stuff of the universe. Other monists include Plotinus (ca. 205–70), Benedict Spinoza (1632–77), and idealist philosophers such as Johann Gottlieb Fichte (1762–1814) who reduced everything to the "I." Both the OT (see Gen 1—3; Job 38:1—40:5) and the NT (see John 1:18; Rom 11:33–35) indicate the radical differences between God and creatures. Catholic teaching has insisted on this fundamental dualism (see DH 3022–23; ND 329–30), as does the Protestant theme of the Deus *totaliter aliter* (Lat. "God as completely other") and Orthodoxy's apophaticism (Gr. "negative theology"). See *Apophatic Theology*; *Deification*; *Dualism*; *Essence and Energies*; *Idealism*; *Materialism*; *Pantheism*.

Monoenergism (Gr. "sole activity"). A seventh-century attempt to reconcile the so-called Monophysites with the teaching accepted by the Council of Chalcedon (451) and developed by Constantinople II (553). According to the compromise formula of monoenergism, proposed by Patriarch Sergius of Constantinople in 633 and supported by Patriarch Cyrus of Alexandria, there are two natures but only one form of activity in Jesus Christ after the Incarnation. That activity, the "theandric" activity, stems from the one person of Christ, the Incarnate Word, and not from the natures. Through the opposition of the monk St. Sophronius (ca. 560–638), who became Patriarch of Jerusalem in 634, monoenergism was abandoned. See *Chalcedon, Council of*; *Constantinople, Second Council of*; *Essence and Energies*; *Monophysitism*; *Monotheletism*.

Monogamy (Gr. "one marriage"). The ideal of being married to only one person (see Matt 5:31–32; 19:1–9; Mark 10:2–12; Luke 16:18). Many societies have allowed polygamy (Gr. "many marriages"), or the practice of having more than one wife either simultaneously or successively. Some societies have accepted polyandry (Gr. "many husbands"), the practice of a woman having more than one husband. The OT patriarchs were initially polygamous, while the Law of Moses allowed for divorce and remarriage. Christ ascribed this custom to the "hardness" of the human heart and aimed at restoring God's initial monogamous plan for marriage. In the Catholic Church, a previous valid marriage rules out a second marriage so long as the other partner is still alive (see DH 777–79, 1798, 1802, 3706–9; ND 1805, 1809, 1828–29). See *Marriage*; *Marriage Impediments*; *Polygamy*.

Monophysitism (Gr. "one nature"). The heresy attributed to those who refused to accept the teaching of the Council of Chalcedon (451) that in Christ there is "one person in two natures" (DH 300–303; ND 613–16) and who broke away from the patriarchates of Constantinople and Rome. None of the parties, however, clearly defended a full-blown version of Monophysitism: namely, that the Incarnation meant either the fusion of Christ's divinity and humanity into a third "nature" or the absorption of his human nature into his divine nature like a drop into an ocean. The difference over Chalcedon seems to have been partly terminological; some experts attribute the origin of real monophysitism to Apollinarius (ca. 310–ca. 390). Among the dissidents, Timothy Aerulus (d. 477) became the Monophysite patriarch of Alexandria; and Peter the Fuller (d. 488), patriarch of Antioch. Monophysite churches were eventually organized by Severus of Antioch (ca. 465–538), deposed from being patriarch of Antioch in 518. The Monophysite churches are now generally called Oriental Orthodox. See *Apollinarianism*; *Chalcedon, Council of*; *Constantinople, Second Council of*; *Coptic Christianity*; *Ethiopian Christianity*; *Eutychianism*; *Hypostatic Union*; *Oriental Orthodox*.

Monotheism (Gr. "one God"). The belief in one (and only one), personal, all-powerful, all-knowing, and all-loving God, who is the creator and Lord of everyone and everything, and, yet, exists distinct from and beyond the whole universe. Initially Israel may have worshiped only one God and practiced only monolatry (Gr. "worship of one God") without necessarily denying the existence of (lesser) heathen deities. By the sixth century, however, Israel's monotheism clearly entailed rejecting the reality of any other gods (Isa 43:10–13; 44:8). The NT revelation that in the one God there are three persons is not opposed to genuine monotheism. Judaism and Islam, however, reject belief in the Trinity as incompatible with their monotheistic faith. In the field of comparative religion, some have argued either that monotheism evolved from an earlier polytheism (belief in many gods) or that a primitive, pure monotheism often lapsed into later polytheism. However, the actual development of various religions does not seem to correspond easily and clearly to either of these master theories. See *God*; *Islam*; *Judaism*; *Mystery*; *Pantheism*; *Polytheism*; *Revelation*; *Transcendence*; *Trinity, Theology of*; *Tritheism*.

Monotheletism (Gr. "one will"). The heresy that maintained that Christ, while having a human nature, lacked a human will and possessed only one (divine) will. After the Council of Chalcedon (451) taught the personal unity but duality of natures in Christ, various attempts were made to reconcile the Monophysite dissidents, who stressed the unity of Christ. A compromise notion of two natures but only one "energy" (i.e., monoenergism) was proposed by Sergius of Constantinople (patriarch 610–38) and then withdrawn by him, since talking of one or two energies was likely to confuse the faithful. Misunderstanding the fundamental issues, Honorius I (pope 625–38) proposed talking of "two natures but only one will" in Christ, a formula for which Honorius was later censured (DH 487–88; 496–98). The *Ekthesis* (Gr. "exposition of faith") promulgated by Emperor Heraclius in 638 endorsed the one-(divine)-will formula. In 638 and 639. synods held in Constantinople upheld this formula, but the Lateran Synod of 649, held under Pope St. Martin I and led by St. Maximus the Confessor, condemned it as incompatible with the full humanity of Christ. On the principle of one will/one nature, the sixth ecumenical council, Constantinople III (680/81), solemnly defined that in Christ there are not only two natures, but also two wills, which, nonetheless, operate harmoniously in his one person (see DH 550–64; ND 635–37). See *Chalcedon, Council of*; *Constantinople, Third Council of*; *Dyotheletism*; *Monoenergism*; *Monophysitism*.

Montanism. An enthusiastic revival movement initiated by Montanus, a converted pagan priest, in second-century Phrygia (in modern-day Turkey), that won many adherents, including even Tertullian (ca. 160–ca. 220). Announcing the consummation of the world, Montanus saw the activities of ecstatic prophets and prophetesses (such as his associates, Priscilla and Maximilla) as signs of the end. Ascetic in its demands, the movement forbade remarriage after the death of one's partner and imposed severe rules of fasting. Montanus came to regard himself as the Incarnation of the Holy Spirit. The movement's contempt for institutional structures, expressed by its freelance way of administering the sacraments, met with church condemnation (see DH 211, 478). See *Parousia*.

Moral Development. Growth in awareness of one's responsibilities and a corresponding maturation in personal freedom. Official church teaching spoke of children reaching "the age of reason" at around seven years of age and beginning then to act as responsible human beings. Modern psychology, however, has illustrated that children often behave under constraint and only slowly interiorize moral principles to start acting freely as responsible persons. Christian communities should foster conditions that encourage development toward moral responsibility in full freedom. See *Faith Development*; *Moral Theology*.

Moral Theology. That field of theology which studies and teaches how Christians (and others) ought to live. This systematic reflection on Christian conduct draws from the Bible (e.g., the Decalogue, the Sermon on the Mount, and the parenesis of Paul), philosophical reason, the traditional teaching of the church, and human experience. It should be based on a full vision of what is entailed by the original creation (Gen 1:26–27) and the refashioning of humanity in Christ (Rom 6:4; 8:28–30; 1 Cor 15:49; 2 Cor 5:17; Eph 4:24; Col 3:10). After St. Thomas Aquinas (ca. 1225–74), moral theology often became isolated from its dogmatic and scriptural roots, and at times a healthy casuistry lapsed into empty legalism. The moral teaching of St. Alphonsus Liguori (1696–1787) was marked by great learning and deep pastoral concern. Johannes Baptist Hirscher (1788–1865) of Tübingen systematically presented morality in terms of the kingdom of God. By the late-twentieth-century, biblical studies, the human sciences, philosophical developments, and, most of all, a renewal in Christology, ecclesiology, and anthropology have challenged and enriched moral theology. Since Leo XIII (pope 1878–1903), papal teaching has more and more encouraged moral theologians not only to study questions of individual morality, but also to take up wider questions of social justice, church-state relations, and international peace. Vatican II's pastoral Constitution on the Church in the Modern World, *Gaudium et Spes* (1965), constituted the first far-reaching and fairly complete official document on the moral life of Christians and, for that matter, of all human beings. Pope John Paul II's 1993 encyclical *Veritatis Splendor* ("the Splendor of the Truth") was the first detailed presentation of fundamental moral principles made by the official magisterium. Eastern moral theology highlights our "life in Christ," for which dogma is reflected spirituality and spirituality lived dogma. Moral issues concerning faith are solved by *akribeia* (Gr. "exactness") and those concerning pastoral practice by *oikonomia* (Gr. "management"). See *Anthropology*; *Casuistry*; *Church and State*; *Decalogue*; *Ethics*; *Fundamental Option*; *Holiness*; *Jansenism*; *Justice*; *Magisterium*; *Parenesis*; *Perfection*; *Probabilism*; *Rigorism*; *Social Teaching*; *Tübingen and Its Schools*.

Mormonism. The teaching of the Church of Jesus Christ of Latter-Day Saints, founded in New York State by Joseph Smith (1805–44) in 1830. *The Book of Mormon*, which he claimed to have discovered through revelation, tells of a prophet Mormon and of Jewish refugees—in a story that runs from the time of the Tower of Babel until the establishment of Mormonism in the United States. An 1843 revelation led Smith to endorse polygamy. When he was murdered, Brigham Young (1801–77) established the sect in the desert, where they founded Salt Lake City, Utah. Mormons expect Christ to return and establish a kingdom on earth for his saints. See *Millenarianism*; *Polygamy*.

Morning Prayer. See *Lauds*.

Mortal Sin. See *Sin*.

Mortification (Lat. "putting to death"). The discipline and self-denial required for growth in the new life given through faith and baptism (Rom 8:13; Gal 5:24). Jesus stressed the cost of discipleship (Matt 10:34–39). Paul describes vividly the struggle with sin and deadly forces that faces those who live with God in Christ (Rom 5:1–19). See *Asceticism*; *Cross*; *Fasting*.

Motu Proprio (Lat. "of one's own accord"). A personal letter written by the pope to the whole church, a local church, or some particular group. When Blessed John XXIII (pope 1958–63) set up a commission to prepare for Vatican II, he sent out a *motu proprio* (*Acta Apostolicae Sedis* 52 [1962], 433–37). If an episcopal conference wishes to enact laws for its territory, it should request from the Holy See a special mandate unless the pope grants it by a *motu proprio*. See *Episcopal Conference*; *Holy See*.

Muratorian Fragment. Probably the oldest list of NT books, named after Ludovico Antonio Muratori (1672–1750), priest, librarian, and archivist, who discovered it in the Ambrosian Library (Milan) and published it in 1740. Mutilated at the beginning and at the end, this eighty-five-line Latin manuscript generally has been dated to the end of the second century AD and has been considered to have come from Rome. Five books, later officially recognized as part of the NT (Hebrews, James, 1 and 2 Peter, and 3 John), are missing from the list. See *Canon of Scripture*; *Marcionism*.

Muslim. Adherent of Islam. See *Islam*.

Myron. See *Chrism*.

Mystagogy (Gr. "leading to the secrets"). Instruction into the secret rites and mysteries of a religion. In his mystagogical Catecheses given during Lent and Eastertide, St. Cyril of Jerusalem (ca. 315–86) prepared catechumens for baptism on Holy Saturday and further instructed them afterward. St. Maximus the Confessor (ca. 580–662) called his mystical interpretation of the liturgy mystagogy. Currently some use the term for a catechesis and theology drawn from and aimed at promoting a deeper experience of God. Karl Rahner (1904–84) argued that the basic theological courses, while distinct from mystagogy, must be close to it and illuminate the personal experience of grace. See *Catechesis*; *Catechumenate*; *Disciplina Arcani*; *Experience, Religious*; *Mystery*; *RCIA*.

Mystery (Gr. "secret"). Not a merely obscure or inexplicable matter, but God's loving plan for human salvation now disclosed through Christ (Rom 16:25; Eph 1:9; 3:9; Col 1:26–27; 2:2; 4:3). While definitively revealed in Christ, the mysterious reality of God transcends human reason and comprehension. It is not the human mind that grasps God; the divine majesty grasps us. Protestant theology has followed Luther's theme of Deus *revelatus sed absconditus* (Lat. "God revealed but still hidden"). Orthodoxy has cultivated its apophatic theology, which stresses the divine inaccessibility. In the nineteenth century, the First Vatican Council (1869–70) (DH 3015–20; ND 131–36), Matthias Scheeben (1835–88), and others spoke of the revealed mysteries or truths (in the plural) about God. Recent theology and official teaching have stressed the unity of God's self-revelation. Karl Rahner (1904–84), the Second Vatican Council (1962–65), and encyclicals by John Paul II (pope 1978–2005) favor the language of the "mystery" rather than the divine "mysteries." For Rahner, there is ultimately only one mystery: that of the tripersonal God who through Christ's saving work and the mission of the Spirit invites us to share the divine life. See *Apophatic Theology*; *Deification*; *Mystagogy*; *Paschal Mystery*; *Salvation History*.

Mystery Religions. Religions of Greek origin (such as Orphism) or of Oriental origin (such as Mithraism) in which rites were often secret and reserved for the initiates. Unlike Judaism and Christianity, which are based on God's involvement in human history, these religions were based on a mythic interpretation of natural phenomena such as the seasons, vegetation, and, especially, fertility. Key roles were assigned to female and male deities, whose heroic deeds were celebrated in such cultic acts as a bath of purification or a sacrificial meal—acts that superficially resembled Christian sacraments. The mystery religions were much in vogue from the first century BC to the fourth century AD. See *History of Religions School*; *Mystery*; *Myth*; *Religion*.

Mystical Body of Christ. See *Body of Christ*.

Mysticism. A special, deep experience of union with and knowledge of the divine reality, freely granted by God. Mystical experiences, which may be accompanied by ecstasy, visions, and other such phenomena, are usually preceded by the serious practice of contemplation and asceticism. While found in all the great world religions, mysticism in Christian experience has a highly personal quality, enhancing rather than suppressing the sense of distinction between the mystic and God. Genuine mysticism always produces more generous love toward others and seems to be found frequently among Christians who are dedicated to prayer and sensitive to God's presence in their lives. Joseph Maréchal (1878–1944), Evelyn Underhill (1875–1941), and other modern authors have encouraged a renewed interest in mysticism. See *Contemplation*; *Mystery*; *Visions*.

Myth (Gr. "fable," "story"). A symbolic story about ultimate realities. Myth has often been understood to be a story about purely fictitious persons, events, and things. While *logos* offers a rational and true account of reality and its causes, an imaginative *mythos* (e.g., about the scandalous activities of gods) may be entertaining but is essentially false. The NT also reflects this negative view of the term *myth* (1 Tim 1:4; 4:7; Titus 1:14; 2 Pet 1:16). The human mind, however, does not operate on the basis of abstract concepts alone. It needs symbolic-imaginative language to find and express the truth about our existence. In his *Dialogues*, Plato (427–347 BC), at times, skillfully uses myths to guide his reader toward the truth. See *Analogy*; *Demythologization*; *Narrative Theology*; *Symbol*.

N

Narrative Theology. A modern attempt to renew Christian theology as the theology of a historical religion that not only has something to say, but also a story to tell. Breaking away from abstract doctrinal statements, narrative theology finds its home in biblical and other religious stories. While usefully correcting tendencies to cut theology off from life and worship, narrative theology needs critical criteria to establish meaning and truth. Among Eastern Christians, the narrative element in theology is safeguarded by the liturgy and icons. See *Icon*; *Liturgy*; *Theology*.

Nativity. See *Christmas*.

Natural Law. The universal, moral law given by God in the very act of creating human beings and open to being known by the light of reason (see GS 79, DHu 2). Pagan literature, as in the Antigone passage of Sophocles (ca. 497–406 BC); the Western legal tradition; the Bible (e.g., Rom 2:14–15); and other voices witness to the natural law, which points to the right way of acting freely and responsibly as a human being. Sin makes it harder to discern and obey the natural law (see Matt 19:1–9), the main principles of which are enumerated in the Decalogue. In the light of the natural law alone, it is often difficult to reach moral certainty on specific issues in areas such as international relations, social justice, and sexual behavior. Since it seems to suggest structures independent of God, Eastern Christians tend to distrust talk of natural law and insist on the union between morality and spirituality. See *Decalogue*; *Eastern Churches*; *Freedom*; *Law*; *Moral Theology*; *Sin*.

Natural Theology. The discipline dealing with the knowledge of God available through reason alone (see Ps 19:1–4; Wis 13:1–9; Acts 14:17; 17:22–31; Rom 1:18–23; 2:14–15). Developed by St. Thomas Aquinas (ca. 1225–74), natural theology was challenged from the time of the Enlightenment, when the validity of the arguments for God's existence came under fire. The First Vatican Council (1869–70) taught that "from the things that were created, God can be known with certainty through the natural light of human reason" (DH 3004; ND 113; see DV 6). The council affirmed a possibility ("can be known"), but did not indicate ways of knowing God (by logical proofs? intuition? mystical experience?). It did not claim that anyone had ever actualized this possibility without the hidden help of grace. Karl Barth (1886–1968) and other exponents of dialectical theology, arguing that sin has made human reason by itself simply incapable of knowing God, vigorously excluded any kind of natural theology. Mostly natural theology has been practiced by Christian believers, such as William Paley (1743–1805). Even if they stand aside from what they know through revelation, nevertheless, they can raise questions about God only because they are already familiar with the answers. Finally, a purely natural-theology approach presents an abstract, philosophical view of humanity— quite different from the concrete view of sinful humanity found in salvation-history theologies. The Second Vatican Council (1962–65) set the knowledge of God through creation (and, hence, natural theology) within the context of the history of revelation and salvation (DV 2–6, 14–17). In recent years, Alister McGrath (b. 1953) and others continue to endorse the practice of natural theology. See *Arguments for the Existence of God; Dialectical Theology; Enlightenment; Five Ways, The; Salvation History; Theodicy; Theology.*

Nature (Lat. "that which is born"). The entire cosmos, which is good because it is created by God (Gen 1–2), or else something acting according to its own essential characteristics. In the latter sense, Christian doctrine refers to the one nature of God and the two natures (divine and human) in Christ. Catholic theology has distinguished grace (or what comes to us through God's redeeming activity in Christ) from nature (that which belongs to human beings as human beings). A classical axiom states that grace does not destroy, but presupposes, elevates, and perfects nature. Here it is important to recall that a purely natural order is an abstraction. The order of grace has existed right from the beginning, in that God has freely called all men and women to the supernatural destiny of eternal life. Calvinists and some other Protestants have pessimistically stressed the way sin has thoroughly corrupted human nature (see DH 1521, 1555; ND 1925, 1955; GS 13). See *Concupiscence; Cosmos; Creation; Creature; Depravity, Total; Ecology, Human; Entelechy; Grace; Original Sin; Potentia Oboedientialis; Supernatural.*

Negative Theology. Like apophatic theology, an approach to the divine mystery that insists that we can say more about what God is not than about what God is. It is a way of doing theology that may put more stress on *sapientia* (Lat. "wisdom") than *scientia* (Lat. "science"). The Orthodox theologian Vladimir Lossky (1903–58) criticized Western negative theology for seeking a compromise between faith and reason instead of accepting antinomies or seeming contradictions between beliefs. What may not be resolved at the level of ideas may find its solution at the personal level of self-purification. See *Apophatic Theology; Cataphatic Theology; Mystery; Theology; Wisdom Literature.*

Neocatechumenate. A post–Vatican II itinerary of Christian initiation, started by Kiko Arguello (b. 1939) and Carmen Hernández, which aimed at helping baptized Christians to discover or rediscover what faith and baptism involve. This "way" of formation for the baptized, which follows the structures of the catechumenate in the early church, reinitiates believers into their Christian life and aims either at reevangelizing traditionally Christian countries or at helping to root the gospel more deeply in recently evangelized areas. There are now 40,000 parish-based communities of between twenty to fifty persons, making in all an estimated one million members. Laypersons, priests, and families, formed through the neocatechumenate, go out as itinerant missionaries to all parts of the world. In 1987 a large diocesan seminary (*Redemptoris Mater*) was opened in Rome for members of the neocatechumenal "way" who have a priestly vocation. There are now seventy-five such missionary seminaries in all five continents. See *Baptism; Catechumenate; RCIA.*

Neo-Chalcedonianism. A term coined by Joseph Lebon (1879–1957) for the attempt to mediate between the defenders of the Council of Chalcedon (451), which taught that there are two natures in the one person of Jesus Christ, and the so-called Monophysites, who maintained the pre-Chalcedonian formula of St. Cyril of Alexandria (d. 444), "the one Incarnate nature of Jesus Christ." The controversy hinged on the word *physis* (Gr. "nature"), which was still being used to mean both a concrete, subsisting individual (or person) and the nature of that individual—or natures in the case of Christ. Those Cyrillian theologians who considered Chalcedon a surrender to Nestorian theologians (guilty, in their eyes, of having divided Christ into two individuals) sought to reinterpret Chalcedon in terms of Cyril's condemnation of Nestorianism. In his "Third Letter to Nestorius" (DH 252–63; ND 606/1–12), Cyril stressed Christ's one divine person, anathematizing anyone who failed to proclaim that God, in Christ, had suffered on the cross. At Chalcedon this letter had been read, recorded, but not acclaimed. Neo-Chalcedonianism, or the interpretation of Chalcedon in terms of Cyril's theology of God's suffering, was officially endorsed at the Second Council of Constantinople in 553 (DH 421–38; ND 620–23); its chief exponent was Leontius of Jerusalem, confused at times with Leontius of Byzantium (both sixth century). See *Chalcedon, Council of*; *Constantinople, Second Council of*; *Ephesus, Council of*; *Enhypostasia*; *Monophysitism*; *Suffering of God*.

Neo-Orthodoxy. A post–World War I movement inspired by Karl Barth (1886–1968) and developed in various ways by theologians such as Emil Brunner (1889–1966), Reinhold Niebuhr (1892–1971), and Helmut Richard Niebuhr (1894–1962). Dissatisfied with the optimistic humanism of Liberal Protestantism, they sought to recover the essential insights of the Reformation and stressed the revealing and judging word of God. In a prophetic way, they insisted on God's sovereign transcendence over against a sinful world. Neo-Orthodoxy has been applied to the work of others such as Karl Rahner (1904–84), but in the strict sense the term applies only to the movement initiated and led by Barth. See *Dialectical Theology*; *Liberal Protestantism*; *Reformation, The*.

Neo-Palamism. An attempt launched at the First Panorthodox Conference (Athens, 1936) to develop an Orthodox theological synthesis by retrieving the thought of St. Gregory Palamas (ca. 1296–1359). Palamite theology highlights both human transformation into the divine image and the real distinction between the essence and energies in God, who always remains transcendent and radically different from creatures. Some of the most famous Orthodox theologians of the twentieth century may be classified as Neo-Palamite: George Florovsky (1893–1979), Vladimir Lossky (1903–58), Paul Evdokimov (1901–70), John Meyendorff (1925–92), Dumitru Staniloae (1903–95), and Metropolitan Kallistos of Diokleia (Timothy Ware) (b. 1934). See *Palamism*; *Thomism*.

Neoplatonism. A revival and religious interpretation of the philosophy of Plato (427–347 BC) that flourished from the third to the sixth century AD. Plotinus (205–70) was the most important representative of this movement, other exponents being Porphyry (ca. 232–ca. 303), Iamblichus (ca. 250–330), and Proclus (410–85). Plotinus argued for the soul or psyche, the mind or nous, and the One or *hen*, from which the world of matter has come about through a system of emanations. Behind and beyond all experience is the One, from which we have come and to which we should return through purification, knowledge, and love. Highly mystical, Neoplatonism has often been interpreted as pantheistic. It had some influence on St. Augustine of Hippo (354–430) and other Fathers of the Church. See *Fathers of the Church; Pantheism; Platonism*.

Neo-Scholasticism. A revival of medieval Christian philosophy and theology, often considered synonymous with Neo-Thomism, but, in fact, somewhat wider in its content and method. At the Roman College (later the Gregorian University), Jesuits such as Luigi D'Azeglio Taparelli (1793–1862), Matteo Liberatore (1810–92), and Joseph Kleutgen (1811–93) began to restore Scholasticism. One of Taparelli's former students, Gioacchino Pecci (1810–1903), as bishop of Perugia and later as Pope Leo XIII, decisively encouraged the movement. His encyclical *Aeterni Patris* (1879) prescribed the teaching of Thomism in Catholic faculties (see DH 3135–40). Up until Vatican II (1962–65), Neo-Scholasticism helped to give a structure and clarity to Catholic theological thought. But progress in biblical, historical, liturgical, and patristic studies showed this clarity to be at times merely formal, verbal, and lacking in substance. On the philosophical side, such new currents as existentialism, linguistic analysis, personalism, and process thought have created a situation of pluralism. See *Neo-Thomism; Scholasticism; Thomism*.

Neo-Thomism. A modern retrieval of the thought of St. Thomas Aquinas (ca. 1225–74), generally considered the greatest medieval philosopher and theologian. The most important Neo-Thomists include Louis Billot (1846–1931), Cardinal Désiré Joseph Mercier (1851–1926), Ambrose Gardeil (1859–1931), Antonin Gilbert Sertillanges (1863–1948), Maurice de Wulf (1867–1947), Maurice de la Taille (1872–1933), Réginald Garrigou-Lagrange (1877–1964), Jacques Maritain (1882–1973), Étienne Gilson (1884–1978), Marie-Dominique Chenu (1895–1990), and Yves Congar (1904–95). See *Neo-Scholasticism; Scholasticism; Thomism*.

Nestorianism. The heresy (condemned in 431 at the Council of Ephesus) that in Christ there are two different persons, one human and the other divine, who are separate subjects linked by a manifest union of love. It was wrongly attributed to Nestorius (d. ca. 451), a monk from Antioch who became patriarch of Constantinople (428–31). He opposed a popular Marian title,

Theotokos (Gr. "Mother of God"), apparently fearing that it threatened the full and distinct divinity and humanity of Christ, but was willing to accept the title if interpreted correctly. See *Antiochene Theology; Apollinarianism; Arianism; Chalcedon, Council of; Church of the East, Assyrian; Ephesus, Council of; Eutychianism; Monophysitism; Theotokos.*

New Eve. A title for Mary, the physical mother of Christ and spiritual mother of all human beings. The parallel and contrast between the first Eve, "the mother of all the living" (Gen 3:20), and Mary as the new Eve go back to St. Justin Martyr (d. 165). The contrast builds not only on language about Jesus as the "last" or new Adam (Rom 5:14; 1 Cor 15:22, 45–49; see DH 901), but also on the faith shown by Mary. As the Fathers of the Church reflected, where Eve's disobedience brought death, Mary's obedient love brought life to all humanity through the redemptive activity of her Son (LG 56, 63). See *Adam; Co-Redemptrix; Eve; Mariology.*

New Testament. The twenty-seven books in the Bible that follow the OT (made up of forty-five books, most of which are shared in common with Jews). Christians recognize these books (the four gospels, Acts of the Apostles, twenty-one letters, and the book of Revelation) as written under the special inspiration of the Holy Spirit, normative for faith, and belonging to the canon of scripture. "In a most excellent way" the church finds in the NT, and, in particular, the gospels, a "perpetual and divine witness" to the reality of Jesus Christ (DV 17–20). See *Bible; Canon of Scripture; Covenant; Infancy Gospels; Inspiration, Biblical; Marcionism; Old Testament.*

Nicaea, First Council of (325). The first ecumenical council, which was convoked by Emperor Constantine the Great (d. 337) and met at Nicaea (now Iznik in Turkey) to deal with the Arian heresy that threatened to disrupt the unity of the church and the Roman Empire. Arius, an Alexandrian priest, had been claiming that Christ, far from being fully and truly divine, was merely the first among God's creatures. In answer, the council taught that Christ was the "only-begotten" Son of the Father and homoousios (Gr. "one in being" or "consubstantial") with the Father (see DH 125–30; ND 7–8). It also recognized the patriarchal rights of Rome, Alexandria, and Antioch, and, for all, it prescribed the Alexandrian solution for the date of Easter. A rising star at the council was St. Athanasius, later bishop of Alexandria (d. 373), who came as an archdeacon to accompany his bishop, St. Alexander of Alexandria (d. 328). See *Arianism; Council, Ecumenical; Creed, Nicene; Homoousios; Patriarch.*

Nicaea, Second Council of (787). A council convoked by the Empress-regent Irene and Patriarch St. Tarasius of Constantinople (d. 806), and attended by about 350 bishops, including a delegation from the West. Being under Muslim domination, the patriarchates of Alexandria, Antioch, and Jerusalem could send only two monks each. In condemning the heresy of iconoclasm (Gr. "image-smashing"), the council endorsed a letter sent by Hadrian I (pope 772–95) and distinguished between *proskynesis* (Gr. "veneration"), the devotion shown to images insofar as they represent God and saints, and *latreia* (Gr. "adoration"), the absolute cult due to God alone. The council also condemned simony and declared the elections of bishops by secular authorities to be null and void (see DH 600–609; ND 206, 1251–52). This council is regarded by Eastern Orthodox as the seventh—and last—ecumenical council. It forms a summary and epilogue to the previous six. See *Eastern Churches; Icon; Iconoclasm; Seven Ecumenical Councils, The; Veneration of Saints.*

Nihilism (Lat. "accepting nothing"). A general term for philosophies which claim that in itself reality is ultimately meaningless. Such an essentially atheistic attitude may affirm life and impose meaning by exercising one's will—as was the case with Friedrich Nietzsche (1844–1900). By professing the absurdity of the universe, the philosophy of Albert Camus (1913–60) and some other existentialists contains elements of nihilism. In his October 1998 encyclical *Fides et Ratio*, Blessed John Paul II (pope 1978–2005) argued against the various forms of nihilism that have taken root during the war-weary twentieth century. See *Atheism; Existentialism.*

Nominalism. A philosophy that developed during the Middle Ages and claims that names (Lat. *nomina*) for things, while useful for purposes of classification, do not validly describe reality. Every substance is irreducibly individual, there are no common natures, and universal concepts exist only in the mind. William of Occam (ca. 1285–1347) was the most famous of the nominalists. This philosophy affected theology, especially the doctrines of God, justification, and sacraments. Through Martin Luther's (1483–1546) teacher, Gabriel Biel (ca. 1420–95), nominalism exercised an influence on the Reformation. Elements of nominalism are found in some forms of modern language philosophy and existentialism. See *Existentialism; Philosophy; Platonism; Reformation, The; Universals.*

Nomocanon (Gr. "law" and "rule"). A term used in Eastern Christianity for collections of ecclesiastical canons and civil law that affected the life of the church. The earliest example is attributed to John III, patriarch of Constantinople (d. 577), called Scholasticus (Gr. "lawyer") because he practiced law as a young man in Antioch. See *Canon Law, Sources of Oriental; Symphony.*

Non-Chalcedonian Churches. The Eastern churches that did not accept the Council of Chalcedon (451). See *Chalcedon, Council of; Oriental Orthodox.*

Nonviolence. The theory and practice of those who, like Mohandas Gandhi (1869–1948), Leo Tolstoy (1828–1910), and Martin Luther King Jr.

(1929–68), work to remedy political and religious injustice without having recourse to physical attacks on people or straight-out war. Such contemporary, nonviolent movements have drawn on Hindu thought, the endorsement of civil disobedience toward unjust laws by Henry David Thoreau (1817–62), and, above all, Christ's example and teaching—in particular, the Beatitudes and the Sermon on the Mount (Matt 5:1—7:29; see GS 78). See *Beatitudes; Law; Peace.*

Notes of the Church. See *Marks (Notes) of the Church.*

Notes, Theological. See *Qualifications, Theological.*

Nous (Gr. "mind"). Reason or the human faculty of understanding. In what has been called a Nous-Logos ("Mind-Word") Christology, Evagrius Ponticus (346–99) proposed that Christ's soul was preexistent and that the mind was the point of union between the eternal Logos and Christ's humanity. See *Christology; Origenism.*

Novatianism. A schism that arose over the treatment of those who lapsed from Christian faith during the persecution (249–50) of Emperor Decius. Novatian, a Roman priest and the author of a thoroughly orthodox work on the Trinity, at first went along with the policy of reconciliation, but later he advocated a rigorous treatment of the apostates. The catalyst of this volte-face may have been his disappointment over the election in 250 of Pope St. Cornelius I. Novatian had himself consecrated as the rival bishop of Rome and died a martyr in the persecution (257–58) under Emperor Valerian. His community continued until the fifth century (see DH 109). At the First Council of Nicaea (325), his followers were mildly condemned for pretending to be *catharoi* (Gr. "pure") and to form an all-holy church that excluded sinners (DH 127; ND 1601). Later they were criticized for re-baptizing heretics (DH 183, 211–12, 214; see also 705, 1670; ND 1404, 1617). See *Donatism; Penance, Sacrament of; Rigorism; Schism.*

Novice (Lat. "new"). A probationary member of a religious institute. Novices live together in a special residence called a novitiate, may wear the religious dress of their institute, and must follow a course of formation for at least a full year (see CIC 641–53, 1196; CCEO 448, 450, 453, 456–59, 893 §3) before being admitted to their first vows. See *Monasticism; Religious Life; Vow.*

Numinous (Lat. "appertaining to the deity"). The awe-inspiring divine presence. In *The Idea of the Holy* (German original 1917), Rudolf Otto (1869–1937) argued that religion originates with the numinous experience of the *mysterium tremendum et fascinans* (Lat. "the mystery that is both awe-inspiring and fascinating"). See *Experience, Religious; Holiness.*

O

Obedience. The willingness to comply with laws and commands or accept as true statements coming from authority. Only God has supreme and absolute authority. Human beings share in various, limited degrees in that divine authority (e.g., parents toward their children, the state toward its citizens, and church leaders toward believers). In fulfilling his Father's will, Christ became "obedient unto death" (Phil 2:8; see Heb 5:8), leaving us the perfect example of loving obedience (John 15:10). Radically opposed to the disobedience that is sin, faith means obedience to God and the divine commands (Matt 7:21; Rom 1:5; 16:26). Within the church, all owe respectful obedience to the pope and bishops—the nature of submission involved being affected by the degree of authority exercised (LG 25, 27). Those who have a vow of religious obedience in religious life owe a particular obedience to their superiors and the rule of their religious institute (PC 14; CIC 573, 590, 598, 601, 618; CCEO 410–12, 421, 426, 555, 564). Diocesan priests owe a special obedience to the pope and their bishops (PO 15; CIC 273; CCEO 370). See *Authority; Magisterium; Religious Life.*

Obediential Potency. See *Potentia Oboedientialis.*

Occasionalism. A philosophy that denies the causal activity of all created things. God is the sole cause of everything that happens; there are no real secondary causes. While anticipated by some Muslim and other medieval thinkers, classical occasionalism emerged as a response to the problem raised by the dualism of René Descartes (1596–1650): How can mind have a causal influence on matter? The occasionalism of Arnold Geulincx (1624–69), and, especially, that of Nicolas Malebranche (1638–1715) simply denied any such causality. Created things, including the human mind, do not act; they simply provide the occasion for God's innumerable interventions. In theology, occasionalist trends have at times denied genuine sacramental causality, reducing the sacraments to mere excuses for the gift of God's grace. See *Causality; Creation.*

Octoechos (Gr. "eight tones"). Liturgical book used in the Byzantine liturgy for the offices of propers for the movable cycle from the first Sunday after Pentecost (which in the Byzantine rite is All Saints' Day) to the first Sunday of the pre-Lenten period. It covers what the Latin liturgy calls the "ordinary time" of the year and is used with the *Triodion* until it is replaced entirely by the latter for Palm Sunday and Holy Week. The name *Octoechos* refers to the eight-scale character of its tones: in the first week after Pentecost, the first tone is used, followed by the second tone in the second week, and so forth. Through this repetition, an eight-week cycle of fifty-six propers, one for each weekday in each of the eight tones, is reenacted during most of the liturgical year. Originally used only on Sundays, the *Octoechos* was later extended to include weekdays in what was called the great *Octoechos*, or *Parakletike*. See *Pentecostarion; Rite; Triodion.*

Office, The Divine (Lat. "duty," "service"). The Liturgy of the Hours or official prayers (mainly the psalms) used by priests, religious, and others (SC 83–101). In this Christian practice, derived from the Jewish custom of praying at fixed hours of the day or night, the church praises God and intercedes for the salvation of the world. The divine office was called *opus Dei* (Lat. "work of God") by St. Benedict of Nursia (ca. 480–ca. 550). See *Acoemetae; Breviary; Liturgy of the Hours.*

Oikoumene or **Oikumene** (Gr. "the inhabited earth"). The inhabited world or the Roman Empire, which was said to correspond to the whole world (see Luke 2:1). Those who spoke of the Mediterranean (Lat. "middle of the earth") as the center of the world saw the countries sharing the Greek culture as the oikumene or whole civilized world. Thus an "ecumenical" council, which initially meant a council of the Byzantine Empire, came to mean a "universal" council. From the sixth century, the patriarch of Constantinople was called ecumenical patriarch, in the sense of enjoying a primacy for Byzantine Christianity. See *Autocephalous; Council, Ecumenical; Ecumenism; Patriarch.*

Old Believers. Those Russians, especially peasants, who rejected the reforms (mainly liturgical) of Nikon, patriarch of Moscow (1605–81); they are also known as Old Ritualists. Excommunicated in 1667 as *Raskolniki* (schismatics), they were persecuted by the state, especially under Peter the Great (1672–1725); their leader, archpriest Avvakum, was burned at the stake (1682). When no bishop joined them, the Old Believers divided into two groups: those who sought to have priests, and those who tried to survive without them. In 1846 a deposed bishop, Ambrose of Bosnia, joined the first group; state recognition followed in 1881. Since the 1970s, efforts have been made to have the 1667 excommunication lifted.

Old Catholics. Catholics who have left the Roman Catholic Church over various issues while retaining much of the same tradition. The most important group is the German-speaking one that left in protest over the dogmas of the infallibility and the universal jurisdiction of the pope proclaimed at Vatican I (1869–70) in 1870 (DH 3050–75; ND 818–40). This group felt encouraged to do so by Bavarian priest and church historian Johann Joseph Ignaz von Döllinger (1799–1890), who never himself joined the group. In 1889 the Jansenist Church of Utrecht, which had broken with Rome in 1724, joined the Old Catholics. In 1932 the Old Catholics entered into full communion with the Church of England. See *Infallibility; Jansenism; Jurisdiction; Pope; Vatican Council, First.*

Old Testament. Those sacred books accepted by Jews and Christians as inspired and canonical (NA 4). The Jews have a threefold division: (1) the Law or the Pentateuch (Genesis, Exodus, Leviticus, Numbers, and Deuteronomy); (2) the Prophets, which include most of the historical books, plus the major and minor prophets (excluding Daniel); and (3) the Writings, which include such books as Psalms, Proverbs, Job, and Daniel. The church recognizes some other books, such as the Wisdom of Solomon and Judith, making an Old Testament of forty-five books that are divided as follows: the Pentateuch, the historical books, the wisdom literature, and the prophets. Against Marcion (d. ca. 160) and others, the church has always held that the OT books are divinely inspired and belong to the canon of scripture. Vatican II (1962–65) underlined the permanent value of the OT scriptures (DV 11, 14–15), which record and interpret the history of preparation for the coming of Christ and his church (DV 16; LG 2, 6; SC 5). See *Bible; Canon of Scripture; Deuterocanonical Books; Inspiration, Biblical; Marcionism; New Testament.*

Omega Point (Gr. last letter of the alphabet). The final goal (see Rev 1:8; 21:6; 22:13) of the evolving and converging universe in the thought of Pierre Teilhard de Chardin, a French Jesuit and paleontologist (1881–1955). Synthesizing Christian faith with the data of science in his *Phenomenon of Man, Le Milieu Divin,* and other (posthumous) works, he pictured a world of growing complexity being progressively humanized and "christified" or evolving toward its culmination in the cosmic Christ (see 1 Cor 15:28; Eph 1:3–10; Col 1:15–20). See *Christocentrism; Entelechy; Eschatology; Parousia.*

Omnipotence (Lat. "being all-powerful"). The divine attribute of being infinitely powerful (2 Cor 6:18; Rev 1:8; 4:8). In the creeds, omnipotence is usually "appropriated" or assigned to God the Father, but the other persons of the Trinity are also confessed to be omnipotent (see DH 29, 75, 164, 169, 173, 441; ND 16; 306/12, 17). The existence of evil has often been invoked as an objection against the existence of a God who is all-powerful, all-good, and all-wise. Omnipotence does not mean that God can do what is logically impossible (e.g., make a square circle) or do what is opposed to other divine attributes. See *Albigensianism; Appropriation; Attributes, Divine; Dualism; Evil, Mystery of; Pantocrator; Theodicy.*

Omnipresence (Lat. "presence everywhere"). The divine attribute of being present everywhere (Ps 139:7–12; Acts 17:24–28). While present everywhere as the creative source of all things, God is present in various other ways, for example, through human persons, the Bible, community worship, and the sacraments (SC 7). See *Creation; Panentheism; Pantheism; Transubstantiation.*

Omniscience (Lat. "knowledge of everything"). The divine attribute of knowing comprehensively everything that is and can be. God's knowledge of the future seems to compromise the exercise of human freedom—a mystery that has drawn "rational" explanations from Western thinkers (e.g., God knows future events in time but from the standpoint of eternity), but which Eastern Christians accept with prayerful praise and respect. See *Attributes, Divine; Eternity; Freedom; God; Molinism; Predestination; Scientia Media; Time.*

Ontological Argument. A way of "demonstrating" God's existence developed by St. Anselm of Canterbury (ca. 1033–1109). Since what we mean by God is *id quo nihil majus cogitari possit* (Lat. "that than which nothing greater can be conceived"), the very idea of God demands the objective existence of God. Otherwise we would be involved in a contradiction, being able to imagine something greater than God—namely, a God who exists. St. Thomas Aquinas (ca. 1225–74), Immanuel Kant (1724–1804), and others have rejected the argument for moving fallaciously from the level of mere thought to that of actual existence. Other philosophers, however, in various ways, have defended the argument: René Descartes (1596–1650), Baruch Spinoza (1632–77), Gottfried Wilhelm Leibniz (1646–1716), and Georg Wilhelm Friedrich Hegel (1770–1831). More recently, some have claimed that, instead of being a "proof," the ontological argument simply explicates the implicit knowledge of God we already possess. See *Five Ways, The; Ontologism.*

Ontologism. A nineteenth-century epistemology endorsed by many Catholic thinkers in Belgium, France, and Italy that argued that we have an immediate, innate knowledge of God. The term was first used in *Introduction to the Study of Philosophy* (1840) by Vincenzo Gioberti (1801–52), who was followed by Blessed Antonio Rosmini-Serbati (1799–1855). With some justification the ontologists claimed to stand in the line of Plato (427–347 BC), St. Augustine of Hippo (354–430), St. Anselm of Canterbury (ca. 1033–1109), and St. Bonaventure (1221–74). Nevertheless they dealt inadequately with the role of sense-perception and the limited nature of our knowledge of God in this life (see John 1:18; 1 John 3:2). In 1861 the Holy Office condemned several propositions from ontologism as ambiguous (see DH 2841–47). In arguing that some prior presence of God in our knowledge is the logical condition for any further knowing, transcendental Thomists such as Bernard Lonergan (1904–84) and Karl Rahner (1904–84) have preserved, in a modified form, a central insight from ontologism. See *Augustinianism; Beatific Vision; Epistemology; Ontological Argument.*

Ontology (Gr. "study of being"). The study of the necessary truths of beings as existent beings. Brought into common use by Christian Wolff (1679–1754), ontology is often synonymous with metaphysics. See *Causality; Metaphysics; Philosophy.*

Option for the Poor. A policy for church life popularized by the theologians of liberation. It urges Christians to work in a special way to effect social justice for those many millions who are deprived of proper food, housing, medical services, education, employment, and other basic human rights. This has been a theme of the Latin American bishops since their Second General Council held at Medellín in 1968. In his 1987 encyclical *Sollicitudo Rei Socialis*, Blessed John Paul II (pope 1978–2005) called for a solidarity with and preferential love for the poor that would be expressed in concrete activity at the local level (42, 43, 47). His 1999 apostolic exhortation *Ecclesia in America* again stressed "the preferential option for the poor" (55, 58, 67). This special concern for the exploited, defenseless, and marginalized draws its inspiration from the OT prophets (e.g., Isa 1:10–20) and from the message and practice of Jesus (Luke 6:20–21; 16:19–31; 17:11–19). In both the OT and the NT, God is revealed as having a preferential, although not exclusive, love for the poor. In a special way, God's presence and activity are revealed in the poor. The Second Vatican Council (1962–65) called on all Christians, especially those of rich nations, to exercise greater justice and love in promoting the cause of the poor (GS 69, 88). See *Anawim; Beatitudes; Liberation Theology; Poverty; Social Teaching.*

Ordinary. The bishop of a diocese (the local ordinary), his vicar general, and episcopal vicars that he may also appoint, all of whom exercise normal jurisdiction in the diocese and have the chief responsibility for this particular church (CIC 134; CCEO 984, 987). In the case of institutes of clerical religious, the major superiors (e.g., the provincial or head of a province) exercise ordinary jurisdiction over those under their charge. See *Bishop; Clergy; Cleric; Diocese; Jurisdiction; Local Church.*

Ordination. The liturgical ceremony through which candidates become deacons, presbyters (priests), or bishops. At the end of the Liturgy of the Word and before the Liturgy of the Eucharist begins, the sacrament is conferred by the imposition of hands and the recital of the prescribed formula. Following ordination, the deacon is vested with the stole and the priest with the chasuble. Both are presented with the book of gospels, while the priest receives as well the chalice and paten. After ordination, the bishop receives his ring, miter, and crozier or pastoral staff, and is seated on his throne as the symbol of his teaching authority. See *Bishop; Deacon; Enthronement; Holy Orders; Presbyter; Priests.*

Oriental and Eastern Orthodox. A distinction that arose in the context of recent ecumenical dialogue. Eastern Orthodox comprise those Eastern churches that accept the first seven ecumenical councils and recognize the Patriarch of Constantinople as their spiritual leader and symbol of unity. They are distinguished from the Oriental Orthodox who accepted the first three ecumenical councils, but rejected the Council of Chalcedon (451) as betraying

St. Cyril of Alexandria (d. 444) and capitulating to a Nestorian *dyophysism* (Gr. "two natures"). See *Armenian Christianity; Autocephalous; Chalcedon, Council of; Constantinople, First Council of; Eastern Churches; Ephesus, Council of; Monophysitism; Nestorianism; Nicaea, First Council of; Patriarchates, Orthodox; Seven Ecumenical Councils, The.*

Origenism. The doctrines and school of thought inspired by Origen of Alexandria (ca. 185–ca. 254). He developed a biblical hermeneutic in terms of the literal, moral, and allegorical senses of scripture. As the first great systematic theologian of Christianity, he stressed images (with sensible reality symbolizing the invisible spiritual world) and our deification through grace. His liking for allegory and, much more, his theses about the ultimate salvation of all (*apocatastasis*), the preexistence of human souls (including Christ's), and an apparent subordination of the Son to the Father met with repeated criticism and opposition. Emperor Justinian I had Origenism condemned at a synod in 543 and again in 553 at a synod prior to Constantinople II (see DH 298, 353, 403–11, 433, 519; ND 401/1, 8; 618/2–3). Nevertheless it is still not clear how far Origen himself was at fault, how far he was simply exploring a variety of views, and how far false views were ascribed to him after his death. It is difficult to decide, since his works were to a large extent destroyed. Any fair judgment on Origen should also take into account Fathers of the Church who greatly admired him, such as St Gregory Thaumaturgus or "Wonder-worker" (ca. 213–ca. 270), St. Athanasius of Alexandria (ca. 296–373), St. Basil the Great (ca. 330–79), and St. Gregory of Nazianzus (329–89). See *Alexandrian Theology; Allegory; Apocatastasis; Constantinople, The Second Council of; Exegesis; Hermeneutics; Platonism; Senses of Scripture.*

Original Justice. The graced state of the first human beings before they fell into sin. Interpreted for centuries as a historical period of time, this original righteousness is better understood to be a way of speaking of our goodness as created and sanctified by God (Gen 1:26–31). Up to recent times, theologians elaborated a whole range of preternatural or special gifts that Adam and Eve were supposed to have received. Not all of his successors imitated St. Augustine (354–430) in his careful language; for example, he interpreted the "immortality" of Adam and Eve as *posse non mori* ("the possibility of not dying") rather than as *non posse mori* ("the impossibility of dying"). See *Adam; Concupiscence; Eve; Fall, The; Grace; Original Sin; Preternatural Gifts.*

Original Sin. Traditionally understood as the loss of grace and wounding of nature suffered by our first parents, which affected all later generations, the notion was developed on the basis of scripture (above all, Gen 3:1–24; Ps 51:5, and Rom 5:12–21) and the ancient practice of baptizing infants for the forgiveness of sins. St. Augustine of Hippo (354–430) argued against the Pelagians that, because infants cannot commit personal sins, the sin from which they are delivered in baptism must be an inherited sinfulness. The doctrine of original sin (DH 496, 621, 1510–16; ND 507–13) expresses not only the sinful condition into which, through no personal fault of our own, all human beings are born and which conditions the exercise of their freedom, but also the fact that the new life of grace coming through baptism is no "natural" right but the free gift of God. Thus original sin refers to our human solidarity in sin and common call to the supernatural life in Christ. The *Exultet* or proclamation sung during the Easter Vigil names original sin as a *felix culpa* (Lat. "happy fault), since it brought the Son of God to come and rescue us. Eastern Christianity, while maintaining infant baptism, calls original sin the sin of our first parents or simply "the fall," and thinks of its consequences in terms of inherited mortality. Protestants have often overemphasized original sin and its evil effects. See *Concupiscence; Depravity, Total; Fall, The; Immaculate Conception; Infant Baptism; Lutheranism; Natural Theology; Pelagianism; Supernatural.*

Orthodoxy (Gr. "right belief"). Belief and teaching recognized by the church as truly based on the divine self-revelation in Jesus Christ. The OT used various criteria to distinguish between true and false prophets (Deut 13:1–7; 18:21–22; Jer 23:9–40; 28:9, 15–17; see Matt 7:15–20). St. Paul's letters reflect his deep concern to maintain the genuine revelation and doctrine he and others have transmitted (Rom 16:17; 1 Cor 11:2; 15:1–11; Gal 1:6–9). Later books of the NT reflect a similar commitment to a teaching that is sound and faithful to the original revelation (1 Tim 1:3–11; 6:3–5; 2 Tim 1:13–14; 4:3–4; Titus 1:9; 2:1; Jude 3). Orthodoxy entered the church's terminological repertoire during the great christological and trinitarian controversies of the third, fourth, and fifth centuries. In the East, it came to be used of the churches united to Constantinople and Rome, as opposed to the dissident Nestorian and Monophysite churches. When the crisis of iconoclasm finally ended in 842, a feast of Orthodoxy was established in the East for the first Sunday of Lent. In the *Synodikon*, or summary of synods read on that day, a litany of orthodox teachers and saints is contrasted with a list of anathematized heretics. The popular etymology linking orthodoxy with "right worship" indicates how the liturgy guarantees the truth and vitality of teaching in the Eastern churches. See *Creed; Deposit of Faith; Dogma; Eastern Churches; Heresy; Heterodox; Iconoclasm; Monophysitism; Nestorianism; Oriental and Eastern Orthodox; Tradition.*

Orthodoxy, Old Protestant. That fidelity to Christian beliefs derived from scripture and the early church that was championed by the mainline churches of the Reformation in the sixteenth and seventeenth centuries. See *Calvinism; Lutheranism; Neo-Orthodoxy; Protestant; Reformation, The.*

Orthopraxis (Gr. "right conduct"). Self-critical activity that aims to "do the truth" (John 3:21; see Gal 5:6), practice Christian discipleship, and transform human society. From the early 1960s, this term was popularized by Johann Baptist Metz (b. 1928), Nikos Nissiotis (1925–86), the World Council of Churches, and liberation theology. Orthopraxis draws its inspiration from Jesus' preaching of the kingdom and his praxis, which led to his death. Orthopraxis leads to and is nurtured by prayer and public worship. Authentic orthopraxis lends credibility to orthodoxy, while true orthodoxy is manifested in orthopraxis. On the one hand, a purely formal orthodoxy is no better than verbal conformity to a set of doctrinal statements. On the other hand, a one-sided emphasis on orthopraxis can deteriorate into mere activism divorced from Christian faith and worship. See *Basic Communities; Black Theology; Feminist Theology; Frankfurt School; Liberation Theology; Orthodoxy; Pluralism; Political Theology; Praxis.*

Our Father. See *Lord's Prayer, The.*

Ousia (Gr. "being," "essence," "substance"). The term used at Nicaea I (325) for one divine nature shared by God the Father and the Son (DH 125–26; ND 7–8). Constantinople I (381) taught the divinity of the Holy Spirit (DH 150–51; ND 12–13). That all three divine persons share the same ousia was made explicit at Constantinople III (553) (DH 421; ND 620/1). In Latin, *ousia* is translated not only by *essentia* ("essence"), but also by *substantia* ("substance"), a term too easily associated with a Greek word for "person" (*hypostasis*). See *Constantinople, First Council of; Constantinople, Second Council of; Constantinople, Third Council of; Homoousios; Hypostasis; Nicaea, First Council of; Person.*

Oxford Movement. An Anglican movement (1833–45) centered in Oxford University and led by John Keble (1792–1866), Blessed John Henry Newman (1801–90), and Edward Bouverie Pusey (1800–82) that formed the first period of Anglo-Catholicism. Inspired by the High Church (rather than the Low Church or evangelical) tradition, it aimed to reform Anglicanism, stressed the apostolic and sacramental character of the church and priesthood, resisted the inroads of liberalism, promoted a Catholic tradition of worship, worked for the poor, and encouraged the formation of male and female communities of religious. To further its cause, the Oxford Movement produced *Tracts for the Times* (1833–41); Newman's *Tract 90* (1841) roused much debate because of its pro-Catholic tendency. In 1836 Keble, Newman, and Pusey started publishing the *Library of the Fathers*, a series that revealed the inspiration they found in a return to the Fathers of the Church. Keble's 1833 sermon "National Apostasy" marked the start of the movement. Its end is generally considered to be Newman's entry into the Catholic Church in 1845. See *Anglican Communion; Anglo-Catholicism; Evangelicals; Fathers of the Church; Liberalism; Religious Life.*

P

Pagans (Lat. "country dwellers"). A term initially used for those in the Roman Empire who lived out in country villages, and, being evangelized after the urban population, became Christians later. In the OT, the *goyim* (Heb. "nations"), or Gentiles, were those who did not acknowledge the one true God (Deut 7:1; Ps 147:20). While denouncing their idolatry, the OT also witnessed to God's saving concern for the pagans (Isa 2:1–4; 49:6; 60:1–3; Amos 9:7; Jonah). Abraham was called to mediate divine blessings to the whole human race (Gen 12:1–3). The OT introduces "holy pagans" such as Melchizedek, the Queen of Sheba, Job, and Ruth. St. Paul proclaims God's desire to justify both Jews and Gentiles (Rom 3:29; 9:24; 15:8–12; see Luke 2:29–32). The followers of some non-Christian religions have been called (in a derogatory sense) pagans or heathens. Superstitions still found among those converted to Christianity have been labeled pagan. The Second Vatican Council (1962–65) avoided altogether the terms pagan and paganism, speaking rather of the "nations" (Lat. *gentes*) to be evangelized. See *Animism; Anonymous Christians; Evangelization; Idolatry; Inculturation; Polytheism.*

Palamism. The theological synthesis of Gregory Palamas (ca. 1296–1359), a monk of Mount Athos and a defender of the method of prayer called hesychasm, practiced on the Holy Mountain. Palamas is a saint of the Greek Orthodox Church and is considered the greatest Byzantine theologian of late medieval times. To maintain that human beings genuinely become like God through deification without jeopardizing God's transcendence, he distinguished between the inaccessible divine essence and the energies through which God becomes known to us and makes us share in the divine life. After a controversy with Barlaam (ca. 1290–1348), a monk from Calabria and an expert on Pseudo–Dionysius the Areopagite (fifth or sixth century), a synod held in Constantinople (June 1341) censured Barlaam. Another synod (August 1341) imposed silence on both. In 1344 Palamas was even excommunicated for heresy. In 1347, however, a synod in Constantinople upheld his orthodoxy, and he was consecrated archbishop of Thessalonica. He had to cope with criticisms coming from the monk Gregorios Akindynos (ca. 1300–49), a one-time friend turned enemy. Yet another attack came from the humanist philosopher Nikephoros Gregoras (ca. 1294–ca. 1359). A synod held in Constantinople in 1351 condemned Gregorios Akindynos posthumously and silenced Nikephoros Gregoras, while recognizing the full orthodoxy of Palamas. In 1368, nine years after his death, Palamas was canonized. His feast is celebrated both on the second Sunday in Lent and on November 14. See *Athos, Mount; Deification; Essence and Energies; Hesychasm; Neo-Palamism.*

Pallium (Lat. "cloak"). A band of white wool worn around the neck and adorned with six black crosses and supporting two strips. As a symbol of his apostolic authority, it was peculiar to the pope, but since early times he has granted it to archbishops as a sign of communion and to certain bishops as a sign of honor. Today, within three months of his appointment, a Western metropolitan (archbishop who presides over a region) must ask for the pallium, and should request a new pallium if subsequently transferred to another metropolitan diocese. He wears it within his ecclesiastical province and then only on occasions prescribed by the liturgy (CIC 437). During the liturgy in the Eastern Church, bishops wear an *omophorion*, a woolen scarf embroidered with crosses that corresponds to the pallium. At his inauguration in 2005, Pope Benedict XVI (pope 2005–13) retrieved an earlier form of the pallium decorated with five red crosses that recall the passion of Christ. See *Archbishop; Pope.*

Palm Sunday. A feast celebrated by all Christians at the start of Holy Week (or the Great Week, as Greek Orthodox call it) to commemorate the entry of Christ into Jerusalem. It is one of the twelve major feasts of the Eastern Orthodox calendar, preceded by Lazarus Saturday, which recalls Christ raising Lazarus from the dead (John 11:1–44). The Western liturgy of Palm Sunday begins with the blessing and distribution of palms and a procession; in the Mass itself, the passion story from Matthew, Mark, or Luke is read. From the end of the fourth century, Egeria the Pilgrim reports the celebration of Palm Sunday in Jerusalem. See *Calendar, Liturgical; Holy Week; Twelve Feasts, The.*

Panentheism (Gr. "everything in God"). A system developed in various ways by philosophers such as Karl Christian Friedrich Krause (1781–1832), Friedrich Heinrich Jacobi (1743–1819), and Charles Hartshorne (1897–2000), according to which God so penetrates the universe that everything is in God. Unlike pantheism, which holds that the universe and God are identical, and, thus, everything is God, panentheism maintains that, while including the universe, God's being goes beyond it. See *God; Pantheism; Process Theology; Theism.*

Panorthodox Conferences (Gr. "all Orthodox"). A movement aimed at fostering unity of action within the various autocephalous churches that make up the Orthodox Church and at promoting relations with other churches. The first Panorthodox consultation took place in Constantinople in 1923. The second, which met on Mount Athos in 1930, discussed the agenda for a future Panorthodox pre-council, which was to prepare for a Holy and Great Panorthodox Council. The first Panorthodox Conference was held in 1961; the second, on the island of Rhodes in 1963, discussed sending observers to Vatican II; the third took place on Rhodes in 1964 and officially expressed commitment to dialogue with the Roman Catholic Church. The fourth met in

1968 at Chambésy, near Geneva, and it was decided to open there a secretariat to prepare for a future Great Council and to revise its agenda. Themes such as marriage impediments, calendar reform, fasting, and the position of Orthodox churches outside their traditional territories figured prominently. A preparatory meeting took place in 1971 at Chambésy. This led to three Panorthodox preconciliar conferences (in 1976, 1982, and 1986) held at the same place to discuss in depth these themes and also ecumenical relations with other churches. See *Dialogue; Eastern Churches; Ecumenism; Vatican Council, Second.*

Pantheism. (Gr. "all [is] God"). Doctrine that identifies God with the universe. Although the word appears for the first time in 1709, pantheistic (or apparently pantheistic) systems of thought are at least as old as Hinduism. Some interpret the divine in natural terms (naturalistic pantheism), as does Benedict Spinoza (1632–77); others interpret nature in divine terms (emanationistic pantheism), a temptation for mystical and Neoplatonic thinkers. Pseudo-Dionysius the Areopagite (fl. 500), John Scottus Eriugena (ca. 810–ca. 877), Cardinal Nicholas of Cusa (1401–64), Meister Eckhart (ca. 1260–1327), Giordano Bruno (1548–1600), and Jacob Boehme (1575–1624) have all been accused, justly or unjustly, of including elements of pantheism in their thought. A modern form of pantheism interprets God as the big "I," a view at least closely approached by such idealists as Georg Wilhelm Friedrich Hegel (1770–1831), Friedrich Wilhelm Joseph von Schelling (1775–1854), and Francis Herbert Bradley (1846–1924). While often described as a form of atheism, pantheism can also be seen as a form of imprisoned theism. The First Vatican Council (1869–70) condemned pantheism (DH 3023; see also DH 285, 722, 976–77, 1043, 2843, 2901, 3201–3216; ND 141–42, 406/26–27, 411/1, 416). See *Atheism; Emanation; Hinduism; Idealism; Immanence, Divine; Monism; Nature; Neoplatonism; Panentheism; Theism; Transcendence.*

Pantocrator (Gr. "ruler of all"). A majestic representation of Christ as sovereign ruler of the universe, usually with his hands raised in blessing. Four famous examples are those in the Church of the Apostles in Constantinople, in the Cathedral of Hagia Sophia (Gr. "Holy Wisdom") in Kiev, and in the cathedrals of Cefalù and Monreale in Sicily. See *Icon; Kingdom of God; Omnipotence; Theocracy.*

Papalism. An attitude toward church teaching and life that exaggerates the Petrine ministry of the pope, while ignoring the role of other bishops and what can be learned from the whole people of God. See *Collegiality; Petrine Ministry; Pope; Sensus Fidelium; Ultramontanism.*

Parable (Gr. "comparison"). A comparison drawn from nature (e.g., the mustard seed in Mark 4:30–32) or from human life (e.g., the marriage feast in Matt 22:1–14) and told as a story to embody and evoke some moral or religious insight. While already found in the OT (2 Sam 12:1–14; and, perhaps, Isa 5:1–7), parables characterize in a special way the preaching and teaching of Jesus. The Synoptic Gospels report many parables used by Jesus in challenging his hearers to recognize God's final rule and decide accordingly. Strictly speaking, John's gospel contains no parables, although the language about the good shepherd (John 10:1–19) and the vine and the branches (John 15:1–8) show clear parabolic elements. Adolf Jülicher (1857–1938), Charles Harold Dodd (1884–1973), and Joachim Jeremias (1900–1979) have enriched our understanding of Jesus' parables. They are not, for example, allegories in which every detail carries an intended meaning. Parables convey one point, although long parables (e.g., the Prodigal Son [better called the Merciful Father] in Luke 15:11–32) can also yield meaning through their subordinate details. See *Allegory; Biblical Criticism; Exegesis; Hermeneutics; Johannine Theology; Senses of Scripture.*

Paraclesis (Gr. "supplication"). The little office of Our Lady used in the Byzantine rite for fifteen days immediately preceding the feast of the Dormition (*koimesis*) of the Mother of God (celebrated on August 15). See *Assumption of the Blessed Virgin; Liturgy of the Hours.*

Paraclete (Gr. "helper" or "attorney"). A term used of Jesus himself, who intercedes with the Father on behalf of sinners (1 John 2:1–2). In St. John's gospel, the word is applied to the Holy Spirit as the Helper (14:16; 14:26; 15:26; 16:7), the Spirit of truth who will be sent to dwell in the disciples and guide them by witnessing to Jesus and his teaching. See *Holy Spirit.*

Paradise (Persian "enclosed garden"). A walled park, or pleasure garden, containing exotic plants, trees, and animals. In the Septuagint (LXX), this is the garden of Eden, where Adam and Eve once lived and from which they were expelled after falling into sin (Gen 2:8–10, 15; 3:23–24; Ezek 28:13; 31:8; 36:35). Paradise came to designate the place of blessedness after death (Luke 23:43), the "third heaven" above the earth to which St. Paul was once carried in ecstasy (2 Cor 12:2–4). Revelation promises life in God's "paradise," where the blessed will eat from "the tree of life" (Rev 2:7; 22:1–2, 14). See *Eschatology; Fall, The; Heaven; Septuagint.*

Paradosis (Gr. "handing on, tradition"). In the NT, tradition handed on within a community. It can be a question of Jewish religious traditions (Gal 1:14), even wrong-headed and reformable ones (Mark 7:1–13). Paradosis can be generic Christian teaching that is handed on (2 Thess 3:6), or else specific traditions of great importance (1 Cor 11:2, 23; 15:3–5). See *Bible; Tradition.*

Parenesis (Gr. "advice"). Preaching aimed at building up community by practical recommendations or warnings. In the only NT appearance of this verb,

St. Paul "advises" the crew of a storm-battered ship on its way to Malta (Acts 27:9, 22). He, St. Peter, and St. Barnabas "exhort" different audiences (Acts 2:40; 11:23; 14:22). Parenetical passages turn up in the Pauline letters (see Rom 6:1–4; 1 Cor 5:7–8; Col 3:1–4), sometimes as lists of virtuous actions (e.g., Rom 12:1–21) or of vices (Rom 13:13). The parenesis can be rather general (as is the case toward the end of most Pauline letters) or it can be aimed at particular problems (1 Cor 11:17–22, 27–34). See *Moral Theology*.

Parish (Gr. "neighborhood"). A subdivision of a diocese that has its own priest and enjoys a certain degree of autonomy under the jurisdiction of the local bishop (see CIC 374, 515–52; CCEO 279–303). Since a bishop cannot preside everywhere in his diocese, he appoints parish priests and sets up parishes (SC 42; CD 32). There people are incorporated into the church through baptism (CIC 858); the young receive religious education; mission work takes place (AA 10; AG 37); and care is given to the sick, the needy, and the aged. The center of parish life is the celebration of the Eucharist and the proclamation of the word of God (see CD 30). See *Bishop; Chaplain; Diocese; Ordinary; Pastor*.

Parousia (Gr. "presence," "arrival"). The official visit of a ruler. From the earliest Christian documents (1 Thess 4:15; 1 Cor 15:23), the parousia designated the return of Christ in glory at the end of history to judge the world (Matt 24:29–31; 25:31–46). This will be "the day of the Lord" (1 Cor 1:8) when Christ "will appear a second time" (Heb 9:28)—an appearance for which Christians wait with patience (Jas 5:7–8; 2 Pet 1:16; 3:4, 12; 1 John 2:28). The Synoptics link the expectation of the end with a warning to keep watching (Matt 24:36–25:13; Mark 13:1–37; Luke 21:5–36). John's gospel speaks of the resurrection to come on the "last day" (John 6:39–40, 44, 54; 11:24). Christ's future coming in glory to judge the living and the dead is confessed by various creeds (see DH 6, 10, 13–17, 19, 30, 40–42, 76, 125, 150; ND 2–7, 9–10, 12). More than Western Christianity, the East highlights the collective dimension of that future consummation when God will be "all in all" (1 Cor 15:28). Some modern theologians prefer not to speak of the "second coming," since the parousia is only the ultimate consequence of Christ's first coming in the Incarnation. With Karl Rahner (1904–84), we might say that it is the world which will come to God in the parousia rather than Christ to the world. See *Eschatology; Heaven; Hell; Last Judgment; Resurrection*.

Parrhesia (Gr. "boldness in speaking"). The fearless openness with which the apostles publicly proclaimed the message of the crucified and risen Christ despite imprisonment and the threat of punishment and death (see Acts 2:29; 4:13, 29, 31; 28:31). Paul shows this frankness in dealing with his communities (2 Cor 7:4). Christians should have a similar boldness as they relate to God (see 1 John 3:21; 5:14) and wait for the day of judgment (1 John 2:28;

4:17). Christian *parrhesia* finds its model in the way Jesus openly proclaimed his message to a hostile world (John 7:26; 18:20). See *Virtues, Cardinal*.

Parthenogenesis (Gr. "virgin birth"). The generation of a child without the intervention of a human father. Some continue to allege that the story of Jesus' conception was derived from pagan legends about women producing remarkable children through the intervention of male gods. But such legends are quite different from the account of the virginal conception found in the infancy narratives of Matthew and Luke. In his *Greek Myths and Christian Mysteries*, Hugo Rahner (1900–1968) showed the superficiality of such comparisons. See *Virginal Conception of Jesus*.

Pasch (Gr. "passover"). A term previously used for the Passover of the Jews and the Christian Easter. See *Easter; Passover*.

Paschal Mystery. The redemption effected by Christ, above all through his death, resurrection, and ascension (SC 5; GS 22), in which Christians participate through baptism, the Eucharist, the other sacraments, and their whole life (SC 6–10; see Rom 6:3–4; 1 Cor 11:23–26). See *Easter; Redemption; Resurrection*.

Passion (Lat. "suffering"). In Aristotelian philosophy, as applied to a contingent being and contrasted with action, passion means being changed. In Christian terminology, the passion refers to the suffering and crucifixion Jesus endured for our salvation (see 1 Pet 2:21–25). All four gospels end with a detailed account of Jesus' passion (Matt 26–27; Mark 14–15; Luke 22–23; John 18–19). On Palm Sunday, the story of the passion is read from one of the Synoptic Gospels; and on Good Friday, from the gospel of John. See *Atonement; Good Friday; Holy Week; Redemption; Salvation*.

Passover. The Jewish family feast celebrated in the spring at the time of the full moon and commemorating the Exodus from Egypt (Exod 12:1–28; Deut 16:1–8). On the afternoon of Nisan 14, the paschal lambs were sacrificed; that evening at the Passover meal, unleavened bread was eaten with roast lamb. Whether it was a Passover meal (the Synoptic Gospels) or not (John), the Last Supper, followed by Jesus' crucifixion and resurrection, coincided with the Passover and its associated week-long feast of Unleavened Bread (Mark 14:1–2, 12–16). Christians quickly came to understand Jesus' dying and rising to have fulfilled the original Exodus and its commemoration in the Passover festival. He was seen as the paschal lamb whose sacrifice of deliverance took away the sin of the world (John 1:29; 1 Cor 5:7). See *Easter; Holy Week; Lord's Supper, The; Pasch; Resurrection*.

Pastor (Lat. "shepherd"). Term used of rulers in the OT (Jer 2:8; 3:15) and of God as the good shepherd (Ezek 34:1–31; Ps 23:1–4). Christ was sent to the lost sheep of Israel (Matt 10:6; 15:24; see Luke 15:3–7). As the good shepherd, he lays down his life for the sheep (John 10:11–16; see Heb 13:20; 1 Pet 2:25). He calls others to be pastors in the church, but the people remain his sheep (John 21:15–17; 1 Pet 5:1–4). Among Protestants, the ordained minister serving a local church is often called pastor, as is the case with Catholic priests in certain parts of Germany (see CIC 519). See *Bishop; Minister; Parish; People of God; Priests.*

Pastoral Office. The ministry of clergy, as pastors serving the people of God. The term may be applied to those whom the bishop has put in charge of particular ministries, such as religious education and family welfare. See *Clergy; Jurisdiction; Laity; Ministry.*

Pastoral Theology. Theology inasmuch as it is concerned with and reflects on (a) the passage to preaching and catechetics from the study of scripture and systematic theology, (b) the practice of liturgical and sacramental life, (c) moral and spiritual counseling, (d) the care of people facing special problems (e.g., refugees, drug addicts, the sick, the old, and the dying), (e) struggles for justice and peace, and (f) the care of people of different ages and in different life situations. Many see pastoral theology as synonymous with practical theology or critical reflection on the church's manifold mission in the world. Over the centuries, outstanding contributions to pastoral theology have come from such figures as St. John Chrysostom (ca. 347–407), St. Gregory the Great (ca. 540–604), and Karl Rahner (1904–84). See *Catechesis; Evangelization; Homiletics; Ministry; Mission, Theology of; Pastoral Office; Theology.*

Patriarch (Gr. "father who rules"). Name given to Abraham, Isaac, Jacob, the twelve sons of Jacob, and David (Gen 12–50; Acts 2:29; 7:8–9; Heb 7:4). From the sixth century onward, the title was given to the bishops of Rome, Constantinople, Alexandria, and Antioch (in that order). These patriarchs exercised wide authority in ways such as appointing bishops to major dioceses and judging appeals to their jurisdiction. The First Council of Nicaea (325) recognized this role of Rome and acknowledged Alexandria to take precedence over Antioch. The First Council of Constantinople (381) gave Constantinople a "primacy of honor after Rome, because it is a second Rome" (canon 3), which the Council of Chalcedon (451) in its twenty-eighth canon (that Pope Leo I never approved) extended so as to make Constantinople second only to Rome in jurisdiction. The Fourth Council of Constantinople (869–70), usually considered by Catholics to be the eighth ecumenical council, acknowledged the primacy of Rome and listed the patriarchates in this order of dignity: Rome, Constantinople, Alexandria, Antioch, and Jerusalem (recognized as a patriarchate at the Council of Chalcedon) (see DH 661). The Fourth Lateran Council (1215) formally and solemnly recognized that order at a time when Constantinople had become a Latin patriarchate; the Council of

Florence (1438–45) repeated that same list of patriarchates and in the same order (DH 811; 1307–8; ND 809). In the case of those Eastern churches in communion with Rome, the Second Vatican Council (1962–65) recognized their traditions, rights, privileges, and jurisdiction (OE 7–10). It indicated that, where necessary, an ecumenical council or the pope could set up new patriarchates (OE 11)—a suggestion made by many theologians for future unions among sister churches and Rome. Vatican II also proposed general guidelines toward a reunion with the Eastern churches separated from Rome (UR 13–18), among which "the Patriarchal Churches hold first place" (UR 14). See *Autocephalous; Eastern Churches; Oriental Orthodox; Orthodoxy; Pentarchy; Primacy.*

Patriarch, Ecumenical (Gr. "universal patriarch"). A title used by the patriarchs of Constantinople since the sixth century. See *Oikumene; Primacy.*

Patriarchates, Orthodox. Autonomous Orthodox churches ruled by patriarchs, the oldest being the Assyrian Church of the East, whose patriarch now resides near Chicago, and bears the title "Catholicos-Patriarch of the Church of the East." The other Orthodox patriarchates comprise two groups: those that recognize the Council of Chalcedon (451) and are known as Eastern Orthodox, and those that do not and are known as Oriental Orthodox. In the first group, four go back to the time of Chalcedon or earlier (in order of dignity, Constantinople, Alexandria, Antioch, and Jerusalem) and five are more recent (Bulgaria, Georgia, Romania, Russia, and Serbia). Among the Oriental Orthodox, Armenians are ruled by the Catholicos of All Armenians, resident in Etchmiadzin, Armenia; the Copts, by the patriarch (also called pope), resident in Cairo; the Ethiopians, by the patriarch, resident in Addis Ababa; and the Malankara Orthodox Syrian Church, by the Catholicos of the East (also called Catholicos of the Apostolic Throne of St. Thomas), resident in Kottayam (Kerala, India). In this group of the Oriental Orthodox churches, the last patriarchate to be erected was that of Eritrea in 1998. See *Chalcedon, Council of; Church of the East, Assyrian; Eastern Churches; Oriental Orthodox; Patriarch; Pope; Primacy.*

Patripassianism (Lat. "suffering of the Father"). A term coined by Tertullian (ca. 160–ca. 220) for that form of Monarchianism that we call modalism, in his campaign against Praxeas (lived ca. 200), whom he mocked as having driven out the Spirit and crucified the Father. Another modalist, Noetus (fl. 200), asserted that it was the Father who had been born and had suffered on the cross. See *Modalism; Monarchianism; Suffering of God.*

Patristics (Lat. "study of the Fathers"). The study of the theology of the Church Fathers. The term has often been used inaccurately as a synonym for patrology. See *Fathers of the Church; Patrology.*

Patrology (Gr. "study of the Fathers"). A term coined in the seventeenth century for the study of the Fathers of the Church. A 1989 instruction on the study of the Church Fathers (issued by the Vatican's Congregation for Catholic Education) distinguishes patrology, the historical and literary study of the Church Fathers, from patristics, the study of their theological thought. See *Fathers of the Church; Patristics*.

Pauline Privilege. The right to remarry of persons who are already married, convert to Christianity, and find that their non-Christian marriage partner either wishes to separate or will not let them practice their religion in peace (CIC 1143). St. Paul first laid down this privilege (1 Cor 7:12–15). See *Marriage; Marriage Impediments*.

Pauline Theology. The theology developed by St. Paul (d. ca. 67), whose call/conversion around 34 AD (1 Cor 9:1; 15:8–11; Acts 9:3–9) changed him from a zealous Pharisee (Phil 3:5–8; Acts 22:3–5) persecuting Christians (1 Cor 15:9; Gal 1:13–14; Acts 7:58—8:3; 9:1–2) to the great Apostle of the Gentiles (Gal 1:12; 15–16; 2:7; Acts 9:15). Radically centered on the resurrection of the crucified Jesus (Rom 4:25; 1 Cor 1:17–25; 15:14–15; Phil 2:6–11), Paul taught that our justification comes by faith and Christ's reconciling grace (Rom 5:6–11) and not through the works of the Law (Gal 2:16—4:31). By baptism believers exist "in" Christ (Rom 8:1; 16:7; 1 Cor 15:22; Phil 3:8–9) and through the Holy Spirit live a new life (Rom 5:1—8:39), being progressively changed into the image of Christ (Rom 8:29) and forming together the Temple of the Spirit (1 Cor 3:16–17) and the body of Christ (1 Cor 12:12–27). In the new "Israel of God" (Gal 6:16), all the baptized enjoy a basic unity (Gal 3:26–28) and are called to use their different charisms (1 Cor 12:1–31) to build up the community in love (Rom 5:5; 1 Cor 12:31—13:13) and to show in their lives the fruits of the Spirit (Gal 5:16–26). Along with Johannine theology, Pauline theology is the primary NT theology and has had the greatest influence in the history of Christianity. See *Appearances of the Risen Lord; Body of Christ; Charisms; Grace; Holy Spirit; Justification; Law*.

Peace. Called by St. Augustine of Hippo (354–430) "the tranquillity of order." For both the OT and NT, peace is more than freedom from war (see Isa 2:4; Mic 4:3; Matt 26:52). *Shalom* (Heb. "health," "peace") is the comprehensive welfare given through union with God—in particular, the saving peace associated with the Messianic Age (Isa 9:1–7; 11:1–9; 32:15–20). Jesus blessed the peacemakers (Matt 5:9). Risen from the dead, he brought that peace "the world cannot give" (John 14:27; 20:19, 21; Col 3:15), which entails a new solidarity (Gal 3:28; Eph 2:13–18) effected by his death and resurrection (Col 1:20). His followers are to proclaim peace, the message of eschatological salvation (Acts 10:36; Rom 10:15; see Matt 10:12–13). In his 1963 encyclical *Pacem in Terris*, Blessed John XXIII (pope 1958–63) placed his hopes for international peace in a social order based on freedom, justice, love, and truth. Pope Paul VI's 1967 encyclical *Populorum Progressio* called development "the new name for peace" (14). The Second Vatican Council (1962–65) pleaded for greater effort in fostering peace and community among the nations (GS 77–90). Through its Peace and Justice Commission and in many other ways, the Holy See has constantly tried to promote international peace. In the United States, the National Conference of Catholic Bishops spoke out prophetically in *The Challenge of Peace: God's Promise and Our Response* (1983). But in this world, "peace comes dropping slow" (William Butler Yeats [1865–1939]). See *Justice; Just War; Kingdom of God; Messiah; Nonviolence; Salvation; Tolerance.*

Pelagianism. A heresy concerning grace initiated by Pelagius (fl. 400), a monk from Britain or Ireland, who, first in Rome and then in North Africa, taught that human beings can achieve salvation through their own sustained efforts. Original sin amounted to no more than Adam's bad example, which did not harm interiorly his descendants, and, in particular, left intact the natural use of free will. Reducing grace to the good example provided by Christ, Pelagius encouraged a strongly ascetical life and the emergence of a church for the morally elite. His disciples, Celestius (fifth century) and Julian of Eclanum (ca. 386–454), developed Pelagianism as a system. Strongly opposed by St. Augustine of Hippo (354–430), this heresy was condemned by two councils in North Africa (DH 222–30; ND 501–2, 1901–6), then in 431 by the Council of Ephesus (DH 267–68). See *Augustinianism; Messalians; Original Sin; Semi-Pelagianism.*

Penance, Sacrament of. One of the seven sacraments instituted by Christ for the forgiveness of sins after baptism. This sacrament answers a deep need to confess sin, receive pardon from God, and be reconciled with the community harmed by our sins (2 Sam 12:1–25; Ps 51; Mark 1:4–5; Luke 7:36–50; 15:11–32; 18:9–14). That reconciling role is suggested by some words from St. Augustine of Hippo (354–430): "pax cum ecclesia dimittit peccata" (Lat. "it is peace with the church that forgives sins") (see PO 5). The gospels present Christ as forgiving sins (Mark 2:5–11; Luke 7:36–50) and giving his disciples the power to forgive sins (John 20:19–23). In the early church, baptized Christians who committed murder, apostasy, or adultery and then repented had to undergo a long, severe, and public period of penance before they were readmitted by the bishop to holy communion. From the sixth century, Irish and other missionaries spread the practice of repeated private confession to priests; the penances imposed on penitents became less rigorous. The Fourth Lateran Council (1215) prescribed confession at least once a year for those who had fallen into mortal sin (see DH 812; ND 1608). The Council of Florence (1438–45) declared that the sinner's confession is the matter of the sacrament, whereas the words of absolution are the form (see DH 1323; ND

1612). Martin Luther (1483–1546) recognized penance as a sacrament, but subsequent reformers considered only baptism and the Eucharist to be sacraments. The Council of Trent (1545–63) reaffirmed the sacramentality of penance (DH 1667–93; ND 1615–34). In the East, there is a "medicinal" approach to the sacrament, which aims at healing human beings from their wounds and evil inclinations. Conditions for the fruitful reception of the sacrament are a real contrition for sin, the confession of at least all mortal sins, a genuine intention not to sin again and to avoid all occasions of sin, and willingness to do the penance imposed by the priest. This penance, which can take various forms (e.g., prayer, fasting, almsgiving, or some other good work), should facilitate the conversion from sin to God. See *Attrition; Confession; Contrition; Forgiveness of Sins; Reconciliation; Sacrament; Sin.*

Penance, Virtue of (Lat. "repentance"). The real desire to turn from sin and be once again oriented toward God. See *Attrition; Contrition; Conversion; Metanoia.*

Pentarchy (Gr. "rule of five"). A theory, especially popular in the first millennium, that the one and undivided Christian Church was to be governed by the patriarchs of Rome, Constantinople, Alexandria, Antioch, and Jerusalem (in that order). With the schism between East and West (definitive only with the rejection of the Council of Florence), Greek Orthodox churches spoke of the tetrarchy (Gr. "rule of four"). But the idea of a pentarchy has never been completely abandoned and suggests some ecumenical possibilities. See *Code of Canons of the Oriental Churches; Council, Ecumenical; Florence, Council of; Patriarch; Primacy; Schism.*

Pentateuch (Gr. "five books"). The usual Catholic and Orthodox name for the first five books of the Bible (Genesis, Exodus, Leviticus, Numbers, and Deuteronomy), which Jews call the Torah and some Protestants call the first five books of Moses. The tradition about Moses as the author of these books should be understood in the sense of his having inspired much of the story and legislation recorded in the Pentateuch. Following some insights of Jean Astruc (1684–1766), Johann Gottfried Eichhorn (1752–1827) postulated as sources for the Pentateuch the Yahwist Document (J) and the Elohist Document (E). Julius Wellhausen (1844–1918) claimed a further source, the Priestly Code (P), to which a Deuteronomistic Source (D) was later added to complete the four-source theory. Today more attention to oral traditions and other factors has modified any neat theory about four preexisting documents (J, E, P, and D) from which the books of the Pentateuch were written. See *Bible; Old Testament; Torah.*

Pentecost (Gr. "the fiftieth day"). Along with the Passover (fifty days before) and the subsequent (autumn) feast of the Tabernacles, Pentecost is the third major Jewish feast that celebrated initially the harvesting of the grain, and, later, the giving of the Law to Moses on Mount Sinai. As a Christian feast, Pentecost recalls the day that the Holy Spirit descended upon the disciples, Peter preached to the people and pilgrims in Jerusalem, and around three thousand accepted his message and were baptized (Acts 2:1–42). From the pilgrim Egeria, we have evidence that in the Holy Land, Christians already celebrated this feast in the fourth century. The twentieth canon of the First Council of Nicaea (325) speaks of the season of Pentecost, in effect the whole fifty-day Easter feast, as a time when one should not kneel during prayers but say them standing up. The feast of Pentecost is also called Whitsunday (Old English "White Sunday"), probably because that was a day (perhaps the last day?) when the newly baptized wore their white garments. In the Byzantine liturgy, Pentecost takes two consecutive days: on Sunday the liturgy celebrates the completion of the revelation of the Trinity (a feast celebrated in the Latin rite on the Sunday following Pentecost, known as Trinity Sunday); and on Monday, the descent of the Spirit on the apostles. See *Holy Spirit; Passover; Pentecostarion.*

Pentecostals. Certain Christian communities that stress baptism in the Spirit and special gifts such as healing, prophecy, and speaking in tongues (1 Cor 14:1–40). These assemblies originated in Kansas and California during the first years of the twentieth century. Since the 1960s, many charismatic prayer groups have appeared in the Catholic Church and other mainline Christian churches. They are open to renewal in the Spirit and use their charisms (1 Cor 12:4–11) to serve the whole people of God. Unlike the Pentecostals, however, this renewal does not set up distinct assemblies, but aims to help all baptized Christians experience their new life in the Spirit. See *Charisms; Glossolalia; Holy Spirit; Miracle; Prophecy.*

Pentecostarion. The book of seasonal liturgical propers used in the Byzantine liturgy for the divine services from Easter Sunday until Pentecost Sunday inclusive. See *Easter; Octoechos; Pentecost.*

People of God. Israel as God's chosen people, set apart from other nations and cherished by God through a special covenant (Exod 5:1; 19:3–6; Deut 4:20; 7:6–8; Isa 43:20–21; Jer 31:33; Ps 100:3). Those who believe in Christ form the new people of God (Rom 9:25–26; 1 Pet 2:9–10; Rev 21:3). The Second Vatican Council (1962–65) used "people of God" as a central designation for the church (LG 9–17), and the theme has been developed by some exponents of liberation theology. See *Berith; Church; Covenant; Ecclesiology; Liberation Theology.*

Perennial Philosophy. A theme, popularized by Neo-Scholasticism, that goes back to a book written by Augustinus Steuchus (1496–1548), bishop of Kissamos in Crete, who in his *De perenni philosophia* (1540) argued for an essential harmony between the thought of Christian Platonists, such as Marsilio Ficino (1433–99) and Giovanni Pico della Mirandola (1463–94), and the philosophy of classical antiquity. Subsequently other writers such as Gottfried Wilhelm Leibniz (1646–1716) developed this thesis and maintained a basic unity in the whole history of Western thought. Aldous Huxley (1894–1963) and others have used perennial philosophy in a broader sense, claiming that all great religious traditions share the same ancient wisdom. See *Neo-Scholasticism; Neo-Thomism; Platonism; Scholasticism; Thomism.*

Perfection. The condition of those who are mature, complete, and blameless (Job 1:1). The Sermon on the Mount names God as the standard of our perfection (Matt 5:48), an aim that is closely connected with total commitment to the law of love (Mark 12:28–34; Col 3:14) and constitutes a lifelong quest (Phil 3:12). All the baptized are called to perfection (LG 39–42), and some to the practice of the three counsels of perfection: voluntary poverty (Matt 19:21), complete abstention from sexual relationships (see Matt 19:10–12), and obedience to a religious superior (LG 43–47). These evangelical counsels promote a life resembling that of the poor and chaste Christ, who showed an unswerving obedience to his loving Father. See *Holiness; Imitation of Christ; Love; Religious Life.*

Perichoresis, Christological (Gr. "going around"). The interpenetration of the divine and human natures of Christ. While remaining intact and not confused one with one another, they coinhere without separation or division (see DH 112–13, 115, 1301, 1331; ND 301–3, 323, 326). See *Chalcedon, Council of; Hypostatic Union; Incarnation.*

Perichoresis, Trinitarian. The reciprocal presence, interpenetration, or inter-relationship of the three persons of the Trinity (DH 1331; ND 326). St. Gregory of Nazianzus (329–89) used the term, but it acquired its full technical meaning with St. John Damascene (ca. 675–ca. 749). See *Immanent Trinity; Relations, Divine.*

Pericope (Gr. "selected passage"). A passage from the scriptures read in church or examined in a homily or in scholarly research. See *Exegesis; Hermeneutics; Homily.*

Person (Lat. "actor's mask"). The word originally employed to designate the role someone plays on the stage or in life, and then applied to a subsistent, rational individual. Boethius (ca. 480–ca. 524) classically defined person as "rationalis naturae individua substantia" (Lat. "an individual substance of rational nature"). Applied to the Trinity, this definition might imply three centers of reason, thus conflicting with orthodox belief of one reason held in common by the three divine persons. Over the centuries, various aspects of what it is to be a person were explicitated or added: relationship, incommunicability, self-consciousness, freedom, duties, inalienable rights, and dignity. For Immanuel Kant (1724–1804), the human person is an absolute that may never be used as a means, but must always be respected as a moral end-in-itself. Today, to overcome the notion of persons as autonomous selves, some stress the way persons are always persons-in-relationship, constituted through relations with other persons and the environment. See *Hypostasis; I and Thou; Immanent Trinity; Personalism; Persons of the Trinity; Prosopon.*

Personalism. A philosophy centered on the unique value of human persons. On the one hand, it opposes totalitarian ideologies (which subordinate the welfare of individuals to that of the collectivity), behaviorism, and any psychology that understands human beings as case studies to be interpreted simply in terms of their functions and reactions. On the other hand, true personalism excludes any selfish individualism bent on furthering one's own "interests" at the expense of others. Many (rather diverse) thinkers can be called personalists, for instance, Nicholas Berdyaev (1874–1948), E. S. Brightman (1884–1953), Martin Buber (1878–1965), Ferdinand Ebner (1882–1931), Emmanuel Mounier (1905–50), and Michael Polanyi (1891–1976). See *Person.*

Persons of the Trinity. The Father, Son, and Holy Spirit, who share in the one divine nature and subsist in relationship to each other. When speaking of the divine persons, the Greek Fathers often preferred the word *hypostasis* (Gr. "subsisting individual") over *prosōpon* (Gr. "face"), with its suggestion of mere modalism ("three faces of God"). They had their difficulties also with the Latin *persona*, even though Tertullian (ca. 160–ca. 225) had adopted the term precisely to combat the modalism of Praxeas. The Council of Chalcedon (451) used *hypostasis* and *prosōpon* as equivalents. Contemporary social models of the Trinity often tend toward tritheism or a doctrine of "three Gods"—a tendency opposed by Karl Barth (1886–1968) with his "three ways of being" and Karl Rahner (1904–84) with his "three distinct ways of subsisting." See *Father, God as; Holy Spirit; Hypostasis; Logos; Modalism; Ousia; Patripassianism; Person; Relations, Divine; Son of God; Tritheism; Trinity, Theology of.*

Pessimism. (Lat. "tendency to expect the worst"). A view of the world that underlines the presence of evil and expects its victory, at least in the short run. Over against the optimism of Gottfried Wilhelm Leibnitz (1646–1716) and his claim that "this is the best of all possible worlds," Voltaire (1694–1778), moved by the disastrous earthquake in Lisbon, wrote his play *Candide* (1759). Arthur Schopenhauer (1788–1860), the pessimistic philosopher par excellence, went as far as to claim that, even if this were the best of all possible worlds, it would not justify its existence. While recognizing how sin and other evils overshadow and harm our human condition, Christians find hope through their life of grace and expect the ultimate victory of the general resurrection (Rom 8:18–25; Rev 21:1–4). See *Antichrist; Eschatology; Evil, Mystery of; Grace; Original Sin.*

Petrine Ministry. The special service for Christian faith, life, and unity performed by St. Peter and handed on to his successor, the bishop of Rome, the city where Sts. Peter and Paul died as martyrs. The Petrine office meant witnessing to Christ's resurrection (Luke 22:31–32; 24:34; Acts 2:22–36) and exercising pastoral authority with love (Matt 16:17–19; John 21:15–19; 1 Pet 5:1–4). St. Ignatius of Antioch (ca. 35–ca. 107) called the Church of Rome "the one that presides in love," a phrase repeated by Patriarch Demetrios (patriarch 1972–1991) when Pope John Paul II (pope 1978–2005) visited Constantinople in 1979. St. Irenaeus of Lyons (ca. 130–ca. 200) appealed to apostolic succession, in general, and that of the bishop of Rome, in particular, as a criterion for recognizing Christian truth. When the "Tome" (his letter to the patriarch of Constantinople, St. Flavian) of St. Leo I (pope, 440–61) was read at the Council of Chalcedon (451), the members of the council exclaimed, "Peter has spoken through the mouth of Leo." The First Vatican Council (1869–70) expressed this Petrine office in terms of universal jurisdiction and infallibility (DH 3050–75; ND 818–40). The Second Vatican Council (1962–65) spelled out the collegial character of this office, exercised together with all the bishops who with and under Peter's successor share responsibility for the whole church (LG 22). Recent ecumenical dialogues with Anglicans, Orthodox, and Protestants have shown a growing sensitivity to the need for a central church office as a visible sign and agent of Christian unity in faith, but no agreement appears yet in sight on the concrete exercise of the Petrine ministry. In the 1995 encyclical *Ut Unum Sint* (no. 96), Blessed John Paul II appealed to the leaders and theologians of other churches to engage with him in "patient and fraternal dialogue" on the Petrine ministry. See *Apostle; Apostolic Succession; Catholicism; Collegiality; Conciliarism; Febronianism; Gallicanism; Infallibility; Jurisdiction; Pentarchy; Pope; Protestant; Reformation, The.*

Pharisees (Heb. "separated ones"). A pious Jewish group formed in the second century BC that accepted both the oral and the written Law, and scrupulously observed many practices (guided by 366 positive norms and 250 negative ones). The group criticized Jesus for forgiving sins, breaking the Sabbath, and associating with sinners. In his turn, he objected to the Pharisees' external legalism and self-righteous formalism (Mark 7:1–23; Luke 18:9–14). Nevertheless, the gospels also record how he was defended and entertained by some Pharisees (Luke 7:36; 13:31; John 7:50–51; 19:39). St. Paul's teacher, the Pharisee Gamaliel, urged restraint in dealing with the apostles (Acts 5:34–39). Not only Paul, but also other Pharisees (Acts 15:5) became Christians. After the revolt of Bar-Cochba (AD 135), the traditions of the

Pharisees were preserved by the rabbis and the Mishnah. See *Mishnah; Sadducees; Talmud.*

Phenomenology (Gr. "study of appearances"). The study of phenomena as opposed to noumena (Gr. "things that are apprehended"), or things as they are in themselves and not simply as they appear to be. After Immanuel Kant (1724–1804) had drawn a sharp distinction between the noumenal and the phenomenal world, Georg Wilhelm Friedrich Hegel (1770–1831), in his *Phenomenology of the Spirit* (1807), claimed to trace various phases that the mind passes through: from naive consciousness, sensible certitude of phenomena, and on to the absolute knowledge of the Spirit. By studying the contents of human consciousness, the phenomenology of Edmund Husserl (1859–1938) aimed at describing the way that things, as they really are, actually manifest themselves. Max Scheler's (1874–1928) work on feelings and values took phenomenology in a somewhat Augustinian direction, as did that of Husserl's assistant, St. Edith Stein (1891–1942). Phenomenology may also be existential, as with Maurice Merleau-Ponty (1908–61), who aimed at describing "my" world rather than the world as it is in itself. With Martin Heidegger (1889–1976), phenomenology became a philosophy of existence based on historicity and time. See *Existentialism; Experience, Religious; Philosophy.*

Philocalia (Gr. "love of what is beautiful"). (a) An anthology drawn from the writings of Origen (ca. 185–ca. 253) by St. Basil the Great (ca. 330–79) and St. Gregory of Nazianzus (329–89). (b) The same title was chosen for an anthology on asceticism, solitude, and the prayer of the heart called hesychasm, drawn from thirty-eight Fathers of the Church and published in 1782 by St. Macarius Notaras, bishop of Corinth (1731–1805), and St. Nicodemus Hagiorita ("of the Holy Mountain," i.e., of Mount Athos) (ca. 1749–1809). Inspired by this anthology, Paisy Velichkovsky (1722–94) translated into Slavonic his own selection from the Greek Fathers and published it in 1793 as *Dobrotoliubie* (Slav. "love of what is good"). Bishop Theophan Zatvornik (Russ. "the Recluse") (1815–94) made a free translation into Russian from the 1782 anthology, considerably enlarging it and giving it the title of Velichkovsky's collection. Both editions of the *Dobrotoliubie* have greatly influenced Russian spirituality and affected a wide public, as evidenced by the anonymous *The Way of a Pilgrim* (published in Kazan, Asian Russia, in 1870). In the last decades, the rediscovery of the *Philocalia* has greatly contributed to make Orthodox spirituality (and the spirituality of the Fathers generally) known in the West. See *Cappadocian Fathers; Fathers of the Church; Hesychasm; Jesus Prayer; Mysticism.*

Philosophy (Gr. "love of wisdom"). The study of the most general principles of things and our knowledge of them. After Socrates (ca. 469–399 BC) and Plato (ca. 428–ca. 348 BC), Greek philosophy reached its climax with Aristotle

(384–22 BC). He set philosophy within a unified scheme for learning that for centuries had a massive influence both in the East and the West. An introductory study of logic or the science of reasoning was to serve as the *organon* (Gr. "instrument") for further knowledge. Then followed (a) *theoria* (Gr. "contemplation"), which was divided into the first philosophy (metaphysics), mathematics, and physics; (b) *praxis* (Gr. "action," "behavior"), which was divided into ethics and politics; and (c) *poiesis* (Gr. "making," "production"), which was divided into rhetoric, poetics, and economics. After René Descartes (1596–1650) and Immanuel Kant (1724–1804), the problem of the nature, conditions, and limits of human knowledge has often occupied center stage in philosophy. In the twentieth century, various forms of existentialism, analytic philosophy, Marxism, process philosophy, Thomism, and other philosophies have produced a situation of pluralism—at least in the Western world. Theology needs help from some well-based philosophy if it is to clarify critically its concepts, language, questions, and method. See *Aristotelianism; Epistemology; Ethics; Existentialism; Hermeneutics; Idealism; Materialism; Metaphysics; Neoplatonism; Neo-Scholasticism; Neo-Thomism; Nominalism; Perennial Philosophy; Personalism; Phenomenology; Platonism; Pragmatism; Process Theology; Scholasticism; Structuralism; Theology.*

Philosophical Theology. A philosophical study of revealed truth, undertaken, unlike the philosophy of religion, in the light of faith and proved an exercise of "faith seeking understanding." By considering such themes as revelation, faith, tradition, and biblical inspiration, philosophical theology, while typically taking a speculative rather than an historical approach, overlaps with fundamental theology. Philosophical theology also takes up such topics as the divine attributes, the relationship between the divine and human minds of Christ and the Eucharist, which do not enter fundamental theology. Philosophical theologians, who often come from the ranks of American and British analytic philosophers, aim at exploring intellectually revealed truths and providing evidential considerations in support of such truths. *The Oxford Handbook of Philosophical Theology* (2009) illustrates clearly the scope of this discipline. See *Faith; Fundamental Theology; Inspiration, Biblical; Philosophy of Religion; Revelation; Theology; Tradition.*

Philosophy of Religion. The philosophical study of religious language, beliefs, experience, and practice. This rather vaguely focused discipline was created by David Hume (1711–76), Immanuel Kant (1724–1804), Georg Wilhelm Friedrich Hegel (1770–1831), and other figures of the Enlightenment, who often played down the significance of revelation and wished to develop a religion within the limits of reason alone. Some use this discipline today to elaborate grounds for religious belief or to study the relations between philosophical reason and religious faith. In philosophizing about religion, this discipline normally prescinds from the standpoint of personal faith and studies all world religions, without endorsing the preeminence, let alone uniqueness, of any one religion. Hence it is usually to be distinguished from philosophical theology, which does not prescind from Christian faith and partly coincides with fundamental theology. See *Fundamental Theology; Natural Theology; Philosophical Theology; Philosophy; Religion; Revelation.*

Pietism. A revival movement in Protestantism that was shaped by Philipp Jakob Spener (1635–1705) and that (over against the prevailing, formal orthodoxy of the official church) stressed prayer, reading of the Bible, religious experience, and committed Christian life in small communities. Other notable names in the movement include the hymn-writer Paul Gerhardt (ca. 1607–76), Nikolaus Ludwig Graf von Zinzendorf (1700–1760), and the mystic Gerhard Tersteegen (1697–1769). Pietism helped the rise of Methodism as well as influencing theologians such as Friedrich Daniel Ernst Schleiermacher (1768–1834). See *Liberal Protestantism; Lutheranism; Methodism; Protestant.*

Pilgrimage. Journey of devotion to holy places—a practice common to Christianity and other world religions. After the conversion of Emperor Constantine in AD 312, pilgrimages to the Holy Land and to the tombs of the martyrs in Rome increased. The oldest extant account of a pilgrimage to the Holy Land, the *Itinerarium Burdogalense*, was written around 333 by an anonymous traveler from Burdigala (modern Bordeaux) in Southern Gaul. Other traditional and modern places of Christian pilgrimage include Santiago de Compostela (Spain), the Marian shrines of Lourdes (France), Fatima (Portugal), and the island of Tinos (Greece), where the Orthodox celebrate in a special way the dormition of Our Lady. See *Assumption of the Blessed Virgin; Holy Week; Martyr; Palm Sunday; Pentecost; Vigil.*

Platonism. The philosophy inspired by Plato (427–347 BC), whose Academy remained a center of learning, though not necessarily of Platonism itself, until closed by the Emperor Justinian I (reigned 527–65) in AD 529. The famous *Dialogues*, in which Plato presents Socrates (ca. 469–399 BC) debating with Sophists and others, converge on a central theme: statements about justice, truth, goodness, beauty, and other things in our changing and visible world are valid if they can be "universalized," and this points to a higher world of eternal, changeless, universal Ideas. Our souls preexisted in that world and enjoy an innate knowledge which derives from their previous vision of the Ideas. Clement of Alexandria (ca. 150–ca. 215) and Origen (ca. 185–ca. 254) drew much from Plato, and Origen accepted the preexistence of human souls (see DH 403–4). Initially it was "middle" Platonism, with its stress on God's absolute transcendence, that influenced the Fathers. In a sense, the crisis of Arianism was a crisis of this form of Platonism; an utterly transcendent God needed an intermediary or "demiurge" to create the world. Neoplatonism had some impact on St. Augustine of Hippo (354–430), his followers, and

Renaissance Platonists such as Marsilio Ficino (1433–99). Unlike the West, where Aristotelianism eventually more or less prevailed; in the East, Platonism dominated with humanists such as Michael Psellus (ca. 1019–ca. 1078) and theologians who clarified deification through the Platonic notion of participation. Matthew Arnold (1822–88) suggested that everyone is born either a Platonist or an Aristotelian. Alfred North Whitehead (1861–1947), however, gave the precedence to Aristotle's teacher by claiming that all (Western) philosophy is only a series of footnotes to Plato. See *Alexandrian Theology; Arianism; Aristotelianism; Augustinianism; Deification; Demiurge; Fathers of the Church; Idealism; Neoplatonism; Origenism; Universals.*

Pleroma (Gr. "plenitude"). In the Pauline letters, the term refers to the fullness of God (Eph 3:19); the full measure of Christ's divinity (Col 1:19; 2:9); the church as the complement of Christ (Eph 1:23); and the fullness of time, when the Son of God was sent (Gal 4:4). Gnostics applied *pleroma* to the Son's attributes, which through a series of emanations prepare the transition to the *kenoma* (Gr. "emptiness, void"). See *Emanation; Gnosticism; Kenosis.*

Pluralism. Any philosophical outlook that does not attempt to reduce everything to one ultimate principle. According to whether it accepts a variety of cultures, political parties, or religious confessions, pluralism takes a cultural, political, or religious form. Over against a rigid uniformity, the Second Vatican Council (1962–65) endorsed a proper diversity in Christian traditions and worship (SC 37; UR 14–17). On January 25, 1959, Blessed John XXIII (pope 1958–63) announced his plan to convoke the Second Vatican Council; a few months later, he recalled the traditional maxim "in essentialibus unitas, in dubiis libertas, in omnibus caritas" (Lat. "unity in essentials, freedom in debatable matters, charity in everything"). Some distinguish pluralism, which they see as fracturing the true unity of faith and theology, from a legitimate pluriformity, through which the Christian faith is variously expressed. Apropos of the world's religions, many distinguish between pluralism *de facto* (the pluralism that actually exists) from pluralism *de iure* (a plualism in principle and willed by God). Karl Rahner (1904–84) characterized postmodernism as marked by an irreducible intellectual pluralism. See *Church and State; Classical Consciousness; Dualism; Eastern Churches; Liberty, Religious; Monism; Postmodernism; Rite; World Religions.*

Pneumatology (Gr. "study of the Spirit"). The branch of theology that studies the Holy Spirit. St. Paul's letters testify to the role of the Spirit in revealing God, enabling faith, inspiring prayer, dwelling in the church, blessing the community with various charisms, and working toward the final consummation of all things in Christ (Rom 8:1–27; 1 Cor 2:10–16; 12:1–11; Gal 4:6). Often the Holy Spirit has not been studied alone, but in the context of other main themes of theology, such as Trinity, church, grace, and sacraments. This "neglect" corresponds to what St. John Damascene (ca. 675–ca. 749) called the "kenotic" (Gr. "emptied") character of the Spirit, who comes anonymously to confirm in us the image of the Son, a doctrine given fresh impetus by Vladimir Lossky (1903–58). To borrow from Gustave Flaubert (1821–80), the Holy Spirit functions somewhat like an author in his or her works: being everywhere present and nowhere in particular. The study of the Spirit, as the Christian East knows, belongs everywhere in theology and life, rather than being limited to one particular sector. The Second Vatican Council (1962–65), for example, in its teaching on the church (LG 3–4, 9–17), illustrates how christological and pneumatological reflections require and complement each other. See *Christology; Grace; Holy Spirit; Trinity, Theology of.*

Pneumatomachians (Gr. "Spirit-fighters"). A late fourth-century group that denied the full divinity of the Holy Spirit. Its members are also improperly called Macedonians, possibly because they were joined after his death by followers of Bishop Macedonius of Constantinople (d. ca. 362). They were condemned at the First Council of Constantinople (381), which defined the divinity of the Spirit in vital and biblical terms, but without calling the Spirit "of one being" or "consubstantial" with the Father and the Son (see DH 150–51; ND 12–13). See *Constantinople, First Council of; Holy Spirit; Homoousios; Macedonians; Nicaea, First Council of.*

Political Theology. A theology that protests the privatization of religion and insists on the social responsibility of Christians. After the perestroika of Constantine the Great (ca. 280–337) brought them religious liberty, Christians, such as Eusebius of Caesarea (ca. 260–ca. 340), at times used their beliefs to legitimate the imperial policies and practices. A new, false association of the political order and religion sometimes has encouraged war and persecution, not to mention contemporary "ethnic cleansing." The Enlightenment went to the other extreme by encouraging the view that religion and politics should be kept apart and that faith is a private matter for the individual's conscience. Far from seeking to politicize religion, the political theology of Johann Baptist Metz (b. 1928) and others aims rather to express the implications of Christian faith for the social and political order—above all by protesting against the massive injustice in our world and emphasizing solidarity with the crucified Jesus and the countless victims of the world's past and present history. This theology of praxis has found a kind of official counterpart in Blessed John Paul II's encyclicals, *Sollicitudo Rei Socialis* (1987) and *Centesimus Annus* (1991). See *Black Theology; Church and State; Enlightenment; Feminist Theology; Liberation Theology; Option for the Poor; Praxis; Symphony.*

Polygamy (Gr. "many marriages"). Having more than one wife at the same time. In the period of the OT patriarchs and later (Deut 21:15–17), polygamy was accepted. Appealing to God's original plan (Gen 2:24), Jesus supported monogamy (Gr. "one marriage") and rejected divorce and remarriage, which amounts to subsequent or "serial" polygamy (Mark 10:2–12). The Second Vatican Council (1962–65) condemned polygamy as against the true dignity of marriage (GS 47). See *Marriage*.

Polygenism (Gr. "many origins"). The view that the human race has not come from an original pair of ancestors. but from many. Before the nineteenth century, Christians commonly traced human origins back to a single pair of parents (monogenism). This seemed indispensable to safeguard the unity of the human species and its common fate in the history of salvation: all sinned in Adam and all were redeemed in Christ, the New Adam. Some modern theologians, however, while accepting that God directly created the soul of each individual, envisaged human beings emerging through evolution and not necessarily from an original couple. Pius XII's encyclical *Humani Generis* (1950) cautiously warned against polygenism as not being clearly reconcilable with the doctrine of original sin and its transmission to all the descendants of Adam and Eve (DH 3896–97; ND 420). Since 1950 some reputable theologians, supported by an improved exegesis, and, in particular, by a more accurate interpretation of Romans 5:12–21, have proposed ways of reconciling belief in original sin with polygenism. The universality of human solidarity for good and evil (expressed by the doctrines of creation and original sin) can be safeguarded without necessarily subscribing to biological monogenism. At the same time, however, some evolutionary biologists today hold that our race derives not from many families, but from one. See *Creation; Evolution; Original Sin*.

Polytheism (Gr. "belief in many gods"). The belief that there are many gods, who are often grouped around a supreme deity in a pantheon (Gr. "all gods") of hierarchical importance and who personify various experiences and functions of life. Polytheistic religions were and are found in many ancient and modern cultures. Some writers have argued that in the religious history of the human race, polytheism led to the higher stage of monotheism or that a primitive monotheism declined into polytheism. The historical and anthropological data seem to be too complex to support such simple theories. See *Monotheism; Theism*.

Pope (Gr. "father"). Title originally reserved in the East for the bishop of Alexandria, but now applied also to priests, because of their spiritual parentage. The Orthodox Patriarch of the Copts is also known as "pope" and enjoys extensive powers. In the West, the title was originally used for important bishops, but by the eleventh century had come to be limited to the bishop of Rome alone. The head of the Catholic Church has also been called successor of Peter, vicar of Jesus Christ, and patriarch of the West. In March 2008, Pope Benedict XVI (pope 2005–13) dropped his title of "Patriarch of the West," since it could suggest that his primacy is only that of being "primus inter pares" or "first among equal" patriarchs. Blessed John Paul II (pope 1978–2005) preferred to be called "Bishop of Rome," a title that goes back to early Christian times and is widely acceptable. See *Bishop; Collegiality; Conclave; Coptic Christianity; Infallibility; Jurisdiction; Petrine Ministry; Patriarch; Priests; Primacy.*

Positive Theology. A branch of theology that deals with historical data and particular facts (drawn from the Bible and tradition) to determine the doctrines Christians believe, as opposed to natural theology, which treats of universal religious principles known from reason. An epoch-making protagonist of positive theology was the French Jesuit Denys Petau (1583–1652). Today positive theology seldom appears among the schemes for dividing the whole field of theology; its place has often been taken by historical theology. See *Biblical Theology; Dogmatic Theology; Fundamental Theology; Moral Theology; Pastoral Theology; Patristics; Systematic Theology; Theology.*

Positivism. The philosophy popularized by Auguste Comte (1798–1857), who held that we know only what we can perceive through the senses, rejected theological and metaphysical claims, and wished to reorganize society on scientific lines. Between the two world wars, logical positivists, such as Alfred Jules Ayer (1910–89), argued that only statements which are either tautological or can be tested by empirical observation are meaningful—a principle that is itself neither tautological nor open to be verified by such observation. See *Materialism; Metaphysics; Science and Religion.*

Possession, Diabolical. The frenzied, violent, or obscene state of persons controlled by demonic forces. The NT, but not John's gospel, speaks of such possession and deliverance from it through Christ's saving power (Mark 1:23–28; 5:1–20; Luke 11:14–20; Acts 19:13–16; Matt 8:28–34). The Christian tradition has accepted the possibility of diabolical possession. At the same time, many alleged cases can be explained as psychological disturbance rather than literal enslavement by the devil. A famous case involved the Jesuit Jean Joseph Surin (1600–1665), a noted spiritual writer, who set out to exorcize an Ursuline convent in Loudun and wound up suffering for twenty years in a pathological state interpreted by many as diabolical possession. See *Demons; Devil, The; Exorcism.*

Postmodernism. A term first used by Arnold Toynbee in 1946, and, from the 1970s, widely applied to a Western culture disenchanted with reason, scientific method, and faith in progress. At the end of the First World War, Oswald Spengler (1880–1936) wrote of "the decline of the West." During the Second World War, Dietrich Bonhoeffer (1906–45) reflected on a world "come of age"—an idea that would encourage secular and even "death of God" theology. Immediately after the Second World War in lectures held in Munich and Tübingen, Romano Guardini (1885–1968) argued that the Modern Age had come to an end. Jacques Derrida (1930–2004), Michel Foucault (1926–84), Jean-François Lyotard (1924–98), and others have explored the fragmented, even traumatized, reality of human existence. Jürgen Habermas (b. 1929) and further writers have resisted postmodernism as a faddish, misguided abandonment of rational thought. Postmodernist trends are to be found in architecture, art (e.g., the work of Andy Warhol [1930–87]), literary criticism, philosophy, biblical exegesis, and other disciplines. See *Death of God Theology; Enlightenment; Frankfurt School; Hermeneutics; Pluralism; Rationalism.*

Potentia Jurisdictionis. See *Hierarchy; Jurisdiction; Ordination.*

Potentia Oboedientialis (Lat. "potency under obedience"). Human nature, insofar as it is open to divine grace. The term goes back to St. Thomas Aquinas (ca. 1225–74) and Blessed Peter of Tarantaise (ca. 1224–76), who is also known as Innocent V (pope 1276). In post-Tridentine theology, this human openness to God was often interpreted in a static way. Henri de Lubac (1896–1991) and others have used the term to indicate how human beings are dynamically open to God's initiatives. See *Grace.*

Potestas Ordinis. See *Hierarchy; Holy Orders; Jurisdiction; Ordination.*

Poverty. (a) The state of being without such essential goods and services as food, clothing, and shelter, and, by analogy, the state of those who in various ways are spiritually poor. Down to Blessed John Paul II's 1987 encyclical *Sollicitudo Rei Socialis* (see 14–19) and beyond, like many other Christians, church leaders have prophetically denounced the subhuman conditions of life to which war, military expenditure, the greed of rich nations, and other factors have condemned millions of people. (b) As an evangelical form of life, poverty means the voluntary renunciation of private property so as to follow Christ more closely (see Mark 10:17–22; 2 Cor 8:9), serve others more freely, and witness more clearly to the absolute value of God's final kingdom (PC 13; LG 42, 44). Both the Eastern and the Western codes of canon law sum up what the practice of the evangelical poverty involves in institutes of consecrated, religious life (CIC 600, 668; CCEO 460, 467–68, 529 §3). See *Anawim; Beatitudes; Evangelical Counsels; Justice; Liberation Theology; Option for the Poor; Religious Life; Rights, Human; Social Teaching; Vow.*

Practical Theology. See *Pastoral Theology.*

Pragmatism (Gr. "belief in things"). An American philosophical movement initiated by Charles Sanders Peirce (1839–1914) and developed by William James (1842–1910) and John Dewey (1859–1952). Highlighting the reality of experience, this school tested the truth of assertions by their practical results. Dewey, in particular, had a profound influence on American thought and education. Pragmatism also influenced George Tyrrell (1861–1909) and some other modernists. See *Modernism; Philosophy.*

Praxis (Gr. "doing, performing"). Self-critical activity that is not satisfied with a merely theoretical vindication of truth, but aims to verify truth by transforming society. Christian discipleship requires a praxis centered on Jesus and, far from denigrating the church's public worship, leads to it and issues from it. See *Frankfurt School; Orthodoxy; Orthopraxis; Political Theology.*

Prayer. Traditionally defined by Evagrius Ponticus (346–99) as "the dialogue of the mind with God" or by St. John of Damascus (ca. 675–ca. 749) as the "elevation of the mind to God." Mind should not be understood here in a merely intellectual way, because prayer involves also our freedom and emotions. God is present in a way that goes far beyond the presence of human partners in dialogue. To pray is to invoke, adore, praise, thank, express sorrow, and ask blessings from our personal creator and Lord. Prayer may be uttered aloud or occur silently in the heart, can take place alone or with others, within the official liturgy of the church or beyond it. Jesus prayed publicly and in private (e.g., Mark 1:35; 6:46; 14:12–26, 32–42), taught his disciples to pray (Matt 6:9–13; 7:7–11; Luke 11:1–4), and with them inherited the OT tradition of prayer represented classically by the psalms. The richest collection of NT prayers occurs in the opening chapters of Luke's gospel (Luke 1:46–55, 68–79; 2:14, 29–32). Acts 4:24–30 records a moving prayer in time of persecution. Christians believe that the Holy Spirit makes possible their life of prayer (Rom 8:15, 26–27; Gal 4:6). See *Acoemetae; Apophatic Theology; Asceticism; Cataphatic Theology; Contemplation; Hesychasm; Impetratory Prayer; Intercession; Jesus Prayer; Liturgy; Liturgy of the Hours; Lord's Prayer, The; Meditation; Mysticism; Philocalia; Retreat; Worship.*

Preaching. Proclaiming the word of God within Christian worship or as an invitation to conversion and worship. Preceded by John the Baptist (Mark 1:1–8), Jesus proclaimed the good news of God (Mark 1:14–15) and sent the Twelve to preach (Mark 6:7–13). Peter (Gal 2:7–8), Paul, and other Christian missionaries proclaimed the gospel of Jesus crucified and risen from the dead as Christ, Lord, and Son of God (Rom 1:1–6, 15–16; 10:14–18; Gal 1:15–16). Great Christian preachers have included St. Ephraem (ca. 306–73), St. John Chrysostom (ca. 347–407), St. Augustine of Hippo (354–430), St. Leo the Great (pope 440–61), St. Antony of Padua (1195–1231), Martin Luther (1483–1546), George Fox (1624–91), Bishop Jacques Bénigne Bossuet (1627–1704), Louis Bourdaloue (1632–1704), John Wesley (1703–91), and John Henry Newman (1801–90). The Order of Preachers was the name given to the religious institute founded by St. Dominic Guzman (1170–1221). Faced with the modern revolution in social communications, styles of preaching have been changing to serve better the challenge of evangelization. See

Catechesis; Evangelization; Homiletics; Kerygma; Parenesis; Proclamation; Word of God; Worship.

Preambles of Faith. Those presuppositions of Christian faith that can be made explicit to show how the act of faith is also a reasonable human act. On the one hand, human experience, especially in its deepest aspects, can make people open to hearing and believing the word of revelation. On the other hand, accepting God's self-communication in Christ presupposes some knowledge of God, of human destiny (see Rom 1:19–20; 2:15; Heb 11:6), and of Jesus' earthly history. See *Analysis of Faith; Faith*.

Precious Blood. See *Blood of Christ*.

Predestination (Lat. "being foreordained"). Being elected for salvation through the eternal foreknowledge and will of God (see Matt 20:23; John 10:29; Rom 8:28–30; Eph 1:3–14). The Pelagian controversy provoked from St. Augustine of Hippo (354–430) some extreme assertions about God electing only some people for eternal salvation. Disallowing the universal saving will of God, John Calvin (1509–64) held a double predestination: some human beings are elected by God for eternal salvation and others for eternal damnation. This view had been held by the monk Gottschalk (ca. 804–ca. 869) and was repeatedly condemned (see DH 621, 685, 1567; ND 1967). While properly vindicating the primacy of the divine grace on which we depend utterly, predestination should not be pushed to the point of denying either God's universal saving will (1 Tim 2:3–6) or human freedom (see DH 396–97; ND 1921–22). See *Apocatastasis; Augustinianism; Calvinism; Foreknowledge; Freedom; Grace; Merit; Molinism; Omniscience; Pelagianism; Providence; Salvation; Semi-Pelagianism*.

Preexistence. The belief that Jesus of Nazareth was/is personally identical with the Son of God, who has existed from all eternity and who entered the world to be revealed in human history (John 1:14; 1 Cor 8:6; 2 Cor 8:9; Phil 2:5–11; Col 1:15–17; Heb 1:2–3). Although pre-Christian Jewish thought envisaged intermediaries between God and the world, there are no demonstrable antecedents for the notion of Christ's fully personal preexistence as the Son of God and Logos who truly "descends" to earth. In pre-Christian Judaism, Wisdom and the Logos are only vivid metaphors for God's attributes and activities. Plato (427–347 BC) argued for preexisting Ideas that provided the pattern for the demiurge in fashioning the world. His philosophy encouraged Origen (ca. 185–ca. 254) to propose that God created spirits whose use or misuse of free will either made them angels or devils, or else turned them into souls inhabiting human bodies. See *Christology from Above; Demiurge; Eternity; Incarnation; Logos; Origenism; Wisdom Literature*.

Preface (Lat. "spoken before"). Originally, in the Latin rite, any prayer "spoken before" the people. It now refers only to the prayer that introduces the canon in the Latin Mass and enumerates reasons for giving praise to God. Prefaces vary with the time of the year (e.g., Advent, Lent, Easter, and Pentecost) as well as for the various feasts (e.g., those of Our Lady, apostles, and martyrs). The corresponding part in Eastern liturgies comes immediately before the anaphora. See *Anaphora; Eucharist; Eucharistic Prayer; Liturgy.*

Presbyter (Gr. "elder"). Term used for officials of a synagogue, members of the Jewish Sanhedrin or supreme council in Jerusalem, and those who led early Christian communities (see Acts 11:30; 14:23). Originally presbyters seem to have been synonymous with the *episkopoi* (Gr. "overseers") (see Phil 1:1; Titus 1:5, 7). In the Jerusalem church, the presbyters were associated with the apostles (Acts 15:2, 4, 6, 22–23; 16:4). By the time of St. Ignatius of Antioch (ca. 35–ca. 107), the presbyters (or priests) were a group coming after the overseers (or bishops) and before the deacons. The decree of the Second Vatican Council (1962–65) on priests is entitled *Presbyterorum Ordinis* (1965). See *Bishop; Deacon; Elders; Priests.*

Presbyterianism. A form of church government distinguished, on the one hand, from episcopalianism or the rule of bishops, and, on the other, from congregationalism or the rule of the community. It involves rule through a series of courts, up to the General Assembly—with the representative ministers and elders participating after being elected. Presbyterians stand in the tradition of John Calvin (1509–64) and the Scottish reformer John Knox (ca. 1505–72). The Church of Scotland is the only Presbyterian Church that is also an established or state church. See *Calvinism; Congregational Theology; Elders; Episcopalians.*

Preternatural Gifts. Special endowments that enhanced the human nature of Adam and Eve apart from the basic, supernatural gift of grace. Official church teaching spoke of integrity (or freedom from concupiscence) and immortality (DH 222, 371–72, 396, 1508–9, 1512, 1926, 1955, 1978, 2616–17, 3514; ND 501, 504–5, 508–9, 512, 514/26), while theological speculation suggested further privileges. See *Concupiscence; Original Justice; Original Sin; Paradise; Polygenism; Supernatural.*

Priests. Members of the community set apart to offer sacrifice and mediate between God and human beings—in a cultic way like the OT Levitical priesthood (Exod 28:1; 32:25–29; Lev 8:1—9:24), or as priest-kings such as Melchizedek (Gen 14:18–20), or in a prophetic way such as Ezekiel. The one supreme mediator between God and humanity (1 Tim 2:5), Jesus, is called the great high priest by Hebrews (Heb 4:14—5:10), which expounds the nature of his sacrifice, mediation of the new covenant, and priesthood as being superior to the Levitical priesthood (Heb 6:20—10:18). (a) Through their baptism all believers share in Christ's royal priesthood (1 Pet 2:4–10; SC 14; AA 3); this is called the priesthood of all the faithful. (b) Through the sacrament of holy orders priests are consecrated, by the Holy Spirit and for the good of the whole church, to a special ministry of word, sacraments, and pastoral leadership (PO 2, 4–6). This is often called the ministerial priesthood, but some prefer the name presbyterate, to underline the essential difference from the priesthood of all the faithful. Besides being confessors, anointing the sick, and administering other sacraments, the ministry of ordained priests means offering the sacrifice of the Mass "in the person of Christ and as representing the church" (LG 10, 28). There is one priesthood, that of Jesus Christ, in which in their own different ways the baptized and ordained ministers share. See *Baptism; Bishop; Celibacy; Clergy; Deacon; Holy Orders; Initiation; Mediation; Ministry; Ordination; Pastor; Presbyter; Prophet; Protestant.*

Primacy (Lat. "first seat"). The office of the leading bishop or primate in a church and the respect due to his rank. A primacy of honor means presiding at synods and conferences, but does not entail special authority beyond one's own diocese or country, as is the case with the archbishop of Canterbury in the Anglican Communion. The pope's primacy of jurisdiction means real authority in the pastoral government of the whole church (see DH 875, 3059–60, 3063–64, 3074; ND 804, 825–26, 829–30, 839). Many Orthodox recognize the pope's primacy of honor, but not his real jurisdiction. However when Blessed John Paul II (pope 1978–2005) visited Constantinople in 1979, Patriarch Demetrios I (patriarch 1972-1991) greeted him with the words of St. Ignatius of Antioch (ca. 35–ca. 107) describing the Roman see as "presiding in love," a venerable title that indicates a pastoral service for the whole church. In some Eastern churches, for example, the Georgian Orthodox, the Armenian Apostolic and several Syrian churches, the primate is called *catholicos* (Gr. "general superior"), a title that is equivalent to that of patriarch and may also indicate being autocephalous. Primacy can be universal or regional. Thus, among the Oriental Orthodox churches, the patriarch of Alexandria enjoys a primacy of honor over the Ethiopian and Eritrean Churches. See *Armenian Christianity; Autocephalous; Authority; Bishop; Church of the East, Assyrian; Diocese; Eastern Churches; Jurisdiction; Patriarch; Petrine Ministry; Pope; Synod.*

Priscillianism. A fourth-century heresy associated with the Spaniard Priscillian, preacher, and one-time bishop of Avila. This dualistic heresy borrowed from Gnosticism and Manichaeism, and followed Modalist tendencies by interpreting Father, Son, and Holy Spirit as merely three modes or facets of the same God. Reaction against this heresy accelerated developments in trinitarian doctrine. In 386, despite the protests of St. Martin of Tours (d. 397), Priscillian was put to death by state authorities in Trier, becoming the first heretic executed by Christians in government (see DH 188–208, 283–86, 451–64). See *Dualism; Gnosticism; Manichaeism; Modalism; Patripassianism.*

Probabilism. System of moral theology characterized by the principle that, if after seeking to arrive at certainty, an objective doubt remains about a law's existence or application, it is lawful to act on a merely probable opinion, even when the opposite opinion favoring a stricter interpretation may seem more probable. This system, supported by Jesuits and others, was challenged by probabiliorism, a system adopted by the Dominicans in 1656, which allowed one to follow only those opinions that have more evidence in their favor. St. Alphonsus Liguori (1696–1787), the founder of the Redemptorists, through his mediating position lent support to probabilism, the system commonly accepted today (see DH 2725–27). See *Jansenism; Laxism; Moral Theology; Rigorism.*

Process Theology. The theological movement inspired by Alfred North Whitehead (1861–1947), whose philosophy, like some other philosophies, stresses the priority of becoming over being. Whitehead, however, goes beyond them in trying to synthesize this approach to reality with the results of the natural sciences. Whitehead understands the ultimate constituents of reality to be "actual entities" rather than substances, and makes his point of departure "actual occasions" or entities in interaction with the whole universe. Through love, God is at work non-coercively, being "the great companion— the fellow-sufferer who understands." Whitehead's translation of traditional metaphysics into dynamic terms has attracted followers in the United States, the British Isles, and elsewhere. Some, such as Charles Hartshorne (1897–2000), have developed process thought in a somewhat different way. Although recognizing his valuable stress on personal categories, commentators have criticized Whitehead's philosophy over such matters as his notion of a "finite God," who changes in interaction with a world that evolves. See *Panentheism.*

Processions. A theological term for the way in which the second and third persons of the Trinity originate from the Father. The derivation of the Son from the Father is also called generation or filiation, whereas that of the Spirit from the Father and the Son is also called spiration (see DH 150, 804; ND 12, 318). St. Augustine of Hippo (354–430), followed by the medieval Scholastics, interpreted the generation of the Son as the act of self-knowledge by the Father, with the Spirit proceeding through the mutual love of Father and Son. See *Filioque; Immanent Trinity; Relations, Divine; Scholasticism; Spiration; Trinity, Theology of.*

Proclamation. Announcing Christ (Col 1:28) and the gospel (1 Cor 9:14) with praise and thanksgiving. This may take place through the evangelization of "outsiders," or within the liturgy—as in the *Exultet* or Easter proclamation and the Eucharist, which "proclaims the death of the Lord until he comes" (1 Cor 11:26). See *Anamnesis; Doxology; Evangelization; Homily; Kerygma; Preaching; Prophet.*

Prolepsis (Gr. "anticipation"). The principle of real anticipation that comes from the way in which Christ's resurrection represents in advance what will happen at the end of history (1 Cor 15:20, 28) and illuminates the nature of grace and sacraments as the real beginning of our life in glory (John 6:54; Rom 6:3–8; 1 Cor 11:26). Thus, St. Thomas Aquinas (ca. 1225–74) understood the sacraments to be anticipatory signs. Munich theologian Wolfhart Pannenberg (b. 1928) has appealed to the principle of *prolepsis* in facing a wide range of theological and philosophical questions. See *Eschatology; History.*

Prophecy. See *Prophet.*

Prophet. Someone inspired by the Spirit of God to speak and/or act in a certain way. Interpreting past and present events and announcing coming events, the OT prophets spoke from a deep knowledge of God, preached fidelity to the covenant, and opposed a merely external observance of the Law. Called by God (Isa 6:1–13; Jer 1:4–19; Ezek 1:1—3:27), they delivered God's word to the people. Conflicts between prophets highlighted the challenge of identifying those who were genuinely authorized to speak in God's name (1 Kgs 22; Jer 27–28). The NT witnesses to similar problems in testing and discerning prophecy (1 Cor 14:37–40; 1 Thess 5:19–21). Acknowledged as a prophet (Mark 6:15; 8:28) or the prophet (John 6:14; 7:40; see Deut 18:15, 18), Jesus spoke and acted prophetically (Mark 11:15–18; 13:1–2; Luke 11:29). While placing himself in the prophetic line (Matt 13:57; Luke 13:34), Jesus claimed that he was "more than" the prophetic, royal, and sacred persons and places of the OT (e.g., Matt 12:15–21, 41–42). The NT repeatedly notes how the OT prophetic expectations were fulfilled in Jesus. The prophetic charism continued in the NT communities (Rom 12:6; 1 Cor 12:28–30; 14:29, 32) and the later church. The Second Vatican Council (1962–65) emphasized that all the baptized through their insight and witness share in Christ's prophetic office (LG 12, 35). See *Charisms; Islam; Jesus Christ; Old Testament; Priests.*

Propitiation. An explanation of redemption in terms of God's anger being appeased through Christ's sacrificial death. This explanation rests on a misinterpretation of some NT passages (e.g., Rom 3:25; 8:3; 2 Cor 5:21; Gal 3:13). The appropriate terms for the atonement (e.g., *expiation* and *sacrifice*) should be sharply distinguished from the language of propitiation, which a number of Catholic and Protestant authors have unfortunately used down to the twentieth century. See *Atonement; Expiation; Redemption; Sacrifice; Satisfaction.*

Proselytes (Gr. "those who have come over"). Gentile converts to Judaism (see Matt 23:15; Acts 2:10) or else "God-fearers" who observed only part of the Jewish Law (see Acts 10:2; 13:43).

Proselytism. In the past, proselytism was often synonymous with evangelization. In fact, the Second Vatican Council (1962–65) affirmed the church's right to evangelize and make converts (AG 7; DHu 13–15). However, proselytism often has the negative meaning of forcing or otherwise manipulating people into accepting a particular faith. Religious and civil societies have often condemned this type of proselytism, which was also decried by Vatican II (1962–65) (AG 13; DHu 4). In ecumenical dialogue with the Eastern Orthodox churches, proselytism is one of the questions for the official agenda. See *Conversion; Evangelization; Liberty, Religious; Uniates.*

Prosopon (Gr. "face," "mask," "role"). Initially, a mask worn on stage; later, a term for "person". Some Fathers of the Church and councils spoke of the three *prosōpa* of the Trinity and the one *prosōpon* in Jesus Christ (see DH 250, 302; ND 604, 615). For Nestorius (d. ca. 451), who valued the language of "form/appearance" in Philippians 2:6–7, *prosōpon* meant whatever makes up someone's "appearance" or public "manifestation." But *hypostasis* was the more common term for a person or a rational individual. See *Hypostasis; Nestorianism; Person.*

Protestant. Person, church, theology, or institution related in some way to the sixteenth-century Reformation. The beginning of Protestantism is symbolically dated to October 31, 1517, when Martin Luther published his ninety-five theses on indulgences, in which he attacked various abuses regarding the doctrine, preaching, and practice of penance. The term "Protestant" comes from the non-Catholic minority at the Imperial Diet held at Speyer in 1529, who presented a "protest" against the religious policies of the Catholic Emperor Charles V. Often identical with evangelical, Protestant sometimes expresses an antagonism to Catholicism. The common theological principles of Protestantism include the doctrine of justification by faith alone and not by works, the sole authority of holy scripture, and the universal priesthood of all believers. See *Baptists; Calvinism; Catholicism; Congregational Theology; Depravity, Total; Dialectical Theology; Evangelicals; Faith and Works; Hussites; Imputation; Justification; Law and Gospel; Liberal Protestantism; Lutheranism; Methodism; Neo-Orthodoxy; Penance, Sacrament of; Presbyterianism; Puritans; Reformation, The; Sola Fides; Sola Gratia; Sola Scriptura; Theologia Crucis; Theologia Gloriae; Zwinglianism.*

Protocanonical (Gr. "first-time members of the canon"). Term applied to thirty-nine OT books accepted by all as inspired and canonical. See *Apocrypha; Canon; Deuterocanical Books.*

Protoevangelium (Gr. "first gospel"). The story of the infancy of Jesus in the apocryphal Book of James. The term also refers to a traditional interpretation of the woman crushing the serpent's head (Gen 3:15) as the first promise of salvation and Our Lady's role in it. See *Apocryphal Gospels; Eschatology; Infancy Gospels; Senses of Scripture.*

Protology (Gr. "study of first things"). Doctrine about the origin of the world and human beings. Protology corresponds to eschatology, since God's plan at the beginning is best illuminated by its full unfolding at the end. See *Adam; Creation; Eschatology; Eve; Fall, The; Original Justice; Original Sin.*

Providence (Lat. "foresight"). God's all-wise, all-loving, and all-encompassing guidance of nature, history, and the course of individual lives (see Matt 6:25–34; 10:29–31). The Christian doctrine of providence allows for both human freedom and the mysterious ways of God, who can "write straight on/with crooked lines." See *Deism; Foreknowledge; Freedom; Omniscience; Predestination; Scientia Media; Theism.*

Prudence (Lat. "foresight"). The first of the cardinal virtues, entailing the capacity to translate general norms and ideals into practice. Christian prudence is more than a mere shrewdness that foresees difficulties and avoids undesirable consequences. It involves the exercise of a practical imagination that makes a coherent whole of one's moral life. See *Virtues, Cardinal.*

Psalms (Gr. "songs"). OT religious songs that express to the all-holy God the adoration, thanksgiving, complaints, sorrow, trust, and other feelings of individuals and the whole people. Though traditionally attributed to King David (d. ca. 970), perhaps only a few of the 150 psalms go back to him. This Jewish liturgical book is used by Christians everywhere for their public worship and private prayer. A landmark of OT scholarship was the study by Hermann Gunkel (1862–1932) of the psalms according to their literary forms (see DH 3521–28). See *Biblical Criticism.*

Pseudepigrapha (Gr. "false title"). Books attributed to someone who did not write them. The term is often limited to certain Jewish works written shortly before or after the beginning of the Christian era (e.g., the Book of Enoch and the Assumption of Moses).

Pulpit. See *Ambo.*

Purgatory (Lat. "purification"). State of those who die in God's friendship, but who still need their personal sins to be expiated (through the merits of Christ) and who should grow spiritually before enjoying the beatific vision. The scriptural passages that have been adduced (2 Macc 12:38–46; Matt 5:25–26;

12:31–32, and 1 Cor 3:11–15) do not as such establish the existence of purgatory. It can be validated in the light of divine justice and by the fact of Christians praying (attested at least since the second century, as in the tomb inscription of Abercius, bishop of Hierapolis in Phrygia [in modern Turkey], who died ca. 200), and celebrating the Eucharist (attested at least since the third century) for their dead. In line with this practice, Greek authors such as Clement of Alexandria (ca. 150–ca. 215), Origen (ca. 185–ca. 254), and St. John Chrysostom (ca. 347–407), and Latin authors such as Tertullian (ca. 160–ca. 225), St. Cyprian (d. 258), and St. Augustine of Hippo (354–430) wrote in various ways of purification after death and our communion through prayer with our dear departed. Praying for the dead has remained a typical feature of Eastern and Western liturgies. The Second Council of Lyons (1274) and the Council of Florence (1438–45) taught the cleansing suffering endured after death (by those not yet fit for the beatific vision) and the value of prayers and pious works offered on their behalf (DH 856, 1304–5; ND 26, 2308–9)— avoiding, however, the language of fire, which the Orthodox oppose. Martin Luther (1483–1546) rejected first the value of indulgences for the dead and then the very existence of purgatory. The Council of Trent (1545–63) maintained the doctrine of purgatory, said nothing about the nature and duration of purgatory, and reiterated the value of offering prayers and the Eucharist for those in purgatory (DH 1580, 1820; ND 1980, 2310). The Second Vatican Council (1962–65) briefly recalled our communion with those being purified after death and endorsed the teaching of Florence and Trent (LG 49, 51). The state of purgatory can be understood as a final process of loving but painful maturation before we see God face to face. With the last judgment, purgatory will come to an end (DH 1067). See *Beatific Vision; Communion of Saints; Death; Eschata; Indulgences.*

Puritans. An umbrella term for those influential groups within the Church of England who opposed the religious settlement of Elizabeth I (queen 1558–1603), and, following a Calvinist theology, aimed at purifying the church of nonbiblical elements. They insisted on preaching, a strict observance of Sunday, and an austere moral code. Many Puritans came to reject the episcopal government of the church. Leading English puritans included Thomas Cartwright (1535–1603), the Lord Protector Oliver Cromwell (1599–1658), and the poet John Milton (1608–74). In the early seventeenth century, Puritan refugees established the Massachusetts Bay Colony. The most notable theologian to emerge among the New England Puritans was Jonathan Edwards (1703–58). In the British Isles "Low Church" Anglicans, Baptists, Congregationalists, Presbyterians, and Quakers have all inherited elements from the original Puritans. See *Anglican Communion; Baptists; Calvinism; Congregational Theology; Episcopacy; Friends, Society of; Presbyterianism; Protestant; Reformation, The.*

Q

Qaddis (Heb. "holy"). A very old Jewish doxology used for daily prayer in the synagogue. It glorifies God's name for its grandeur and holiness, parallels two petitions in the Lord's Prayer, and echoes Ezekiel 38:23: "And so I shall be magnified and sanctified and be known among the multitude of pagan nations and they, for their part, will soon realize that I am the Lord." See *Doxa; Doxology; Lord's Prayer, The; Synagogue.*

Quakers. See *Friends, Society of.*

Qualification, Theological. An evaluation of a particular theological proposition in its relationship to revealed truth and church doctrine. If found in the sources of revelation, a statement can be qualified as *de fide divina* (Lat. "of divine faith"). If it has been solemnly defined by the extraordinary magisterium, it becomes *de fide definita* (Lat. "of defined faith"). Other theological notes include such qualifications as *de fide ecclesiastica* (Lat. "of the church's faith"), *fidei proximum* (Lat. "close to faith"), and *theologice certum* ("theological certain") (see DH 2269, 2374). Negative qualifications have included "heresy," a "rejected opinion" (Lat. *opinio reprobata*), and a position that "offends pious ears" (Lat. *piis auribus offensiva*). The use of theological notes, which were once a constant feature of Catholic theological remarks, has been largely dropped. A 1989 document of the International Theological Commission ("The Interpretation of Dogma") called for their revival. In its current correspondence, the Congregation for the Doctrine of the Faith applies such negative qualifications as "errors," "grave doctrinal ambiguities," and "dangerous ambiguities." Some Orthodox theologians follow the qualifications proposed by the Russian patristic scholar Vasilij Bolotov (d. 1900): dogma (which is certain), theologoumenon (which is probable), and mere opinion (which is possible). See *Council, Ecumenical; Heresy; Hierarchy of Truths; Infallibility; Magisterium; Theologoumenon; Theology.*

Quelle or **Q** (German "source"). A hypothetical lost document composed largely of sayings or logia of Jesus and used as a major source by Matthew and Luke. Many scholars accept this hypothesis, which explains numerous close similarities between Matthew and Luke. See *Synoptic Gospels; Two-Source Theory.*

Quietism. School of spirituality developed by Miguel de Molinos (ca. 1640–97), who preached a total abandonment to God that reduced human responsibility and dismissed outward acts of religion as superfluous. In 1687 he was condemned by his former friend, Blessed Innocent XI (pope 1676–89) (see DH 2201–69; ND 2007). Charges of quietism were also made against a renowned mystic, Madame Guyon (1648–1717), and a leading spiritual writer, François de Salignac Fénelon, archbishop of Cambrai (1651–1715), who was condemned by Innocent XII (pope 1691–1700) in 1699 (DH 2340–74). See *Spirituality*.

Quinisext Synod. A synod convoked by Justinian II (emperor 685–711) and held in Constantinople (692) in the *trullus* (Gr. "domed room") of the imperial palace, and, hence, often called the council in Trullo. Its aim was to deal with some canonical matters, since the fifth ecumenical council, Constantinople II (553), and the sixth, Constantinople III (680–81), had not enacted any disciplinary measures. For this reason, the synod is called the *Quinisext* (Lat. "fifth-sixth"). The legislation concerned marriage impediments, the age of ordination, clerical marriage, and clerical dress. It forbade representing Jesus under the image of a lamb, considering that a Monophysite aberration. This prohibition also hinted at coming iconoclasm. From the viewpoint of Eastern canon law, the synod was one of the most important, even if it met resistance in the East itself, and its legislation, owing to a supposed anti-Latin bias, was never fully accepted in Rome. Hadrian I (pope 772–95) gave its canons some approval, after they were mistakenly presented as the canons of Constantinople III. The Byzantines intended the canons of the Quinisext Synod to bring conformity of practice between East and West. See *Canon Law, Sources of Oriental; Constantinople, Second Council of; Constantinople, Third Council of; Iconoclasm; Islam; Monophysitism*.

Qumran Scrolls. Religious texts in Hebrew, Aramaic, or Greek copied or composed between 20 BC and AD 60 and discovered in 1947 (and later) in caves at Qumran, eight miles south of Jericho and close to the Dead Sea. Hence the manuscripts are also known as the Dead Sea Scrolls. The manuscripts, which seem to have belonged to a nearby Jewish community of Essenes, include sections, sometimes extensive ones, from nearly all of the books of the OT, as well as from other religious works. This discovery has proved of major importance for research into the OT and the environment in which Christianity was born. See *Bible; Essenes; Old Testament*.

R

Rationalism. Any system that privileges reason in the search for truth, including religious truth. A strongly rationalist strain characterizes the Enlightenment. Some of its figures used reason to reject revelation; others went on to reject all religious belief. While acknowledging (against the fideists) the capacity of human reason to know God from the created world, Vatican I (1869–70) asserted against rationalists the supernatural, divine revelation to which we owe the assent of faith (DH 3004–5, 3008; ND 113–14, 118). As a synonym for atheism or agnosticism, rationalism is no longer used much. But Eastern Christians often couple rationalism with Western individualism that loosens ties with the real habitat of faith, the community. See *Enlightenment; Fideism; Liberalism; Revelation; Vatican Council, First.*

Ratum et Consummatum (Lat. "ratified and consummated"). A term in canon law for a marriage that has been validly contracted and sexually consummated in a way that is humanly dignified and open to the procreation of children (CIC 1061; see CCEO 853, 862, 1384). A marriage is indissoluble if it is both ratified and consummated; if it is only ratified, it may be dissolved for good reasons. See *Marriage; Validity.*

RCIA (The Rite of Christian Initiation of Adults). A course of preparation for adults (introduced in 1972) who wish to be baptized and enter the church. Once enrolled as catechumens, the candidates are instructed in the faith and obligations of Christians—normally during Lent. From the third to the fifth Sunday of Lent, they undergo "scrutinies," or soul-searching examinations of conscience, to detect their weaknesses and pray to be delivered from them. Those undergoing these demanding exercises are supported by the prayers of the community. At the Easter Vigil, they receive the sacraments of baptism, confirmation, and Eucharist—thus following as adults the order the Eastern Church follows for the Christian initiation of children, who in one ceremony are baptized, confirmed, and receive communion. See *Catechumenate; Easter Triduum; Holy Week.*

Real Presence. Among the various presences of the risen Christ in our world, the presence par excellence (SC 7). After the consecration at Mass, he is present with his body, blood, soul, and divinity under the appearances of bread and wine (see DH 1637, 1640–41, 1651–54; ND 1514, 1517–18, 1526–29). See *Consecration; Epiclesis; Eucharist; Transubstantiation.*

Recapitulation. See *Anakephalaiosis.*

Reception. (a) The process by which official teachings and decisions are accepted, assimilated, and interpreted by the whole church. It has often taken time before the pronouncements of an ecumenical council or pope have been known, understood, and received by the local churches and their leaders. While Orthodox theology generally believes the validity of a council and its teaching to depend on its reception, Catholic theology follows the First Vatican Council (1869–70) (DH 3074; ND 839) in holding that such validity does not depend on reception. (b) In a broader sense, *reception* refers to the whole process by which each generation accepts the revelation transmitted through scripture and tradition (DV 8–9). See *Council, Ecumenical; Deposit of Faith; Magisterium; Sensus Fidelium; Sobornost.*

Reconciliation. Reestablishing friendship after a situation of conflict and alienation has been overcome. (a) A term with an ordinary, secular meaning (see 1 Cor 7:11), reconciliation is applied by St. Paul to God's loving initiative in redeeming us and to our need to accept this new situation of being reconciled through Christ (Rom 5:8–11; 2 Cor 5:18–20). In an extended fashion, reconciliation is applied to the effect of redemption on the whole world (Col 1:19–20). (b) As it brings reconciliation with God and the church, the sacrament of penance is now often called the sacrament of reconciliation (see LG 11; PO 5). See *Penance, Sacrament of; Redemption; Salvation.*

Redaktionsgeschichte (German "story of editing"). The name given by Willi Marxsen (1919–93) to the work of the final editors or writers of our biblical texts. Redaction criticism, as it is often called, studies the motivation of these authors in editing earlier material, the changes they introduced, and the message they wished to communicate to their particular audience (see DV 19). See *Biblical Criticism; Exegesis.*

Redeemer (Lat. "one who pays to liberate somebody"). A title given to Jesus (but not as such by the NT) for delivering us from sin and evil through his Incarnation, life, death, resurrection, and sending of the Holy Spirit. While having a different origin, in actual usage the title is synonymous with Savior, a title given to Jesus sixteen times by the NT. See *Salvation.*

Redemption (Lat. "buying back"). God's activity in delivering human beings from the bondage of sin and evil. The liberation from oppression in Egypt was the paradigmatic case in the OT of the divine redemptive activity (Exod 15:1–21; Deut 7:8; 13:5; 24:18). The deliverance from the Babylonian Exile (587–538 BC) also revealed God's loving fidelity as redeemer (Isa 41:14; 43:14; 44:24; 54:8). Through his death and resurrection (Mark 10:45; Rom 4:25; Eph 1:7; 1 Pet 1:18–21), Christ delivered us from the power of sin and evil (Col 1:13–14) in a redemption that is appropriated by faith (Rom 3:24–30) and will be completed in the resurrection to come (Rom 8:23; Eph 4:30). From the time of the NT, redemption has been understood not only as deliverance from oppression (1 Cor 15:20–28, 54, 56–57), but also as purification from guilt (1 Cor 6:11; Eph 5:25–26; Heb 2:17–18) and a love that changes the human heart (Mark 7:21–23; Rom 5:5; 1 John 4:9–10), and brings a new covenant of friendship with God (Mark 14:24; 1 Cor 11:25). See *Atonement; Cross; Covenant; Expiation; Justification; Reconciliation; Salvation; Satisfaction.*

Reductionism. Any attempt to explain or explain away the complex data of reality by appealing to only one of its aspects. Thus a philosopher may identify reality at large with the immediately available sense-data. Rejection of faith in God usually takes the form of reductionism. In his *Essence of Christianity* (German original, 1841), Ludwig Feuerbach (1804–72) argued that belief in God was nothing but the projection of human desires and aspirations. A concern to speak to the culture of their age has often led deists, liberal Protestants, and rationalists to oversimplify and dilute the full Christian revelation. See *Deism; Liberal Protestantism; Rationalism.*

Reformation, The. At least since the Council of Vienne (1311–12), a cry for "reform in head and members" was heard in the church, whose life at all levels had become marked by many grave abuses. The situation was aggravated by the "Babylonian Captivity" of the papacy in Avignon (1305–74); the Great Western Schism, when there were two or three popes (1378–1417); the Conciliarist Movement; and the scandals associated with the Renaissance papacy. Various attempts at reform within the Catholic Church gained strength, and, finally, broke through at the time of the Council of Trent (1545–63). The Protestant Reformation, often simply called the Reformation, must be seen in the same perspective. At the center of this movement stood Martin Luther (1483–1546), and, for a second generation, John Calvin (1509–64). Other leading figures were Ulrich Zwingli (1484–1531), reformer of Zurich, and Philipp Melanchthon (1497–1560), collaborator of Luther in Wittenberg. The English Reformation began over the marital problems of Henry VIII (1491–1547) and the failure of Cardinal Thomas Wolsey (ca. 1474–1530) to secure him a divorce. Papal authority was rejected and the monasteries suppressed. The leading reformers in England included Archbishop Thomas Cranmer (1489–1556), Bishop Hugh Latimer (ca. 1485–1555), and Bishop Nicholas Ridley (ca. 1500–1555). Undoubtedly nationalism and economic interests helped the cause of the Reformation. But it was often a deeply felt religious movement that aimed to purify church life and base Christian living on the scriptures (UR 21). Vatican II (1962–65) honestly acknowledged the need for "that continued reformation" to which Christ always calls his church (UR 6). See *Anabaptists; Anglican Communion; Augsburg Confession; Baptists; Calvinism; Conciliarism; Counter-Reformation; Hussites; Lutheranism; Nominalism; Presbyterianism; Protestant; Puritans; Trent, Council of; Vernacular; Vienne, Council of; Waldensians; Zwinglianism.*

Regeneration (Lat. "new birth"). The spiritual rebirth brought by baptism (John 3:5; Titus 3:5; 1 Pet 1:3). St. Paul speaks equivalently of baptism as death to the old state of sin and new life in the risen Christ (Rom 6:1–11; 2 Cor 5:17). See *Baptism.*

Regula Fidei (Lat. "rule of faith"). Norm of faith as a public, ecclesial criterion for discerning the true revelation communicated by Christ to the church. St. Irenaeus of Lyons (ca. 130–ca. 200) appealed to this norm against Gnostic claims to special revelations accessible only to the elite. By expressing its content, the emerging creeds took over the role of the regula fidei. See *Creed; Faith; Gnosticism; Revelation; Scripture and Tradition; Sola Scriptura; Tradition.*

Reign of God. See *Kingdom of God.*

Reincarnation. The belief, also called *metempsychosis* (Gr. "animate afterward"), that souls inhabit a series of bodies and can live many lives on this earth before being completely purified and so released from the need to migrate to another body. According to this belief, the soul preexists its embodiment and after death exists in a disembodied state before animating once again a body of the same or a different species. In various forms, reincarnation has been accepted by Buddhists, Hindus, Neoplatonists, and others. Belief in resurrection and official rejection of the preexistence of souls (see DH 403, 854, 1440; ND 25) rule out reincarnation. By maintaining an indefinite series of chances, the doctrine of reincarnation reduces the seriousness of God's grace and of human liberty exercised in one life that is terminated by a once-and-for-all death (1 Cor 15:20–28; 2 Cor 5:10; Heb 9:27). See *Buddhism; Death; Hinduism; Neoplatonism; Resurrection; Soul.*

Relations, Divine. The ordering of the divine persons among themselves in a way that constitutes three persons in one God. There are four such relations: paternity, filiation, active spiration, and passive spiration. Paternity constitutes the Father, filiation the Son, and passive spiration the Spirit. Active spiration is common to the Father and the Son, and does not form a new person. See *Filioque; Immanent Trinity; Processions; Spiration; Trinity, Theology of.*

Relativism. The view that there are no absolutes, that truths and values are all determined by particular periods, cultures, societies, and persons. Pure relativism ("all claims and truths are relative") is self-contradictory. Milder forms of relativism stress the way that historical, cultural, and religious presuppositions condition one's grasp of meaning and truth. The relativizing approach of Ernst Troeltsch (1865–1923) left contemporary theology with the major challenge of elucidating Christ's absoluteness in order to show that in a unsurpassable manner he is the fullness of divine revelation and salvation for all peoples of all times. In the area of dogmatic definitions, historically conditioned formulations should be distinguished from the lasting truths being taught. Both before and after being elected pope in 2005, Benedict XVI highlighted the dangers and weaknesses of the relativism that characterizes the Western world. See *Biblical Criticism; Christology; Classical Consciousness; Dogma; Idealism; Modernism; Pluralism.*

Relics (Lat. "remains"). The bodily remains of saints or objects closely connected with them (such as their clothing and letters). From early centuries, the tombs and remains of martyrs and other saints were venerated. The crusades brought a traffic in relics, but those taken back to Europe were often spurious. Since Trent (DH 1821–23; ND 1255–57), official church teaching has tried to correct abuses connected with relics (see CIC 1190; CCEO 888), and, in general, to relate the veneration of saints, their images, and their relics to the central worship of God (SC 111, LG 51). In the West, relics of martyrs and other saints are inserted under fixed altars (CIC 1237; see Rev 6:9). In the Orthodox East, relics enjoy an even greater role in popular piety than they do in the Catholic West. See *Crusades; Eastern Churches; Icon; Iconoclasm; Nicaea, Second Council of; Saint; Trent, Council of; Veneration of Saints.*

Religion (Lat. "being bound"). The basic attitude human beings should take toward God, their creator and redeemer. The moral virtue of religion expresses itself in adoration and wholehearted service of our loving God. Karl Barth (1886–1968) opposed faith (as founded in the word of God and utterly dependent on divine grace) to religion, which he dismissed as the worthless product of merely human aspirations. See *Adoration; Creation; Love; Redemption; Worship.*

Religions. Systems of belief in and response to the divine, including the sacred books, cultic rituals, and ethical practices of the adherents. Christians, in general, and Catholics, in particular, are called to live the tension between evangelization and dialogue represented, respectively, by the Decree on the Church's Missionary Activity (*Ad Gentes*) and the Declaration on the Relationship of the Church to Non-Christian Religions (*Nostra Aetate*) of the Second Vatican Council (1962–65). See *Animism; Anonymous Christians; Buddhism; Christianity; Dialogue; Evangelization; Hinduism; Islam; Judaism; Mission, Theology of; World Religions.*

Religious Life. A form of Christian existence that practices the evangelical chastity, poverty, and obedience, and involves a common life under a superior. A period of novitiate comes at the beginning and vows regulate the lifestyle. In the West, the approved forms of religious life include the monastic orders (such as the Benedictines, Carthusians, and Cistercians), the canons regular (such as the Premonstratensians, founded by St. Norbert [ca. 1080–1134] in the twelfth century), the mendicants (such as the Franciscans and the Dominicans, founded in the thirteenth century), and the clerics regular (such as the Jesuits and the Theatines, founded in the sixteenth century). Institutes of consecrated life founded in more recent times are called congregations if their members pronounce only simple vows (unlike orders whose vows are solemn). Religious life is followed by both nonordained laypersons and ordained clergy. The Second Vatican Council (1962–65) taught that all the baptized are called to the fullness of Christian life and the perfection of love (LG 39–42), and that religious follow their way of life in order to be consecrated with greater liberty to the love and service of God and others (LG

43–47; PC 1). The council also called for an *aggiornamento* of religious institutes by a return to the original spirit of their founders and foundresses (see PC 2; CIC 573–709). Secular institutes (associations of laypersons, priests, or both), which have come into existence since World War II, are a form of consecrated Christian life, but not a form of religious life as such (CIC 710–30; CCEO 563, 566; CCEO 410–572). Among the enduring results of the Oxford Movement has been the revival of religious life in the Anglican Communion. Similar revivals of religious life have come among Protestants, such as the Christusbruderschaft in Germany and the ecumenical community at Taizé. Orthodox theologians such as Paul Evdokimov (1901–70) speak of "spiritual monasticism" to express the universal call to holiness. Both in the East and in the West, monks and religious differ from laypersons only in the means, not in the common goal, of holiness. See *Anachoretism; Celibacy; Cenobites; Chastity; Evangelical Counsels; Hermit; Monasticism; Obedience; Oxford Movement; Perfection; Poverty; Vow.*

Reparation. Making amends for an offense committed against or damage done to another. Reparation can refer to the compensation to be made when, for instance, someone's property or good reputation has been unjustly damaged. In the area of devotion to the Sacred Heart, reparation refers to prayers and good works undertaken to make amends for sins against Jesus' love expressed in the gift of the Blessed Sacrament and in the suffering through which he redeemed us. See *Atonement; Blessed Sacrament; Expiation; Heart, Sacred; Penance, Sacrament of; Satisfaction.*

Repentance. See *Metanoia.*

Reprobation. Act whereby God excludes those in the state of unrepented mortal sin from final salvation and condemns them to eternal punishment (see Matt 25:41–46). See *Calvinism; Hell; Jansenism; Predestination; Sin, Mortal and Venial.*

Reservation of the Blessed Sacrament. The practice of keeping in a tabernacle consecrated hosts to serve for the communion of the sick and the adoration of the faithful (CIC 934–44; CCEO 714 §1). Orthodox Christians and some Anglicans also reserve consecrated hosts for distribution to the sick. A lighted lamp near the tabernacle indicates the presence of the Blessed Sacrament. See *Adoration; Blessed Sacrament; Real Presence.*

Res et Sacramentum (Lat. "thing signified and its sign"). To be distinguished from (a) *sacramentum tantum* (Lat. "only a sign"), such as bread and wine destined for use in the Eucharist, and (b) *res sacramenti (tantum)* (Lat. "the thing signified [taken by itself]") or the grace signified and produced by a sacrament. *Res et sacramentum* goes beyond the immediate grace effected by a sacrament, and refers to such enduring realities as the real presence of Christ in the Eucharist (and not merely the grace of holy communion), and the indelible character imparted by baptism, confirmation, and holy orders. See *Character; Communion; Grace; Sacrament; Sign; Sphragis; Symbol.*

Resurrection (Lat. "rising," "being raised"). Not a mere return to earthly life, like the resuscitation of the daughter of Jairus (Mark 5:22–24, 35–43), but the passage of Jesus through death to his definitive, transformed life (Rom 1:3–4; 1 Cor 15:42–50) that has inaugurated the final resurrection of human beings and their world (1 Cor 15:20–28). What happened to the transfigured body of Christ prefigures what will happen to our bodies. This central truth of faith formed the initial proclamation of Christians (Acts 2:22–24, 32–33, 36; 1 Cor 15:1–11), who almost defined God (the Father) in terms of having raised Jesus from the dead (Rom 10:9; 1 Cor 6:14; Gal 1:1; 1 Thess 1:10; see 1 Cor 15:15). Later NT traditions, church teaching, and creeds (John 10:17–18; DH 359, 539; ND 634) spoke of Christ (as divine) rising by his own power. Through his appearances (e.g., 1 Cor 15:5–8; Mark 16:7; Matt 28:9–10, 16–20), the first disciples came to know that Jesus was risen from the dead. The discovery of the empty tomb by Mary Magdalene (probably with one or more women companions) served as a secondary, negative sign confirming the event of the resurrection (Mark 16:1–8; John 20:1–2). As the climax of divine revelation (DV 4, 17), the resurrection of the crucified Jesus, together with the sending of the Holy Spirit, contains implicitly all the basic Christian truths. Hence the paschal mystery needs to be explored not only in its factuality, but also as the mystery of revelation, redemption, faith, hope, and love. See *Appearances of the Risen Lord; Ascension; Descent into Hell; Easter; Eschatology; Mystery; Paschal Mystery; Passover.*

Resurrection of the Dead. Final life after death effected by the divine power for the whole human being (in "body and soul"). Although as such it surfaced late in the OT, hope for a general resurrection emerged from ancient Jewish faith in God as the faithful, just, and all-powerful Lord of life. Interpretations of the nature of resurrection varied from images of a physical reanimation (2 Macc 7:1–42; 12:44–45; 14:46) to hopes for a glorious, transformed existence (Dan 12:1–4), similar to but not identical with St. Paul's expectations of a "spiritual" body (1 Cor 15:35–54). Jesus' preaching of the final reign of God presupposed a general resurrection (Matt 8:11; Mark 9:43–48; Luke 11:31–32). His refutation of the Sadducees showed that he understood the resurrection of the dead to involve a new form of human existence (Mark 12:18–27; see Rom 14:9; 1 Cor 15:22–23; Col 1:18; Rev 1:5) in a world renewed and transformed (see LG 48–49, 51; GS 14, 22). See *Apocalyptic Literature; Communion of Saints; Eschatology; Eternity; Heaven; Parousia; Soul.*

Retreat. An individual or group withdrawal (normally to a religious house set apart for this experience) to awaken and deepen one's spiritual life through silence, prayer, and such exercises as the examination of conscience. Frequently male or female directors are available to guide retreatants toward discerning God's will in their present state of life or, sometimes, in a new state of life. Retreats range from a weekend to thirty days, a length popularized by St. Ignatius of Loyola (1491–1556), who composed the *Spiritual Exercises*. In recent decades, some retreats have adapted Asian methods of asceticism and prayer. See *Prayer; Spirituality; Zen.*

Revelation (Lat. "taking away the veil"). The disclosure by God of what was previously unknown. The OT records the divine revelation communicated primarily through words (Jer 23:18, 22) and events of history (Exod 15:1–21) and secondarily through the created world (Ps 19:2; Wis 13:1–9). As major mediators of God's revelation, the classical prophets also spoke of the saving revelation to come (Isa 40:1–11; Jer 31:31–34). In his Incarnation, life, death, resurrection, and sending of the Holy Spirit (DV 4, 17), Christ was the climax of the divine self-revelation (John 1:14, 18; Heb 1:1–2), being simultaneously the revealer (or agent) and the revealed or the content of revelation. For the doctrine of revelation, John's gospel (with its language of glory, light, signs, truth, witness, the "I am" sayings, and, above all, the Incarnation of the Word) is the richest NT book. With Christ and the apostolic age, foundational revelation is completed, and we await only the final, glorious revelation of the parousia (Titus 2:13; 1 John 3:2; DV 4). Since the Middle Ages, and especially since the Enlightenment, the truths of revelation have been contrasted with those of reason, accessible to us without any special communication from God being strictly necessary. This propositional view of revelation characterized the teaching of the First Vatican Council (1869–70) (DH 3004–7, 3026–28; ND 113–14, 116, 216). The Second Vatican Council (1962–65) understood revelation as primarily God's personal self-manifestation that invites our personal response of faith (DV 2, 6) and secondarily as the communication of divine truths (DV 7, 9, 10, 11, 26). Vatican II recognized the essentially salvific and sacramental nature of God's self-revelation, mediated through events (deeds) and words (DV 2, 4, 14, 17). Salvation history and the history of revelation are inseparable, two sides of the same reality. Since the council, some scholars have been advancing the theology of revelation by reflecting on God's symbolic self-communication that human beings experience in faith. Both Catholic theology and official teaching have become more aware of the Holy Spirit mediating revelation and salvation beyond institutional Christianity. The Romanian theologian Dumitru Staniloae (1903–93) interpreted Orthodoxy as a religion of revelation that he understood to be the communication of God's energies. See *Creed; Deposit of Faith; Dogma; Enlightenment; Essence and Energies; Experience, Religious; Grace; Johannine Theology; Logos; Mystery;*

Natural Theology; Palamism; Parousia; Salvation History; Scripture and Tradition; Symbol; Vatican Council, Second; Word of God.

Revivalism. Systematic attempts to rouse new life among lax or nominal believers by enthusiastic preaching and spontaneous praying aimed at evoking a mass religious response. From the eighteenth century, there have been recurrent revivalist movements in the United States, the British Isles, and elsewhere. A revivalist style of worship characterizes the Salvation Army, founded by William Booth (1829–1912) in 1865. See *Baptists; Charismatic; Methodism; Pentecostals; Pietism.*

Righteousness. See *Justification.*

Rights, Human. The things to which human beings are entitled in justice because they are created in the divine image and likeness and called to eternal life with God. These include freedom of conscience and the right to life, work, marriage, education, and property. The third commandment of the Decalogue (Exod 20:2–17; Deut 5:6–21) ensured regular recreation for poor workers and slaves. Many laws of the OT and prophetic denunciations of injustice (2 Sam 11:1—12:14; Isa 5:23) are concerned with basic human rights. The OT repeatedly demands protection for orphans, widows, and strangers (Deut 24:17–22; 27:19). Despite the basic equality of all persons in Christ (Gal 3:28), slavery, oppression of women, antisemitism, and other offenses against human rights continued to disfigure Christian life. At the same time, for many centuries, monks and other church groups often stood almost alone in providing education and in caring for the sick, the destitute, and the dying. The Magna Carta (1215), the American Declaration of Independence (1776), the United Nations' Universal Declaration of Human Rights (1948), and the European Convention on Human Rights (1953) figure among the major statements expressing and encouraging a general awareness of basic human rights. Among the many Christians who have championed human rights we should recall Bartolomé de Las Casas (1484–1566), William Wilberforce (1759–1833), Daniel O'Connell (1775–1847), Bishop Wilhelm Emmanuel Ketteler (1811–77), Cardinal Henry Edward Manning (1808–92), Martin Luther King Jr. (1929–68), Pope Leo XIII (1810–1903), who issued the landmark encyclical *Rerum Novarum* (1891), and Blessed John XXIII (pope 1958–63), whose encyclical *Pacem in Terris* (1963) was the first full acceptance of the theory and practice of human rights by the official magisterium. The Second Vatican Council (1962–65) endorsed a complete range of human rights (GS 27, 29, 66). In particular, a whole document (*Dignitatis Humanae*) was dedicated to the right of persons and communities to social and civil liberty in religious matters—a development in church teaching prepared for and encouraged by the American theologian John Courtney Murray (1904–67). In his social teaching, Blessed John Paul II (pope 1978–2005) insisted that each and every human person has an innate dignity and infinite value, being created in God's image. See *Anthropology; Black Theology; Decalogue; Feminist Theology; Image of God; Justice; Liberty, Religious; Magisterium; Person; Social Teaching.*

Rigorism. A moral system that, in cases open to doubt, insists on law over liberty, even when the case for liberty enjoys a high degree of probability. Such thinking stifles freedom for the sake of safety and was condemned in 1690 (see DH 2303; ND 2009/3). See *Laxism; Moral Theology; Probabilism.*

Rite. Way of celebrating a religious ceremony and, in particular, a sacrament. The term may also refer to the complex of ceremonies observed by a particular church. In the West, such rites as the Ambrosian in Milan differ from the normal Latin rite only through relatively minor liturgical features. In *Summorum Pontificum*, a 2007 *motu proprio*, Pope Benedict XVI (pope 2005–13) has approved as the extraordinary form of the Latin rite the Tridentine Mass, the Latin form of the Roman Missal published in 1962 and derived from the Council of Trent (1545–63); it may also be celebrated in a vernacular translation. The standard form of the Latin rite is the Roman Missal of Pope Paul VI, published in 1970. Among Eastern Catholics, however, *rite* means not only considerable differences in liturgy, but also the whole style of life for a particular church with its specific spirituality and discipline. *Rite* in this sense coincides with the tradition of a specific church; that is, with the particular liturgical, spiritual, theological, and disciplinary patrimony (CCEO 28 §1) enjoyed by an *ecclesia sui iuris,* or self-governing church (CCEO 27). In the East, there are now seven such major rites: the Armenian, the Byzantine, the Coptic, the East-Syrian (sometimes called Assyro-Chaldean), the Ethiopian, the Maronite (or Syro-Maronite), and West-Syrian (or Antiochene). These seven rites are found in both the Catholic and Orthodox traditions, except for the Maronite rite, which is only Catholic. See *Armenian Christianity; Church of the East, Assyrian; Coptic Christianity; Ethiopian Christianity; Liturgy; Liturgy of St. John Chrysostom; Maronites; Motu Proprio; Trent, Council of; West-Syrian Tradition.*

Ritual. An official book containing the prayers and actions prescribed for the celebration of the sacraments, funerals, the public pronouncing of vows, the consecration of a church, and other religious ceremonies.

Roman Catholicism. See *Catholicism.*

Rosary (Lat. "rose garden"). A popular Western prayer said out of devotion to the Blessed Virgin Mary. It consists of twenty decades, each commemorating a mystery concerning Christ or Mary and including the "Lord's Prayer," the "Hail Mary" (ten times), and the "Glory Be." The five joyful mysteries center on Christ's birth and childhood. The five luminous mysteries or mysteries of light (added in 2002 by Blessed John Paul II [pope 1978–2005]) begin with Christ's baptism in the Jordan and end with the institution of the Eucharist at the Last Supper. The five sorrowful mysteries begin with Christ's agony in the garden and end with his death on the cross. The five glorious mysteries begin with Christ's resurrection and end with Mary's sharing in her Son's victory. Although popular tradition says otherwise, the rosary was probably not introduced by St. Dominic (1170–1221). Dominican preachers popularized it, and a Dominican pope, St. Pius V, officially endorsed the rosary in 1569. Because of its repetitions, the rosary has sometimes been called the Jesus Prayer of Western Catholicism. See *Devotions; Jesus Prayer.*

Rubric (Lat. "red"). Directive printed in red alongside the main text (in black) that is read or chanted at liturgical assemblies. Rubrics indicate how some ceremony can or should be performed. See *Liturgy.*

Rule. The written and approved order of life for men or women with vows who belong to a particular religious institute. The Second Vatican Council (1962–65) invited religious institutes to update their various rules (PC 3–4; see CIC 578, 587; CCEO 426). Laypersons associated with a religious order sometimes follow a simplified form of that order's rule. In the East, the rule regulating the liturgy or the life of a monastery is often referred to as *Typikon* (Gr. "decree, norm"). See *Religious Life.*

Rule of Faith. See *Regula Fidei.*

Ruthenian (Lat. "Russian"). A Catholic who belongs to one of the churches that originally depended on the bishop of Kiev. Metropolitan Isidore of Kiev accepted union with Rome immediately after the Council of Florence (1438–45), which eventually led to very many Slavs returning to Catholicism through the Union of Brest (1595–96). The Ruthenian churches were signatories to this union and used to be described as the Slav-speaking Catholics of Byzantine rite in Poland, Hungary, and Bohemia. Today, Ruthenians refers broadly to Belorussians, Slovaks, and Ukrainians. These Catholics were never grouped together under one jurisdiction. The term is also used to refer specifically to Byzantine Catholics who originated in an area known as Carpatho-Ukraine or Transcarpathia. See *Eastern Churches.*

S

Sabbath (Heb. "rest"). Saturday, the last day of the Jewish week, kept holy through worship of God and abstinence from work (Exod 20:10; 31:13–17). That day recalls how God "rested" from the work of creation (Gen 2:2–3; Exod

20:11; 31:17) and how the people were delivered from Egypt (Deut 5:15). Protesting against a Sabbath observance that had become narrowly legalistic (Matt 12:9–14; Mark 2:23–28; Luke 13:10–17), Christ roused opposition by claiming that the "Son of Man is lord even of the Sabbath" (Mark 2:28; see John 5:2–18). The Seventh-Day Adventists observe Saturday as their holy day, as does the Ethiopian (non-Chalcedonian) Church. See *Ethiopian Christianity; Seventh-Day Adventists; Sunday.*

Sabellianism. See *Modalism; Monarchianism; Patripassianism.*

Sacrament (Lat. "public pledge of fidelity"). A visible sign, instituted by Christ, that reveals and communicates grace. The Catholic Church and the Orthodox accept seven such sacraments: baptism, confirmation, Eucharist, marriage, holy orders, anointing of the sick, and penance (see CIC 840–1165; CCEO 667–852). Eastern Christians speak of a sacrament as *mysterion* (Gr. "hidden reality"); "mystery" lends itself to more general use than "sacrament" (see DH 860, 1310; ND 28, 1305). Protestants generally recognize only two sacraments, baptism and the Eucharist. Three sacraments (baptism, confirmation, and holy orders) confer a permanent character and cannot be repeated (see DH 781, 1313, 1609, 1767, 1774; ND 1308, 1319, 1410, 1710, 1717). Since the Middle Ages, sacraments have often been analyzed according to their form (words) and matter (elements such as water, bread, wine, or oil used for their administration). For the sacrament of penance, the acts of the penitent are considered the quasi-matter of that sacrament (see DH 1620; ND 1673). Outstanding contributions to sacramental theology have come from St. Augustine of Hippo (354–430); Pseudo-Dionysius the Areopagite (ca. 500); Peter Lombard (ca. 1100–60); Hugh of St. Victor (ca. 1096–1142), whose symbolic interpretation of reality brings him closer to Eastern theology; St. Thomas Aquinas (ca. 1225–74); Matthias Joseph Scheeben (1835–88); and Odo Casel (1886–1948). Modern theology speaks of (a) Christ as the primordial sacrament (*Ursakrament*) or the efficacious sign of God's grace; and (b) the church he established as the foundational sacrament (*Grundsakrament*), which is realized concretely in the life of the seven sacraments—a vision of sacramental life developed by Otto Semmelroth (1912–79), Karl Rahner (1904–84), and Edward Schillebeeckx (1914–2009) (see SC 27; LG 7, 11). See *Anointing of the Sick; Baptism; Character; Confirmation; Donatism; Eucharist; Ex Opere Operantis; Ex Opere Operato; Grace; Holy Orders; Marriage; Minister; Penance, Sacrament of; Res et Sacramentum; Sign; Sphragis; Symbol, Theology of; Validity.*

Sacramental. A sacred sign, instituted by the church, that resembles the sacraments and that signifies and obtains spiritual effects through the church's intercession (CIC 1166). By expanding the definition of sacramentals from things (e.g., the palms distributed on Palm Sunday) or practices (e.g., the rosary) to speak of all-inclusive signs, the Second Vatican Council (1962–65) indicated that every event of life can be sanctified (SC 60). Usually only clerics could be legitimate ministers of sacramentals. Now laypersons can administer some of them in accord with the judgment of the local bishop and the norms of the liturgical books (SC 79; CIC 1168). Examples of laypersons administering sacramentals include the distribution of ashes on Ash Wednesday and parents leading their children in saying the rosary, as they have done for years. See *Ash Wednesday; Cleric; Holy Week; Laity; Palm Sunday; Ordinary; Rosary; Sacrament.*

Sacrifice (Lat. "making holy"). The offering of a gift to God in worship (Gen 4:2–5). Sacrifices can express praise, thanksgiving, and repentance toward God, expiate sin (Heb 9:22), support prayers of intercession, seal a covenant (Exod 24:4–8), and strengthen communion between God and worshipers. Both within the Jewish-Christian tradition and beyond, the nature and reality of sacrifice usually involve a priest offering a victim in a cultic setting. The OT, especially the prophets, insisted on the proper intention and just life of those worshiping God through sacrifices (Isa 1:2–31; Hos 6:6; Amos 5:21–24; Ps 51:15–17). Jesus echoed Hosea in stressing the priority of mercy over sacrifice (Matt 9:13; 12:7). He understood his own coming death as a sacrifice that would atone for sins and bring a new and enduring covenant (Mark 14:22–24; 1 Cor 11:23–26). See *Blood of Christ; Covenant; Eucharist; Expiation; Holocaust; Intercession; Passover; Priests; Worship; Yom Kippur.*

Sacrifice of the Mass. The re-presentation in the Eucharist of the perfect sacrifice of Christ's death and resurrection (Rom 3:25; 4:25; Heb 10:12, 14). So far from being another sacrifice, the Mass is the daily offering "in memory of" Christ (Luke 22:19; 1 Cor 11:24–25), re-presenting what happened once and for all on the first Holy Thursday, Good Friday, and Easter Sunday. There are many Masses, but only one sacrifice. The Council of Trent (1545–63) insisted on the sacrificial nature of the Mass, which in a bloodless and sacramental way perpetuates for the benefit of all the one sacrifice of Calvary (see DH 1738–59; ND 1545–63). The Second Vatican Council (1962–65) gave a richer teaching on the Mass (PO 2; SC 7; LG 3, 28), noting, for instance, that it is a paschal banquet or sacrificial meal (SC 47). The Byzantine tradition highlights the uniqueness of Christ's sacrifice by not celebrating more than one Eucharist a day in any church. See *Anamnesis; Eucharist; Mass.*

Sacrilege (Lat. "bringing the sacred under one's control"). Violating sacred persons, events, places, and things. Examples would be profaning a church, stealing chalices, and doing violence to persons leading a consecrated life. See *Consecration.*

Sadducees. Traditionally considered descendants of the priest Zadok (2 Sam 8:17; 1 Kgs 1:8). From the second century BC, this priestly aristocratic group exercised strong economic and political influence. Basing themselves on the

Torah, they rejected oral traditions, the resurrection of the dead, and the existence of angels (Mark 12:18–27; Acts 23:6–8). The high priest Caiaphas and other Sadducees had their political and religious reasons for helping to bring about Jesus' execution by Pontius Pilate (see also Acts 4:1; 5:17). After the fall of Jerusalem in AD 70, the Sadducees disappeared as a group. See *Angels; Pharisees; Resurrection; Torah.*

Saint (Lat. "one who is holy or set apart"). One called to full personal perfection or already enjoying that condition in eternal life with God. All baptized Christians receive a vocation to holiness (LG 39–42). After their death some are officially recognized for their outstanding sanctity (SC 8, 104, 111; LG 50–51). As Léon Bloy (1846–1917) summed up life, "the only sadness is not to love God, not to be a saint." See *Beatification; Canonization; Holiness; Holiness of the Church; Perfection; Trisagion; Veneration of Saints.*

St. Thomas Christians. Various groups of Eastern-rite Christians who reside in or come from the state of Kerala (Southwest India). They trace their origin to St. Thomas the apostle's arrival in India and activity among them (52–72 AD); his tomb at Mylapore (near Chennai) became a pilgrimage center. Besides the Fathers of the Church who refer to his activities in India, the third-century *Acts of Thomas* tells the story of his evangelizing the region and dying a martyr's death. The St. Thomas Christians belonged to what was known as the Church of the East (East of Constantinople and the Byzantine Empire), and, subsequently, also mainly for polemical reasons, as the Nestorian Church, which, in the sixteenth century, branched into the East Syrian Church (also known as the Assyrian Church of the East) and the Chaldean Catholic Church. Ishoyahb III, patriarch of the Church of the East (649–60), raised the Indian Church to the status of a metropolitan church, whereas Timothy I (patriarch 780–833) reserved to himself the right to ordain its metropolitan, known as the Metropolitan of All India; up to the sixteenth century, these metropolitans were ordained and sent from Mesopotamia to India by the patriarch of the Church of the East.

After Portuguese missionaries arrived in the sixteenth century, the St. Thomas Christians were forced to renounce their allegiance to the Mesopotamian patriarch and abjure their "Nestorian" errors at the Synod of Diamper (1599), a synod that was never approved by Rome. The compulsory latinization of their rite, suppression of their autonomous metropolitan status, and imposition of Portuguese patronage led to a protest in 1653 (known as the Coonan Cross Oath) and a schism in 1663. (1) The vast majority of St. Thomas Christians remained in the Catholic Church and formed what came to be known as the Syro-Malabar Church, now the second largest Eastern Catholic Church after the Ukrainian Greek Catholic Church. In 1896 Trichur, Ernakulum, and Changanacherry in Kerala were established as apostolic vicariates led by Syro-Malabar clergy. A return to the oriental liturgy began under

Pope Pius XI (pope 1922–1939) in 1934, and the restoration of the Chaldean Pontifical was finished in 1959. A project to restore the other liturgical books started in 1954, but has not yet been completed. In 1992 Blessed John Paul II (pope 1978–2005) made the Syro-Malabar Church a major archiepiscopal church, led by Cardinal Antony Padiyara (1921–2000) of Ernakulum-Angamly. In February 2012, George Alencherry, who was Major Archbishop since 2011, was created a cardinal. (2) The community that broke away in 1653, known as the Malankara Orthodox Church, was led by the Archdeacon Thomas Parampil, ordained bishop in 1653 by the laying on of hands by twelve of his priests. It eventually joined the Syrian Orthodox Church (still known as the Jacobite Church), but the West-Syrian liturgy was adopted only in the nineteenth century. The second largest Eastern church in Kerala, it has been rocked by several schisms. (3) After disagreements with the legitimately ordained Mar Thomas VI of the Malankara Orthodox Church, one of the bishops sent by the Patriarch of Antioch to ordain him, Mar Gregorios, ordained Abraham Koorillos bishop in 1772. After failing to establish his authority, the latter went to British Malabar and founded the Church of Thozhiyoor, a city in the district of Trichur. Known also as the Independent Syrian Church of Malabar, it belongs to the Syrian Orthodox tradition. (4) The (Catholic) Syro-Malabar Church also suffered divisions through the activity of Mar Thomas Rokos in 1860–62) and Mar Elias Mellus in 1874–82. The Mellusian Schism has endured as a tiny Nestorian Church and now goes by the name of the Assyrian Church of the East in India. (5) Another group left the Malankara Orthodox fold in the nineteenth century after being influenced by some Anglican missionaries and eliminating veneration of Mary as the Mother of God, prayers for the dead, and the use of icons. When its leaders, Mar Mathew Athanasius Palakunnathu (1818–77; metropolitan from 1840) and his successor Mar Thomas Athanasius refused to participate in an 1876 synod under the auspices of the Syrian Orthodox patriarch, the latter excommunicated them. Although the patriarch, in 1889, won a legal battle for property, some of the pro-Anglican section founded the Mar Thoma Syrian Church. (6) Eventually the Malankara Orthodox Church became divided between those who sided with the Syrian Orthodox patriarch and those who sided with their own Catholicos. In 1911 the patriarch's party took the name of the Malankara Syrian Orthodox Church, and the Catholicos' party took the name of the Malankara Orthodox Syrian Church. (7) Dissatisfied with this situation, in 1930, under Mar Geevarghese Ivanios, a group joined the Catholic Church and gave rise to the Syro-Malankara Catholic Church.

If we are to appreciate the variegated and vibrant life of St. Thomas Christians today, we must recall the seven churches and their origins. Contact with the West brought a fluctuation between the Church of the East (of "Nestorian" leanings) and the Syrian Orthodox Church (of "Monophysite" tendencies). Efforts continue to restore communion between the seven churches; they celebrate the feast of St. Thomas on the same day and sometimes do so together. See *Church of the East, Assyrian; Eastern Catholic Churches; Fathers of the Church; Four Ranks of; Liturgy; Monophysitism; Nestorianism; Rite; Syrian Orthodox Church; Ukrainian Catholic Church.*

Salvation (Lat. "making safe," "rescuing"). A comprehensive term for being delivered from personal or collective suffering and evil. The Passover recalls the deliverance through the water (Exod 12:1–28; 14:15–31) of a people threatened with genocide (Exod 1:8–22). Human deliverers often play a part, but in salvation God's role alone is decisive (Exod 15:1–21; Pss 46; 48; 76). The OT may highlight the this-worldly nature of salvation (Deut 33:28–29; Isa 2:1–5), but the Sinai covenant and its aftermath always include spiritual, other-worldly elements (Ezek 36:22–32). Prophetic (Jer 31:1–34; Ezek 37:1–14), eschatological (Isa 43:5—44:5), and clearly apocalyptic (Dan 12:1–3) promises point to a future salvation to come from God. The NT stresses liberation from the bondage to sin and death (Mark 1:5; Rom 5:12—7:25; Heb 2:14–18). Mary's Son is called Jesus ("God is salvation") because "he will save his people from their sins" (Matt 1:21; see Acts 4:12). The "rule of God" and the "kingdom of heaven" are reverent circumlocutions for the divine salvation that will reach its climax at the *eschaton* (Rom 5:8–10; 8:18–25; 13:11; Heb 9:28; 1 Pet 1:5). Almost every page of the Bible has something to say, directly or indirectly, about salvation, its nature, its mediation, and the human need for salvation. The *Benedictus* is perhaps the finest biblical prayer of thanksgiving for God's saving interventions (Luke 1:67–79). See *Apocalyptic Literature; Atonement; Covenant; Eschaton; Evil, Mystery of; Grace; Holy Spirit; Justification; Kingdom of God; Messiah; Parousia; Passover; Reconciliation; Redemption; Resurrection of the Dead; Sin; Soteriology.*

Salvation History. The whole story of human beings and their world seen as a drama of redemption running from creation to the parousia and finding its center in Christ (Eph 1:3–14; Col 1:15–20). Developed by Protestant scholars such as Johann Christian Konrad von Hofmann (1810–77), the theme of salvation history provided the key to OT theology for Gerhard von Rad (1901–71). He presented Israel's history as first confessed in ancient creeds (Deut 26:5–9; Josh 24:2–13). That history of salvation is marked by ever-increasing expectations as divine promises point to future fulfillment. For Oscar Cullmann (1902–99), the reality of external events is central to God's saving acts that reach their climax in Christ. Luke's scheme of salvation history, which presents Christ as the center of time, is for Cullmann the heart of NT theology. The Second Vatican Council (1962–65) used the theme of salvation history, understanding it as more or less synonymous with the history of revelation (DV 2–4; 14–15; AG 3). See *Creed; Hope; Parousia; Prophet; Redemption; Revelation; Salvation.*

231

Sanctification (Lat. "being made holy," "making holy"). God's action in enabling human beings, whose sins have been forgiven, to participate more fully in the divine holiness and perfection. Through the Holy Spirit (1 Pet 1:2), sanctification continues and completes a process that begins with justification (see 1 Cor 1:30; 6:11). Sanctification consists of charity and comes through the gracious help of Jesus Christ (see DH 225–30; ND 1901–6). Whereas Protestants tend to emphasize that sanctification in this life is radically incomplete, the Council of Trent insists that it is possible through God's abundant grace (see DH 1530–32; ND 1933–35). Eastern Christians prefer to speak of deification (2 Pet 1:4). See *Deification; Grace; Holiness; Justification.*

Sardica, Council of (ca. 343). A council held in Sardica (now Sofia, capital of modern Bulgaria) and convoked by the Eastern emperor Constantius II (324–61) and the Western emperor, his brother Constans (ca. 323–50), to heal a rift between East and West occasioned by Arianism and the question of the orthodoxy of St. Athanasius of Alexandria (ca. 296–373). Angered that he had already been rehabilitated by Rome, most of the Eastern bishops pretended that their emperor had won a victory and retired to celebrate in nearby Philippopolis. The Westerners, under the presidency of Hosius of Cordoba, affirmed the orthodoxy of Athanasius and even of Marcellus of Ancyra (Ankara), who died ca. 374. This council is also important because of its disciplinary canons, which allowed for appeals to the pope (see DH 133–36). See *Arianism; Modalism; Primacy.*

Sarx (Gr. "flesh"). The flesh of animals and human beings (1 Cor 15:39), the human body (Acts 2:31), the human condition (John 1:14), earthly descent (Rom 1:3), merely natural standards of life (1 Cor 1:26), and the force of bodily existence that leads to sin, as opposed to living by the Spirit (Gal 5:16–26). See *Logos-Sarx Christology; Nature; Soma; Spirit.*

Satan (Heb. "opponent"). Understood, at first, as an adversary who plots against someone (Job 1:6—2:10) and, later, as the devil or supremely evil leader of the fallen angels who seeks to disrupt God's plan of salvation for humanity (Matt 13:39; Mark 1:13; 4:15; Luke 10:18; 13:16; John 13:2, 27). For opposing his suffering destiny, Jesus rebukes St. Peter and calls him Satan (Mark 8:33). See *Angels; Demons; Devil, The.*

Satisfaction (Lat. "making amends"). (a) An interpretation of the Incarnation and redemption in terms of Christ, by his freely accepted death, vicariously making amends for the offense to the divine honor caused by sin. St. Anselm of Canterbury (ca. 1033–1109) developed the classical version of this view and won a wide following in the Middle Ages, the Reformation period, and later. Through his sinlessness, humanity, and divinity, Christ (and only Christ) could sufficiently satisfy on our behalf for the infinite dishonor to God that is sin.

Anselm's theory has been falsely criticized for highlighting legalistic and punitive elements. One of its real weaknesses, however, is that it interprets the redemption without taking into account the resurrection (see Rom 4:25). (b) Satisfaction also refers to the third stage (after contrition and confession) in the sacrament of reconciliation: the penance imposed by the priest to repair in some small way the harm caused by sin and receive further healing grace from God (DH 1689–93, 1711–15; ND 1630–34, 1651–55). See *Atonement; Confession; Contrition; Expiation; Incarnation; Penance, Sacrament of; Redemption; Reparation.*

Scandal (Gr. "stumbling block"). Some deed or word that tempts others to sin (Rom 14:13; 16:17). Christ warns against scandalizing others (Matt 16:23; Mark 9:42) or allowing oneself to be scandalized (Mark 9:43–47). The 1983 Code of Canon Law both alerts us to ways of avoiding or causing scandal and imposes penalties on those who cause serious scandal (CIC 277, 326, 695–96, 703, 903, 990, 1132, 1184, 1211, 1455, 1560, 1722,1727; see CCEO 500 §2, 503, 703 §1, 840 §2, 877, 1113, 1241, 1473, 1481). In the NT, scandal can also refer to something good that nevertheless arouses disapproval and opposition (John 6:61–62; 1 Cor 1:23). See *Canon Law; Sin.*

Schism (Gr. "division"). Separation into opposed groups (John 7:43; 1 Cor 1:10–13; 11:18; 12:25). Prefigured by the OT division between the Northern and Southern kingdoms that followed Solomon's death (931 or perhaps 926 BC), schisms have harmed the life and unity of the church. Heresy and schism are not always clearly distinguishable, but whereas real heresy means sinning against faith by willfully rejecting revealed truths, schismatics offend against love by breaking off communion with other members of the church. Schisms are not primarily provoked by doctrinal matters, but by differences over authority and church order. The most serious schism in Christianity has been that between the Catholic West and the Orthodox East. Although conventionally dated to 1054, this schism had been preceded by many earlier tensions, and, yet, was not fully felt by rank-and-file Christians on both sides for a long time afterward. Despite the reconciliation between Rome and Constantinople expressed by ceremonies in the Vatican (Rome) held by Paul VI (pope 1963–78) and in the Phanar (the patriarch's residence in Istanbul) by Athenagoras I of Constantinople (patriarch 1948–72) on December 7, 1965, this schism is not yet fully healed today. Vatican II (1962–65) acknowledges separations and divisions (UR 3, 13), but never uses the terms schism or schismatics; nor, for that matter, does it ever speak of heresy or heretics. See *Dialogue; Ecumenism; Filioque; Florence, Council of; Heresy; Primacy; Vatican Council, Second.*

Scholasticism (Gr. "leisure"; Lat. "study," "teaching"). An academic and monastic tradition that used Aristotelian and Platonic philosophy to understand, interpret systematically, and speculate about the truths of faith. Building on St. Augustine of Hippo (354–430), Boethius (ca. 480–ca. 524), and others,

Scholasticism really began with St. Anselm of Canterbury (ca. 1033–1109) and his program of *fides quaerens intellectum* (Lat. "faith seeking understanding"). After Peter Abelard (1079–1142) and Peter Lombard (ca. 1100–60), it found its greatest exponents in St. Thomas Aquinas (ca. 1225–74), St. Bonaventure (ca. 1217–74), and Blessed Duns Scotus (ca. 1265–1308). With William of Occam (ca. 1285–1347), Scholasticism declined into empty nominalism. See *Aristotelianism; Neo-Scholasticism; Neo-Thomism; Nominalism; Perennial Philosophy; Philosophy; Platonism; Schools of Theology; Summa; Thomism.*

Schools of Theology. Various groups of theologians who investigate and systematically present the data of scripture and tradition in their own characteristic ways. Their methods and standards are affected by their setting (e.g., a university, a monastery, or a seminary), their audiences (e.g., seminarians, the general public, or the church at large), and their philosophical differences (e.g., Aristotelianism, existentialism, Platonism, or process thought). In the Middle Ages, the great schools of theology (Augustinian, Dominican, and Franciscan) were mostly associated with such new universities as Bologna, Cambridge, Cologne, Naples, Oxford, and Paris and/or with such great teachers as the Franciscan St. Bonaventure (1221–74), the Dominicans St. Albert the Great (ca. 1200–80), and St. Thomas Aquinas (ca. 1225–74), and, a little later, the Franciscans Blessed Duns Scotus (ca. 1265–1308) and William of Occam (ca. 1285–ca. 1347). In the nineteenth and twentieth centuries, schools of theology have likewise been associated with particular institutions (e.g., the University of Tübingen, the University of Chicago, and the Gregorian University in Rome), and/or with figures such as Karl Barth (1886–1968), Karl Rahner (1904–84), Bernard Lonergan (1904–84), Hans Urs von Balthasar (1905–88), and Paul Tillich (1886–1965). See *Augustinianism; Neo-Scholasticism; Neo-Thomism; Nominalism; Scholasticism; Scotism; Thomism; Tübingen and Its Schools.*

Science and Religion. The tension that, from the seventeenth century, emerged between (a) scientific discoveries, laws, and methods; and (b) religious beliefs. Difficulties have come from disciplines such as astronomy, biology, paleontology, physics, psychology, and sociology. Ironically, it can be argued that the Jewish-Christian faith in God the creator made possible the very rise of Western science. The trial of Galileo Galilei (1564–1642) created the enduring image of an official church refusing to accept new discoveries and trying to limit proper scientific freedom. That case, like the debate over the theory of evolution developed by Charles Darwin (1809–82), also highlighted the issue of the proper interpretation of biblical texts. In the twentieth century, scientific and technological growth became spectacular. Along with that growth has come the now widely held conviction that science alone cannot answer ultimate questions about meaning and values, may prove dehumanizing and extremely dangerous (e.g., nuclear weapons), and should respect the different methods employed in philosophy and theology. Progress in theories of knowledge has shown that even in the natural sciences broad claims to pure, impartial objectivity should be abandoned. For many, the French priest-paleontologist Pierre Teilhard de Chardin (1881–1955) has symbolized the end of the old antagonism between science and religion. Whether found in religion or in science, all truth is based in God and can never be opposed to itself (see GS 36). Blessed John Paul II (pope 1978–2005) made this point, with reference to the Galileo case, in his 1992 address to the Pontifical Academy of Sciences (ND 184a-c). Previously, in 1983, at a symposium of scientists commemorating Galileo's work, John Paul II had endorsed a new dialogue between the official church and science (ND 173). The work of priest-scientists such as Sir John Polkinghorne (b. 1930) and the contribution of the John Templeton Foundation have done much to further the dialogue between science and faith. See *Autonomy; Biblical Criticism; Creationism; Evolution; Fundamentalism; God of the Gaps; Positivism; Truth.*

Scientia Media (Lat. "middle knowledge"). A theory first developed by the Jesuit Luis de Molina (1535–1600) to reconcile real human freedom with the divine foreknowledge of everything that will happen. He suggested that God knows and takes into account decisions that rational creatures would freely make in any situation in which they might be placed. Molina called it "middle" knowledge, because it is more than a knowledge of mere possibilities, but less than a vision of actual future events. Since the 1970s, Alvin Plantinga (b. 1932) and others have revived interest in and stirred up fresh debate about this theory. See *Foreknowledge; Molinism.*

Scotism. The system developed by the Franciscan Blessed Duns Scotus (ca. 1265–1308), who came from Scotland; taught in Cambridge, Oxford, Paris, and Cologne; and, for his great speculative capacity, was called *doctor subtilis* (Lat. "subtle doctor"). Unlike St. Thomas Aquinas (ca. 1225–74), he gave the primacy to love and will (instead of knowledge and reason), and, hence, argued that our heavenly happiness will consist primarily in our love for (rather than our vision of) God. Scotus also differed from Aquinas by championing the doctrine of the Immaculate Conception. He held that the Incarnation was no "rescue operation" mounted primarily because of the fall, but would have happened anyway. Scotus's notion that particular beings are individuated through a *haecceitas* (Lat. "this-ness") that is somehow intelligible, and his speculations about *possibilia* (Lat. "possibilities") exercised an influence on Martin Heidegger (1889–1976). See *Beatific Vision; Fall, The; Immaculate Conception; Incarnation; Love; Scholasticism; Schools of Theology; Thomism.*

Scribes. Originally copiers and keepers of records whose further skills could lead to their official advancement (Ps 45:1; Ezra 7:6; Sir 38:24—39:11; see Jer 8:8). At the time of Jesus, they came mainly, but not exclusively, from the

Pharisees, and with the chief priests and the elders made up the seventy-one members of the Sanhedrin or supreme Jewish council in Jerusalem. Because of their work in interpreting and applying scripture, they were called doctors of the law or lawyers (Luke 7:30). See *Bible; Pharisees; Torah.*

Scripture. See *Bible.*

Scripture and Tradition. The relationship between the written and inspired word of God and the wider reality of the church in its "doctrine, life, and worship" handing on "to every generation all that she herself is, all that she believes" (DV 8). Against the reformers' principle of *sola scriptura* (Lat. "scripture alone"), the Council of Trent (1545–63) taught that the gospel was "the source of all saving truth and rule of conduct." It was "contained" not only in the "written books," but also in the "unwritten traditions that have come down to us" (DH 1501; ND 210). Although the council had spoken of one source ("the gospel"), this teaching led many Catholics to develop the "two-source" theory, according to which some revealed truths could be contained in tradition and not in scripture. The Second Vatican Council (1962–65) understood revelation as being primarily the living self-communication of God (DV 2–6), rather than a body of revealed propositions "contained" in the Bible or other sources. The council stressed the process of tradition (singular) rather than individual traditions (or particular teachings or practices); insisted on the way tradition and scripture are united in their origin (revelation), function, and goal (DV 9); and, while speaking only of the scripture as the word of God, recognized the role of tradition in clarifying and actualizing revelation (DV 8). The council's documents on ecumenism (UR 14–17) and the Eastern churches (OE 5–6) expressed the way Tradition (in upper case) is passed on through traditions (lower case). Thanks to a 1963 meeting of the Faith and Order Commission of the World Council of Churches and the influence of Yves Congar (1904–1995), Gerhard Ebeling (1912–2001), Hans-Georg Gadamer (1900–2002), and others, more and more Protestants have accepted that an exclusive appeal to scripture alone is not possible. Tradition is an essential means for understanding revelation, while scripture has its special role in judging and reforming traditions. The Orthodox have an organic sense of the relationship between scripture and tradition, and often speak of tradition as including both. See *Bible; Holy Spirit; Lutheranism; Magisterium; Protestant; Reformation, The; Sola Scriptura; Sufficiency of Scripture; Tradition; Trent, Council of; Vatican Council, Second; Word of God.*

Second Coming. See *Parousia.*

Secularism (Lat. "belief in the world"). (a) An atheist or agnostic ideology that rules out religious beliefs and values, and that explains everything exclusively in this-worldly terms. (b) This is to be distinguished from secularity, or the attitude of being concerned with this world and its affairs but not necessarily in an antireligious way. (c) Secularization refers to any social and historical process that brings a change away from ecclesial control and sacred purposes, for example, the suppression of the monasteries in sixteenth-century England, the impact of the French Revolution in France itself, and the policy of Napoleon Bonaparte (1769–1821) in Germany. Land and buildings originally used for religious life were appropriated by nobles, merchants, and others for thoroughly mundane, this-worldly purposes. (d) The secular (diocesan) clergy are priests under obedience to the bishop of their diocese, as distinguished from priests who belong to religious orders or congregations. See *Autonomy; Church and State; Clergy; Diocese; Ordinary; Religious Life.*

Self-Communication. Term used by Friedrich David Ernst Schleiermacher (1768–1834), Herman Schell (1850–1906), Romano Guardini (1885–1968), and others, including Karl Rahner (1904–84) and the Second Vatican Council (1962–65) (DV 6), to designate the self-manifestation and self-giving of God in the process of revelation and grace. In his 1986 encyclical on the Holy Spirit, *Dominum et Vivificantem*, Blessed John Paul II (pope 1978–2005) applied this term to the mission of the Spirit. See *Deification; Grace; Idealism; Revelation.*

Semi-Arianism. The teaching of Bishop Basil of Ancyra (Ankara) and others after Nicaea I (325). They excluded the Arian view of Christ being only the first among creatures, but did not yet endorse the orthodox doctrine of his being *homoousios* (Gr. "of one being/essence") with the Father. They called the Son *homo-i-ousios* (Gr. "of a similar nature") to the Father. Although their term was heretical, the difference of only an "i" created a platform of dialogue that helped many Semi-Arians toward full orthodoxy. See *Arianism; Homoousios; Nicaea, First Council of.*

Semi-Pelagianism. The view that derives from St. John Cassian of Marseilles (ca. 360–435), St. Vincent of Lérins (d. before 450), and other monks in southern France, and that asserts that human beings can make their first step toward God without the help of divine grace. While accepting that grace is indispensable for salvation and so rejecting Pelagianism, those who developed Semi-Pelagianism (as it came to be called in the late sixteenth century) did so at least partly because of their opposition to the extreme version of predestination advanced by St. Augustine of Hippo (354–430). Eventually Semi-Pelagianism was condemned at the Second Council of Orange (529); unfortunately, the acts of this council, after being forgotten for centuries, became known again only at the end of the sixteenth century. Official church teaching, while following Augustine's teaching on grace (see DH 370–97, 2004–5, 2618, 2620; ND 504–05, 1915–22, 1989/4–5), has never endorsed his interpretation of predestination. See *Anthropology; Grace; Pelagianism; Predestination; Synergism.*

Sense of Faith. See *Sensus Fidelium.*

Senses of Scripture. The various meanings that biblical texts can convey. The literal sense is the meaning intended by the original author writing for a particular audience in given historical circumstances and using specific literary forms. Once written, however, a biblical text, like other texts, begins to have a life of its own. It will be read and interpreted in contexts very different from that in which it was originally composed. It will communicate and evoke meanings that go beyond what the original author intended. Over the centuries, those who hear, read, and use biblical texts for prayer bring to this dialogue their own questions and interests; they can, thus, discover fresh ranges of meaning. By looking for and often establishing, at least in part, the literal sense, biblical criticism remains essential; among other things it can check wild flights of subjective interpretation. At the same time, the Holy Spirit, who first inspired the writing of the biblical texts, enlightens individuals and the whole community to find meaning and life in those texts today (see DV 12, 21–25). In its 1993 document "The Interpretation of the Bible in the Church," the Pontifical Biblical Commission presented skillfully the literal and spiritual senses of scripture (ND 273–76). From Origen (ca. 185–ca. 234) to Pope Benedict XV (1854–1922) and beyond, believers have witnessed to their conviction that the whole Bible is centered on Christ and finds its meaning in him. See *Alexandrian Theology; Allegory; Antiochene Theology; Biblical Criticism; Exegesis; Fundamentalism; Hermeneutics; Inspiration, Biblical; Origenism; Sensus Plenior; Typology.*

Sensus Fidelium (Lat. "sense of the faithful"). The instinctive sensitivity in matters of faith exercised by the whole body of believers (LG 12, DV 8), whose appreciation and discernment of revelation are guided by the Holy Spirit (John 16:13; 1 John 2:20, 27). This sense of faith gives rise to and manifests itself in the *consensus fidelium* (Lat. "consensus of the faithful"), as a cause produces its corresponding effects. Those who have helped to develop this idea include Blessed John Henry Newman (1801–90), Matthias Joseph Scheeben (1835–88), and Johann Adam Möhler (1796–1838). See *Faith; Grace; Hierarchy; Holy Spirit; Indefectibility; Laity; Sobornost.*

Sensus Plenior (Lat. "fuller sense"). The way that the scriptures (e.g., OT texts) can have meanings that go beyond the literal sense (the meaning explicitly intended by the original human author[s]). Such meanings, intended by the principal author (God), have emerged in the light of later events that make up the divinely guided history of salvation. See *Senses of Scripture.*

Septuagint (Gr. "seventy"). The most important Greek version of the OT, indicated as LXX because of the legend that the translation was made by seventy (or seventy-two) scholars working independently. According to Jewish tradition, it was commissioned by Ptolemy Philadelphus (285–46 BC) for his famous library in Alexandria. While seeming to be a joint work of many translators, it was probably finished later—by about 132 BC. In important respects, it differs from the Hebrew Bible. It includes books that are simply not found in the Hebrew Bible (such as Tobit, Judith, Wisdom, Sirach, and Baruch). It adds extra sections to some books (e.g., Esther). These further books and additions, called Apocrypha in the Protestant tradition, are considered Deuterocanonical by Catholics and Orthodox. When citing the OT, NT authors often followed the LXX rather than the original Hebrew. Many early Fathers of the Church considered the LXX to be the standard version of the OT. The Greek Orthodox Church recognizes the LXX as inspired. Before the Greek Constitution of 1978 came into force, one needed permission from the Holy Synod to translate the LXX into modern Greek; even then, the original text had to be printed on a facing page. See *Apocrypha; Bible; Canon of Scripture; Deuterocanonical Books; Old Testament; Vulgate.*

Seven Ecumenical Councils, The. Those general councils from Nicaea I (325) to Nicaea II (787) recognized as ecumenical by both Roman Catholics and the Greek Orthodox. They enjoy a unique importance in any dialogue between East and West. Although the Greek Orthodox later held important councils, such as those of Constantinople in 1351 and Jerusalem in 1672, none of them was considered ecumenical. Roman Catholics have normally counted twenty-one ecumenical councils down to the Second Vatican Council (1962–65). See *Chalcedon, Council of; Constantinople, First Council of; Constantinople, Second Council of; Constantinople, Third Council of; Council, Ecumenical; Ephesus, Council of; Nicaea, First Council of; Nicaea, Second Council of.*

Seventh-Day Adventists. A group that derived from mainline Adventists, a denomination that had formed when William Miller (1742–1849) began to proclaim in 1831 that 1844 would be the end of the world and the second coming of Christ. Ellen G. White (1827–1915) was a prominent figure among the Seventh-Day Adventists. They observe the Sabbath instead of Sunday, practice adult baptism by complete immersion, abstain from alcohol and tobacco, and live in expectation of the parousia, without, however, now predicting a definite year for Christ's return. See *Advent; Parousia; Sabbath; Sunday.*

Shekinah (Heb. "abode, dwelling-place," formed from the verb "to pitch a tent"). God's glorious presence in our midst. Although it does not use the word, the OT refers to the Tent of Encounter in the desert where God's glory was manifested (see Exod 33:7–11; Num 11:16–25; 12:1–10). In the Talmud, the term can be a reverent circumlocution for God. John's Gospel uses the notion of the *shekinah* by speaking of the Incarnation as the Word "pitching his tent amongst us" and our "seeing his glory" (John 1:14). See *Doxa; Glory; Talmud.*

Shema (Heb. "listen!"). The first word of a prayer that, in its full form, was composed from Deuteronomy 6:4–9; 11:13–21 and Numbers 15:37–41, but runs as follows in its shorter form: "Hear, O Israel, the Lord Our God is the Lord. You will love the Lord your God with your whole heart, with your whole soul, and with your whole power" (Deut 6:4–5). Christ quoted the opening line of this prayer when answering a scribe's question about the greatest commandment (Mark 12:28–30). The Shema occupies in Jewish piety the central place that the Our Father does in Christian piety. See *Love; Prayer.*

Sheol (etymology uncertain). The place in the underworld where in earlier OT thought all the dead lead the same shadowy existence (Gen 37:35; Num 16:30–34; Deut 32:22; Job 3:13–19; 26:5–6; Isa 14:9–11). Long life on earth is desirable, because the dead can no longer praise God (Pss 6:5; 88:3–6, 11–12; Isa 38:18). See *Eschatology; Heaven; Hell; Purgatory.*

Sign. Something indicating a state or quality (e.g., a label on a bottle), a distinguishing mark or gesture conveying information (e.g., movements of the hand). All symbols are signs, but not all signs (e.g., road signs) are symbols. Signs can often be more conventional (e.g., directions in an airport terminal) and less "natural" than symbols, which may correspond more closely to the things symbolized. Symbolic words and gestures (e.g., a kiss) let us share in the thing symbolized (e.g., love); signs usually point to something else (e.g., "To Chicago"), without mediating its presence. But certain signs (e.g., the sign of the cross) can be deeply symbolic and allow us to participate in something (e.g., the passion of Jesus). (a) Jesus spoke of the "signs of the times" (Matt 16:3), language taken up by Vatican II (1962–65) (GS 4, 11). (b) John's Gospel did not follow the Synoptic Gospels in applying to the miraculous deeds of Jesus the language of "wonder" (Gr. *teras*) or "deed of power" (Gr. *dunamis*), but called those deeds "signs" (Gr. *sēmeia*) (that revealed his identity and called people to faith in him (e.g., John 2:11; 11:47). (c) Often catechists have spoken of sacraments as outward (visible) signs of inward (invisible) grace. (d) Vatican II's teaching (LG 1) encourages understanding the Church as a sign of salvation for the whole world. See *Ecclesiology; Miracle; Res et Sacramentum; Sacrament; Symbol; Vatican Council, Second; Word and Sacrament.*

Simony. Dealing with spiritual goods as if they were for sale. Selling or buying a church office or sacrament constitutes the sin of simony. The name comes from a magician Simon who wanted to buy from Peter and John the power to impart the Holy Spirit (Acts 8:9–25). At times, simony has disfigured the life of the church and has been repeatedly condemned (see DH 304, 473, 586, 691–94, 707, 715, 751, 820; CIC 149, 188, 1380). See *Lateran Council, Second.*

Simplicity. The characteristic of being indivisible, not made up of various parts. Being spiritual and entirely self-present, God is simple in this ontological sense (John 4:24; see DH 297, 800, 805, 1880, 3001; ND 19, 319). In the moral sphere, simplicity refers to the uncomplicated rightness of intention with which the truly religious person acts (see Matt 10:16). In Eastern spirituality, it characterizes a person whom the Holy Spirit has integrated and made "all of a piece." See *Immutability; Prudence; Suffering of God*.

Simul Justus et Peccator (Lat. "being sinful and righteous at the same time"). A phrase summarizing the Lutheran conviction that we always have to confess ourselves sinners, when we look at ourselves in the light of the accusing law and of our own natural possibilities. As Blessed John XXIII (pope 1958–63) admitted, "If you peep into your conscience, you spot a sinner." At the same time, we should admit that we are really justified when we believe in God's promise of forgiveness and mercy through Christ. See *Depravity, Total; Imputation; Justification; Lutheranism; Protestant; Sin*.

Sin. Any thought, word, or deed that deliberately disobeys God's will and in some way rejects the divine goodness and love. Starting from the sin of Adam and Eve (Gen 3:1–24), the OT tells a story of human sin and bondage to sin (see GS 37). Repeatedly denouncing idolatry and injustice, the prophets affirmed personal responsibility for sinful failures (Jer 31:29–30; Ezek 18:1–4). The OT calls sin *hatta* (Heb. "missing the mark"), *pesha* (Heb. "transgression of orders," "revolt against superiors"), and *awon* (Heb. "guilt stemming from iniquity") (see Ps 51:3–5). Like the OT (Gen 6:5; 8:21; Jer 17:9), Jesus saw that sin comes from the heart (Mark 7:20–23). St. John's gospel understood sin as disbelief in Christ, a preference for darkness over the Light of the world (John 3:16–21; 9:1–41; 11:9–10). From the outset, Christians acknowledged that Christ had died "for our sins" (1 Cor 15:3; see Rom 4:25; Heb 2:11–14). The Protestant tradition has been impressed by St. Paul's reflections on the power of sin to corrupt and enslave human beings (Rom 1:18—3:23; 5:12–21; 6:15–23). The Orthodox tradition sees that sin destroys *koinonia* (Gr. "communion") with God, with other human beings, and with nature. The Catholic tradition, like Western Christianity, generally has tended to think of the sins of individuals rather than of the community wounded by sin. But the 1987 encyclical of Blessed John Paul II, *Sollicitudo Rei Socialis* (see 36–37), witnesses to a renewed sense of the societal dimension of sin (see GS 25). See *Atonement; Expiation; Fall, The; Grace; Heart; Koinonia; Metanoia; Original Sin; Penance, Sacrament of; Reparation; Salvation*.

Sin, Mortal and Venial. A distinction between sins that "exclude from the kingdom of God" (1 Cor 6:9–10; Gal 5:19–21; Eph 5:5) and those that do not do so (Jas 3:2; 1 John 1:8; 5:16–17). A mortal (Lat. "deadly") or grave sin means a deliberate and radical turning away from God that comes through clear knowledge and full consent in a truly serious matter (see DH 1537, 1544, 1680–82; ND 1626, 1938, 1945). It brings the loss of sanctifying grace and the risk of eternal damnation. Venial (Lat. "excusable") sins truly harm one's relationship with God and others, but do not entail a fundamental option against God. The CIC speaks of venial sins and grave sins (CIC 988), but not of mortal sins; likewise, the CCEO speaks of grave or serious sins (CCEO 719–20), but not of mortal sins. The *Catechism of the Catholic Church*, first promulgated in 1992 by Blessed John Paul II (pope 1978–2005) and with a definitive edition in 1997, retains the distinction between mortal and venial sins (nrs. 1854–64). See *Fundamental Option; Grace, Habitual; Hell; Penance, Sacrament of.*

Sin, Original. See *Original Sin*.

Sins, Seven Deadly. The sins traditionally considered to be the root of all other sins. As developed by Evagrius Ponticus (346–399), St. Gregory the Great (ca. 540–604), and others, the list includes pride, covetousness, lust, envy, gluttony, anger, and sloth. "Sloth" translates inadequately *acedia* (Gr. "indifference"), which means apathy, torpor, or a distaste for spiritual matters.

Sitz im Leben (German "place in life," "life context"). Term popularized by Hermann Gunkel (1862–1932) and other pioneers of form criticism. It refers to the function that a particular biblical unit (e.g., a hymn, saying, or story) could have enjoyed in the life and worship of the community. In the case of the NT, it refers especially to the way specific traditions about the earthly Jesus were shaped and handed on (orally or perhaps sometimes in writing) during the post-Pentecost period (AD 30–ca. 67) until Mark and the other evangelists wrote their gospels. Sometimes scholars speak of the *Sitz im Leben Jesu*—that is, the historical circumstances in which Jesus told a parable, cured some sick person, or pronounced on a given issue. See *Biblical Criticism*.

Skepticism (Gr. "inquiring, doubting"). Doubting the possibility of knowing anything for certain. Gorgias (d. 376 BC) and Pyrrhon of Elis (ca. 360–ca. 270 BC) held that the human race cannot reach certainty about anything whatsoever. Such absolute skepticism, sometimes called Pyrrhonism, is obviously self-contradictory. Relative skepticism limits itself to some areas of knowledge, for instance, religious and moral truth. See *Relativism*.

Sobornost (Russian "conciliarism"). Term used by Yuri Samarin (1819–76) in the Russian translation of the English and French works of Alexej Chomjakow (1804–60), Russian Orthodox layman and theologian; it can be rendered by "conciliarity" or "collegiality" (from the Russian *sobor* meaning "gathering," "synod"). From the eleventh century, the word *soborny* had been used in the Slavonic version of the creed to translate "Catholic" in "the Catholic Church."

Chomjakow held *sobornost* to be the distinguishing characteristic of the Orthodox Church: the loving collaboration of the faithful and hierarchy in their life, belief, and worship. He argued that Catholics have unity without freedom, Protestants freedom without unity, and the Orthodox unity and freedom in the bond of love. *Sobornost* amounts to the collegiality of all church members. See *Catholicity; Collegiality; Eastern Churches; Orthodoxy; Synod.*

Social Teaching. Church teaching concerning the rights and obligations of different members of society in their relationship to the common good, both national and international. Jesus' message of repentance called on the financially secure to care for the poor, the maimed, the lame, and the blind (Luke 14:12–14). The future judgment should encourage us to attend now to the earthly needs of the hungry, strangers, the naked, the sick, and prisoners (Matt 25:31–46). In general, the NT shows the same practical concern for needy people (Acts 4:32—5:11; Rom 12:8; 1 Cor 13:3; Heb 13:16; 1 John 3:17; Jas 1:27; 2:14–17). St. Ambrose (ca. 339–97), St. John Chrysostom (ca. 347–407), and other Fathers preached the same message. For centuries, church institutions stood almost alone in caring for the socially deprived, such as widows, orphans, the sick, and prisoners as well as in providing education through monastic orders such as the Benedictines. St. Vincent de Paul (ca. 1580–1660); the Daughters of Charity, the Sisters of Mercy; Blessed Frédéric Ozanam (1813–53); St Joseph de Veuster (1840–89), known as Father Damien; Adolf Kolping (1813–65); Mother Teresa of Calcutta (1910–97), beatified in 2003; and many others spent their lives meeting the needs of the poor and suffering. The first great social encyclical was Leo XIII's (pope 1878–1903)1891 *Rerum Novarum*, which addressed itself to such questions as just wages and private property. Forty years later, in 1931, Pius XI (pope 1922–1939) took up these and related themes in his *Quadragesimo Anno*. Blessed John XXIII's (pope 1958–1963) *Mater et Magistra* updated the church's social teaching with an eye to state intervention in the case of the needy, whereas his 1963 *Pacem in Terris* advocated an international social order based on a thorough respect for human rights. The Second Vatican Council (1962–65) defended religious freedom in its declaration *Dignitatis Humanae* (1965). The same council encouraged at every level a truly just social order (GS 9, 63–93), calling on church members to participate actively in social causes (AA 7, 8, 13). Although the mission Christ gave his church does not primarily concern the political, economic, and social areas, religious faith heightens our obligations to neighbors in need (GS 42). In his 1967 *Populorum Progressio,* Paul VI (pope 1963–1978) called economic development that attended to the whole human person the new name for peace. Social justice, international solidarity, and human rights were constant themes of Blessed John Paul II's (pope 1978–2005) teaching, expressed, in particular, through his 1981, 1987, and 1991 encyclicals: *Laborem Exercens, Sollicitudo Rei Socialis,* and *Centesimus Annus*. In *Caritas in Veritate* (2009), his first social encyclical,

Pope Benedict XVI (pope 2005–13) has taught that if our globalized world is to achieve truly human progress, economic development must be imbued with respect for life and a civilization of love. See *Encyclical; Justice; Liberation Theology; Moral Theology; Option for the Poor; Rights, Human; Subsidiarity.*

Socinianism. A religious system that denies the Trinity and the divinity of Christ and draws its name from the Italians Lelio Francesco Maria Sozini (1525–62) and his nephew Fausto Paolo Sozzini (1539–1604; his name was spelled differently from that of his uncle) (see DH 1880; ND 648). Fausto Sozzini spent the last part of his life in Poland. Eventually many Socinians joined other forces to form the Unitarian Church. See *Trinity, Theology of; Unitarianism.*

Sola Fides (Lat. "faith alone"). A basic axiom Martin Luther (1483–1546) gave to the Protestant Reformation. Justification comes by faith in Jesus Christ (Rom 1:17) and not through the works of the law (Rom 3:28). See *Faith; Justification; Law and Gospel; Merit; Protestant; Reformation, The.*

Sola Gratia (Lat. "grace alone"). A basic principle of the Protestant reformers expressing as a matter of fact the same conviction as *sola fides*. We are justified only by God's mercy and Christ's merits, to which we cling by faith, and not by our own observance of the law and meritorious works. Catholic theology also teaches the absoluteness of God's grace, but stresses the importance of human "collaboration" with and within the all-embracing initiative of God's work. God and human beings are not in competition; every human success has God as its necessary inspirer and supporter. See *Faith and Works; Imputation; Justification; Pelagianism; Sanctification; Semi-Pelagianism; Synergism.*

Sola Scriptura (Lat. "Scripture alone"). Another Reformation principle coming from Martin Luther (1483–1546) and recognizing the highest religious authority in the word of God as witnessed to in scripture. In this sense, the principle can be aligned with the Second Vatican Council's (1960–65) statement that "the teaching office of the church is not above the Word of God but serves it" (DV 10). Luther's principle is unacceptable (and indeed unworkable) if it is taken to exclude the interpretative and actualizing role of tradition (DV 9, 21, 24). See *Bible; Magisterium; Revelation; Scripture and Tradition; Sufficiency of Scripture; Tradition; Word of God.*

Soma (Gr. "corpse," "body"). A living body (Mark 5:29) or a dead corpse (Mark 15:43). Over against Platonism and Neoplatonism, the biblical concept of *soma* shows no hostility toward matter, as if the soul were imprisoned in the body. In St. Paul's letters, unlike *sarx* (Gr. "flesh"), which may denote the whole human being as oriented toward sin, *soma* is more neutral. It can simply refer to the body as distinguished from soul or spirit (1 Thess 5:23). *Soma* is used of Christ's body in the Eucharist (Mark 14:22; 1 Cor 11:24), of his church (Rom 12:4–5; 1 Cor 12:12–27), and of our earthly body, which will be glorified and "spiritualized" through the resurrection (1 Cor 15:35–58; Phil 3:21). With an eye on our ultimate, bodily destiny, Orthodox Christians speak of transfigured love, a love that goes beyond merely carnal love and aims at transforming society. See *Body of Christ; Eucharist; Neoplatonism; Platonism; Resurrection; Sarx.*

Son of God. Used in the OT of angels, the chosen people (e.g., Hos 11:1), and sometimes of such individuals as the anointed king (e.g., Pss 2:7; 89:26–27) and righteous individuals (but never of prophets) to indicate a special relationship to God and vocation from God. The voice from heaven at Jesus' baptism and transfiguration, his intimate address to God as Father (e.g., Mark 14:36), and then his resurrection from the dead (e.g., Rom 1:4; Gal 1:16) helped to establish this title, which enjoyed a central place in the gospels of Matthew and John as well as in the Letter to the Hebrews. Jesus never called himself the Son of God, but at least three times he implied that he was the Son (Matt 11:25–27; Mark 12:6–8; 13:32). Believers were understood to become adopted sons and daughters in the Son (e.g., Gal 4:4–7) or "children of God" through God's "only Son" (John 1:12–14). From the time of the First Council of Nicaea (325), Son of God became (with Lord) the central high title for Jesus. See *Abba; Adoption as God's Children; Christological Titles; Christology; Jesus Christ; Kyrios; Nicaea, First Council of.*

Son of Man. A Hebrew (and Aramaic) phrase used repeatedly in Ezekiel to indicate someone who is weak and mortal (i.e., the prophet) and once in Daniel to point to a heavenly, apocalyptic figure (Dan 7:13–14). Jesus repeatedly applied this designation to himself with reference to (a) his work and life on earth (e.g., Matt 8:20; 11:19), (b) his death and resurrection (e.g., Mark 8:31), and (c) his coming in glory at the final judgment (e.g., Mark 8:38; 13:26–27). Outside the Synoptic Gospels, the title hardly appears; the proclamation and teaching of the early church preferred Son of God, Lord, and Christ. In the patristic period and later, the title reappeared simply as a way of indicating his humanity—a usage that ignored the divine implications of the Son of Man coming to exercise God's prerogative of judging all men and women. See *Christological Titles; Christology; Jesus Christ; Kyrios; Messiah; Son of God.*

Sophia (Gr. "wisdom"). (a) A practical knowledge and discerning judgment, classically represented in the OT by Solomon (1 Kgs 3:1–28; 4:29–34). Revealed through creation and human history (Wis 10:1—11:4), *Hokmah* (Heb. "wisdom") is personified as God's agent in creation and a prophetess (Prov 8:1–36) who invites to her feast those who are not yet wise (Prov 9:1–6). Wisdom is a sure and beneficial guide for life (Wis 6:1–25). The NT sees in

Wisdom a prefiguration of Christ (Matt 12:42; 1 Cor 1:24–30; Col 2:3), a wisdom, however, which expresses itself in the folly of the cross (1 Cor 1:17–25). (b) For the Valentinians and some other ancient Gnostics, *Sophia Prounicos* and *Sophia Achamoth* had an important cosmological and ecclesial role. (c) The most famous church in Eastern Christianity was *Hagia Sophia* or *Santa Sophia* (Gr. and Lat., respectively, for "Holy Wisdom"), dedicated to Christ, the divine Wisdom/Logos in person. Built in Constantinople and consecrated under the Emperor Justinian I in 538, *Santa Sophia* became a model for many other Byzantine churches. After the fall of Constantinople in 1453, it became a mosque and later a museum. Churches dedicated to Holy Wisdom in Ukraine and Russia have been understood by some to refer to Mary, the Mother of God, revered in the West as "seat of wisdom." (d) A *sophiology* (Gr. "study of wisdom") or theology in the key of wisdom has been developed by Russian theologians such as Vladimir Solovi'ev (1853–1900), Sergius Bulgakov (1871–1944), and Pavel Florenskij (1882–ca. 1937). See *Christology; Creation; Fools for Christ's Sake; Gifts of the Holy Spirit; Gnosticism; Valentinians; Wisdom Literature.*

Soteriology (Gr. "doctrine of salvation"). The systematic interpretation of Christ's saving work for human beings and the world. Recognizing how Christ died and rose to save sinful humanity (Mark 14:24; John 11:49–52; Rom 4:25; 5:6–11; 1 Cor 15:3; 1 Pet 1:3), the NT holds together inseparably the saving function and personal identity of Christ as Son of God. Just as the NT applies various christological titles to Jesus, so it understands his saving work in a variety of ways—above all, as victorious liberation, expiation, and transforming love (John 1:29; 13:1; 16:33). Through the influence of Philipp Melanchthon (1497–1560) and others, reflection on Christ's saving work was often partly separated from Christology. Some treatises on soteriology examined "objective" salvation apart from its "subjective" appropriation through grace. In general, recent Western theology has tried to end the divorce between soteriology and Christology. Except where Western influence prevailed, Eastern theology has always considered together Christ's person and saving work. See *Atonement; Christology; Economy; Expiation; Grace; Love; Redemption; Salvation; Satisfaction.*

Soul. The spiritual principle of human beings that survives their death. According to the OT, the *nephesh* (Heb. "breath of life") comes from God (Gen 2:7) and disappears at death. "My *nephesh*" can mean "myself" or "my soul" (Ps 3:2–3; see Mark 8:34–36). Like the LXX, the NT often uses *psyche* (Gr. "soul") as the principle of life (Rom 16:4; Phil 2:30). Toward the end of the OT, Greek language and thought introduced a sense of the human soul as distinct from the body and endowed by God with immortality (Wis 3:1–9; 9:15; 16:13). Here and there, the NT reflects a certain dualism between body and soul (Matt 10:28; Luke 16:22; 23:43; 2 Cor 5:6–10; Phil 1:23; 1 Pet 1:9), but primarily thinks of human beings as animated bodies destined for final resurrection.

Under Stoic influence, Tertullian (ca. 160–ca. 220) seems to have believed the soul to be material, whereas Origen (ca. 185–ca. 254), at the other end of the spectrum, held that our souls were not only spiritual but even preexistent. St. Thomas Aquinas (ca. 1225–74) understood the soul to be the form of the body. This became official teaching at the Council of Vienne in 1312 (DH 902; ND 405). Against the Neo-Aristotelianism of Pietro Pompanazzi (1464–1525), the Fifth Lateran Council taught in 1513 the individuality and immortality of human souls (DH 1440; ND 410). See *Animism; Anthropology; Aristotelianism; Death; Life after Death; Matter and Form; Preexistence; Reincarnation; Resurrection; Stoicism; Vestigia Trinitatis; Vienne, Council of.*

Soutane. See *Cassock*.

Sphragis (Gr. "seal"). A word used in secular Greek for an official seal (e.g., that of the emperor) or a mark indicating the owner of something (see also Rev 5:1–9; 6:1–12). In the language of the Greek Fathers of the Church, the word refers to the cross made on catechumens during the rite of baptism to show that they belong to Christ. The formula for confirmation uses the verb: "Be *sealed* with the gifts of the Holy Spirit." *Sphragis* also refers to what the Latins call the sacramental character. See *Baptism; Character; Confirmation.*

Spiration (Lat. "breathing"). A technical term based on John 3:8 and used in the doctrine of the Trinity for the way the Spirit proceeds from the Father and (or through) the Son. The NT calls the Holy Spirit the "Spirit of the Father" (Matt 10:20), the "Spirit of the Son" (Gal 4:6), and "the Spirit of Christ" operating through the OT prophets (1 Pet 1:10–12). Latin theology adds that the Spirit is "breathed" from both Father and Son, and distinguishes between active and passive spiration. Precisely because it is common to the Father and the Son, active spiration does not constitute a new person, whereas passive spiration is another name for the Holy Spirit, who is "breathed" but does not "breathe" within the Trinity. In this way, the Latin church distinguished between the spiration by the Father, who is a principle without principle and an origin without origin, and the spiration by the Son, who is a principle originating from another principle, namely, the Father. Most theologians of the Greek Church, however, deny the Son's participation in the procession of the Spirit, as this would impair the *monarchy* (Gr. "sole principle") or originless origin of the Father. Both the Second Council of Lyons (1274) and the Council of Florence (1438–45) specified that the Holy Spirit is breathed from the Father and the Son as through a single principle (DH 850, 1300; ND 321–22). See *Filioque; Florence, Council of; Lyons, Second Council of; Processions; Relations, Divine.*

Spirit. See *Holy Spirit; Soul.*

Spiritism or **Spiritualism**. System of practices based on the belief that the souls of the dead can communicate with the living, especially through the help of a medium. While efforts to contact the dead were common enough in the past (e.g., 1 Sam 28:3–25), modern spiritualism goes back to 1848 and the abnormal experiences that Margaret and Kate Fox had in Hydesville, New York. Their influence spread séances with mediums across North America and the British Isles. Spiritualism has often been characterized by fraud and commercial exploitation. In 1882 Frederic W. H. Myers (1843–1901) founded the Society for Psychical Research in London. The society still operates and investigates parapsychological or abnormal phenomena. But the academic world at large is still reluctant to recognize parapsychology as a genuine science.

Spirituality. Systematic practice of and reflection on a prayerful, devout, and disciplined Christian life. In its practice, Christian spirituality has always called for an ascetical and prayerful life in which a spiritual guide and the light of the Holy Spirit help discern the direction in which individuals and communities are being led (1 Thess 5:19–22; 1 John 4:1). Schools or styles of spirituality have often followed the charisms of such orders as the Benedictines, Carmelites, Carthusians, Dominicans, Franciscans, and Jesuits. As a field of study, spirituality involves theological (including liturgical), scriptural, historical, psychological, and social elements. Eastern theology differs from Western through the primacy it assigns to the Spirit, and, consequently, to Christian life, spirituality, and to theology itself, spirituality being viewed as theology "from within." See *Asceticism; Contemplation; Devotion; Discernment of Spirits; Experience, Religious; Grace; Hesychasm; Holy Spirit; Imitation of Christ; Monasticism; Mysticism; Pneumatology; Prayer.*

Sponsor. Another word for godfather or godmother, that is, the adult who supports a candidate for baptism or confirmation. Canon law lays down that at least one sponsor but possibly two, one of each sex, should be present for the ceremony or at least fulfill their task by proxy. The sponsors have to be appointed either by the candidate (if an adult), or candidate's parents or guardians, or the parish priest. A sponsor must be a Catholic who has already received baptism, confirmation, and the Eucharist; should normally be at least sixteen years of age; and may not be a parent of the candidate. The names of the sponsors are entered in the baptismal register. Besides giving good example and encouragement in Christian living, the godparents take responsibility for the Christian education of those whom they have sponsored if the parents or guardians fail in their duty (see CIC 774, 851, 872–74; CCEO 618, 684–85). If the circumstances suggest this, a non-Catholic Eastern Christian may function as a sponsor, provided that the other sponsor is Catholic (CCEO 685 §3). In Western practice, a non-Catholic Christian may function as a witness (CIC 874 §2). At confirmation, it is desirable that the sponsor or sponsors be the same as at baptism, since the duties assumed resemble those assumed by the sponsors at baptism (CIC 892–93, 895). See *Baptism; Confirmation; Marriage Impediments.*

Staretz (Russian "old man"). A monk leading a contemplative life to whom younger monks or other people go for spiritual guidance. This kind of direction has been important in Russian religious history and also among the Greeks, who call the director *geron* (Gr. "old man"). See *Apophthegmata Patrum; Spirituality.*

Staurology (Gr. "study of the cross"). See *Theologia Crucis.*

Stoicism (Gr. "teaching of the porch"). A school of philosophy founded by Zeno of Citium (335–263 BC) and called after the *stoa,* or porch, in Athens where he taught. Stoicism proposed a harmony between the human being as a microcosm (Gr. "small world") and the macrocosm (Gr. "big world"). Logos (reason or a world-soul) governed the universe, and human beings needed only to control their passions so as to live in tune with nature and its laws. Primarily a moral philosophy, Stoicism held a pantheistic cosmology in which God and the divine energy pervaded everything. Dominant for centuries among intellectuals in the Greco-Roman world (see Acts 17:18), Stoicism numbered among its adherents Seneca (ca. 4 BC– AD 65) and Marcus Aurelius (emperor 161–80). In the NT, the tripartite anthropology of 1 Thessalonians 5:23 ("body, soul, and spirit") reflects Stoic thought, as do catalogues of virtues in the letters of St. Paul, who also quotes the Stoic poet Aratus: "for we too are his [God's] offspring" (Acts 17:18). The influence of Stoicism on Christian theology is seen with St. Theophilus of Antioch (late second century), who adopted the Stoic distinction between Logos *endiathetos* (Gr. "immanent word") and Logos *prophorikos* (Gr. "expressed word") to interpret God and the process of revelation by which the Father expresses the Word. Stoic ideas exercised some influence on the Cappadocian Fathers and in the trinitarian and christological controversies. The Christian tradition of natural law owes much to Stoicism. See *Apologists; Cappadocian Fathers; Cosmology; Immanence, Divine; Logos; Natural Law; Pantheism.*

Structuralism. A method developed by Ferdinand de Saussure (1857–1913) in the area of linguistics, used by Claude Lévi-Strauss (1908–95) to analyze the myths of traditional societies, and applied in disciplines such as psychology and sociology. In biblical exegesis, structuralism is concerned neither with the genesis of a text and the meaning intended by the author (or historical exegesis), nor with readers and their search for self-understanding (or existential exegesis), but with the present meaning conveyed by the text itself. This method reflects on the deep structures of narrative and the symbolic function of language (e.g., in parables). See *Biblical Criticism; Exegesis; Existentialism; Hermeneutics; Senses of Scripture.*

Subdeacon. A church minister who is on the way to becoming either a permanent deacon or a deacon and then a priest. Subdeacons existed as early as the third century. Considered a sacramental rather than a sacrament, the subdiaconate was abolished in the West after the Second Vatican Council (1962–65). In the Eastern Churches, it is considered to be a minor order, and the role of the subdeacon is mainly that of assisting the bishop during the liturgy. See *Clergy; Deacon; Sacramental.*

Subordinationism. Assigning an inferior status to the Son with regard to the Father, and to the Holy Spirit with regard to the Father and the Son. When the doctrine of the Trinity had not yet been worked out and theologians were trying to do justice to the Father's *monarchy* (Gr. "only principle"), the tendency to interpret the Son and Spirit as subordinate agents of an absolutely transcendent Father was shown by St. Justin Martyr (ca. 100–ca. 165), Tatian (d. ca. 160), St. Irenaeus of Lyons (ca. 130–ca. 200), Clement of Alexandria (ca. 150–ca. 215), and, most of all, Origen (ca. 185–ca. 254). By denying that the Son was really and fully divine by nature, Arius (ca. 185–ca. 254) took subordinationism to a heretical extreme that was rejected in 325 by Nicaea I (see DH 125–26; ND 7–8). When the Pneumatomachians (Gr. "denigrators of the Spirit") maintained a similar false subordinationism by declaring the Spirit to be created by the Son, Constantinople I (381) described the Spirit as being equal in dignity with, and worthy of the same worship as, the Father and the Son (see DH 150; ND 12). See *Arianism; Constantinople, First Council of; Homoousios; Macedonians; Monarchianism; Nicaea, First Council of; Pneumatomachians; Trinity, Theology of.*

Subsidiarity (Lat. "assistance"). A principle consistently endorsed by the social teaching of the church according to which decisions and activities that naturally belong to a lower level should not be taken to a higher level. In social and civil life, this means, for example, that the central organs of a state should not intervene unnecessarily at the local level. The Second Vatican Council (1962–65) appealed to the principle of subsidiarity in dealing with international cooperation in economic matters (GS 85–86) and in indicating the limits of the state's responsibility in education (GE 3, 6). Within the church, in theory, subsidiarity has been an operative principle in many post–Vatican II reforms, even if not always put into practice. See *Church and State; Education; Social Teaching.*

Substance and Accidents. A reality that remains the same under change, and the (often changing) characteristics that inhere in it. A substance (Lat. "underlying reality") can exist on its own, whereas accidents (Lat. "happenings") can exist only in a substance and not independently. See *Accident; Aristotelianism; Homoousios; Nature; Person; Transubstantiation.*

Suffering of God. The question whether God can/does suffer or remains impassible in the face of human misery. While God cannot change and suffer in the divine nature, by reason of his human nature, the Incarnate Son of God suffered and died on a cross. That appalling death expressed for all time God's loving concern for and real solidarity with human beings in their pain and suffering. See *Evil, Mystery of; Impassibility; Neo-Chalcedonianism; Patripassianism; Process Theology; Theopaschite Controversy.*

Sufficiency of Scripture. The adequacy of scripture in communicating the foundational revelation that reached its unsurpassable completeness with Christ and the NT church. As long as Christians conceived of revelation as primarily a body of truths (plural) disclosed by God, the question of sufficiency became twofold: do the scriptures "contain" all these revealed truths (material sufficiency)? Are the scriptures "formally" sufficient, in the sense of being their own adequate interpreter? Recognizing the role of tradition (and the magisterium) in canonizing, interpreting, applying, and actualizing the scriptures, even Catholics who accepted the material sufficiency of the scriptures rejected their formal sufficiency. When, however, the Second Vatican Council (1962–65) presented revelation as primarily being the personal self-manifestation to us of the triune God (DV 2–6), it no longer seemed appropriate to talk of this living reality as being "contained" in anything, even the scriptures. Appreciating revelation as an interpersonal event makes it difficult to inquire about the material sufficiency of the scriptures as either "containing" or "not containing" all revealed truths. See *Canon of Scripture; Deposit of Faith; Magisterium; Revelation; Scripture and Tradition; Sola Scriptura; Tradition.*

Summa (Lat. "main part"). A systematic summary of what is known in one field, such as theology. In the Middle Ages, a *summa* was distinguished from both *opuscula* (Lat. "small works"), which debated particular issues, and *Sentences*, or collections of the views of Church Fathers on various topics. Those who produced a *summa* included St. Albert the Great (ca. 1200–1280), Alexander of Hales (ca. 1170–1245), and St. Thomas Aquinas (ca. 1225–74). With his *Summa Theologiae*, Aquinas skillfully followed a dialectical method of first presenting two seemingly contradictory lines of evidence before developing his own response to the given question. See *Scholasticism.*

Sunday (Old English "day of the sun"). The "day of the Lord" (Rev 1:10) when Christians rest from work to remember joyfully Christ's resurrection (Mark 16:1–2), God's creation of the world, and the coming of the Holy Spirit. Eastern Christians call Sunday the eighth day to recall how Christ's resurrection regenerated the universe. The NT indicates that Christians met for the Eucharist on Sunday (Acts 20:7; see 1 Cor 16:2). In the early second century, both St. Ignatius of Antioch (ca. 35–ca. 107) and a Roman governor, Pliny the Younger (62–113), referred to Christians worshiping on that day. The Council of Elvira in Spain (ca. 306) legislated for Sunday observance, and, in 321, Constantine the Great ordered abstinence from work on that day. Church law calls for attendance at Mass on Sunday and a rest from work that allows for a proper religious and human enjoyment of that day (CIC 1246–47; CCEO 880–81; OE 15). In a 1998 apostolic letter, *Dies Domini*, Blessed John Paul II (pope 1978–2005) developed beautifully the theme of keeping Sunday as a truly holy day. See *Sabbath; Seventh-Day Adventists.*

Supernatural (Lat. "above nature"). A term coined by Pseudo-Dionysius the Areopagite (fl. ca. 500) for God, who is above our categories, our experiences, and our nature. From the Middle Ages, the term has referred to God's free and loving self-gift that already in the life of grace raises us above what is due to our human nature and prepares us for the life of glory. See *Grace; Nature; Supernatural Existential.*

Supernatural Existential, The. The situation that was created for human freedom as a result of Christ's redemptive work. The term "existential" was coined by Martin Heidegger (1889–1976) to describe a situation that as a matter of fact preconditions the way human freedom is exercised. Karl Rahner (1904–84) adapted the term for theology. Original sin is an existential in this sense, because it creates hindrances even before human beings can exercise their freedom. The supernatural existential is at the opposite end of the spectrum from original sin, because the supernatural existential means that, even before they accept grace, human beings are positively determined by it and not merely confronted with an external offer of salvation. See *Anonymous Christians; Grace; Justification; Original Sin; Redemption; Salvation; Supernatural.*

Symbol (Gr. "something thrown together"). Something perceptible representing naturally (e.g., lion symbolizing courage) or conventionally (e.g., flag symbolizing a country) something else. By making other things present, symbols enter our imagination, affect our feelings, and influence our behavior. Rational explanations will always fall short of the potential range of meanings expressed by given symbols. Particularly when we take up religious symbols, which represent ultimate, transcendent realities, we can expect these symbols to prove inexhaustible in their significance. The relationship between symbols and signs is much disputed. Many hold symbols to be particular kinds of signs. All symbols are signs, but not all signs are symbols; for example, a traffic sign is not normally reckoned to be a symbol. Karl Rahner (1904–84) understood Christ to be the supreme "real [ontological and not merely conventional] symbol," which, as the grace of God appearing in history, effects what it symbolizes; "he that sees me sees the Father" (John 14:9). See *Creed; Cross; Johannine Theology; Sacrament; Sign.*

Symbol, Theology of. View of the visible world as an image of the invisible. In his *Timaeus,* Plato (427–347), writing about the origin and constitution of the world, says: "Time is the moving image of eternity." The parables of Jesus show that he saw everyday things and events as windows on God and invitations to respond to the divine activity. Origen (ca. 185–ca. 254) developed a strongly symbolic theology. St. Augustine of Hippo (354–430), in his philosophical symbolism and biblical interpretation, gave a fresh impulse to a symbolic interpretation of reality. The Augustinian Hugh of St. Victor (ca. 1096–1141) interpreted everything in the universe as a sort of sacrament of divine realities. A symbolic approach remains central for the Eastern theology of the icon. Hugo Rahner (1901–68) described the theology of his brother Karl Rahner (1904–84) as being essentially a "theology of the real symbol," which characterized Catholic and Orthodox thinking. The Logos (Word) is the real symbol of the Father; Christ's humanity is the real symbol of the Logos; the church is the real symbol of God's grace; sacraments are real symbols of the particular graces being symbolized. See *Icon; Nicaea, Second Council of; Incarnation; Origenism; Sacrament.*

Symbolics. The systematic study of the symbols (Gr. "creeds") and basic beliefs of different Christian confessions. Developed by Georg Callixtus (1586–1656), Johann Adam Möhler (1796–1838), and others, this branch of theology has been given fresh life through the ecumenical movement—in particular, through the bilateral dialogues (or dialogues between official representatives of two Christian churches) and the World Council of Churches' Faith and Order Commission (e.g., its 1982 report Baptism, Eucharist, and Ministry, commonly called BEM). See *Augsburg Confession; Dialogue; Ecumenism; Faith and Order; Thirty-Nine Articles; World Council of Churches.*

Symbolum Apostolicum. See *Creed, Apostles'.*

Symphony (Gr. "harmonious voices/sounds"). The theory in Eastern theology that church and state should act in unison for the glory of God. See *Canon Law, Sources of Oriental; Church and State; Theocracy.*

Synagogue (Gr. "assembly of persons or things"). A Jewish school and place for worship. The corresponding Hebrew word is *knesset,* now used for Israel's parliament. Luke situates Jesus' first sermon in the synagogue at Nazareth (Luke 4:16–30), and we read of further visits to synagogues (Matt 9:35; Mark 1:39; Luke 4:44; 13:10; John 6:59). St. Paul and other early Christians used synagogues for dialogue and debate with Jews (see Acts 13:14–43; 17:1–2, 10–12). First formed in the sixth century BC, synagogues have remained the center for Jewish worship and instruction throughout the ages. Among modern Jews, the reformed speak of temples, whereas the Orthodox refer to schools. See *Israel; Judaism.*

Synaxarion (Gr. "assembly book"). The brief account of the life of a saint or the meaning of a particular feast, read at the *Orthros* or morning service in the Liturgy of the Hours of the Byzantine Church. See *Liturgy of the Hours*.

Synaxis (Gr. "congregation"). An assembly for the Liturgy of the Word, the Eucharist, or some other religious function. Almost synonymous with synagogue (Gr. "assembly"), the word may have first been used by Christians to distinguish their worship from that of the Jews. See *Eucharist*; *Liturgy of the Word*; *Synagogue*; *Worship*.

Syncretism (Gr. "combining of two Cretan cities against a third"). Any attempt to reconcile or merge different or even incompatible principles and practices. Often superficial and transient, syncretism may occur among religions, philosophies, and within Christianity itself. The first to attempt ecumenical syncretism on a large scale was Georg Callixtus (1586–1656), a Protestant theologian who aimed to reconcile Lutherans, Calvinists, and Catholics on the basis of the Bible, the faith of the first five centuries, and the Apostles' Creed. See *Comparative Religion*; *Creed, Apostles'*; *Ecumenism*; *History of Religions School*.

Synergism (Gr. "working together"). The teaching of the Eastern church that God and human beings cooperate in grace and liberty. This doctrine has sometimes been rejected as Semi-Pelagianism, because it is thought to detract from God's absolute sovereignty in the whole process of human salvation—from the first step toward conversion right through to final perseverance. However, this criticism wrongly presupposes that God and human beings are competitors, instead of recognizing that it is God's grace that enables human beings to repent and produce the fruits of conversion in liberty. A doctrine similar to synergism, developed by the Lutheran Philipp Melanchthon (1497–1560), met with similar (unfounded) criticism. See *Semi-Pelagianism*.

Synod (Gr. "council"). An assembly of bishops and others meeting to determine matters of church doctrine and practice. The name is applied to any such official assembly, from a diocesan synod right through to an ecumenical council (CD 36–38). The traditions of Eastern Christian churches are more synodal. See *Collegiality*; *Council, Ecumenical*; *Sobornost*.

Synod, Diocesan. An official assembly of priests and laypersons convoked by the bishop of a particular diocese to help him in the government of that diocese (CIC 460–68; CCEO 235–42). See *Bishop*; *Diocese*; *Ordinary*.

Synod of Bishops. An assembly of bishops that represents all the episcopal conferences and usually meets every three years in Rome through the month of October. Its scope is to promote collegial union between the bishops and the pope by advising him in matters of faith, morals, and church discipline (CD 5; CIC 342–48). The 1987 Synod discussed the role of the laity; the 1990 Synod, the formation of priests. To prepare the Jubilee Year of 2000, synods took place for the various continents; for example, 233 bishops attended the Synod of America (November/December 1997); 191 bishops attended the Asian Synod (April/May 1998). The most recent such assemblies have been the Synod of Bishops on the Bible (2008), the Synod of Bishops on Africa (2009), and the Synod of Bishops on the Middle East (2010). See *Collegiality; Episcopal Conference.*

Synoptic Gospels (Gr. "overview"). The gospels of Matthew, Mark, and Luke, which very frequently parallel each other closely in content and phraseology. The term comes from the Protestant NT scholar Jakob Johann Griesbach (1745–1812), who printed the three gospels in parallel columns, so that one could see at a glance their major convergences and minor divergences. To account for the obvious literary relationship among these gospels, most contemporary scholars favor the "two-source" theory, according to which Mark wrote first. Then Matthew and Luke drew on Mark and on a collection of Jesus' sayings (Q or Quelle) as well as having some other separate sources. See *Quelle; Two-Source Theory.*

Syrian Orthodox Church. Name for the church that Severus (d. 538), patriarch of Antioch and theologian, helped to organize in opposition to the Council of Chalcedon (451). Polemically labeled Monophysite for its opposition to the council's formula regarding Christ's two natures (rather than to the two natures themselves), this church was also called Jacobite after Jacob Baradaeus (ca. 500–78). Ordained bishop of Edessa in 542 at the insistence of Empress Theodora, Jacob went around preaching and ordaining bishops. He wore rags to avoid capture; hence, his nickname Baradaeus ("shabbily clad"). The designation Jacobites is first found at Nicaea II (787), but this church calls itself Syrian Orthodox. Its head bears the title Syrian Orthodox Patriarch of Antioch and all the East, and resides in Damascus, Syria. The liturgy of this church, one of the seven major extant Eastern rites, is known as West-Syrian (or Antiochene). The West-Syrian rite is extremely rich. It has at least seventy eucharistic anaphoras and many variant texts for other ceremonies. The main eucharistic liturgy is that of St. James, which may go back to apostolic times. In general, the liturgy is celebrated in the vernacular; Arabic is used in the Middle East; Malayalam, in India; and English, in the United States. See *Anaphora; Church of the East, Assyrian; Edessa; Monophysitism; St Thomas Christians; West-Syrian Tradition.*

Systematic Theology. The attempt to expound in a coherent and scholarly fashion the main Christian doctrines. While often coinciding in practice with dogmatic theology, systematic theology may differ by including a treatment of moral issues. It may also differ from dogmatic theology by paying even more attention to methodology, terminology, the use of philosophical principles, a strictly unified perspective, and issues concerned with the conditions and limits of theological knowledge. While Western systematic theology has often expounded analytically different treatises (Christology, grace, sacraments, and so forth), Eastern theology has tended to be more synthetic. See *Dogmatic Theology; Eastern Theology; Epistemology; Fundamental Theology; Philosophy.*

T

Tabernacle (Lat. "tent"). An ornamented box or cupboard that houses consecrated hosts for distribution to the sick and dying, for benediction, and for adoration by those who "visit" the Blessed Sacrament. In some churches the tabernacle is placed behind the main altar; in others, in a side chapel. A candle or at least an electric light burns in front of it. Christian tabernacles recall the Jewish tabernacle or portable shrine in which the ark of the covenant, which symbolized the divine presence, was housed during the wandering in the desert. See *Benediction; Blessed Sacrament; Candles; Eucharist; Shekinah; Viaticum.*

Talmud (Heb. "instruction"). The collection of Jewish traditions containing the Mishnah (oral teachings) and the Gemara (discussions about the Mishnah). There are two versions: the Palestinian Talmud and the longer Babylonian Talmud, both completed during the fifth century, but including material that goes back much earlier. See *Haggadah; Mishnah.*

Taoism (Chinese "right way"). A system of religious and philosophical beliefs and practices that, along with Confucianism and Buddhism, has helped to shape Chinese history and culture. It was founded by Lao-Tse, an honorific title ("the wise old man") for Li, a Chinese state archivist who lived around 600 BC, or, perhaps, much earlier. He is credited with having written the *Lao Teh Ching* (On the Primordial Principle of the World and Its Influence), which sees the Tao as the way of ultimate reality: that is, as immanent in the way of the universe (the ordering principle behind all life) and in the way human beings should order their lives in accordance with the Tao. Against the background of the social upheavals occurring while the Chou dynasty was in power (ca. 1127–ca. 256 BC), Taoism taught a harmony to be attained by bringing one's attitudes and conduct in line with the primordial principle. The system was further developed by Chuang Chou (ca. 369–286 BC). See *Buddhism; Confucianism.*

Teleological Argument (Gr. "study of ends and purposes"). The argument that moves from the orderly character of the world to claim the existence of God as the Designer and Final Cause of everything. In their different ways, Aristotle (384–22 BC), St. Thomas Aquinas (ca. 1225–74), and many others interpreted the universe as revealing intelligent purposes and pointing to God as the final end of all things. David Hume (1711–76) challenged transempirical causality in general; and Immanuel Kant (1724–1804), the viability of proofs for the existence of God in particular. The teleological argument had to face further objections when Charles Darwin (1809–82) explained biological design through the survival of the fittest. Mechanistic explanations of order in the world as simply resulting from the random operation of natural forces dominated for years. However, recent advances in astronomy, biology, physics, and other sciences have shown just how massive and far-reaching is the order in a universe that has apparently existed for only a relatively brief time. The odds against such an astonishing order emerging by mere chance give a new plausibility to the argument for an intelligent Designer. See *Arguments for the Existence of God; Causality; Finality; Five Ways, The.*

Temperance (Lat. "moderation"). One of the four cardinal virtues, temperance enables us to moderate our appetites and control our passions. Expressed in Plato's (427–347 BC) image of a chariot drawn by three stallions whom the rider must keep under a tight rein if he is not to finish in a ditch, temperance was made a paramount virtue by Stoics. Later NT books encourage temperance (at times translated as "sobriety," "self-control," or "modesty"), especially (but not exclusively) among church leaders and older people (1 Tim 3:2; Titus 1:8; 2:2, 5). Modern "temperance societies," instead of educating people to be moderate, have required total abstinence from all alcoholic drinks. See *Abstinence; Chastity; Stoicism; Virtues, Cardinal.*

Temple, The. The central religious shrine of the Jews, built in Jerusalem, and the only place where sacrifice could be offered (see Deut 12:1–31). First built during the reign of Solomon (ca. 970–ca. 930 BC), the Temple was destroyed by the Babylonians in 586 BC. The prophets Haggai and Zechariah encouraged the building of the second Temple (520–15 BC; see Ezra 3:1–13; Hag 2:1–9, 15–19). After it was desecrated by King Antiochus Epiphanes in 167 BC (Dan 9:2–7; 11:31; 1 Macc 1:41–64; 2 Macc 6:1–6), Judas Maccabeus purified and rededicated it (1 Macc 4:36–59). *Hanukkah*, a festival of lights held yearly in mid-December, still commemorates this purification of the Temple. Herod the Great, who ruled from 37 to 4 BC, built the magnificent third Temple, destroyed by the Romans in AD 70. On its ruins stands the Al-Aqsisa Mosque, the Dome of the Rock, where tradition places Abraham's coming to sacrifice Isaac, and Mohammed's ascent into heaven. For Muslims, this is the second most sacred place in the world, after El-Kaaba in Mecca. See *Islam; Jerusalem; Synagogue.*

Temptation (Lat. "testing"). A valuable trial of one's worth (Jas 1:2–4, 12) or an inducement to commit sin (Jas 1:14–15). God is said to "tempt" Abraham (Gen 22:1–19; Heb 11:17–19) and to allow Job to be "tempted" (Job 1:1—2:13). The weakness of the flesh (Mark 14:38) and difficult circumstances (Luke 8:13) can lead us to do wrong. As the great tempter, the devil tried to lead Christ into sin, especially during his period in the desert after baptism (Matt 4:1–11; Mark 1:13; Luke 4:1–13). Tempted as we are, Jesus, nevertheless, did not sin (Heb 4:15). Human beings can fail by "tempting" God, through demanding signs (Matt 12:39) and complaining about their situation (Exod 17:1–7; Deut 6:16; 9:22; 33:8; Pss 95:8; 106:32; Heb 3:8–10). Like Christ and the prayer he gave us for times of severe testing (Matt 6:13; Luke 11:4), church teaching recognizes our weakness when faced with temptation and encourages prayer and asceticism as remedies (see DH 1533–35, 2192, 2217, 2224, 2237, 2241–53; ND 1936–37). See *Asceticism; Prayer; Sarx; Sin*.

Tetrarchy. See *Pentarchy*.

Theandric (Gr. "divine-human"). Adjective used by Pseudo-Dionysius the Areopagite (ca. 500) to describe the acts of the God-man Jesus Christ. Some used the term in a Monophysite and/or Monothelite sense, as if Christ had only one (divine) nature and/or only one (divine) will. But St. Maximus the Confessor (ca. 580–662) and St. John of Damascus (ca. 675–ca. 749) used the term in a thoroughly orthodox sense. In and through his two natures and two wills (which are neither confused nor separated), the one (divine) person of Christ performs divine-human acts. See *Chalcedon, Council of; Communicatio Idiomatum; Monophysitism; Monothelitism*.

Theism (Gr. "belief in God"). The belief in a transcendent, personal God who creates, conserves, and acts in special ways (e.g., through miracles) in our world. Unlike pantheism, theism does not push the divine immanence to the point of identifying God with the world. Unlike deism, theism holds that God is not a mere remote creator, but through providence, revelation, and a variety of salvific acts is ceaselessly engaged on our behalf. Cambridge Platonist Ralph Cudworth (1617–88) probably coined the term. Immanuel Kant (1724–1804) clearly distinguished between theism and deism. Despite their major differences, Christianity, Islam, and Judaism may be bracketed together as theistic religions (NA 3–4). See *Deism; God; Pantheism*.

Theocentrism (Gr. "God-centered"). A way of thinking that systematically centers everything on God. It is often contrasted with anthropocentrism (Gr. "human-centered"), which takes human existence, experience, and values as its center and guide. Exaggerated anthropocentrism ignores or even rules out God. At the same time, an exclusive theocentrism is unacceptable, since God made human beings in the divine image and likeness (Gen 1:26–27) and the

Word has become flesh (John 1:14). With reference to Christianity and other religions, a theocentric approach (which sometimes overemphasizes pluralism and the equal value of any belief in God) is often contrasted with a Christocentric approach (which insists that, whether or not they acknowledge this truth, Christ is the revealer and savior for all human beings [John 1:9; 14:6; Acts 4:12; 2 Cor 5:18–19]). See *Anonymous Christians; Anthropocentricism; Christocentricism; Pluralism.*

Theocracy (Gr. "rule of God"). Government by God or by God's representatives. Many ancient nations believed their rulers to be invested with divine authority or even to be identified with divine beings. Flavius Josephus (ca. 37–ca. 100) created the term theocracy and applied it to a classic example, the Jewish people. The royal psalms, often composed for a coronation or a royal wedding, celebrated God's dominion revealed and exercised through the king (e.g., Pss 2, 45, 110). Israel's laws (e.g., the Ten Commandments) not only expressed God's will, but also carried civil sanctions, even the death penalty. After the time of Jesus, theocracy showed up not only in new religious movements such as Islam, but also in Christianity itself. In the Byzantine Empire, the ruler was seen as an image of Christ, the *Pantocrator* (Gr. "all-powerful"); and the state, as an image of celestial order. Theocratic elements were to be found in the reforms of Pope St. Gregory VII (ca. 1021–85). Both Ulrich Zwingli (1484–1531) and John Calvin (1509–64) set out to establish a divine rule in Zurich and Geneva, respectively, examples followed by the Puritan Lord Protector Oliver Cromwell (1599–1658) in England. See *Calvinism; Church and State; Decalogue; Islam; Pantocrator; Symphony; Zwinglianism.*

Theodicy (Gr. "justification of God"). Term introduced by the philosopher Gottfried Wilhelm Leibniz (1641–1716) in his response to Pierre Bayle (1647–1706), who had once again raised the question: If God is all good and all powerful, where does evil come from, and what does it mean? The question is older than the book of Job and finds its most poignant restatement in Jesus' abandonment on the cross (Mark 15:34). How can believers account for the suffering of the innocent and the faithful? Auschwitz, Dresden, Hiroshima, and further scenes of mysterious evil in modern times have more than kept the question alive. One can rightly point out that very often human beings should be put on trial for their murderous misuse of freedom. Nevertheless, a measure of mysterious, unmerited suffering remains. As we wait for the parousia, a provisional answer comes from the way Jesus himself suffered with us and for us. Today, theodicy is often used in a broader sense, as a synonym for natural theology. See *Evil, Mystery of; Natural Theology; Parousia; Suffering of God.*

Theologia Crucis (Lat. "theology of the cross"). An expression coined by Martin Luther (1483–1546) to qualify the right way of doing theology. As saving and merciful, God is known as hidden in Christ crucified and in experiences of suffering and temptation that reveal the nothingness of human beings before God. In ways that go counter to our expectations, God is revealed in the powerlessness and folly of the cross (see 1 Cor 1:17–31). Sergius Bulgakov (1871–1944) understood revelation "kenotically" as the divine glory manifested in God's self-humbling. See *Kenosis; Lutheranism; Theologia Gloriae.*

Theologia Gloriae (Lat. "theology of glory"). (a) Polemically contrasted by Martin Luther (1483–1546) with the theology of the cross and referring to Scholastic and mystical theology. Luther sees in them ways of wanting to know God presumptuously by relying on our own possibilities and capacities, instead of humbly believing and trusting in God. Theology of glory means here a theology of human self-glorification. (b) In another context, the term refers to Eastern theology, which highlights the glorification of Christ and our participating in his glory. This theology draws its inspiration from John's gospel: "The Word became flesh and dwelt among us, and we have seen his glory" (John 1:14). As understood by St. Paul, glory can be associated with Luther's favored theme of justification. "Those whom he [God] has called he has also justified, and those whom he has justified he has also glorified" (Rom 8:30). See *Doxa; Glory of God; Johannine Theology; Mysticism; Natural Theology; Scholasticism; Shekinah; Theologia Crucis.*

Theologoumenon (Gr. "theological dimension/element"). A nonbinding theological thesis that is found clearly neither in scripture nor in the definitive teaching of the magisterium. Theses of great theologians can have the status of *theologoumena* and may later in some way enter the teaching of the church. Some non-Catholic scholars sometimes use the word *theologoumenon* to distinguish the binding definitions of the first seven ecumenical councils from some subsequent pronouncement of the Roman Catholic Church. See *Filioque; Magisterium; Seven Ecumenical Councils, The; Theology.*

Theology (Gr. "science of God"). In the West, the methodical effort to understand and interpret the truth of revelation. As *fides quaerens intellectum* (Lat. "faith seeking understanding"), theology uses the resources of reason, drawing in particular on the disciplines of history and philosophy. In the face of the divine mystery, theology is always "seeking" and never reaches final answers and definitive insights. It breaks up into a number of styles and sub-areas, some of which are indicated below. With their concern for spirituality, Eastern Christians see the contemplation of the Trinity as the heart of all genuine theology. See *Apologetics; Apophatic Theology; Biblical Theology; Black Theology; Cataphatic Theology; Christology; Dogmatic Theology; Ecclesiology; Feminist Theology; Fundamental Theology; Hermeneutics; History; Mission, Theology of; Moral Theology; Mystagogy; Negative Theology; Pastoral Theology; Patristics; Philosophy; Political Theology; Positive Theology; Revelation; Spirituality; Systematic Theology.*

Theology, History of. The orderly attempts to understand and interpret revelation that have continued from the NT to Vatican II (1962–65) and its aftermath. Even more than their OT predecessors, St. Paul, St. John, St. Luke, and other NT authors have left us inspired theological insights and approaches, but no treatises systematically structured through the use of philosophy. With the apologists and the struggle against Gnosticism, Greek culture began providing Christian theology with philosophical language and concepts. While remaining characteristically biblical, liturgical, doxological, catechetical, and pastoral, the Fathers of the Church often developed their theology through great controversies, especially the trinitarian and christological debates of the fourth and fifth centuries. Along with Pseudo-Dionysius the Areopagite (late fifth and early sixth century), St. Maximus the Confessor (ca. 580–662), and St. John of Damascus (ca. 675–ca. 749), the theology of the Cappadocians has left its lasting mark on Eastern theology; for instance, through the distinction between God's essence and energies developed by St. Gregory Palamas (ca. 1296–1359).

By his powerful intellect and style St. Augustine of Hippo (354–430) massively influenced subsequent teaching on such themes as sin, grace, sacraments, and the Trinity. After St. Anselm of Canterbury (ca. 1033–1109) launched Scholasticism, it was perfected by St. Thomas Aquinas (ca. 1225–74) and his synthesis of Aristotelian and Platonic philosophy with the data of revelation. Alongside the academic theology of the new universities, the mystical and monastic theology of St. Bernard of Clairvaux (1090–1153), St. Hildegard of Bingen (1098–1179), St. Gertrude of Helfta (1256–ca. 1302), St. Catherine of Siena (1347–80), and others continued the spiritual, liturgical tradition of the Fathers. Scholasticism declined into the nominalism of the late Middle Ages. The new humanism developed by scholars such as Erasmus of Rotterdam (1469–1536) and the Reformation itself revolutionized the study of the Bible and the Fathers of the Church. For Catholics, the Council of Trent (1545–63) provided a clearer basis for subsequent theology, which featured such outstanding figures as John of St. Thomas (1589–1644), Denis Petau (1583–1652), Francisco de Suarez (1548–1617), and Gabriel Vásquez (1549–1604). First the Enlightenment philosophy and then nineteenth-century biblical and historical criticism, the theory of evolution, various forms of socialism, and the new disciplines of psychology and sociology brought massive challenges to Christian theologians. Not only great progress in philosophical and patristic studies, but also the biblical, ecumenical, and liturgical movements revitalized Catholic theology in the twentieth century, particularly in France, Germany, and the Low Countries. Alongside great Protestant teachers such as Karl Barth (1886–1968), Dietrich Bonhoeffer (1906–45), Rudolf Bultmann (1884–1976), and Paul Tillich (1886–1965), and Orthodox theologians such as Sergius Bulgakov (1871–1944), Vladimir Lossky (1903–58), and Dumitru Staniloae (1903–93), such Catholic theologians as Yves Congar (1904–95) and Karl Rahner (1904–84) led the Catholic revival. Since Vatican

II (1962–65), both within the Catholic Church and beyond, theology has become more anthropological, dialogical, and spiritual. Now less of a clerical and European monopoly, theology is being vigorously developed in the Americas, Asia, and elsewhere. See *Alexandrian Theology; Antiochene Theology; Apologists; Aristotelianism; Augustinianism; Black Theology; Calvinism; Cappadocian Fathers; Dialectical Theology; Doctor of the Church; Doxa; Eastern Theology; Enlightenment; Essence and Energies; Fathers of the Church; Feminist Theology; Gnosticism; Humanism; Jansenism; Kerygmatic Theology; Liberal Protestantism; Liberation Theology; Lutheranism; Modernism; Monasticism; Mysticism; Neo-Palamism; Neoplatonism; Neo-Scholasticism; Neo-Thomism; Nominalism; Origenism; Oxford Movement; Palamism; Platonism; Political Theology; Reformation, The; Scholasticism; Scotism; Stoicism; Thomism; Three Theologians, The; Trent, Council of; Tübingen and Its Schools; Vatican Council, First; Vatican Council, Second.*

Theology, Methods in. Coherent ways of doing theology that vary according to their characteristic questions, central aim, context, audience, use of sources, and criteria. (a) North-Atlantic academics typically raise questions about meaning, look for the truth, prefer theology in a university setting, dialogue with professional colleagues, privilege written texts, and use criteria suggested by reason. (b) Latin American theology of liberation represents another theological method, one that inquires about justice, does theology in a public context, privileges the voices of the poor and suffering, and respects the criteria of praxis. (c) A liturgical and monastic method of theologizing looks for the divine beauty, finds its home in the setting of prayer, aligns itself with fellow-worshipers, and takes its texts and criteria from the church. Each of these three methods can be broken down into subgroups. Method (a), for instance, will be affected by the kind of philosophy it adopts (e.g., Neo-Thomism, various forms of existentialism, analytic philosophy, or process thought). Method (b) will change if it is in contact with the Christian poor in Latin America or the Hindu poor of India. Method (c) will vary according to whether it is practiced by Trappist contemplatives in the United States, Orthodox Christians in Russia, or Zen-trained monks in Japan. Ideally, Christian theology can only be enriched by a proper pluralism in which the three major methods serve to complement one another. See *Beauty, Theology of; Doxa; Eastern Theology; Justice; Locus Theologicus; Option for the Poor; Philosophy; Pluralism; Praxis; Schools of Theology; Truth.*

Theonomy (Gr. "divine law"). An ethics for which God's will mediated through our created intelligence and freedom is the ultimate authority. See *Autonomy; Heteronomy.*

Theopaschite Controversy (Gr. "suffering of God"). A controversy that continued from the fifth century until after Constantinople II (553), and that concerned statements about the Son of God suffering and dying for us. Granted that God as God cannot suffer, the union of the divine and human natures in the one person of Jesus Christ justified the confession of those Scythian monks who, on a visit in Rome around 519, declared, "One of the Trinity suffered for us"—"in the flesh" (added in 534). (See DH 401, 432; ND 617, 620/10.) See also *Communicatio Idiomatum; Constantinople, Second Council of; Suffering of God; Trisagion.*

Theophany (Gr. "appearance of God"). A visible manifestation of God. While repeating that no one can see God and survive (Exod 19:21; 33:20; Judg 13:22), the OT refers to theophanies experienced by Moses and others (Exod 3:1–6; 33:17–23; 34:5–9; Isa 6:1–5). The gospels report quasi-theophanies at Christ's baptism and transfiguration (Mark 1:9–11; 9:2–8). In the early church, the Epiphany or Christ's manifestation to the Gentiles (Matt 2:1–12) was called a theophany—a usage that still continues in the East. See *Christophany; Doxa; Epiphany; Experience, Religious.*

Theotokos (Gr. "God-bearer"). A title given to Our Lady and used at least as early as Origen (ca. 185–ca. 254) to express the fact that she gave birth to the Son of God. In Latin, although the exact equivalent is *Deipara* ("God-bearer"), the title often appears as *Deigenetrix* ("Mother of God"). When Nestorius of Constantinople called into question this popular title, the Council of Ephesus (431) condemned him, and, in upholding the unity of Christ's person, proclaimed the legitimacy of the title *Theotokos* (DH 250–52; ND 604–6/1). It was not just a man (or a humanity) that Mary begot, but the Son of God himself. See *Ephesus, Council of; Mariology; Nestorianism.*

Thirty-Nine Articles. A set of doctrinal propositions adopted by the Church of England in 1571 that partly distinguish the Anglican position on controverted issues from those of Roman Catholicism, on the one hand, and continental Protestantism, on the other. These articles, which often allow for somewhat divergent interpretations, remain a major witness to the faith of the Anglican Communion. See *Anglican Communion.*

Thomism. The philosophical and theological teaching of St. Thomas Aquinas (ca. 1225–74). Enriched by the encyclopedic knowledge of his teacher and fellow Dominican St. Albert the Great (ca. 1200–80), Thomas shaped a mass of insights that had been accumulating over the centuries, especially since St. Anselm of Canterbury (ca. 1033–1109). He created a remarkable synthesis between faith and reason. Although unfinished, his *Summa Theologiae* is the greatest achievement of medieval theology. Thomas is said to have "baptized" Aristotle (384–322 BC), drawing from the Greek philosopher items such as a theory of causality. At the same time, Thomas retained a number of Platonic traits, something connected with his extensive use of St. Augustine of Hippo (354–430) and Pseudo-Dionysius the Areopagite (ca. 500). From 1300 to

1500, interpreters of Thomas (or Thomists) were concerned with opposing Scotism, nominalism, and a revived Neoplatonism. With the sixteenth and seventeenth centuries, came a golden age of Thomists, who included Thomas Cardinal Cajetan (1469–1534), Sylvester of Ferrara (1474–1528), Francisco de Vitoria (ca. 1485–1546), John of St. Thomas (1589–1644), Melchior Cano (1509–60), Domingo Soto (1494–1560), and Domingo Bañez (1528–1604). Whereas the 1917 Code of Canon Law still considered Thomas to be the teacher for philosophy and theology in Catholic seminaries (see the old CIC 589, 1366), the 1983 code simply recommends him as particularly useful (see the new CIC 252; PO 16; GE 10). In his 1998 encyclical letter *Fides et Ratio,* Pope John Paul II (pope 1978–2005), while insisting that there is no "official philosophy of the Church" (no. 76; see no. 49), proposed St. Thomas Aquinas as a master of thought and model for theologians (nos. 43–45). See *Aristotelianism; Augustinianism; Code of Canon Law; Five Ways, The; Locus Theologicus; Molinism; Neoplatonism; Neo-Thomism; Platonism; Scholasticism; Schools of Theology; Scotism; Summa; Transcendentals; Trent, Council of.*

Three Chapters, The. Selected writings from three authors accused of favoring Nestorianism, whom Justinian I (emperor, 527–65) had condemned posthumously as a goodwill gesture to the Monophysite opposition to the Council of Chalcedon (451). The condemnation touched the works and person of Theodore of Mopsuestia (ca. 350–428), the writings that Theodoret, Bishop of Cyrrhus (ca. 393–ca. 466), directed against St. Cyril of Alexandria (d. 444), and the letter that Ibas of Edessa (bishop 435–49) sent in 433 to Maris, bishop of Hardascir in Persia. Though summoned to Constantinople in 547, Pope Vigilius (pope 537–55) refused at first to subscribe to such posthumous condemnation and opposed any tampering with Chalcedon's teaching. After being forced to come to Constantinople, in his *Iudicatum* of 548, he condemned propositions from Theodore, yet only insofar as they might lend themselves to a Nestorian interpretation against Chalcedon. When an ecumenical council, Constantinople II (553), was convoked, Vigilius eventually signed the condemnation of *The Three Chapters*, an act that led to a serious schism in the West, which was healed only around 700. However unfortunate the circumstances, this unusual censuring may be interpreted as a guarantee that there is nothing in church doctrine that would warrant the Nestorian error. See *Chalcedon, Council of; Constantinople, Second Council of; Monophysitism; Nestorianism.*

Three Theologians, The. Those considered in the East to be the theologians par excellence: St. John the Evangelist, St. Gregory of Nazianzus (329–89), and St. Simeon the New Theologian (949–1022). St. John the Evangelist: a prayerful contemplation of the glory of God revealed and experienced in Christ, the Son of God (John 20:31), John's gospel is the most profound of all the gospels. The author of the fourth gospel has been traditionally identified with John the son of Zebedee (see John 21:2) and the disciple "whom Jesus loved" (John 13:23; 19:26–27; 20:2–8; 21:7, 20–24). St. Gregory of Nazianzus: St. Gregory attended the second ecumenical council, Constantinople I (381). He became bishop of Constantinople during the council but some time later resigned his see and retired to Nazianzus (in Cappadocia). His writings include "Five Theological Orations," in which he defends the divinity of the Holy Spirit, many poems, and several letters against Apollinarianism. St. Simeon the New Theologian: after joining the Constantinopolitan monastery of Studios, he left what he found to be a lax religious community to become a monk and for about twenty-five years superior of the monastery of St. Mammas, also in Constantinople. Considered the greatest mystical theologian of the Byzantine Church, his original contribution consisted in the way in which he communicated his own experiences of God in hymns and poems centered on the theme of deification. See *Apollinarianism; Cappadocian Fathers; Constantinople, First Council of; Deification; Doctor of the Church; Johannine Theology; Philocalia.*

Thurible (Lat. "censer"). A vessel that contains hot coals for burning incense during Mass and other ceremonies, such as eucharistic benediction, the Liturgy of the Hours, processions, and funerals. See *Benediction; Ceremony; Eucharist; Funeral Rite; Incense; Liturgy of the Hours.*

Tiara, Papal (Gr. "royal Persian turban"). A large beehive headdress with which popes were crowned and which they wore on solemn, extra-liturgical functions. Pope Paul VI (pope 1963–1978) sold his tiara and gave the money to the poor. John Paul I (pope 1978) refused to be crowned. His successor, Blessed John Paul II (pope 1978–2005), declined to reintroduce the tiara and any solemn crowning at the beginning of his pontificate. See *Pope.*

Time. Defined as "the moving image of eternity" by Plato (427–347 BC) and as the measure of movement by Aristotle (384–322 BC). Scholastics added that time was thus created by reason, because only reason can measure the before and after. The lived time when we wait, suffer, rejoice, and rest is not properly measurable by a clock or even by the passage of day and night and the shift of the seasons. With their memory of the Exodus and messianic expectations, the Jews had a linear concept of time and history. They remembered the past so as to hope for a fuller future. Wherever a sense of history's dénouement is lacking, the Greek cyclical image of history will prevail, which Friedrich Nietzsche (1844–1900) recaptured in "the myth of the eternal return." Christian eschatology highlighted the direction of time and history, which will culminate in Christ's parousia and God's final kingdom (1 Cor 15:20–28; Rev 21:1–22; 20). Interpreting time as duration, Henri Bergson (1859–1941) laid a foundation for his theistic metaphysics. See *Advent;*

Apocalyptic Literature; Eschatology; Eternity; History; Kairos; Lent; Metaphysics; Parousia; Sabbath; Salvation History.

Tithes (Old English "tenth"). The tenth (or other) part of the produce of the land, contributed to maintain the clergy and support the church's mission through schools, hospitals, help to the needy, and works of evangelization. Support for the maintenance of OT priests and places of worship (see Gen 14:16–20; Deut 12:6, 11, 17) was enjoined by law (see Num 18:25–32; Deut 14:22–29). The NT considers it only right that Christian communities should support those who proclaim the good news (see Matt 10:10; Luke 10:7; 1 Cor 9:7–14; 1 Tim 5:18). Eventually, after the conversion of Europe to Christianity, tithes became part of the taxes to be paid. Wherever states no longer recognize and support churches in that way, voluntary contributions are needed. Collections, taken up during the offertory, express in a liturgical setting believers' desire to support the church's mission. See *Church and State; Justice; Koinonia.*

Tolerance (Lat. "enduring"). Leaving in peace those whose beliefs and practices differ from our own. After suffering persecution from some Jewish authorities and then, for centuries, from Roman rulers, Christians gained religious freedom with the so-called Edict of Milan (313). Fairly soon, and especially after Theodosius I (the Great; emperor 379–95) made Christianity the state religion, Christians began showing intolerance toward fellow-Christians (accused of being heretics or schismatics), Jews, Muslims, and, in the Spain shaped by the Catholic sovereigns Isabella of Castile (1451–1501) and Ferdinand V of Aragon (1452–1516), former Jews and Muslims whose genuine conversion to the Catholic faith was suspect. With the Reformation, tolerance was proclaimed, but was normally extended only to one's own party. John Calvin condemned Michael Servetus (1511–53) to death, and another Protestant theologian, Theodore Beza (1519–1605), upheld the decision. The Peace of Augsburg (1555), with its *maxim cuius regio eius religio* (Lat. "whoever runs the state determines its religion") tolerated in each country only one Christian confession, as was the practical case in England under the Elizabethan settlement. Some Baptists, Catholics, Puritans, and Quakers fled from England in search of religious freedom in Europe and North America. The Enlightenment and the American War of Independence served to encourage, at least in the long run, a racial, religious, and cultural toleration based on respect for natural human rights. Today, at least in the area of religion, mere indifference to questions of truth and practice can masquerade as genuine tolerance. The Second Vatican Council (1962–65) encouraged all Catholics to live and proclaim the gospel, but always with loving respect for others (GS 28, 73, 75; AG 11; DHu 1). See *Church and State; Crusades; Enlightenment; Freedom; Inquisition; Pluralism; Priscillianism; Rights, Human.*

266

Tongues, Speaking in. See *Glossolalia*.

Tonsure (Lat. "shearing"). Having the hair of one's head cut to express separation from the world and complete dedication to God—a symbol found not only in Christianity, but also in other religions, such as Buddhism. When conferring minor orders (acolyte, exorcist, lector, and porter), the bishop cut some hair from the candidate's head—in recent times a mere tiny circle at the back of the crown. In the Latin rite, tonsure was abolished along with the minor orders in 1972. However, in some religious orders, mainly contemplative ones, the ceremony of tonsure is still performed by the abbot. Immediately after baptism in the Byzantine rite, there is the ceremony of *trichokuria* (Gr. "haircut"), in which hair is cut from four places on the head to show that the neophyte is completely dedicated to God. In the East, clerics still receive the tonsure before receiving minor orders, as do monks before entering a monastery. See *Acolyte; Baptism; Cleric; Exorcism; Holy Orders; Lector; Monasticism*.

Torah (Heb. "instruction," "law"). The Law God gave to Moses (Deut 1:5; 4:44) and the Pentateuch that contained it. Torah could also refer to parental teaching or authority (see Prov 1:8; 3:1; 4:2), instructions given in God's name by priests (Deut 17:11; 24:8; 33:10), and the law God writes in the human heart (Jer 31:33; Mal 2:7). The Samaritans retained as their Bible only the Pentateuch, an index of how the authority of the Torah was (and is) higher than that of the Prophets and the Writings (the other parts of the Jewish Bible). See *Bible; Old Testament; Pentateuch; Sadducees*.

Tradition (Lat. "transmission"). The process of handing on (tradition as act or process), or the living heritage that is handed on (tradition as content). Through the Holy Spirit (the invisible bearer of tradition) the church, the whole people of God, is empowered to pass on its memory, experience, expression, and interpretation of the foundational self-revelation of God that was completed with Christ and the New Testament community. Thus tradition involves "the Church in her doctrine, life and worship" transmitting to the next generation "all that herself is, all that she believes" (DV 8). Identifying and unifying the church, tradition secures continuity from its origins into the future. Within the whole people of God, bishops and others have a special responsibility as the visible agents and interpreters of tradition. Particular traditions can fail to communicate the gospel and need to be reformed (see Mark 7:1–23; 10:2–12). For the Orthodox, tradition, expressed above all in worship, is indispensable for understanding any issue. Reception by the whole church indicates whether a new development is in line with its tradition. In the late twentieth century, Yves Congar (1904–95), George Tavard (1922–2007), Jean-Marie-Roger Tillard (1927–2000), and others encouraged speaking of tradition as the collective memory of the church. See *Deposit of Faith; Revelation; Scripture and Tradition; Sensus Fidelium; Sola Scriptura.*

Traditionalism. A reaction against the rationalism and individualism encouraged by the Enlightenment. Traditionalism was classically expressed by Félicité de Lamennais (1782–1854) in his four-volume *Essai sur l'indifférence en matière de religion.* Others who held similar views included Louis de Bonald (1754–1840), Joseph de Maistre (1753–1821), Louis-Eugène-Marie Bautain (1796–1867), Gerhard Casimir Ubaghs (1800–1875), and Augustin Bonnetty (1798–1879). The traditionalists maintained that a revelation was granted to humanity at its origins and then transmitted in an unbroken way through subsequent history. This revelation is the authoritative source of our philosophical, moral, and religious truth. De Lamennais held that the common consent of humanity infallibly testifies to the original revelation. The First Vatican Council (1869–70) repudiated the traditionalists' claim that knowledge of God can only come through revelation and our faithful assent to it. By the natural light of reason, human beings can also know God (see DH 3004–5, 3026; ND 113–15). See *Enlightenment; Faith; Fideism; Natural Theology; Rationalism; Tradition.*

Transcendence (Lat. "surpassing"). The otherness of God, whose existence "goes beyond" the universe and is not to be identified with it. See *Apophatic Theology; Immanence, Divine; Incomprehensibility; Natural Theology; Pantheism.*

Transcendental Philosophy. A form of Thomism developed by the Belgian Jesuit Joseph Maréchal (1878–1944) in response to the critical philosophy of Immanuel Kant (1724–1804). After René Descartes (1596–1650), one could not ignore the question about the subject who asks and seeks to know, but is all too aware of the possibility of being deceived. Then David Hume (1711–76) rejected all knowledge that is neither analytical (tautological) nor experiential. Kant put metaphysics into question, in the sense that whoever makes claims concerning the existence of God, the immortality of the soul, and its liberty must first inquire whether such an enterprise is at all possible. What we call "external" reality may be shown to be (at least in part) the product of our mind. In response to Kant, Maréchal defended the theistic realism of St. Thomas Aquinas (ca. 1225–74) by arguing that human beings and their (metaphysical) questions reveal a drive that leads them beyond the immediate data of sense perception toward an Absolute. Maréchal's transcendental method was followed by thinkers such as Bernard Lonergan (1904–84), Emerich Coreth (1919–2006), and Johann Baptist Lotz (1903–92), and it greatly influenced the early Karl Rahner (1904–84). See *Epistemology; Metaphysics; Philosophy; Thomism.*

Transcendentals (Lat. "things that surpass"). A word used by Scholastics for those properties that belong to a being just because it is a being, and that thus "transcend" the categories for classifying things (e.g., essence, quality, time, and space). Six transcendentals were eventually listed: (1) reality; (2) being; (3) unity; (4) truth; (5) goodness; and (6) being something. A being is all this just because it exists. St. Thomas Aquinas (ca. 1225–74) names only three transcendentals: unity, truth, and goodness. The Scholastics often added a fourth, beauty, but were inclined to say that beauty is merely the harmonious functioning of unity, truth, and goodness. However, Hans Urs von Balthasar (1905–88) has argued for the priority of the beautiful as God's first way of attracting us in Jesus Christ. See *Doxa; Glory of God; Scholasticism; Transcendence.*

Transcendental Theology. A theological orientation similar to transcendental philosophy and practiced especially by Bernard Lonergan (1904–84); its use by Karl Rahner (1904–84) has been exaggerated. It asks about the possible answers that open up when we consider the human subject. To use an example from Rahner, penance is not simply an objective duty to be carried out, but a virtue impelling the subject to change. Every objective question has its subjective side, which, when explored, throws new light on the theological issues at stake. See *Method, Theological; Penance, Sacrament of; Theology, Methods in.*

Transfiguration. That episode in Christ's life when on a mountain (probably Mount Tabor near Nazareth) Peter, James, and John saw him radiant with glory and in the company of Moses and Elijah (Matt 17:1–9; Mark 9:2–10; Luke 9:28–36; 2 Pet 1:16–19). Representing, respectively, the Law and the prophets, Moses and Elijah had both seen God's glory (see Exod 24:12–18; 33:7–23; 34:29–35; 1 Kgs 19:1–18). In Oriental mysticism, the "light of Tabor" became synonymous with the deepest experience of God, which completely transforms our being after the arduous climb to the mountain (our asceticism). However, the predominant note was (and is) not the indispensable effort, but the ever-greater glory that is ours if we let God change our being (2 Cor 3:18). In this assimilation to God's own glory through purification (see 1 John 3:2), the Byzantine mystic St. Gregory Palamas (1296–1359) saw God's energies at work. The three apostles saw Christ in a new light because their eyes had changed and they had matured. The feast of the Transfiguration highlights Christ himself, the Son of God by nature, whose eternal glory revealed through suffering supports the Christian pilgrimage in time to God. At least as early as the fourth century, Greeks celebrated this feast, which became widely adopted in the East by the year 1000. In 1457, Pope Callistus III made the Transfiguration a feast of the universal church to thank God for the victory over the Turks the previous year at Belgrade. See *Doxa; Essence and Energies; Hesychasm; Mysticism; Palamism; Theology; Twelve Feasts, The.*

Transfinalization (Lat. "change in purpose"). A term used by some theologians in trying to illuminate what happens in the Eucharist when bread and wine are changed into the body and blood of Christ. Instead of invoking the terminology of substance and accidents (which also applies to subrational beings), they look to the area of interpersonal relationships and note that our human experience changes when something assumes a radically new purpose. Some also speak of a eucharistic transignification (Lat. "change of meaning"), in that the bread and wine undergo a deep change in meaning and express Christ's giving himself to us. In his 1965 encyclical *Mysterium Fidei*, Paul VI warned that these theories can at best complement the traditional church teaching on transubstantiation and on some points seem at odds with it. Do transfinalization and transignification indicate a change in the bread and wine that allows us to confess the real presence of Christ? See *Transubstantiation*.

Transmigration of the Soul. See *Reincarnation*.

Transubstantiation (Lat. "change of substance"). The change (through the eucharistic words of consecration) of the substance of bread and wine into the body and blood of Christ, with the appearances of bread and wine remaining. Lateran IV (1215) used the word transubstantiate in the eucharistic section of its profession of faith (DH 802; see 782, 1642; ND 21, 1502, 1519). At the Reformation, Ulrich Zwingli (1484–1531) took a purely symbolic view of the Eucharist and denied that any change took place, a view anticipated by Berengar of Tours (ca. 999–1088), who rejected transubstantiation and denied the real presence (DH 700; ND 1501). Martin Luther (1484–1531) held that, while the substances of bread and wine remain, the body and blood of Christ do become present for the believer. This view is called consubstantiation (Lat. "with the substance"). In its eucharistic teaching, the Council of Trent restated the belief that by their consecration, bread and wine are transubstantiated into the body and blood of Christ, and should be adored (DH 1651–54, 1656; ND 1526–29, 1531). The Greek Orthodox Church uses *metabole* (Gr. "change") or *metousiois* (Gr. "change of essence"), instead of transubstantiation, but the only real dispute with the Roman Catholic Church concerns the moment of consecration. See *Accident; Consecration; Constance, Council of; Epiclesis; Eucharist; Lateran Council, Fourth; Real Presence; Zwinglianism.*

Trent, Council of (1545–63). Convoked by Paul III (pope 1543–1549) to meet the grave need for reform, held in the northern Italian city of Trent, and considered by Catholics the nineteenth ecumenical council, this great council of the Counter Reformation clarified church doctrine and renewed discipline. It met over three periods. The first eight sessions (1545–47) treated major themes raised by the reformers such as the relationship between scripture and tradition, original sin, justification, and sacraments. Tension between Emperor Charles V and Paul III led to a suspension of the council, which resumed under Pope Julius III (pope 1550–1555) in a second period (1551–52). The achievements of sessions nine through fourteen included decrees on the Eucharist and on the sacraments of penance and extreme unction (now called the anointing of the sick). After various princes revolted against Emperor Charles V, Trent once again adjourned, finally meeting again in a third period (1562–63) under Pope Pius IV (pope 1559–1565). Its sessions fifteen through twenty-five defined doctrines about the Eucharist, the sacraments of orders and matrimony, and purgatory. Disciplinary measures covered such items as the "form" of marriage, indulgences, the need for an index of prohibited books, and a range of church reforms. The decrees of the Council of Trent, approved by Pius IV in 1564, laid a solid and clear basis for subsequent Catholic teaching, theology, institutional reform, and spiritual renewal. See *Anabaptists; Anointing of the Sick; Baptism; Calvinism; Counter-Reformation; Eucharist; Grace; Holy Orders; Justification; Lutheranism; Marriage Form; Penance, Sacrament of; Protestant; Purgatory; Reformation, The; Sacrament; Scripture and Tradition; Sola Fides; Sola Gratia; Sola Scriptura; Zwinglianism.*

Trinity, Theology of. Attempts to understand and interpret even a little the central Christian mystery of one God in three distinct persons, Father, Son, and Holy Spirit (Matt 28:19; 2 Cor 13:13). Drawing on the operations of our intellect and will for his "psychological" model of the Trinity, St. Augustine of Hippo (354–430) interpreted the generation of the Son (or Word) on the analogy of human self-knowledge, whereas true self-love illuminates the origin of the Holy Spirit, the "personified" mutual love of Father and Son. Over the centuries, theologians have followed Augustine or else taken up other analogies from experience and philosophy, such as the "I-Thou-We" of the personalist thought developed by Martin Buber (1878–1965). All such approaches to the tripersonal God can be helpful. Nevertheless, through being drawn from created human reality and common experience, they are not immediately rooted in the self-communication of God in salvation history that reached its climax with the paschal mystery. The famous icon of St. Andrew Roublev (ca. 1360–1430), which is now kept in a Moscow gallery, represents the scene of Abraham's *philoxenia* (Gr. "hospitality"), with three angels seated around a table (Gen 18:1–15), a scene that brings to mind for a Christian the ineffable trinitarian mystery. A chalice on the table links this mystery with the Eucharist, hence with the saving story of Christ's passion, death, and resurrection. That icon reminds us of a basic truth about trinitarian theology: it should move from the economic Trinity (revealed in salvation history) to the immanent Trinity (where analogies from created reality can help us), and not vice versa. In the theology of the Trinity, as elsewhere, the order of redemption takes precedence over the order of creation. See *Constantinople, First Council of; Economy; Father, God as; Filioque; Generation; Holy Spirit; Immanent Trinity; Modalism; Mystery; Nicaea, First Council of; Paschal Mystery; Person; Processions; Relations, Divine; Son of God; Spiration; Tritheism; Unitarianism.*

Triodion (Gr. "three odes"). The book of seasonal propers in the Byzantine liturgy for the divine services from the fourth Sunday before Lent until Holy Saturday inclusive. During this period, normally only three odes or canticles, instead of the usual nine, are sung at matins. See *Chant; Lent; Octoechos*.

Trisagion (Gr. "thrice holy"). An ancient refrain ("Holy God! Holy! Mighty! Holy! Immortal! Have mercy upon us!"), stressing Christ's holiness, power, and immortality against those who ascribed suffering to him in his divine nature. Indeed, we come across the first (documentable) use of the *Trisagion* at the Council of Chalcedon (451), which carefully distinguished between the divine and human natures in Christ, but without separating them (DH 302; ND 615). Then opponents of the council, apparently led by Peter the Fuller (d. 488), Monophysite patriarch of Antioch, added to the hymn, after "immortal," the words: "who was crucified for us." Fearing that the addition would lead to *Theopaschism*, the supporters of Chalcedon rejected the addition and interpreted the original refrain as addressed to the Trinity. The opponents of Chalcedon, such as Peter the Fuller, interpreted the refrain as referring to Christ. With or without the addition, the prayer is found in all the ancient liturgies, normally in the opening rites. Until recently in the Latin rite, the *Trisagion* was sung in Latin and Greek during the adoration of the cross on Good Friday; some continue that practice. See *Aphthartodocetism; Chalcedon, Council of; Monophysitism; Theopaschite Controversy*.

Tritheism (Gr. "belief in three gods"). A belief in three gods that misrepresents Christian monotheism, which accepts three distinct persons in one God. John Philoponus (d. ca. 565), in attempting to reconcile Christian doctrine with Aristotelian philosophy, explained the one nature shared by the divine persons to be only an intellectual abstraction; he was condemned at the Third Council of Constantinople (680/81). In the West, the Council of Soissons (1092) condemned the nominalist philosopher Roscellinus (d. ca. 1125) for claiming the three divine persons to be distinct beings without an identical substance in common. At the Council of Reims (1148), Bishop Gilbert de la Porrée (ca. 1080–1154) was accused of reifying the distinctions among the persons to the point of making them completely independent individuals. See *Constantinople, Third Council of; Monotheism; Nominalism; Person; Trinity, Theology of*.

Trullo, Council in. See *Quinisext Synod*.

Truth. A characteristic of (a) knowledge, (b) being, and (c) activity. (a) Knowledge is true when one's judgments are logically coherent and correspond to the way things are. (b) All reality is true, inasmuch as it is intrinsically knowable and known by God. (c) Our words and deeds are true when we faithfully witness to what we know, live according to our beliefs, and find our theories verified through their practical consequences. The Hebrew word for truth (*emet*) is cognate with *amen* and indicates lived fidelity. God is called "rich in grace (*hesed*) and fidelity" (Exod 34:6; see Ps 117:2), an OT refrain echoed when John describes the Word made flesh as being "full of grace and truth" (John 1:14). As the perfect revelation of the Father, Christ is the truth (John 14:6). His Holy Spirit will lead us into all truth (John 16:13). Believers are set free to "do" the truth (John 3:21; 8:32). Where philosophy has interpreted truth as a property (of knowledge, reality, and activity), the NT understands truth in a deeply personal way—in terms of Christ, the Holy Spirit, and believers. See *Amen; Hesed; Holy Spirit; Revelation; Transcendentals.*

Tübingen and Its Schools. Several quite different orientations in theology that came to be identified with the University of Tübingen. When founding this university in 1477, Count Eberhard of Württemberg was helped by the scholastic Gabriel Biel (ca. 1420–95), whose nominalism significantly influenced Martin Luther (1483–1546). In 1534–35 the faculty of theology became Protestant. Luther's second in command, Philipp Melanchthon (1429–1560), had studied in Tübingen. Other, later students included Georg Wilhelm Friedrich Hegel (1770–1831) and Friedrich Wilhelm Joseph von Schelling (1775–1854).

Between 1573 and 1581, three Lutheran theologians—Jacob Andreae, Lukas Osiander, and Jakob Heerbrand—as well as the Greek scholar Martin Crusius, all from the University of Tübingen, carried on a correspondence with Jeremias II of Constantinople (with some breaks, ecumenical patriarch 1572–95), to whom a Greek translation of the Augsburg Confession had been sent in 1573–74. In spite of the patriarch's friendly reaction, no agreement was reached.

In the early nineteenth century, Ferdinand Christian Baur (1792–1860) founded a renowned Tübingen School that included Adolf Hilgenfeld (1823–1907), Albert Schwegler (1819–57), and David Friedrich Strauss (1808–74). Applying to Christian history and theology the Hegelian dialectic of development (thesis-antithesis-synthesis), Baur argued that, in early Christianity, the dialectic of the Jewish party of Peter and the Gentile party of Paul was overcome by the emergence of Catholicism in the second century. The Baur school declined after the departure of Albrecht Ritschl (1822–89) and Adolf von Harnack (1851–1930). A Catholic Tübingen School emerged when a Catholic faculty of theology moved there from Erlangen in 1819. Important figures in the first period included Johann Sebastian Drey (1777–1853); Johann Baptist Hirscher (1788–1853), who moved to Freiburg in 1837; and Johann Adam Möhler (1796–1838). In the second period of the Catholic Tübingen School, we come across Johann Evangelist Kuhn (1806–87); Franz Anton Staudenmaier (1800–1856), who later moved to Freiburg; and Karl Joseph Hefele (1809–93), the famous historian of the councils and bishop of Rottenburg. A third period was distinguished by the teaching of Paul Schanz (1841–1905), Francis Xavier Funk (1840–1907), Karl

Adam (1876–1966), and Josef Rupert Geiselmann (1890–1970). While the programs differed, common themes included the kingdom of God, dynamic tradition, the church as organism, and the critical study of history. Through the influence of Johannes Michael Sailer (1751–1832), these Catholic theologians of Tübingen confronted the Enlightenment by endorsing some of its tenets. After the Second Vatican Council (1962–65), one can hardly speak of "schools" in Tübingen. But significant Catholic teachers there have included Joseph Ratzinger (b. 1927 and elected Pope Benedict XVI in 2005); Hans Küng (b. 1928); and Walter (later Cardinal) Kasper (b. 1933), from 1999 to 2010 president of the Pontifical Council for Promoting Christian Unity. Among the important Protestant professors, one should mention Gerhard Ebeling (1912–2001), Eberhard Jüngel (b. 1934), Ernst Käsemann (1906–98), and Jürgen Moltmann (b. 1926). See *Augsburg Confession; Enlightenment; Schools of Theology.*

Twelve Feasts, The. The major feasts in the Eastern Orthodox liturgical year, which starts on September 1. With minor variations on some lists, these are the Nativity of the Mother of God on September 9 (the icon often being that of Mary's conception); the Discovery and Exaltation of the Cross on September 14; Mary's Presentation in the Temple on November 21, better known in the East as the Entrance of the Mother of God into the Temple; the Nativity of Christ on December 25; the Epiphany on January 6, better known in the East as the Theophany (or manifestation) of the Three Persons of the Trinity (the icon being that of Christ's baptism); Christ's Presentation in the Temple on February 2; the Annunciation on March 25; Palm Sunday; the Ascension; Pentecost; the Transfiguration on August 6; the *koimesis* (Dormition) of the Mother of God on August 15. As the feast of feasts celebrated every Sunday and on every other feast, Easter does not figure on this list. The paschal mystery occupies the center of the Icon of the Twelve Feasts. See *Ascension; Assumption of the Blessed Virgin; Calendar, Liturgical; Christmas; Easter; Eastern Churches; Epiphany; Hypopante; Palm Sunday; Paschal Mystery; Pentecost; Theophany; Transfiguration.*

Two-Source Theory. (a) The widely accepted hypothesis that the gospels of Matthew and Luke had two major sources: Mark's gospel and Q (a collection of Jesus' sayings). (b) A view commonly held from the sixteenth century down to the Second Vatican Council (1962–65) that there are two "materially" separate and equally valid "sources" of revelation: tradition and scripture. See *Quelle; Redaktionsgeschichte; Revelation; Scripture and Tradition; Synoptic Gospels.*

Typology (Gr. "study of images, prototypes"). Way of interpreting events, persons, and things as types foreshadowing the NT antitypes that fulfilled revelation and salvation. Thus Adam and Melchizedek are types of Christ (Rom 5:14; Heb 6:20—7:28). The story of God's people in the Exodus from Egypt prefigures the challenges that Christians face and the sacraments they receive (1 Cor 10:1–11). The flood foreshadows baptism (1 Pet 3:20–21), and the manna in the desert anticipates "the bread of life" (John 6:48–51). St. Irenaeus (ca. 130–ca. 200) and then the school of Alexandria were attuned to this typical sense of scripture, which Origen (ca. 185–ca. 254) developed in an allegorical direction. In the West, typological interpretation was adopted by St. Ambrose (ca. 339–97), and, even more, by St. Augustine of Hippo (354–430), from whom it passed down to the Latin Middle Ages. See *Alexandrian Theology; Allegory; Antiochene Theology; Origenism; Senses of Scripture.*

U

Ubiquity of God. See *Omnipresence.*

Ukrainian Catholic Church. The largest (around five million members) Eastern Catholic church, which traces its origins to the conversion in 988 of Prince (St.) Vladimir of Kiev in Rus', from where Christianity spread over what is now known as Russia. This strong Catholic minority has been present in Ukraine since the Union Council of Brest (1596), when many Ruthenians became Catholic. In 1946 Joseph Stalin (1879–1953) forced them to join the Orthodox, an affiliation they disowned when they received freedom under Mikhail Gorbachev (b. 1931). Joseph (created Cardinal in 1965) Slipyj (1892–1984), who succeeded Metropolitan Andrew Sheptyckyj (1906–44), spent 1945–63 in Communist prisons, was named Archbishop of Lviv of the Ukrainians in 1963, and died still hoping to see the Ukrainian Catholic Church become a patriarchate. There is a strong diaspora (nearly one million) of Ukrainian Catholics in Canada, the United States, and elsewhere. See *Diaspora; Eastern Churches; Patriarch; Ruthenian.*

Ultramontanism (Lat. "beyond the mountains"). Contemptuous name used by Gallicans for those who maximalized papal authority and looked for all solutions "beyond the Alps" to Rome. The Ultramontanes reacted against movements such as Febronianism, Gallicanism, and Jansenism, which in their different ways supported the jurisdiction of local churches over against the central authority of Rome. Representative Ultramontanists included Joseph de Maistre (1753–1821); Félicité Robert de Lamennais (1782–1854), for part of his life; Louis Veuillot (1813–83); Cardinal Nicholas Wiseman (1802–65), archbishop of Westminster; his successor, Cardinal Henry Edward Manning (1808–92); and William George Ward (1812–82). The restoration of the Jesuits in 1814, the unsettling revolutions of 1830 and 1848, the long pontificate of Pius IX (1846–78), and other factors encouraged many to look for authority as the answer to almost every question. The Ultramontane movement culminated in the definition of papal infallibility at Vatican I (1869–70) in 1870 (see DH 3065–75; ND 831–40). The qualified terms of the definition, however, implicitly criticized the exaggerations of the movement. Through its teaching on the collegiality of all bishops with and under the pope, Vatican II (1962–65) produced a more balanced account of papal authority (LG 22–25). See *Church; Collegiality; Febronianism; Gallicanism; Jansenism; Traditionalism; Vatican Council, First; Vatican Council, Second.*

Uniates. The name given to the Ruthenians who, at the synods of Brest in 1595–96, accepted and ratified full communion with Rome, promulgated at the Vatican in 1595. The term, which was then extended to other Eastern Christians in union with Rome, has been used in a pejorative sense and should be replaced by *Eastern Catholics*. (Incidentally, not all Eastern Catholics have emerged by branching off from an already existing Orthodox Church: for example, the Maronites did not do so and have no parallel among Orthodox churches.) The Orthodox often consider Eastern Catholics a treacherous stumbling block on the way to the one church that Christ wants—examples of false proselytism rather than real ecumenism. However in the official theological dialogue with the Eastern Orthodox, there is a subcommission on the Eastern Catholics of the Byzantine rite in union with Rome, whose purpose is to study this question of proselytism and uniatism. Eastern Catholics are taking full part in this dialogue. At the seventh plenary session of the Joint International Commission for Dialogue between the Roman Catholic and the Orthodox churches in Balamand (1993), while uniatism understood as proselytism was decried as a method belonging to the past and practiced by both sides (arts. 12, 18), the right of Eastern Catholics to exist was formally recognized (art. 16). See *Armenian Christianity; Eastern Catholic Churches, Four Ranks of; Eastern Churches; Ecumenism; Maronites; Melkites; Proselytism; Ruthenian.*

Unitarianism. A view that rejects the divinity of the Son and the Holy Spirit, and, in defense of a strict monotheism, accepts only one divine person. Although various doubts about the divinity of the Son and the Holy Spirit emerged repeatedly in the early history of Christianity, Unitarianism is really a modern heresy, developed by Martin Cellarius (1499–1564), Michael Servetus (1511–53), and Fausto Paolo Sozzini (Socinus) (1539–1604) (see DH 1880; ND 648). In the United States, the intellectual prestige of Unitarianism came from figures such as William Ellery Channing (1780–1842), Ralph Waldo Emerson (1803–82), and Charles William Eliot (1834–1926), who was president of Harvard University for forty years and reformed the Harvard Divinity School. Unitarians have no formal creed and have dwindled in numbers. Many have either become agnostics or else returned to mainline forms of Christianity. See *Adoptionism; Arianism; Monarchianism; Monotheism; Pneumatomachians; Socinianism; Subordinationism; Trinity, Theology of.*

Universalism. A conviction that emerged after the Babylonian Exile (587–538 BC) that through Israel God's salvation was being offered to all the nations (Isa 42:6; 49:6; 52:10; see Jonah; Luke 2:30–32; John 8:12). Universalism also refers to the view that all human beings will eventually be saved. See *Apocatastasis; Hell; Israel; Salvation*.

Universals. General concepts such as rose, house, justice, and creature. With a kind of exaggerated realism Plato (427–347 BC) argued that eternal, subsistent forms or Ideas in a higher world serve as models for the universal terms we apply to individual things in our changing, visible world. The opposite view is the nominalism of William of Occam (ca. 1285–1347) and Gabriel Biel (ca. 1420–95), which holds that only individual beings are real; universal terms are more or less an arbitrary convenience. The moderate realism of St. Thomas Aquinas (ca. 1225–74) argued that general concepts exist in our mind, but are based in the real nature of things. See *Nominalism; Philosophy; Platonism; Thomism*.

Univocity (Lat. "one voice"). Being predicated of different subjects, including God, in exactly the same way. As this procedure may imply no essential difference between God and creatures, the consequence could be monism in philosophy and pantheism in theology. See *Analogy; Equivocity; Monism; Pantheism*.

V

Valentinians. Followers of Valentinus, who founded one of the most important Gnostic sects in the second century. He seems to have been born in Egypt and to have led the Gnostics in Alexandria before leaving for Rome around 135. He stayed there for about twenty years, and, at one point, apparently hoped to become the bishop of Rome. He taught a complicated system of *aeons*, which originally formed the *pleroma*. Later, through *syzigies* (Syriac "coupling," "marrying"), Sophia, a female goddess and one of the lowest *aeons*, gave birth to the demiurge or creator of the universe, identified with the (evil) God of the OT. This system was vigorously challenged by St. Irenaeus of Lyons (ca. 130–ca. 200) (see DH 1341). See *Demiurge; Dualism; Gnosticism; Marcionism; Platonism; Pleroma*.

Validity (Lat. "strong," "efficacious"). A term that entered the standard vocabulary of the church with the Council of Trent (1545–63) (DH 1809) and Pope Benedict XIV (1675–1758); it concerns the conditions that have to be observed for some act to be efficacious—as canon law insists (see CIC 124; CCEO 931). Sacraments, for example, besides being primarily signs of Christ's covenantal love, have their essential elements and thus may be valid or invalid.

A condition for validly receiving any of the other sacraments is the prior reception of baptism (CIC 842.1; CCEO 675.2). Invalidity is synonymous with nullity; an invalid act may be described as null and void. The valid reception of a sacrament means that it "counts"; fruitful reception means that grace is imparted or augmented. A Christian who gets married according to the conditions required by the church but does so in the state of mortal sin is validly married, but has not (yet) received the grace of the sacrament. See *Grace; Marriage Form; Marriage Impediments; Sacrament; Sin.*

Vatican Council, First (1869–70). Convoked by Blessed Pius IX (pope 1846–78) and intended to treat many themes, including the Eastern churches. (The Orthodox patriarchs had been invited to attend the council, but they declined.) Proceedings were suspended when Italian troops occupied Rome in September 1870. By then the council had produced two constitutions: *Dei Filius*, on God the Creator, revelation, faith, and the relationship between faith and reason; and *Pastor Aeternus*, on papal primacy and infallibility. Against fideism and traditionalism, *Dei Filius* taught that, from the works of creation, God can be known with certainty. In the OT and NT, there has been a "supernatural" revelation of divine truths or mysteries (plural). The definition of papal infallibility prompted the schism of the so-called Old Catholics and was misused by the "Iron Chancellor" of Germany, Otto von Bismarck (1815–98), in his *Kulturkampf* (German "cultural fight"), an attempt to subordinate the church to the civil government (see DH 3112–17; ND 841). Vatican I strengthened Catholic faith and papal authority, but its teaching on revelation and infallibility was to be filled out by Vatican II's teaching, respectively, on faith's personal response to the divine self-communication and the collegiality of bishops. See *Fideism; Infallibility; Old Catholics; Primacy; Rationalism; Revelation; Supernatural; Traditionalism; Ultramontanism.*

Vatican Council, Second (1962–65). Convoked by Blessed John XXIII (pope 1958–63) and considered by Catholics the twenty-first ecumenical council. Meeting for one session under Pope John XXIII and three under Paul VI (pope 1963–78), the council aimed at an *aggiornamento* (Italian "updating") of the church's life and doctrinal formulations. Instead of defining new dogmas, it wanted to teach pastorally and encourage the cause of Christian and human unity. The unprecedented number of non-European bishops present led Karl Rahner (1904–84) to divide Christian history into three periods: (1) the church at its origins in Jewish Christianity; (2) the church of a specific culture, Hellenistic or Latin (European), which lasted for centuries; and (3) the church of all nations, which started with Vatican II. The council was attended by over two thousand five hundred Catholic bishops and by non-Catholic observers from the main Christian denominations, enhancing its value as a platform for dialogue and a point of reference for all. On December 7, 1965, Paul VI and the Orthodox patriarch of Constantinople issued a joint declaration, expressing their regret for nine centuries of division and hopes for future reconciliation (see below). The first of the council's sixteen documents was *Sacrosanctum Concilium* (December 4, 1963), a constitution on the liturgy that endorsed reform through (a) a return to earlier and simpler forms, and (b) the use of the vernacular or language of the place. The decree *Inter Mirifica* (December 4, 1963) drew attention to the importance of the communications media. The third session brought the dogmatic constitution on the church, *Lumen Gentium*, one of the council's major achievements. It was approved on the same day (November 21, 1964) as the decree on the Eastern Catholic Churches, *Orientalium Ecclesiarum*, and the decree on ecumenism, *Unitatis Redintegratio*, documents committing the church to ecumenical work that was to bear fruit in subsequent unofficial and official dialogues. At the fourth session, the council issued a decree on the pastoral duty of bishops, *Christus Dominus*, a document that also aimed to renew synodical structures in the church. On the same day (October 28, 1965), the council promulgated two other decrees, *Optatam Totius*, on the training of priests, and *Perfectae Caritatis*, on the renewal of religious life; and two declarations, *Gravissimum Educationis*, on Christian education, and *Nostra Aetate*, on the positive relationship of the church to non-Christian religions. On November 18, 1965, Vatican II approved two further documents: *Dei Verbum*, a constitution on divine revelation that also dealt with faith, scripture, tradition, biblical truth, the interpretation of the gospels, and the role of the scriptures in renewing the whole church; and a decree on the ministry of laypeople, *Apostolicam Actuositatem*. On December 7, 1965, the council issued its last four documents: a declaration on religious liberty, *Dignitatis Humanae*; a decree on the church's missionary activity, *Ad Gentes*; a decree on the ministry and life of priests, *Presbyterorum Ordinis*; and the longest text of Vatican II, *Gaudium et Spes*, a pastoral constitution on the church in the modern world. On December 7, 1965, ceremonies held simultaneously in the Vatican and at the ecumenical patriarch's residence in Constantinople lifted the mutual excommunications between the Orthodox and the Catholic churches. The following day the council, the greatest event in the life of twentieth-century Catholics, ended with a solemn liturgy. See *Byzantine Christianity; Council, Ecumenical; Dogma; Schism; Synod; Synod of Bishops; Vernacular.*

Veneration of Saints. A devotion shown to dead persons of outstanding holiness, seeking to imitate their lives and obtain their intercession before God. Saints are venerated in a special way by the Catholic and Orthodox churches (UR 15), and, to a lesser extent, by the Anglican Communion, in particular, since the Oxford Movement. The Jews drew inspiration from the great figures of their past history (Sir 44:1—50:24; see 2 Macc 15:12–16), a theme taken up by the Letter to the Hebrews, which lists many OT heroes and heroines of faith (Heb 11:1—12:1). The early Christians revered the Blessed Virgin and the martyrs; Origen (ca. 185–ca. 254) was the first to reflect seriously on devo-

279

tion to the saints. The first nonmartyrs to be venerated were St. Antony the Abbot (ca. 251–356) and St. Martin of Tours (d. 397). Both at Nicaea II (787), against Eastern iconoclasts, and at Trent (1545–63), against Protestant iconoclasm, the Catholic Church asserted the importance of venerating saints (see CCEO 884–88). Altars are consecrated only after relics of saints have been fixed in them (CIC 1237 §2). In the Eastern church, the eucharistic liturgy is celebrated on the *antimension* or a piece of cloth containing relics, which is placed on the altar and functions like the Latin corporal (the cloth on which the paten and chalice are placed). See *Beatification; Canonization; Communion of Saints; Hyperdoulia; Martyr; Miracle; Nicaea, Second Council of; Oxford Movement; Pilgrimage; Relics; Saint; Trent, Council of.*

Vernacular (Lat. "dialect, language of the people"). The language of the people used in the liturgy. Liturgies usually started with the local language, except when another language was introduced by missionaries or imposed by a conquering nation. But liturgical history constantly illustrates a deeper religious phenomenon: the tension between the people's need to understand the texts and the desire to acknowledge God's mysterious otherness by using a classical, numinous language. In the West, Greek was used in the liturgy for the first few centuries until Latin gradually took over. Rome and Constantinople encouraged Sts. Cyril (ca. 826–68) and Methodius (ca. 815–85) to employ the vernacular among the Slavs in central Europe. The Reformation leaders, while often continuing to use Latin in theology, introduced the vernacular for public worship. In 1963 the Second Vatican Council (1962–65) officially approved the vernacular for Catholic liturgy (see SC 36, 54, 63, 101) in the Roman rite. In the East, the various national churches used the people's language: Arabic, Armenian, Coptic, Ge'ez (in Ethiopia), Greek, Syriac, and so forth. But with the passage of centuries, the liturgical texts have become archaic and are no longer readily understood. Many Eastern Christians in the United States, Canada, and Australia, for example, have simply switched to English. The issue of using an archaic language or the vernacular in the liturgy will never be fully and finally resolved. In the English-speaking world, the introduction of a new translation in 2011 raised questions about the quality of the language used in the liturgy. See *Evangelization; Liturgy; Liturgy of the Hours; Reformation, The.*

Vespers (Lat. "evening-star"). Evensong or evening prayer in the Liturgy of the Hours. In the 1970 reform of the Latin rite, vespers have the following structure: (a) an introductory verse; (b) a hymn corresponding to the day, the feast, or the liturgical season; (c) three psalms, one of which is sometimes replaced by a biblical canticle; (d) a short reading from scripture; (e) a short responsorial hymn; (f) the Canticle of Our Lady or *Magnificat* (Luke 1:46–55); (g) the intercessions, followed by the Lord's Prayer and the collect of the day; and (h) a final blessing. In the Byzantine rite, evening prayer is called *hesperinos* (Gr.

"evening prayer"); during Lent, it introduces the Liturgy of the Presanctified. See *Lauds; Liturgy of the Hours; Liturgy of the Presanctified.*

Vestigia Trinitatis (Lat. "footprints, traces of the Trinity"). Hints of the tripersonal being of God to be found in the created world and especially in human beings. St. Augustine of Hippo (354–430) saw the Trinity mirrored in human knowing and loving. Other such hints of the Trinity include the "I-Thou-We" of interpersonal relationships, the father-mother-child structure of a family, and the human search for the fullness of life, meaning, and love. See *Analogy; Creation; Image of God; Natural Theology; Trinity, Theology of.*

Via Affirmationis, Negationis, Eminentiae (Lat. "way of affirmation, way of negation, exalted way"). Three rules for speaking analogously about God that were classically formulated by St. Thomas Aquinas (ca. 1225–74). Our experience of human goodness, for example, allows us to predicate goodness of God. At the same time, God is not good in the limited way that human beings may be said to be good. Finally, being Goodness itself, God is good in an excellent way that transcends our understanding and language. See *Analogy; Apophatic Theology; Cataphatic Theology; Five Ways, The; Negative Theology; Transcendence.*

Viaticum (Lat. "food for the journey"). Holy communion given to those in danger of death to prepare them for the next life. Church law lifts every restriction when Christians are dying so that they may confess their sins and receive the Eucharist (see CIC 566, 844, 865, 867, 883, 913, 921, 961). See *Eucharist.*

Vienne, Council of (1311–12). The council convoked by Pope Clement V (1264–1314) that met at Vienne in southern France. French by birth, the pope had transferred his residence to Avignon, southern France, in 1309; there, the popes were to stay until 1377, in the so-called Babylonian Captivity. Wanting to seize the property of the Templars, an order of religious soldiers founded by Hugh de Payens in 1119, King Philip IV ("the Fair") forced the pope and council to condemn them on what seem to have been trumped-up charges of immorality and heresy. The council censured the Beguines, sisters who led a semi-religious common life, and their male counterparts, the Beghards, for holding that one could see God through natural effort (see DH 891–99). The council ordered a levy for a crusade, but the money ended up in the pocket of Philip IV. Without naming Petrus Olivi (ca. 1248–98), the leader of the spiritual Franciscans, the council condemned a series of propositions attributed to him and taught that Christ really suffered, because he had a complete human nature, that the soul is the form of the body, and that it is necessary for their salvation to baptize infants (DH 900–904; ND 405). See *Beatific Vision; Council, Ecumenical; Crusades.*

Vigil (Lat. "waking"). Curtailing or omitting sleep so as to pray, especially on the eve of a solemn feast. The practice goes back to the early church, which, partly on the basis of Jesus' parables that call for vigilance, expected that he would come in glory at midnight, and consequently, held all-night services culminating in the Eucharist. Pliny the Younger (62–113) and Egeria the Pilgrim (end of the fourth century) testify to such vigils. In monasteries, especially those of contemplative orders, night hours have been used for the divine office. The Russian Orthodox hold vigils in parishes, for example, the popular *Pannychida* (Church Slavonic "all-night long"), a funeral service modeled on vespers. In Latin Christianity, the Christmas Vigil ends with midnight Mass, and the Easter Vigil can last until after midnight or even until dawn. Vigil can also designate the day before a solemn feast, which always starts with vespers on the eve of the celebration. See *Acoemetae; Liturgy of the Hours; Monasticism; Vespers.*

Virginal Conception of Jesus. The act by which Mary conceived Jesus through the power of the Holy Spirit without the intervention of a human father. On the basis of the gospels (Matt 1:18–25; Luke 1:26–38), the Christian tradition and ordinary church teaching have always held that Jesus was so conceived—a belief at least implicitly affirmed by the Apostles' Creed: "He was conceived by the power of the Holy Spirit and was born of the Virgin Mary." The fact that Jesus was born of a woman points to his humanity. The fact that he was conceived through a special intervention of the Holy Spirit points to his divinity; he is "Emmanuel, God with us" (Matt 1:23). See *Christology; Holy Spirit; Incarnation; Mariology.*

Virginity. A state of abstention from marriage and sexual intercourse. From the time of the early church, communities of men and women have practiced a life of consecrated virginity, following Christ, living a program of constant prayer, serving the needy, and acting as a sign of God's final kingdom (see LG 42; PC 1, 12; OT 10; CIC 604; CCEO 570). See *Bogomils; Cathars; Celibacy; Chastity; Encratites; Monasticism; Religious Life.*

Virtue (Lat. "force"). A habit of good behavior that enables one to do what is right with ease, pleasure, and consistency. The opposite is vice, or the habitual inclination to do evil. See *Chastity; Ethics; Fundamental Option; Habit; Moral Theology; Personalism.*

Virtue Ethics. An approach to ethics derived from Aristotle (384–22 BC), which promotes virtuous habits that form character and bring human "flourishing" and happiness (hopefully in moral communities that shape life for virtuous individuals), rather than highlighting obligations to be fulfilled (deontological ethics), or the "useful" consequences of one's actions (utilitarian ethics), or the "loving" context of one's actions (situation ethics). Some fear that virtue ethics seem to base moral obligations on the likelihood of one's actions bringing true happiness, and so reduce moral commandments to being conditional rather than categorical. Notable figures in the revival of virtue ethics include Bernard Häring (1912–98) and Alisdair MacIntyre (b. 1929). St. Thomas Aquinas (d. 1274) emphasizes that virtues are more a gift of God than a human achievement. Virtue ethics can cite St. Paul's exhortations to adopt and practice the virtues of the new life (e.g., Col 3:12–17). See *Aristotelianism; Ethics; Habit; Moral Theology; Virtues, Cardinal.*

Virtues, Cardinal (Lat. "hinge"). Prudence, temperance, fortitude, and justice, which together support the whole structure of the moral life. See *Fortitude; Justice; Moral Theology; Prudence; Temperance.*

Virtues, Theological. The faith, hope, and love that are directed immediately toward God as being infinitely trustworthy and lovable, and, hence, the One to whom we should commit our whole life and future (1 Cor 13:13; Gal 5:5–6; Col 1:4–5; 1 Thess 1:3; 5:8; DH 1530–31; ND 1933–34; DV 5). See *Agape; Faith; Hope; Love.*

Visions. Unusual experiences in which other-worldly beings are manifested; these may be merely subjective hallucinations or else genuine communications from God (Isa 6:1–5; Luke 24:23; Acts 7:31; 10:17, 19; 11:5; 12:9; 16:9–10). The official church has pronounced worthy of credence only a few visions of the Virgin Mary, such as those to St. Juan Diego, an Aztec peasant, at Guadalupe, Mexico (1531); to St. Catherine Labouré, at Paris (1830); at La Salette, France (1846); to St. Bernadette Soubirous at Lourdes, France (1858); and to Lucia dos Santos and her cousins, Francisco and Jacinta, at Fatima, Portugal (1917). Visions are corporeal when something is seen, imaginative when the inner imagination is affected (but not the outer senses), and intellectual when the visionary receives a sudden and unmediated grasp of divine truths. Authentic visions never add new "content" to the deposit of faith. Instead they remind Christians of what has already been revealed in Christ, and/or give practical encouragement toward moral and spiritual reform. Alleged visions that, at least in the long run, do not produce "the fruit of the Spirit" (Gal 5:22–23; see Matt 7:15–20) are for that very reason suspect. See *Appearances of the Risen Lord; Deposit of Faith; Mysticism; Revelation.*

Voluntarism (Lat. "will"). Any doctrine that stresses the will at the expense of the intellect. The serious discussion of voluntarism was launched in Plato's (427–347 BC) dialogue *Euthyphro*, when Socrates raised the question: "Do the gods love the law because it is holy, or is it holy because the gods love it?" Affirming the second alternative would be voluntarism. For voluntaristic systems, God's will or the moral agent's preferences have tended to be decisive in establishing moral values. Voluntarism has also played a role in metaphysics, for example, in Scotism and nominalism. See *Ethics; Metaphysics; Moral Theology; Nominalism; Scotism.*

Vow. A promise freely made by an adult to do something good that is not already required by God's commandments, church law, or other obligations. To fulfill one's vows comes under the virtue of religion (see CIC 1191–98; CCEO 889–94). In the OT, vows were practiced (Lev 27:1–33; Deut 23:21–23; 1 Sam 1:11), sometimes with tragic consequences (Judg 11:30–40). The possibility of taking vows continued in the NT (Acts 21:23–26). Vows may be private or public. Vows are public if pronounced in the presence of witnesses, as is the case with the first, simple (or nonsolemn) vows that members of religious institutes take immediately after the novitiate. If these public vows bind for life, they are called perpetual vows. If they no longer bind after a certain period of time, unless renewed, they are called temporary vows. Perpetual vows that are solemn make more severe demands on the one who pronounces them, are recognized as such by competent church authority, and may be dispensed from only by papal authority. See *Chastity; Novice; Obedience; Poverty; Religious Life.*

Vulgate. A name deriving from *vulgata editio* (Lat. "popular edition") and referring to the most widely used Latin translation of the Bible. When the need for a common translation was felt in Rome, St. Jerome (ca. 340–420) translated the gospels and for the rest of the NT revised the already existing *Vetus Latina*. Forced to leave Rome, Jerome learned Hebrew and began translating the OT as well. By 404 he completed translating (or revising existing translations of) the whole Bible. In 1546 the Council of Trent declared the Vulgate to be the authentic Latin translation of the Bible (see DH 1506; ND 214). A revised edition of the text was published under Sixtus V (1590), and another revision under Clement VIII (1592). In 1908 work began on a new edition of the whole Vulgate, but ended with the publication in 1995 of the final (eighteenth) volume of a revised edition of the OT only. A revised edition of the NT will require the completion of the revision of the *Vetus Latina*; in any case, John Wordsworth (1843–1911) and Henry Julian White (1859–1934) published (1889–1911) what is still a good critical edition of the Vulgate NT. From the early fifth century in Syriac-speaking regions, the Syriac version, *Peshitta* (Syriac "simple"), functioned as a kind of Vulgate or text of the Bible accessible in the current language. See *Bible.*

W

Waldensians. Members of a renewal movement that started in the twelfth century and eventually emerged as a church with a Calvinist creed. In 1174 a rich merchant of Lyons, [Peter] Valdes (d. before 1219), after hearing Christ's invitation to the rich young man (Matt 19:21), distributed his wealth among the poor and began preaching the gospel in the south of France. By their frequent attacks on the worldliness of the church, he and his followers provoked constant friction. After the Third Lateran Council (1179) failed to win them back, they were excommunicated at the Council of Verona (1184). Their rejection of any use of violence, refusal to take oaths (DH 913), and preaching without official church approval (see DH 809) made the rift too wide to heal. In 1207 Innocent III launched a crusade against the Albigensians that also affected the Waldensian bases in southern France. Many Waldensians migrated to Spain, Germany, Bohemia, Poland, Savoy, and Piedmont. The Waldensians who returned to the Catholic Church in 1207 were required to make a profession of faith touching the disputed issues (see DH 790–97; ND 403, 640, 1301, 1411, 1504, 1703, 1802). Italian Waldensians looked for contact with the Protestant Reformation at the Synod of Chanforans (1532), and they adopted the Calvinist confession of faith. After the 1655 massacre of Waldensians, mourned by John Milton in his sonnet, "On the Late Massacre in Piedmont," a few mountain communes received permission to practice their religion freely. After 1848 they enjoyed real political and religious freedom. In 1922 the Waldensians moved their school of theology to Rome, just a few blocks from the Vatican. They are a church of about thirty thousand, the strongest Protestant group in Italy. See *Calvinism; Hussites; Lateran Council, Fourth; Protestant; Reformation, The.*

Westminster Confession. A profession of faith produced by the Westminster Assembly of 1643, which became the classical creed of English-speaking Presbyterianism as well as influencing Baptists and Congregationalists. Originally aiming to modify in a Puritan sense the Thirty-Nine Articles of the Anglican Church (1571), the assembly had to shift direction when the Solemn League and Covenant between the Scots and the English Parliament (1643) called for a common creed for the churches of the British Isles. In its thirty-three chapters, the Westminster Confession covered with a Calvinist slant all the elements of Christian faith from creation to the final judgment. To popularize this confession, the Westminster Assembly also published a longer and a shorter catechism. See *Anglican Communion; Calvinism; Congregational Theology; Creed; Puritans; Thirty-Nine Articles.*

West-Syrian Tradition. An ancient tradition from which arose the liturgies of the Syrian Orthodox and of other churches, including (to a certain extent) that of the Maronites. See *Maronites; St. Thomas Christians; Syrian Orthodox Church.*

Will of God. The supreme principle by which all human beings should let their lives be guided (Matt 6:10; see 6:33). Based on God's infinite wisdom and goodness, the divine will is a personal project of love for all men and women, one that aims to bring them to their full and final happiness. Not always easy to discern in practice, the will of God can at times call for painful sacrifice (Mark 14:35–36). See *Conscience; Decalogue; Discernment of Spirits; Holiness; Moral Theology; Perfection; Providence.*

Wisdom Literature. A genre of literature that was developed in the ancient Middle East (and elsewhere) and to which belong five books of the OT: Job, Proverbs, Qoheleth (or Ecclesiastes), Sirach (or Ecclesiasticus), and Wisdom. Sometimes the Song of Songs and the Psalms are added to the list. The Hebrew word for wisdom is *hokmah*; it can refer to the skill of a craftsman (Exod 31:6), administrative ability (Gen 41:39), and political leadership (Deut 34:9). While not avoiding ethical and religious questions, ancient wisdom often highlighted useful maxims for advancing one's career. Israel's wisdom went deeper and even wrestled with such mysteries as the unexplained suffering of those who, like Job, are blameless before God. King Solomon (d. ca. 931) was considered the wise man par excellence (see his famous judgment in 1 Kgs 3:16–28). True wisdom comes from God and helps human beings discern between good and evil (1 Kgs 3:5–9). It is one of the spiritual endowments of the Messiah (Isa 11:2). Like the word of God, wisdom tended to be personified in the OT, foreshadowing the NT revelation of the eternally preexistent Son of God (Prov 8:22–31; Wis 7:22—8:1; Sir 24:1–22). Christ's parables reflect OT wisdom, for instance, the parables of the unjust steward (Luke 16:1–8) and of the wise and foolish virgins (Matt 25:1–12). Yet God's wisdom is folly to the wise (Matt 11:25; 1 Cor 1:18–2:5). See *Deuterocanonical Books; Fools for Christ's Sake; Sophia.*

Word and Sacrament. God's word and its correlative sign, symbol, and/or event. In John's gospel, Christ's words (3:34; 5:24; 8:31; 15:3) and signs (2:11, 18, 23; 3:2; 4:54) harmonize to communicate truth (revelation) and life (salvation). Origen (ca. 185–ca. 254) associated word and symbol in his theology of the preexistent and Incarnate Word, who manifests the Father to us. As regards word and symbol in Christian life, St. Augustine of Hippo (354–430) spoke of a sacrament as visible word. The Reformation, especially in the Calvinist tradition, brought a one-sided stress on word at the expense of sign and sacrament. The Second Vatican Council (1962–65) understood God's self-communication as coming neither by word alone nor by significant event alone, but through the interplay of words and events (see DV 2, 4, 14, 17). See *Revelation; Sacrament; Symbol.*

Word of God. God's self-revelation in history (DV 1–5, 26), as (a) uttered, (b) written, and (c) incarnated. (a) God's word is creative (Gen 1:1—2:4) and effective (Isa 55:10–11). God spoke through the OT prophets (Heb 1:1; 2 Pet 1:21). Jesus proclaimed the word of God (Luke 5:1), as did his apostles (Acts 13:5; 17:13; 1 Thess 2:13) and those who follow them in truly preaching "the gospel of God" (1 Thess 2:9), a reality that is simultaneously revealing and saving (Rom 1:15–17; 1 Cor 1:18; 2 Cor 2:14–16). (b) Written under the special inspiration of the Holy Spirit (Rom 15:4; 2 Tim 3:16; 2 Pet 1:20–21; see DV 11), the scriptures are the word of God, which enlightens and nourishes the church's liturgy, teaching, and life. (c) The preexistent Son of God is the Word who "became flesh" (John 1:14), the personal self-communication of God. See *Inspiration, Biblical; Logos; Preexistence; Prophet; Revelation; Word and Sacrament.*

World. The universe created by God (Matt 25:34; John 17:5, 24). World can also mean the field where the gospel is to be proclaimed (Mark 16:15), or those who do not acknowledge Christ (John 1:9–11) and are hostile to him and his followers (John 8:23; 15:18–20; 17:14). Satan is the prince of this world (John 12:31; 14:30; 16:11), but out of love God sent the Son into the world (understood as humankind) to save it (John 3:16–17). Inspired by this love, Vatican II (1962–65) dedicated its longest text (GS) to "…the Church in the Modern World." In line with the consistent Christian opposition to Gnostic forms of dualism, this document affirmed the essential goodness of the created world. Far from being a screen between God and human beings, the world should be a point of mediation, as the use of matter in the sacraments illustrates (see DH 800, 3025; ND 19, 418). See *Cosmos; Dualism; Gnosticism; Liberation Theology; Manichaeism; Oikoumene; Political Theology; Sacrament; Vestigia Trinitatis.*

World Council of Churches (WCC). A fellowship of churches that was formed by the merger of the Faith and Order Movement and Life and Work at the first assembly of the WCC in 1948 (Amsterdam). The main purpose of the WCC is to call churches to the goal of visible unity in one faith and in one eucharistic fellowship. At the same time, the WCC considers itself a provisional expression of that unity, and, as such, it is a forum for encounter and collaboration among Christian churches. General assemblies were held in Amsterdam (1948); Evanston, United States (1954); New Delhi (1961); Uppsala (1968); Nairobi (1975); Vancouver (1983); Canberra (1991); Harare (1998); and Porto Alegre (2006). The Geneva-based WCC has 349 member churches of various Christian traditions: Anglican, Orthodox, and Protestant. Since 1965 the Roman Catholic Church, though not a member, has enjoyed regular contacts with the WCC through the Joint Working Group. See *Dialogue; Ecumenism; Faith and Order.*

World Religions. Those religions that command world attention because of their age, many adherents, and sophisticated teaching. Any complete list could be debated, but at least Christianity, Judaism, Islam, Buddhism, Hinduism, and Taoism belong among such religions. See *Anonymous Christians; Buddhism; Christianity; Dialogue; Hinduism; Islam; Judaism; Taoism.*

Worship. Adoration of God, which expresses itself in praise, thanksgiving, self-offering, penitence, and petition. Personal worship of God can take place anywhere and at any time (John 4:21–24). Public Christian worship is the liturgy, centered on Christ, who as great high priest has offered on our behalf the sacrifice of the new covenant (Heb 4:14—10:25). Our worship means sharing in Christ's priestly act on our behalf (SC 7), which calls for the living sacrifice of our daily existence (Rom 12:1). See *Adoration; Covenant; Hyperdoulia; Impetratory Prayer; Incense; Liturgical Movement; Liturgy; Liturgy of the Hours; Penance, Virtue of; Priests; Sacrifice*.

Y

Yahweh (origin uncertain). The proper name for the God of the Jews, also frequently called Elohim (the common Semitic name for God). The name Yahweh turns up in the creation and patriarchal narratives (see Gen 2:4; 4:26; 12:8; 26:25). But this may be an anachronism, a name for God that was antedated when the original traditions and texts were later edited by a redactor called the Yahwist. According to another redactor (called the Elohist because he had hitherto used "Elohim" for God), Yahweh as God's name was first revealed to Moses and "explained" as "I am who I am," or "I will be what I will be" (Exod 3:13–15). However, instead of receiving the name Yahweh through a special revelation, the Israelites may have taken it over from others. If understood causatively, as "he who causes to be," the name points to God as creator and Lord of history. Toward the end of the Babylonian Exile (587–538 BC), the Jews stopped pronouncing the name, which was written as the tetragrammaton (Gr. "word of four letters"), YHWH. In its place, they said "Adonai" (Heb. "Lord") when the tetragrammaton appeared. A similar reverence is shown by English versions that translate Yahweh as "the Lord." Given this reverence for God's holy name, some, such as Martin Buber (1878–1965), have suggested that it expresses apophaticism or silence before the name—in the spirit of "never mind what my name is." See *Apophatic Theology; Israel; Jehovah; Pentateuch*.

Yom Kippur (Heb. "day of expiation"). The only obligatory Jewish fast day, celebrated in September/October (Lev 16:1–34; Num 29:7–11). To expiate Israel's sins, an elaborate rite was performed in the Temple. The rite ended with a scapegoat being charged with the people's sins and led out into the desert. The observances of the day are now regulated by the Mishnah. The Letter to the Hebrews uses the imagery of Yom Kippur to express the meaning of the redemption and especially the fact that Christ, having died once and for all for our sins, expiated them and so made the whole ceremony of Yom Kippur superfluous (Heb 9:6—10:18). See *Atonement; Expiation; Mishnah; Temple, The*.

Z

Zealots. Jewish freedom fighters who fought the Romans at the beginning of the first century AD and then during the war that led to the destruction of Jerusalem in AD 70. There is no reliable evidence that the Zealots were active at the time of Jesus. The nickname "Zealot," applied to Simon, one of the Twelve (Luke 6:15), probably referred only to his religious zeal (see John 2:17; Gal 1:14). See *Pharisees; Sadducees; Scribes.*

Zen (Sanskrit "meditation"). A form of meditation that has flourished in the context of Buddhism. Apparently started by Bodhidharma, an Indian monk resident in China, Zen is now mainly associated with Japan. It involves such practices as the tea-drinking ceremony and the art of archery—ways of attaining peace of soul by being "lost" in things. Many Christians, such as the Jesuits William Johnston (1925–2010) and Makibi Enomiya (Hugo Lassalle, 1898–1990), have tried to show that Zen as a method (without the Buddhist credo) is compatible with Christianity. A 1989 letter from the Congregation for the Doctrine of the Faith, while recognizing that Zen could help Christian meditation, warned against dangers and abuses. See *Buddhism; Contemplation; Meditation; Prayer.*

Zeon (Gr. "warm"). A practice (in the Byzantine liturgy) that emerged in the eleventh century of adding warm water to the consecrated wine just before communion, so as to symbolize the blood and water that came from Christ's side when pierced on the cross by a lance (John 19:14). It also designates the small container for serving the warm water. The words said by the priest when adding the water recall the spiritual fervor that ought to characterize communicants. See *Byzantine Christianity; Liturgy.*

Zwinglianism. A movement within the Protestant Reformation, initiated by Ulrich (or Huldreich) Zwingli (1484–1531) with his reformation of the city of Zurich. Rejecting the authority of the pope, the Mass as sacrifice, the invocation of the saints, and the celibacy of the clergy, he tried to establish a theocracy at Zurich. His interpretation of the Eucharist as entailing a purely symbolic presence led to a fruitless dispute with Martin Luther (1483–1546) at Marburg in 1529. Zwingli recalled to Christian attention that the Eucharist is also a community meal (see DH 1635–61; ND 1512–36). He died carrying the banner in Zurich's war against the Swiss Catholic cantons. See *Calvinism; Lutheranism; Protestant; Real Presence; Reformation, The; Theocracy; Transubstantiation.*

	Council	Pope; Saint(s) present; those condemned	Agenda	Results
1	Nicaea I (325), convoked by Emperor Constantine I	Pope St. Sylvester I; St. Athanasius of Alexandria; Arius condemned	Arianism; date of Easter	Nicene Creed; Archbishop of Alexandria to determine Easter date; 20 canons
2	Constantinople I (381), convoked by Emperor Theodosius I	Pope St. Damasus I; when St. Meletius of Antioch died, St. Gregory of Nazianzus, confirmed as archbishop of Constantinople, presided; when he resigned from both charges, St. Nectarius was baptized, became archbishop of Constantinople, and presided; Eunomius of Cyzicus andApollinarius of Laodicea condemned	Radical Arianism; Pneumatomachianism; Apollinarianism	Nicene-Constantinopolitan Creed; 7 canons
3	Ephesus (431), convoked by Emperor Theodosius II	Pope St. Celestine; St. Cyril of Alexandria; Nestorius condemned	Unity of Christ expressed by Marian title *Theotokos* ("God-bearer")	Christ "one and the same" divine person; the church of Cyprus autocephalous (canon 8)
4	Chalcedon, (451), convoked by Emperor Marcian	Pope St. Leo I; St. Flavian; Eutyches condemned	Integrity of Christ's humanity and divinity	One (divine) person of Christ in two distinct natures; 30 canons; the "28th canon," which granted Constantinople primacy second only to Rome, never approved by Pope Leo I; monophysites start drifting away
5	Constantinople II (553), convoked by Emperor Justinian I	Pope Vigilius; Theodore of Mopsuestia, Theodoret of Cyrrhus and Ibas of Edessa condemned	Efforts to re-unite the monophysites	Condemnation of *The Three Chapters,* drawn from writings of Theodore, Theodoret and Ibas; no canons

	Council	Pope; Saint(s) present; those condemned	Agenda	Results
6	Constantinople III (680–681), convoked by Emperor Constantine IV	Pope St. Agatho; St. Maximus the Confessor; Patriarch Sergius of Constantinople and Pope Honorius I condemned	Monotheletism	Peace between East and West; no canons; Synod "in Trullo" (692) enacted canons that the 5th and 6th ecumenical councils ("Quinisext") had not introduced
7	Nicaea II (787), convoked by Empress Irene	Pope Hadrian I; Iconoclasts condemned	Veneration of icons	Devotion to images restored; simony condemned; 22 canons
8	Constantinople IV (869–70), convoked by Emperor Basil I	Pope St Nicholas I; Photius, a saint for Greek Orthodox, condemned	Restoration of order	Constantinople's precedence over Alexandria; in Synod of Constantinople (879) rehabilitation of Photius; 27 canons
9	Lateran I (1123), convoked by the pope	Pope Callistus II	Crisis of Investiture pitted pope against emperor	Investiture crisis ended by confirming the Concordat of Worms (1122); 22 canons
10	Lateran II (1139), convoked by the pope	Pope Innocent II; Anacletus anti-pope and reformer Arnold of Brescia (d. 1155) condemned	Healing the schism	Schism healed largely thanks to St Bernard, but pope less flexible; Arnold of Brescia condemned, and much later executed; 30 canons
11	Lateran III (1179), convoked by the pope	Pope Alexander III, great canonist from the University of Bologna	Dealing with schism caused by anti-pope Callistus III, supporter of Frederick I (Barbarossa)	Pope to be chosen by cardinals by a two-thirds majority; canons on baptism and marriage
12	Lateran IV (1215), convoked by the pope	Pope Innocent III, greatest medieval political pope	Reform of the Church	*Transubstantiation* used for first time by council; yearly confession and communion; Joachim of Fiore (d. 1202) censured; Constantinople recognized as second after Rome

	Council	Pope; Saint(s) present; those condemned	Agenda	Results
13	Lyons I (1245), convoked by the pope	Pope Innocent IV	Pope's opening address on 5 wounds of the Church: bad clergy; Saracens; Greek Schism; Mongols attacking Hungary; Fredrick II in dispute with pope	Fredrick II deposed, despite the eloquence of his defender, Thaddaeus of Suessa; crusade to be preached
14	Lyons II (1274), convoked by the pope	Pope Bl. Gregory X; St. Thomas Aquinas died en route to the council; St. Bonaventure died at council; Bl. Peter of Tarentaise, a partici- pant, became next pope as Innocent V	Greek schism; the crusade, reform of morals	Ephemeral union between RC Church and Michael VIII Palaeologus; conclave rules; urgency of crusade (the reigning pope had been serving in Acre when elected)
15	Vienne (France) (1311–12), convoked by the pope	Pope Clement V; Bl. Raymond Llull	Templars; doctrine of the soul; Franciscan poverty	Council supports stricter poverty of Franciscans; Church reform; Eastern languages to be taught at major universities; Philip IV (the Fair) suppresses and expropriates property of Templars
16	Constance (1414–18), convoked by Pope John XXIII, prompted by Emperor Sigismund	Popes John XXIII, Gregory XII, Benedict XIII; Wyclif and Huss condemned	Great Schism, with Christendom divided between three popes	Great Schism healed; Gregory XII resigned; John XXIII and Benedict XIII deposed; Martin V elected; councils to be held at short intervals
17	Florence (1438–45), convoked by the pope	Pope Eugene IV; St. Antoninus of Florence; heretics, schismatics and unbelievers condemned	Re-union with Eastern churches	Ephemeral union reached; errors of Armenians and Copts listed

	Council	Pope; Saint(s) present; those condemned	Agenda	Results
18	Lateran V (1512–17), convoked and reconvened by two popes	Popes Julius II and Leo X	Against Council of Pisa, a conciliarist pseudo-council instigated by the French king	Church reforms accepted but too late, too little; with Luther's Reformation on the threshold
19	Trent (1545–63), convoked and reconvened by three popes	Popes Paul III, Julius III and Pius IV; St. Charles Borromeo; Protestant reformers condemned, but not by name	Reform of the Church, when challenged by the Protestant Reformation	Almost all aspects of Church doctrine clarified and reformulated; Counter-Reformation launched
20	Vatican I (1869–70), convoked by the pope	Bl. Pius IX; St. Daniel Comboni; rationalists and fideists condemned	Rationalism and Church order	Relations among revelation, faith, and reason defined; primacy and infallibility of the pope defined
21	Vatican II (1962–65), convoked by two popes	Bl. John XIII and Paul VI; Bl. John Paul II; no condemnations	A pastoral council to re-propose doctrines in an updated way	Church prepared for third millennium; ecumenism endorsed; reforms of liturgy and church life

Note: At the early councils, popes were not present. They were not represented either at Nicaea I (led by Emperor Constantine) or at Constantinople I (led by Emperor Theodosius), but were normally represented by delegates. Yet, except for the influence of Leo the Great and his *Tome* at the Council of Chalcedon (451), they had a limited influence on the proceedings.

c. 30	Death and Resurrection of Jesus and the First Pentecost
c. 36	Calling of St. Paul
c. 67	Martyrdom of Sts. Peter and Paul in Rome
70	Destruction of Jerusalem
c.100	Death of last apostles
c. 107	Martyrdom of St. Ignatius of Antioch
144	Marcion the Gnostic breaks with the Roman community
154	Martyrdom of St. Polycarp
189–98	Papacy of St. Victor I; controversy over date of Easter risks schism; St. Irenaeus of Lyons intervenes with the pope
c. 200	Death of St. Irenaeus
c. 213	Tertullian leaves the Church to become a Montanist
230	Origen leaves Alexandria and settles in Caesarea (Palestine)
c. 240	Manichaeism, once a world religion, begins
c. 254	Death of Origen
268	Paul of Samosata deposed by the Origenists at the Synod of Antioch
312	Constantine's victory at Ponte Milvio, Rome
313	The so-called "Edict of Milan" and freedom for Christians; Christianity favored
324	Constantine defeats Licinius to become sole ruler in the Eastern and Western Empire
325	First Council of Nicaea
362	St. Athanasius organizes the Synod of Alexandria
363	Death of Emperor Julian the Apostate
373	Death of St. Athanasius of Alexandria; death of St. Ephrem the Syrian
379	Death of St. Basil the Great
380	Theodosius I makes Christianity the state religion
381	First Council of Constantinople
c. 381	Egeria makes her pilgrimage to Holy Land
399	Death of Evagrius Ponticus
407	Death of St. John Chrysostom
410	Alaric sacks Rome
410	Council of Seleucia-Ctesiphon (Persia)
c. 420	Death of St. Jerome
428	Death of Theodore of Mopsuestia
430	Death of St. Augustine of Hippo
431	Council of Ephesus
444	Death of St. Cyril of Alexandria
451	Council of Chalcedon; Jerusalem becomes a patriarchate
461	Death of Pope St. Leo the Great
c. 461	Death of St. Patrick
489	Emperor Zeno closes the School of Edessa
512–18	Severus patriarch of Antioch
523	Death of St. Brigid
527–65	Justinian I, Emperor
c. 530	Death of St. Benedict
c. 543	Death of St. Scholastica
553	Second Council of Constantinople

590–604	Papacy of St. Gregory I, the Great
630	Emperor Heraclius retrieves the Holy Cross from Persian King, Choroes II
632	Death of Muhammad
636	Death of St. Isidore of Seville, the last of the great Western Fathers
662	Death of St. Maximus the Confessor
680-81	Third Council of Constantinople
692	The Council "in Trullo" ("Quinisext")
717	Emperor Leo III repels Arab invasion at the gates of Constantinople
c. 725	The crisis of Iconoclasm begins in the East
731	Charles Martel repels Arab advance on the plains of Poitiers
735	Death of the Venerable Bede
c.750	Death of St. John Damascene, the last of the great Eastern Fathers
787	Second Council of Nicaea
800	Charlemagne crowned in Rome
843	The crisis of Iconoclasm ends in the East, thanks to Empress Theodora
869-70	Fourth Council of Constantinople: Photius condemned
879	Constantinopolitan Synod: Photius rehabilitated with approval of papal legates
910	Cluny founded and starts a far-reaching monastic reform
1054	Cardinal Humbert of Silva Candida and Patriarch Michael Cerularius excommunicate each other; conventional but incorrect date for the East-West schism
1073–85	Papacy of St. Gregory VII, who promotes reform and centralizes papal power
1095	Pope Urban II launches the first Crusade
1109	Death of St. Anselm of Canterbury
1123	First Lateran Council
1139	Second Lateran Council
1170	St. Thomas à Becket murdered in the Canterbury Cathedral
1179	Third Lateran Council
1204	Venetians plunder Constantinople in the Fourth Crusade; Latin Empire and Patriarchate established in Constantinople (1204–61)
1215	Fourth Lateran Council, a great reform council
1215	Nobles force King John I of England to sign the *Magna Charta* (basic rights)
1221	Death of St. Dominic de Guzman, founder of the Dominican Order
1226	Death of St. Francis of Assisi, founder of the Franciscans
1245	First Council of Lyons
1253	Death of St. Clare
1274	Second Council of Lyons brings an ephemeral reunion between the Greek emperor and the Roman Catholic Church
1274	Death of Sts. Thomas Aquinas and Bonaventure
1303	Pope Boniface VIII humiliated by the troops of Philip the Fair
1311-12	Council of Vienne
1309–77	"Babylonian Captivity" of popes in Avignon
1321	Death of Dante Alighieri

1324	Death of Marco Polo
1359	Death of Gregory Palamas, Orthodox Theologian and Saint
1378–1417	The Great Schism divides Christians between two, three popes
1414–18	The Council of Constance
1415	Reformer John Huss burned at the stake
1417	Martin V elected pope
1431	St. Joan of Arc burned at the stake
1438–45	Council of Florence brings ephemeral union with Eastern Churches
1450	Johannes Gutenberg creates the printing press
1453	Constantinople falls to the Turks
1472	Death of Cardinal John Bessarion
1492	Christopher Columbus discovers America
1498	Vasco da Gama reaches Kerala (India) and meets the St. Thomas Christians
1512–17	Fifth Lateran Council
1517	Martin Luther publishes ninety-five theses against the abuse of indulgences and other abuses
1545–63	The Council of Trent launches the Counter Reformation
1546	Death of Martin Luther
1547	Death of Henry VIII
1556	Death of St. Ignatius Loyola, founder of the Society of Jesus
1571	Battle of Lepanto
1582	Gregorian Calendar introduced by Pope Gregory XIII
1582	Death of St. Teresa of Avila, mystical writer and reformer of the Carmelite Order
1618–48	Thirty Years War ends with the Peace of Westphalia
1640	Death of Matteo Ricci in Beijing
1657	Death of Roberto de Nobili in India
1683	Turks besiege Vienna and King Jan III Sobieski of Poland saves the situation
1704	Pope Clement XI condemns the Chinese Rites; condemnation annulled in 1939 by Pius XII
1740–58	Papacy of Benedict XIV
1773	Suppression of the Society of Jesus, but Frederick II ("the Great"), King of Prussia, and Catherine II ("the Great"), Empress of Russia, keep the Jesuits
1776	American Declaration of Independence
1789	French Revolution starts
1801	Concordat between Pius VII and Napoleon Bonaparte
1814	Pius VII restores the Jesuits
1815	Death of Archbishop John Carroll
1846–78	The papacy of Bl. Pius IX
1869-70	The First Vatican Council
1897	Death of St. Thérèse of Lisieux
1878–1903	Papacy of Leo XIII, the pope who helped shape the Church's social conscience
1890	Death of Bl. John Henry Newman

1894	*Orientalium Dignitas*, the Magna Charta of the rights of Eastern Catholics
1914–18	The First World War
1910	With World Missionary Conference in Edinburgh, the modern ecumenical movement starts
1939–45	The Second World War
1958–63	Papacy of Bl. John XXIII
1962–65	The Second Vatican Council
1964	Paul VI proclaims St. Benedict patron of Europe
1965	December 7, 1965 (eve of Vatican II closing), Paul VI and Patriarch Athenagoras lift the excommunications between Rome and Constantinople
1970	Paul VI declares Sts. Catherine of Siena and Teresa of Avila Doctors of the Church
1978–2005	Papacy of John Paul II
1980	John Paul II proclaims Sts. Cyril and Methodius co-patron saints of Europe
1989	Berlin Wall falls; Eastern Christians emerge from catacombs
1997	John Paul II declares St. Thérèse of Lisieux Doctor of the Church
1999	Sts. Bridget of Sweden, Catherine of Siena, and Edith Stein proclaimed co-patronesses of Europe
2005	After five-year interruption, the dialogue between the Catholic Church and the Orthodox Church resumes
2005-13	Papacy of Benedict XVI
2013	Pope Francis inaugurates his papacy

INDEX OF NAMES

Eberhard of Württemberg, Count, 273
Ebner, F., 195
Eckhardt, Meister, 184
Edesius, Saint, 79
Edwards, J., 213
Egeria, 108, 183, 193, 282
Eichhorn, J. G., 192
Elijah, 136, 269
Eliot, C. W., 276
Elipandus of Toledo, Archbishop, 3
Elizabeth I, Queen of England, 213
Emerson, R. W., 276
Engels, F., 150, 151
Ephraem the Syrian, Saint, 37, 38, 64, 72, 205
Epicurus, 151
Erasmus of Rotterdam, 110, 261
Eriugena, John Scottus, 184
Eugenius IV, Pope, 24
Eunomius of Cyzicus (bishop), 11, 81
Eusebius of Caesarea (bishop), 201
Eustathius of Antioch, Saint, 13
Eutyches of Constantinople, 37, 82
Evagrius Ponticus, 173, 205, 242
Evdokimov, P., 24, 102, 169, 221
Eve, 3, 60, 82, 86, 171, 179, 185, 200, 207, 241
Ezekiel, 207

Father Damien (Saint Joseph de Veuster), 243
Felix V (antipope), 24
Felix of Aptunga (bishop), 65
Felix of Urgel (bishop), 3
Fénelon, François de Salignac (bishop), 215
Ferdinand V of Aragon, King, 119, 266
Feuerbach, L., 151, 218
Fichte, J. G., 161
Ficino, M., 194, 200
Fisher, Archbishop Geoffrey, 10

Flaubert, G., 201
Flavian of Constantinople, Saint, 37, 196
Fletcher, J.,79
Florenskij, P., 24, 246
Florovsky, G., 169
Foucauld, Blessed Charles de, 61
Foucault, M., 204
Fox, G., 92, 265
Fox, K., 248
Fox, M., 248
Francis, Pope, 297
Francis of Assisi, Saint, 91
Francis de Sales, Saint, 54
Francis Xavier, Saint, 157
Francisco of Fatima, Blessed, 283
Franklin, B., 74
Frederick I (Barbarossa), Emperor, 133
Frederick II, Emperor, 133, 145
Frumentius, Saint, 79
Funk, F. X., 273

Gabriel the Archangel, Saint, 9, 11
Gadamer, H.-G., 102, 236
Galerius, Emperor, 150
Galilei, Galileo, 234
Gallandi, A., 16
Gamaliel, 196
Gandhi, Mohandas (Mahatma), 105, 138, 172
Gardeil, A., 170
Garrigou-Lagrange, R., 170
Geiselmann, J. R., 274
George of Laodicea (bishop), 109
Gerhardt, P., 199
Germanus of Constantinople, Saint, 4
Gerson, J., 18
Gertrude of Helfta, Saint, 261
Geulincx, A., 174
Gilbert de la Porrée (bishop), 272
Giles of Rome. *See* Aegidius Romanus

302

Gilson, E., 171
Gioberti, V., 177
Gorbachev, M., 275
Gorgias of Leontini, 242
Gottschalk, 206
Gratian, 53
Gregorios, Mar, 230
Gregorios Akindynos, 182
Gregory I (the Great), Pope Saint, 64, 98, 188, 242
Gregory VII, Pope Saint, 36, 47, 259
Gregory IX, Pope, 53
Gregory X, Pope Blessed, 48, 145
Gregory XII, Pope, 50
Gregory XIII, Pope, 30, 53, 149
Gregory XV, Pope, 158
Gregory the Illuminator, Saint, 18
Gregory of Nazianzus, Saint, 32, 50, 64, 81, 179, 194, 197, 264
Gregory of Nyssa, Saint, 14, 15, 32, 81
Gregory Palamas, Saint, 78, 81, 89, 103, 136, 169, 182, 261, 269
Gregory of Sinai, Saint, 103
Gregory of Thaumaturgus, Saint, 179
Griesbach, J. J., 255
Grillmeier, Cardinal Alois, 33, 74, 143
Guardini, R., 139, 202, 237
Guéranger, P., 98, 139
Gunkel, H., 80, 106, 212, 242
Günther, A., 113
Gutiérrez, G., 137
Guyon, J. M. Bouvier de la Motte, 215

Habermas, J., 92, 204
Hadrian, Emperor, 16
Hadrian I, Pope, 172, 215
Hadrian II, Pope, 51
Haggai (prophet), 257
ha-Nasi, Rabbi Judah, 157
Häring, Bernard, 283

Harnack, A. von, 3, 127, 273
Hartshorne, C., 183, 209
Hausherr, I., 114, 153
Hecker, T. I., 7
Heerbrand, J., 273
Hefele, K. J., 273
Hegel, G. W. F., 112, 177, 184, 197, 198, 273
Heidegger, M., 84, 102, 197, 235, 252
Henry II, Emperor (saint), 89
Henry VIII, King of England, 218
Heraclius, Emperor, 162
Hermes, 102
Hernandez, C., 168
Herod the Great, King, 124, 257
Hilary of Poitiers, Saint, 38, 109
Hildegard of Bingen, Saint, 65, 261
Hilgenfeld, A., 273
Hippolytus of Rome, Saint, 55, 81
Hirscher, J. B., 163, 273
Hofmann, J. C. K. von, 231
Holy Spirit, passim
Honorius I, Pope, 162
Hontheim, J. N. von (bishop), 88
Horkheimer, M., 92
Hosea (prophet), 228
Hosius, Cardinal Stanislaus, 148
Hosius of Cordoba (bishop), 232
Hügel, Baron Friedrich von, 159
Hugh de Payens, 281
Hugh of Saint Victor, 227, 253
Hume, D., 74, 90, 198, 257, 268
Hünermann, P., 60
Huss, J., 50, 110, 148
Husserl, E., 197
Huxley, A., 194

Iamblichus of Chalcis, 170
Ibas of Edessa (bishop), 51, 264
Ignatius of Antioch, Saint, 16, 196, 207, 251
Ignatius of Loyola, Saint, 54, 64, 73, 84, 117, 223

Nicodemus (Hagiorita) of Mount
Athos, Saint, 32, 103, 197
Niebuhr, H. Richard, 169
Niebuhr, Reinhold, 169
Nietzsche, F. W., 59, 172, 265
Nikephoros Gregoras, 182
Nikon of Moscow, Patriarch, 175
Nissiotis, N., 181
Noah, 55
Noetus of Smyrna, 159, 189
Norbert, Saint, 226
Novatian, 172

O'Connell, D., 224
Olympia, Saint, 58
Origen, 2, 5, 14, 64, 84, 143, 179,
197, 199, 206, 213, 238, 247,
250, 253, 263, 279, 286
Osiander, L., 273
Otto, R., 173
Ozanam, Blessed Frédéric, 243

Pachomius, Saint, 160
Padiyara, Cardinal Antony, 230
Paganini, N., 36–37
Paley, W., 167
Palladius, Saint, 61
Pannenberg, W., 210
Panselinos, M., 111
Pantaenus, Saint, 5
Papias of Hierapolis (bishop), 16
Parampil, Thomas (archdeacon), 230
Parsch, P., 139
Pascal, B., 123, 135
Patrick, Saint, 158
Paul III, Pope, 119, 270
Paul IV, Pope, 54
Paul VI, Pope, 10, 26, 33, 52, 64,
117, 119, 145, 157, 191, 233,
243, 265, 270, 278
Paul the Apostle, Saint, passim
Paulos of Ethiopia, Patriarch, 77
Peirce, C. S., 204
Pelagius, 123, 191

Petau, D., 202, 261
Peter the Apostle, Saint, 17, 125,
158, 186, 193, 196, 202, 205,
232, 240, 269
Peter Canisius, Saint, 54
Peter the Fuller, Patriarch of
Antioch, 162, 272
Peter the Great, Tsar, 12, 175
Peter the Hermit, 56
Peter Lombard, 227, 234
Petrus Olivi, 281
Philip II, King, 54
Philip IV, King, 281
Philip the Apostle, Saint, 41
Philip Neri, Saint, 54, 91
Philippos of Eritrea (archbishop), 77
Philo of Alexandria, 79, 142
Phoebe the deacon, 58
Photinus, 159
Photius, Patriarch of Constantinople,
51, 89
Pico della Mirandola, G., 110, 194
Pietro Pompanazzi, 247
Pilate, Pontius, 105, 116, 125
Pirmin, Saint, 56
Pius IV, Pope, 271
Pius V, Pope Saint, 226
Pius IX, Pope Blessed, 114, 275, 278
Pius X, Pope Saint, 139
Pius XI, Pope, 45, 157, 230, 243
Pius XII, Pope, 6, 20, 115, 139, 157,
159, 202
Plantinga, A., 235
Plato, 59, 112, 166, 170, 177, 197,
199, 200, 206, 253, 257, 265,
277, 283
Pliny the Elder, 79
Pliny the Younger, 251, 282
Plotinus, 73, 161, 170
Poemen, 15
Polanyi, M., 195
Polkinghorne, Sir John, 235
Polycarp, Saint, 16
Porphyry, 170

Praxeas, 159, 189, 195
Priscilla (a Montanist), 163
Priscillian of Avila (bishop), 208
Proclus, 170
Prosper of Aquitaine, Saint, 136
Psellus, M., 200
Pseudo-Dionysius the Areopagite,
    40, 104, 182, 184, 227, 252,
    258, 261, 263
Ptolemy II Philadelphus, King, 234
Pulcheria, Saint, 37
Pusey, E. B., 181
Pushkin, A., 91
Pyrrhon of Elis, 242

Quadratus, Saint, 16
Queen of Sheba, 182

Rad, G. von, 231
Rahner, H., 129, 187, 253
Rahner, K., passim
Ramakrishna, 105
Ramon Lull, Blessed, 91, 110
Ramsey, Archbishop Michael, 10
Raphael the Archangel, Saint, 9
Ratzinger, Joseph. *See* Benedict XVI,
    Pope
Raymond of Peñafort, Saint, 53
Reitzenstein, R., 106
Ricci, M., 157
Ridley, Nicholas (bishop), 218
Ritschl, A., 273
Roberson, R., 68
Rokos, Mar Thomas, 30
Romanos the Melodian, Saint, 4,
    130
Roscellinus, 272
Rosmini-Serbati, Blessed Antonio,
    177
Rossi, G. de, 34
Rousseau, J.-J., 74
Rublev, Saint Andrei, 111, 271
Rufinus of Concordia (Aquileia), 55
Russell, C. T., 123

Ruth, 182
Rutherford, J. F., 123

Sabellius, 159
Sailer, J. M., 274
Samarin, Y., 242
Sarah, 55
Sartre, J.-P., 85
Satan, 61, 156, 258, 287
Saussure, F. de, 249
Savonarola, G., 54
Schanz, P., 273
Scheeben, M. J., 165, 197, 228, 238
Scheler, M., 197
Schell, H., 237
Schelling, F. W. J. von, 184, 273
Schillebeeckx, E., 227
Schleiermacher, F. D. E., 137, 199,
    237
Schopenhauer, A., 195
Schwegler, A., 273
Schweitzer, A., 78, 124
Segundo, J. L., 137
Selassie, Emperor Haile, 79
Semmelroth, O., 227
Seneca, 249
Septimius Severus, Emperor, 150
Serafini da Bascio, Matteo, 54
Sergius of Constantinople, Patriarch,
    4, 161, 162
Sertillanges, A. G., 170
Servetus, M., 266, 276
Severus of Antioch, Patriarch, 162,
    255
Shaw, G. B., 99
Sheba, Queen of, 182
Shenouda III of Egypt, Pope, 52, 77
Sheptyckyj, Metropolitan Andrew,
    275
Sigismund, Emperor, 50
Simeon, 110
Simeon the New Theologian, Saint,
    103, 264, 265
Simon the Apostle, Saint, 18, 289

Valerian, Emperor, 150, 173
Valla, L., 110
Vásquez, G., 261
Velichkovsky, P., 197
Veuillot, L., 275
Veuster, Saint Joseph de (Father Damien), 243
Vigilius, Pope, 51, 264
Vincent of Lérins, Saint, 61, 237
Vincent de Paul, Saint, 243
Vishnu, 104
Vitoria, F. de, 264
Vivekananda, Swami, 105
Vladimir of Kiev, Prince, 29, 275
Voltaire (Arouet, F.-M), 74, 195

Wainwright, G., 66, 155
Ward, Venerable Mary, 54
Ward, W. G., 275
Ware, Metropolitan Kallistos, 169
Warhol, A., 204
Wattson, P. J. F., 72
Wellhausen, J., 192
Wesley, C., 155
Wesley, J., 155, 205
White, E. G., 239
White, H. J., 284
Whitehead, A. N., 200, 209

Wilberforce, W., 224
William of Occam, 172, 234, 277
William of Orange (King William III), 9
Williams, Roger, 138
Wiseman, Cardinal Nicholas, 275
Wolff, C., 160, 177
Wolsey, Cardinal Thomas, 218
Wordsworth, J., 284
Wulf, M. de, 170
Wyclif, J., 50, 110, 148

Ximénez de Cisneros, Cardinal Francisco, 54

Yeats, W. B., 191
Young, Brigham, 164

Zadok (priest), 228
Zarathustra, 147
Zatvornik, Theophan (Theophan the Recluse), 7, 197
Zechariah (prophet), 257
Zeno, Emperor, 43, 72
Zeno of Citium, 249
Zinzendorf, N. L. von, 199
Zizioulas, John (bishop), 9, 71
Zuzek, I., 45
Zwingli, U., 218, 259, 270, 289